Ethical and Scientific Issues in Studying the Safety of Approved Drugs

AF896521

Committee on Ethical and Scientific Issues in Studying the Safety of Approved Drugs

Board on Population Health and Public Health Practice

INSTITUTE OF MEDICINE
OF THE NATIONAL ACADEMIES

THE NATIONAL ACADEMIES PRESS
Washington, D.C.
www.nap.edu

THE NATIONAL ACADEMIES PRESS 500 Fifth Street NW Washington, DC 20001

NOTICE: The project that is the subject of this report was approved by the Governing Board of the National Research Council, whose members are drawn from the councils of the National Academy of Sciences, the National Academy of Engineering, and the Institute of Medicine. The members of the committee responsible for the report were chosen for their special competences and with regard for appropriate balance.

This study was supported by Contract No. HHSF223200810020I between the National Academy of Sciences and the Food and Drug Administration. Any opinions, findings, conclusions, or recommendations expressed in this publication are those of the author(s) and do not necessarily reflect the view of the organizations or agencies that provided support for this project.

International Standard Book Number-13: 978-0-309-21813-9
International Standard Book Number-10: 0-309-21813-6
Library of Congress Control Number: 2012944110

Additional copies of this report are available from the National Academies Press, 500 Fifth Street, NW, Keck 360, Washington, DC 20001; (800) 624-6242 or (202) 334-3313; http://www.nap.edu.

For more information about the Institute of Medicine, visit the IOM home page at: **www.iom.edu.**

Copyright 2012 by the National Academy of Sciences. All rights reserved.

Printed in the United States of America

The serpent has been a symbol of long life, healing, and knowledge among almost all cultures and religions since the beginning of recorded history. The serpent adopted as a logotype by the Institute of Medicine is a relief carving from ancient Greece, now held by the Staatliche Museum in Berlin.

Suggested Citation: IOM (Institute of Medicine). 2012. *Ethical and Scientific Issues in Studying the Safety of Approved Drugs.* Washington, DC: The National Academies Press.

"Knowing is not enough; we must apply.
Willing is not enough; we must do."
—Goethe

INSTITUTE OF MEDICINE
OF THE NATIONAL ACADEMIES

Advising the Nation. Improving Health.

THE NATIONAL ACADEMIES

Advisers to the Nation on Science, Engineering, and Medicine

The **National Academy of Sciences** is a private, nonprofit, self-perpetuating society of distinguished scholars engaged in scientific and engineering research, dedicated to the furtherance of science and technology and to their use for the general welfare. Upon the authority of the charter granted to it by the Congress in 1863, the Academy has a mandate that requires it to advise the federal government on scientific and technical matters. Dr. Ralph J. Cicerone is president of the National Academy of Sciences.

The **National Academy of Engineering** was established in 1964, under the charter of the National Academy of Sciences, as a parallel organization of outstanding engineers. It is autonomous in its administration and in the selection of its members, sharing with the National Academy of Sciences the responsibility for advising the federal government. The National Academy of Engineering also sponsors engineering programs aimed at meeting national needs, encourages education and research, and recognizes the superior achievements of engineers. Dr. Charles M. Vest is president of the National Academy of Engineering.

The **Institute of Medicine** was established in 1970 by the National Academy of Sciences to secure the services of eminent members of appropriate professions in the examination of policy matters pertaining to the health of the public. The Institute acts under the responsibility given to the National Academy of Sciences by its congressional charter to be an adviser to the federal government and, upon its own initiative, to identify issues of medical care, research, and education. Dr. Harvey V. Fineberg is president of the Institute of Medicine.

The **National Research Council** was organized by the National Academy of Sciences in 1916 to associate the broad community of science and technology with the Academy's purposes of furthering knowledge and advising the federal government. Functioning in accordance with general policies determined by the Academy, the Council has become the principal operating agency of both the National Academy of Sciences and the National Academy of Engineering in providing services to the government, the public, and the scientific and engineering communities. The Council is administered jointly by both Academies and the Institute of Medicine. Dr. Ralph J. Cicerone and Dr. Charles M. Vest are chair and vice chair, respectively, of the National Research Council.

www.national-academies.org

COMMITTEE ON ETHICAL AND SCIENTIFIC ISSUES IN STUDYING THE SAFETY OF APPROVED DRUGS

RUTH R. FADEN (*Co-Chair*), Philip Franklin Wagley Professor of Biomedical Ethics and Executive Director, Berman Institute of Bioethics, Johns Hopkins University, Baltimore, MD

STEVEN N. GOODMAN (*Co-Chair*), Professor of Medicine and Health Research and Policy, Associate Dean for Clinical and Translational Research, Stanford University School of Medicine, CA

ALASDAIR BRECKENRIDGE, Chairman, Medicines and Healthcare Product Regulatory Agency, London, UK

LISA EGBUONU-DAVIS, Executive Advisor, Booz Allen Hamilton, Washington, DC

MIGUEL A. HERNÁN, Professor of Epidemiology, Harvard School of Public Health, Boston, MA

GRACE M. LEE, Associate Professor of Population Medicine & Pediatrics, Harvard Pilgrim Health Care Institute, Harvard Medical School & Children's Hospital Boston, MA

MICHELLE MELLO, Professor of Law and Public Health, Harvard University, Cambridge, MA

ERIC M. MESLIN, Director, Indiana University Center for Bioethics, Associate Dean for Bioethics, Indiana University School of Medicine, Indianapolis

LARRY I. PALMER, (Retired), Professor, Department of Health Administration, Virginia Commonwealth University and Professor of Law, College of William & Mary Law School, Richmond, VA

BRUCE M. PSATY, Professor, Medicine, Epidemiology, and Health Services; Co-Director, Cardiovascular Health Research Unit, University of Washington; Investigator, Group Health Research Institute, Seattle

THOMAS R. TEN HAVE, Professor of Biostatistics, Perelman School of Medicine, University of Pennsylvania, Philadelphia

WILLIAM K. VAUGHAN, (Retired), Health Policy Analyst, Consumers Union, Washington, DC

Consultants

THOMAS J. BOLLYKY, Senior Fellow, Council of Foreign Relations, Washington, DC

RICHARD A. MERRILL, Professor of Law Emeritus, University of Virginia, Charlottsville

EMILY L. EVANS, Ph.D. Candidate, Georgetown University, Washington, DC

IOM Staff

MICHELLE C. CATLIN, Study Director
ALEJANDRA MARTÍN, Research Assistant
ALLISON L. BERGER, Senior Project Assistant (June 2010–August 2011)
THOR YOUNG, Senior Project Assistant (August 2011–November 2011)
NORMAN GROSSBLATT, Senior Editor
ROSE MARIE MARTINEZ, Director, Board on Population Health and Public Health Practice
CAROL MASON SPICER, Associate Program Officer

Reviewers

This report has been reviewed in draft form by persons chosen for their diverse perspectives and technical expertise, in accordance with procedures approved by the National Research Council's Report Review Committee. The purpose of this independent review is to provide candid and critical comments that will assist the institution in making its published report as sound as possible and to ensure that the report meets institutional standards for objectivity, evidence, and responsiveness to the study charge. The review comments and draft manuscript remain confidential to protect the integrity of the deliberative process. We wish to thank the following individuals for their review of this report:

Jesse Berlin, Janssen Research & Development
Dan Carpenter, Harvard University
Perry D. Cohen, Project Director for the Parkinson Pipeline Project
Susan Ellenberg, University of Pennsylvania School of Medicine
Barbara Evans, University of Houston
Thomas R. Fleming, University of Washington
Sean Hennessy, University of Pennsylvania
Peter Honig, AstraZeneca
Karen Jenni, Insight Decisions, LLC
Cato T. Laurencin, University of Connecticut
Bernard Lo, University of California, San Francisco
Jon Merz, University of Pennsylvania
Richard Platt, Harvard Medical School
Joseph Rodricks, ENVIRON
Paul D. Stolley, University of Maryland School of Medicine

Although the reviewers listed above have provided many constructive comments and suggestions, they were not asked to endorse the conclusions or recommendations, nor did they see the final draft of the report before its release. The review of this report was overseen by **Ron Brookmeyer,** University of California, Los Angeles, and **Brian L. Strom,** University of Pennsylvania School of Medicine. Appointed by the National Research Council and the Institute of Medicine, they were responsible for making certain that an independent examination of this report was carried out in accordance with institutional procedures and that all review comments were carefully considered. Responsibility for the final content of this report rests entirely with the authoring committee and the institution.

Preface

This report comes, not coincidentally, at an extraordinary time for both the US Food and Drug Administration (FDA) and this country. With half of all Americans taking at least one prescription drug daily and many older Americans using five or more, and with an increasing array of drugs available to treat more illnesses and more people, the public health consequences of drug exposure—both negative and positive—could not be higher.

At the same time, the costs of health care consume a steadily increasing proportion of our nation's budget, with drug expenditures representing a sizable fraction of total health care dollars. Finally, there is the role of US academic and industry pharmaceutical research as an engine of innovation, bringing enormous economic, scientific, and medical benefits to our populace.

In the middle of this stands FDA, whose goal is to balance those pressures appropriately and to ensure that the drugs it approves do not have risks that outweigh their benefits, while not acting in ways that stifle biomedical innovation. The passage of the FDA Amendments Act of 2007 has afforded FDA broad new powers to monitor the safety of drugs after they reach the marketplace and to take corrective action if drugs' risks are judged to be unacceptable in light of their benefits.

Over the last few decades, there has been a series of high-profile episodes in which drugs in wide use after approval were found to cause harms that justified their withdrawal or restricted use. The highest-profile of these involved Vioxx® (rofecoxib), selective serotonin reuptake inhibitors (SSRIs) in children, Fen-Phen (fenfluramine and phentermine), and most recently, Avandia® (rosiglitazone). It is no secret that the present report was born amid the challenges that FDA was facing in its consideration of the cardiovascular risks associated with the antidiabetic drug Avandia. FDA first requested a letter report from this committee to aid in its deliberation about the scientific and ethical issues surrounding the continuation of the Thiazolidinedione Intervention with Vitamin D Evaluation (TIDE) trial, which had been required of the Avandia manufacturer by FDA. The letter report was presented during the Avandia hearings and is included as an appendix.

But both the letter report and this longer, final report are about much more than the Avandia case. The final report was prepared in response to a series of questions about the kinds of studies and protections for research participants that could or should be mounted by FDA in response to drug safety concerns in the postmarketing period. The committee quickly recognized that the questions posed were not readily answerable when framed from the vantage of a postmarketing crisis where there are few, if any, good options. To provide useful guidance, the committee found itself inexorably drawn to how FDA could have avoided these moments of crisis when the costs in human suffering and dollars to get the evidence it needed were seen by many as unacceptable. The committee hopes that its recommendations, if adopted, will go much further toward resolution of the questions that were posed to it than would have been the case if it had taken a more narrow approach.

This journey took longer than we expected it to, but it produced a report that should stand the test of time. The committee's most important recommendation is that FDA, in its role as a public health agency, be active in shaping its postmarketing drug safety monitoring role, taking it as seriously as it does its responsibility to approve safe and efficacious drugs. The committee calls this, as did an Institute of Medicine (IOM) committee that preceded it, "the lifecycle approach". Obtaining new information about a drug's benefits and risks in the postmarketing context is expected in the lifecycle approach. If acquired and responded to in a timely way, new information need not and should not result in controversies of the Avandia or Vioxx type. The committee hopes that if FDA adopts its findings and recommendations, these kinds of controversies will be minimized in the future and the public will have renewed faith in the agency as protecting of its health while allowing access to the marketplace for drugs that have great potential to cure disease and relieve suffering.

The committee thanks colleagues, organizations, and agencies that were willing to share their expertise, time, and information during the committee's information-gathering meetings (see Appendix C for the names of speakers). Their contributions informed the committee deliberations and enhanced the quality of this report. The committee learned a great deal about drug safety in the context of regulatory science, pharmacovigilance, science and ethics, and the perspectives of both public and patient interest groups. The study sponsor, FDA, gladly provided information and responded to questions. The committee is particularly grateful to Joshua Sharfstein and Janet Woodcock, who provided valuable information and feedback during the committee's deliberation process; to Joshua Sharfstein and Margaret Hamburg for commissioning this study; and to

Carolyn Clancy and Francis Collins for their interest and their agencies' financial support of the study.

We are honored to have worked with wise, creative, and indefatigable committee members, whose names are listed in this volume. The IOM staff, including board director Rose Marie Martinez, study director Michelle Catlin, and research assistant Alejandra Martin, as well as Allison Berger, Thor Young, Carol Mason Spicer, Joel Wu, Erin Rusch, and Hope Hare, were critical in shepherding the report through all its stages and incarnations. The committee was also assisted in its work by study consultants Emily Evans, Thomas Bollyky and Richard Merrill, and by senior editor Norman Grossblatt.

Finally, with deepest gratitude and great sorrow, we dedicate this report to a member of our committee, Thomas Ten Have, who succumbed to a chronic illness during the creation of the report and did not survive to see his contribution take flight. We hope that the report serves as an appropriate capstone to his brilliant and productive career in biostatistics and public health.

Ruth R. Faden and Steven N. Goodman, *Co-Chairs*
Committee on Ethical and Scientific Issues in Studying the Safety of Approved Drugs

In Memoriam

This report is dedicated to
Dr. Thomas Ten Have,
a leader in biostatistical analysis of health outcomes,
a humanitarian,
a valued member of the committee,
and an irreplaceable colleague and friend.

Contents

Abstract

Pharmaceutical products are crucial for preventing and treating diseases, but they can also have harmful effects. Until a drug has been used by a large, diverse population of patients over time, substantial uncertainties about its benefits and risks will remain. The US Food and Drug Administration (FDA) has recently made progress in monitoring drug safety after approval, but the committee finds that FDA needs to embrace more fully a lifecycle approach to drug safety oversight. The lifecycle approach requires FDA to take an anticipatory role in shaping the directions of safety research, starting at the time of drug approval. The process should continue throughout the drug's market lifetime, and its intensity should be dictated by the strength of signals that a drug's risks might outweigh its benefits for everyone or for a definable subgroup. The committee recommends that FDA adopt a specified decision framework for evaluating benefit–risk information that addresses scientific and ethical disagreements and public values. The committee also recommends that FDA create, at the time of approval, a single, publicly available, living document to track its oversight of each drug across its lifecycle, called a Benefit and Risk Assessment and Management Plan (BRAMP).

No general algorithm can dictate when FDA should require a postmarketing study or what type of studies to require if it makes that decision, but the committee identifies circumstances that should cause heightened concern about a drug and the scientific and ethical advantages of various study designs to resolve specific public health questions as they emerge. Circumstances under which postmarketing investigations should be required include not only those specified by the FDA Amendments Act (FDAAA) and the 2011 FDA guidance, such as accelerated approval using surrogate endpoints and new evidence about a drug's benefit–risk balance, but such conditions as approval of first-in-class drugs on the basis of surrogate endpoints, and when surrogate indicators point to potential harms of a drug. The committee finds that although randomized controlled trials (RCTs) remain the gold standard for studying efficacy, there can be ethical and scientific reasons to prefer observational designs when the postmarketing research question focuses on a drug's risks; such designs can often provide safety evidence of sufficient quality for decision-making. When requiring postmarketing RCTs, FDA has special obligations to protect patient-participants' rights and interests, including working with relevant institutional review boards and data monitoring committees. FDA should also establish a new body to provide advice on the ethical challenges that can be posed by requiring observational studies and surveillance activities. For both ethical and scientific reasons, required postmarketing RCTs should include an accepted active treatment as at least one comparator if one is available that would probably be used if access to the drug in question were restricted.

Finally, an increased monitoring role requires that FDA establish effective interdisciplinary teams with the expertise necessary to design safety research and interpret resulting data; the necessary expertise goes beyond that necessary for drug approval. The expanded expertise includes observational study design, analysis and interpretation, Bayesian and causal inference methods, ethics, pharmacoepidemiology, outcomes research, and the design and analysis of clinical trials for safety outcomes.

Summary

Prescription drugs[1] provide great benefit to the public's health. However, most drugs also pose risks to health, and often these risks cannot be identified or fully characterized until after a drug has entered the marketplace. Because the US Food and Drug Administration (FDA) is the agency responsible for ensuring that the benefits of a prescription drug outweigh its risks, the timely identification of and response to risks from marketed drugs are central to its mission. Before 2007, FDA's options in responding to risks of concern that emerged postmarketing were limited. It could either withdraw a drug from the market altogether or negotiate with sponsors to get them to accept a change in its regulatory status with regard to labels, warnings, and the like. The FDA Amendments Act of 2007 (Public Law [PL] 110-85; FDAAA) provided FDA with new postmarketing regulatory tools to better protect the health of the public, including the authority to require an industry sponsor to conduct a clinical trial or other research study in the postmarketing setting (called postmarketing requirements).[2] That expanded authority brought a new set of ethical and scientific questions for FDA to consider; FDA asked the Institute of Medicine (IOM) to conduct a study to address these questions.

[1]For simplicity, the committee uses the term *drugs* throughout this report, but similar considerations would apply to biologics. The committee's charge is related to the Food and Drug Administration's regulation of the drug and biologics supply. When discussing FDA's regulatory authority and mission, therefore, the committee does not address FDA's roles related to other products, such as tobacco, medical devices, veterinary medicines, the food supply, and animal feed.

[2]A postmarketing requirement (PMR) is an FDA-required research study that a sponsor must conduct after a drug has been approved and is released on the market.

CHARGE TO THE COMMITTEE

In April 2010, FDA asked IOM to "convene a committee to evaluate the scientific and ethical issues involved in conducting studies of the safety of approved drugs". The five specific questions posed by FDA appear in Box S-1. In response to FDA's request, IOM convened a committee of 12 members who have expertise in bioethics, biostatistics, clinical trials, epidemiology, health policy, law, patient safety, pharmacoepidemiology, and regulatory science.

FDA requested two reports: a letter report due in July 2010[3] and this final report. In its letter report, *Ethical Issues in Studying the Safety of Approved Drugs: A Letter Report*, released on July 9, 2010, the committee addressed the first question of the committee's charge by presenting a conceptual framework for analyzing the ethics of postmarketing randomized controlled trials required by FDA. In this final report, the committee addresses all five specific questions posed to the committee by FDA.

COMMITTEE'S APPROACH TO ITS CHARGE

The committee met in person six times, including two open information-gathering sessions. The committee used the conceptual framework in its letter report as a starting point for this final report but conducted further research and deliberations related to its full charge. The following underpinnings of that conceptual framework, as well as additional themes that emerged as the committee deliberated its full charge, shaped this report: (1) an understanding of FDA's public health mission; (2) the importance of adopting a lifecycle approach to drug safety and benefit–risk assessment; (3) FDA's ethical obligations in making regulatory decisions, including the centrality of transparency and communication to those decisions; and (4) a commitment to using best practices in regulatory science and high-quality evidence in regulatory decision-making.

BENEFIT–RISK ASSESSMENT AND MANAGEMENT THROUGHOUT A DRUG'S LIFECYCLE

In Chapter 2, the committee explains the need for FDA to adopt a consistent process for factoring in different evidence in the making of regulatory decisions throughout a drug's lifecycle. Using a consistent framework for regulatory decision-making will facilitate stakeholder understanding of decisions and the process by which decisions are made, emphasize the dynamic nature of benefit and risk assessments, provide an opportunity to consider the value of additional

[3]FDA requested that IOM complete the letter report before a July 13–14, 2010, joint meeting of FDA's Endocrinologic and Metabolic Drugs Advisory Committee and Drug Safety and Risk Management Advisory Committee on rosiglitazone.

BOX S-1
Charge to the Committee

The US Food and Drug Administration (FDA) has requested that the Institute of Medicine convene a committee to evaluate the scientific and ethical issues involved in conducting studies of the safety of approved drugs. Questions to be explored by a committee include

1. What are the ethical and informed consent issues that must be considered when designing randomized clinical trials to evaluate potential safety risks?
2. What are the strengths and weaknesses of various approaches, including observational studies, including patient registries, meta-analyses, including patient-level data meta-analyses, and randomized controlled trials, to generate evidence about safety questions?
3. Considering the speed, cost, and value of studies, what types of follow-up studies are appropriate to investigate different kinds of signals (detected pre-approval or postapproval) and in what temporal order?
4. Under what circumstances should head-to-head randomized clinical trials for safety be required?
5. How should FDA factor in different kinds of safety evidence in considering different kinds of regulatory actions?

postmarketing studies, and minimize delays and increase transparency in the agency's decisions. The committee proposes a three-stage framework that FDA could apply to regulatory decisions prompted by new information that could affect a drug's benefit–risk profile, and to use for periodic re-evaluations of the benefit–risk profile during a drug's lifecycle.[4] Central to the framework is the importance of eliciting and incorporating the perspective of the patient.[5] In the first stage (Stage I) of the framework, FDA should define the public health question that prompted the need for a regulatory decision, including identifying the specific characteristics of the drug and health problem at issue, available information about the drug, alternative treatments that are available, and plausible regulatory actions and their potential consequences. In the second stage (Stage II) of the framework, FDA should evaluate the quality of evidence on both the benefits

[4]Given its charge, the committee focuses on the use of the framework in the postmarketing setting, but it could also be useful in the premarketing setting.

[5]FDA should ensure that patient advocacy groups represent the views of patients rather than the views of commercial entities that provide funding to the organizations.

and the risks associated with the drug, including any new information that has triggered the need to consider regulatory action. The output of this stage includes estimates of the likelihood and magnitude of a drug's benefits and risks and a characterization of the scientific evidence on which the estimates are based. The third stage (Stage III) of the framework is the stage in which regulatory decisions are made and implemented. This stage involves synthesizing and integrating the estimates of benefits and risks and the quality of the evidence on which these are based (from Stage II) with the public health question (as specified in Stage I); deciding on the appropriate regulatory actions, including whether further study should be required; communicating the decision; implementing the regulatory actions; evaluating the effects of the regulatory actions; and, particularly in the case of complex or difficult decisions, evaluating the decision-making process and the impact of the action taken on the public's health.

In order to formalize and make concrete a commitment to a lifecycle approach to drug oversight and benefit–risk management, the committee proposes that FDA develop and make public a living document, which the committee calls a Benefit and Risk Assessment and Management Plan (BRAMP), that FDA would update whenever it re-evaluates a drug's benefit–risk profile. The document would serve as a guide that supports organizational adherence to the lifecycle approach, increases the transparency of FDA's decisions, and fosters collaboration between FDA and drug sponsors.

In light of its charge, the committee focuses on the ethical and scientific issues associated with one of the regulatory actions available to FDA: imposing a postmarketing requirement on a drug's sponsor to conduct additional research, including studies that employ observational and RCT designs.[6] When FDA imposes a postmarketing requirement, it is expressing not only scientific uncertainty about the harms or benefits of a drug but a judgment that the public health interests served by requiring additional research outweigh the burdens placed on pharmaceutical manufacturers and—more important from an ethical standpoint—any risk of harm to or burdens on research participants. Because it has required the studies, FDA bears a measure of ethical responsibility for any adverse outcomes that research participants experience. When requiring postmarketing research, therefore, FDA should be confident that the information from the study is necessary to answer the public health question that prompted the consideration of a regulatory action, that the required study is designed and conducted in such a way that it can provide the necessary information, that it will use the study findings in a timely manner in its regulatory decisions, and that the

[6]In this report, the committee uses the term *studies*, in accordance with ordinary usage in the scientific literature, as a parent or generic term that encompasses research projects of all types regardless of design. Thus, as the committee uses the term *studies*, it applies to both clinical trials and non–clinical-trial investigations, such as observational investigations. When referring specifically to either *observational designs* or *randomized controlled trial* (RCT) designs, the committee uses those specific terms.

design and conduct of the study adequately protect the rights and interests of research participants.

FDAAA provides FDA the authority to require postmarketing research under specific circumstances, and FDA has interpreted its authority in guidance to industry about postmarketing requirements. The committee identifies, more specifically, circumstances that typically increase the uncertainty surrounding the benefit–risk profile of a drug under which FDA should seriously consider requiring postmarketing studies and, if it decides not to require research, it should make public its reasoning for that decision.

EVIDENCE AND DECISION-MAKING

FDA's drug-related regulatory decisions are based, to a large extent, on scientific evidence. Statistical inferences must be made in order to use scientific evidence in decision-making. The two main approaches to statistical inference are the standard "frequentist" approach and the Bayesian approach. The frequentist approach to statistical inference is familiar to medical researchers and is the basis of most FDA rules and guidance. The Bayesian approach is less widely used and understood, and it has many attractive properties that can both elucidate the reasons for disagreements and provide an analytic model for decision-making that can allow decision-makers to combine the chance of being wrong about benefits and risks with the seriousness of those errors to support optimal decisions. Bayesian, frequentist, and other relevant methods can be useful for integrating new information about a drug into our current understanding about its association with harms or benefits to inform decisions, and FDA should develop a sufficient body of internal expertise of these approaches.

Scientists and technical experts often disagree about the available evidence. Those disagreements can result from different prior beliefs about the existence of a given benefit or risk, different opinions about the quality of a new study, different opinions about the relevance of the new evidence to the public health question, and different ideas about how to synthesize and weigh all evidence relevant to the public health question. In addition, even if scientists do not make the final decision about what regulatory action FDA should take, they often have opinions about what level of certainty there should be for a given regulatory decision, and that opinion can shape their assessment of the strength of the evidence. Decisions where scientists and technical experts disagree about the available evidence, such as in the case of rosiglitazone (Avandia®), are often the most difficult ones that FDA must make.

If the underlying reasons for disagreements are not properly expressed or elicited, however, it will be difficult to reach a consensus on the appropriate regulatory action. A lack of clarity about those disagreements makes it extraordinarily difficult for those involved in the decision-making process to understand the reasons for the disagreements, adjudicate them, and make decisions. The nature of scientific differences should be identified and explicitly stated so that all participants in the decision-making process—including scientists, technical experts, patients and other stakeholders, and the decision-makers themselves—understand the underlying sources of scientific disagreement. To maintain the public's trust in the agency, it is important that the public can understand how FDA weighs the factors that lead to disagreements in its decisions. FDA's handling of its recent regulatory decision to place restrictions on the distribution of rosiglitazone provides a good example of how it can make public both the disagreements among agency scientists about evidence and how those disagreements were considered in the agency's decision. The three-stage framework discussed above provides a process for eliciting and resolving those differences, and the BRAMP document constitutes a mechanism to provide transparency to the public about the disagreements and how they affected the decision.

The reanalyses of data from rosiglitazone trials revealed discrepancies and judgment calls that occurred from ascertaining clinical events through data analysis that affected the interpretation of the evidence and, later, the regulatory decision. That example highlights the importance of adherence to principles of reproducible research, that is, presenting analyses in such a way that the reader of results can understand most of or all the process that occurred from the gathering of the data to the reporting of specific analyses. At a minimum, that requires provision of study protocols with statistical-analysis plans, statistical code, and information about how decisions were made to produce the analytic dataset from the raw measured data. Optimally, it involves some form of data sharing. Adhering to those principles, for both premarketing and postmarketing data, would facilitate a better understanding of FDA's decisions by the public and allow analysts both in and outside FDA to investigate the sensitivity of conclusions to different analytic approaches.

SELECTION AND OVERSIGHT OF REQUIRED POSTMARKETING STUDIES

As a public health agency, FDA has ethical obligations both to protect the public from unsafe drugs and to safeguard the rights and interests of participants in the research that supports the agency's decisions about drug benefits and risks. Once it has decided to require postmarketing research, FDA must balance those two obligations when determining what type of study or studies to require. FDA may be justified in requiring studies that might expose participants to more net risk than they would probably face in regular clinical practice, that offer participants no reasonable expectation of clinical benefit, or both.[7] This is only justified

[7] Although there may not be any potential clinical benefit from the drug, research participants could benefit from participation through improved clinical care and being provided at no cost a drug that they could not afford.

when a question of pressing public health importance is at stake, no other design with a better benefit–risk balance for participants could supply the evidence needed for a responsible regulatory response to that question, FDA uses the findings of the research in formulating its regulatory response, and special safeguards are in place to protect the rights and interests of the research participants.

As discussed in Chapter 4, FDAAA allows FDA to require an RCT only when observational studies are not sufficient to provide the information the agency needs. The challenge for FDA is to determine when one or more postmarketing observational studies are necessary and adequate to inform its regulatory decision, when one or more postmarketing RCTs are necessary and adequate, or when some combination of studies are required.

To make that decision, FDA should consider the advantages and disadvantages of observational studies and RCTs in the postmarketing setting, which poses distinct scientific and ethical challenges. In contrast to the premarket context, the drug of interest, once approved, will be in general use, making observational studies feasible, and patients will have access to it without having to participate in FDA-required research. After approval, evidence about the drug's benefits and risks can be generated by multiple investigators, supported by various funders, and generated from a wide variety of observational studies and RCTs. Concerns about a drug's benefit–risk profile are likely to involve comparisons with other active treatments that are considered to be therapeutic alternatives.

In theory, an ideal RCT could provide the evidence that regulators need to identify the best regulatory response to a public health question of interest. In practice, however, a number of constraints can make the ideal trial infeasible and increase the potential for imprecision, bias, and decreased transportability[8] of results: patients may refuse to participate, making the study population less representative of the target population taking the drug; adherence may not reach desired levels; and patients may withdraw from the trial. Other practical considerations can limit an RCT or observational study's ability to address the public health question. Those limitations include the ability to measure the endpoints of primary interest, the determinants of drug choice, timeliness, the quality of available data sources or easily obtainable information for observational studies, the frequency of the endpoint being studied, the availability of participants, and the effect size of interest. The public health question also greatly affects the choice of design, with RCTs having advantages over observational studies when the public health question focuses primarily on a drug's benefits or a relative effect size is likely to be small; observational studies have some advantages over

[8]The term *transportability* is used in this report, rather than *external validity* or *generalizability*, because the committee thinks that it reflects a nonbinary characteristic better. Different effects can occur in a variety of settings, and study results may be transportable to some populations or settings but not others, so transportability may not be a simple binary property.

RCTs when the primary focus is on rare or delayed risks, and the relative risks are moderate or large.

Virtually every study type has tradeoffs dictated by either its design or its conduct. Regardless of the type of design chosen, the study should have prespecified protocols, endpoints, analytic plans, and procedures in place to ensure adequate and uniform followup, ascertainment and adjudication of endpoints, and other steps to ensure data quality.

While often methodologically superior to observational studies that use existing data, in the required postmarketing context a prospective cohort study that is designed so that followup starts at the initiation of drug treatment can raise some of the same ethical issues that are raised by an RCT, assuming both occur at the same time in the drug's lifecycle. In these circumstances, there may be ethical advantages to FDA's requiring observational designs examining the effects of past exposures, which may yield results sooner and enable faster regulatory action to protect the public's health. The ability of such designs to provide the information FDA requires for regulatory action rests not only on the availability of high-quality data but also on access to those data. Access is itself a function of ethical considerations related to privacy and authorization.

In deciding what type of RCT to require, FDA should consider which RCT would best approximate the ideal hypothetical trial. As with observational studies, the choice of a comparator for a drug is an important element in the design of an RCT. If an effective treatment is available for the same indication, an active-controlled design (a head-to-head trial, defined as a comparison of two active treatments indicated for the same patients with the same conditions) is often preferred on both ethical and public health grounds. It may be ethically acceptable, however, for FDA to require a placebo-controlled postmarketing trial under some specific circumstances even if an alternative treatment is available—such as studies of interventions intended to provide symptomatic relief for minor, self-limiting, or reversible conditions and in short-term trials to evaluate surrogate endpoints.

When FDA requires postmarketing research, it has an obligation to ensure that the research is conducted ethically. One component of that obligation is to ensure that, when appropriate, the study secures the voluntary informed consent of research participants. However, the ethical obligation to obtain prior informed consent is not applicable to all required postmarketing research.

There are not always ethically relevant distinctions between some kinds of observational research that FDA could require manufacturers to conduct and FDA surveillance activities that are classified as public health practice. It is unclear whether FDA's human subjects regulation (21 CFR 50) or the Common Rule (45 CFR 46) is the operative regulation for FDA-required, postmarketing observational studies, nor is it clear whether some or all types of observational designs qualify as clinical investigations under 21 CFR 50. It is important that FDA clarify whether its human subjects regulations govern required postmarketing observational studies and, if so, how FDA will address and expect institutional review boards (IRBs) to address any differences between 21 CFR 50 and 45 CFR 46 in oversight and research participant protections for different observational designs.

The desirability of linking datasets and of obtaining additional information from patients, or otherwise needing access to some identifying information about patients, will probably increase. That increase could lead to additional ethical questions about the adequacy of data-security practices, authorization for access to different datasets, and the difference, if any, between research and public health goals. To ensure the public that such activities are being conducted with appropriate controls and protections, an independent review body should be formed to advise FDA on the ethics of the postmarketing research and surveillance activities involving large datasets that it conducts or requires.

With regard to required RCTs, there are specific aspects of informed consent that are more salient in the postmarketing setting than in the premarketing setting. In postmarketing trials, patients may be asked to submit to a drug regimen when a safety signal has prompted concerns about risk and possibly about the acceptability of the drug's benefit–risk profile. In that context, it is important to provide information to potential participants about why a new study is required and why it is still ethically acceptable to ask them to consider participating in the study. Provisions may need to be made to ensure adequate discussion of how well patients' existing treatment is working for them. Potential participants also need to know how the care that they will receive in an RCT may differ from the care that they would ordinarily receive. If clinical practice shifts during the trial period, that should be communicated to participants.

For all postmarketing research that it requires, FDA should provide the relevant oversight bodies, such as the IRB and data-monitoring committee (DMC), information about the public health question at issue; the specifics of the study design intended to address that question, including any design features that it views as necessary to the ethical justification of the study; and any changes in clinical practice or professional standards that arise over the course of the study that might affect the benefit–risk profile of a drug and influence a person's decision to join or remain in the study. The IRB should consider dissemination of that information to potential and current study participants.

RESPONSES TO THE CHARGE QUESTIONS[9]

How should FDA factor in different kinds of safety evidence in considering different kinds of regulatory actions?

Since no single algorithm can determine how to factor different kinds of safety evidence into regulatory decision-making, the committee specifies pro-

[9]The committee presents the questions in the order in which they are discussed in the chapters of the report, not the order in which they are presented in the charge.

cesses and principles to guide FDA in deciding among postmarketing regulatory actions. The committee identifies the following five actions FDA can take to improve its decision-making process for postmarketing regulatory decisions in response to different kinds of safety evidence: (1) adopt a specified decision-making framework; (2) create a BRAMP document for each drug; (3) characterize the nature of any disagreements about scientific evidence; (4) create effective multidisciplinary teams with wide ranging expertise, including expertise in observational study design and interpretation, outcomes research and pharmacoepidemiology, and Bayesian methods and modern causal inference approaches; and (5) adhere to the principles of reproducible research.

What are the strengths and weaknesses of various approaches, including observational studies, including patient registries, meta-analyses, including patient-level data meta-analyses, and randomized controlled trials, to generate evidence about safety questions?

A wide variety of designs, data sources, and context-specific facts and priorities affect the strengths and weaknesses of studies, such as whether an adverse event is rare or common, mild or serious, or known or unknown and whether the relative size of risk increase posed by a drug is large or small. A clinical trial of too short a duration to find a delayed effect is going to provide less relevant safety evidence than a design based on patient registry data with long follow-up. These and other contextual and situation-specific factors can be expected to trump broad principles.

The committee does, however, outline some general considerations that are important for evaluating the value of various designs for decision-making purposes. The initial considerations are how strong the signal that motivates the design is and whether it involves primarily an increase in risk, a decrease in benefit, or both, for either the general population or a definable subgroup. Second is how time-urgent the need for a regulatory response is on the basis of the nature of the signal. The third consideration involves how large the change in benefits or risks must be, on both relative and absolute scales, to justify a regulatory response. Fourth is what the other causes of a given adverse event (or failure of benefit) might be and how predictive they are. Fifth is the quality of data likely to be gathered as part of any given design with respect to drug exposure, outcomes, confounders, and other relevant patient, disease, or contextual characteristics. Sixth is a judgment of how study design, conduct, or context is likely to affect the transportability of the study results. Seventh is what the logistical requirements of a design will be, including data access, cost, and feasibility. Finally, there are considerations of ethical burden, consent, confidentiality, and study oversight. These factors can lead to the choice of either a single design type or a combination of studies with counterbalancing strengths and weaknesses.

Considering the speed, cost, and value of studies, what types of follow-up studies are appropriate to investigate different kinds of signals (detected pre-approval or postmarketing) and in what temporal order?

All the issues listed in the preceding question about design choice also affect the optimal sequencing of study designs in response to a given signal. The main difference is that the outcome of one study may affect the design, conduct, or initiation of subsequent studies. There are general principles to guide FDA beyond the statutory requirement in FDAAA[10] to require a clinical trial only if sufficient information to address the public health question and the attendant decision cannot be obtained with an observational study. All research strategies will work best if anticipated and planned for early, even evidence synthesis. The committee identifies a number of characteristics—consistent with FDA's authorities under FDAAA and with FDA guidance on postmarketing requirements—that, if evident in the premarketing phase, should cause heightened concern about the possibility that harm will outweigh benefit in the postmarketing context.

Under what circumstances should head-to-head randomized clinical trials for safety be required?

The public health question that underlies FDA's regulatory decisions in the postmarketing setting is most likely to be addressed by comparing the drug at issue with the therapies likely to be used if the drug were removed from the market or its use were restricted. That is, it is most likely to be addressed by a head-to-head trial involving a comparison of two active treatments that are both indicated for the same patients who have the same condition. However, for such a study to be scientifically valid and ethical, the active comparator must have a well-defined benefit–risk profile and be a clinically acceptable alternative to the drug being tested. If no comparator treatment exists or no comparator has a well-defined benefit–risk profile, typically at least one arm of the study should be some form of "usual care" or a placebo if usual care is not a proven or active treatment. If there are ethical reasons for not having a usual-care or placebo arm in the study—for example, if the treatment in question is for an irreversible and fatal disease—a treatment that does not have a well-defined benefit–risk profile might be the only ethically acceptable comparator. In such cases, FDA should take the questionable benefit–risk profiles of the drug and its comparator into account when interpreting the results of the study.

What are the ethical and informed consent issues that must be considered when designing randomized clinical trials to evaluate potential safety risks?

The ethical justification for FDA to require a trial to resolve a postmarketing benefit–risk profile question rests on the determination that (1) a responsible

---

[10]21 USC § 355(o)(3)(2010).

regulatory decision cannot be made on the basis of existing evidence or evidence that could be obtained from new observational studies, (2) an RCT can be properly designed and implemented to inform a responsible regulatory decision, (3) FDA will use trial results in making a regulatory decision in a timely fashion, and (4) the RCT can be carried out in a manner that provides sufficient protection of and respect for research participants. Informed consent obligations may be especially salient in the fourth consideration because patients may be asked to submit to a drug regimen about which a safety signal has prompted concerns about risk and potentially about the acceptability of the drug's benefit–risk profile. FDA should work with manufacturers, investigators, and IRBs to ensure that prospective research participants understand why additional research about an approved drug is needed, why it is reasonable to ask them to consider participating in the study, the state of current evidence about the drug's risks (including any boxed warnings, the "major statement" currently listed in direct-to-consumer advertisements, and any formal conclusions about adverse effects made by FDA staff or an FDA advisory committee), and how the care that participants in the RCT will receive may differ from the care that they would ordinarily receive. The last consideration is particularly crucial in cases in which medical practice has shifted away from prescribing the study drug because accumulating evidence from passive surveillance, observational studies, and small trials or meta-analyses suggests that another therapy is as effective and has a more favorable benefit–risk profile. It should be communicated in this situation that a potential participant who does not enroll in the trial is more likely to have a different drug prescribed. If clinical practice continues to shift during the trial period, the statement should be strengthened and communicated to research participants.

FINDINGS AND RECOMMENDATIONS

Finding 2.1

FDA's current approach to drug oversight in the postmarketing setting is not sufficiently systematic and does not ensure consistent assessment of benefits and risks associated with a drug over its lifecycle. Use of a standardized regulatory decision-making framework that is flexible enough to adapt to decisions of different complexity could make FDA's decision-making process more predictable, transparent, and active, allowing FDA to better anticipate postmarketing research needs and to plan for such research early when more design options with fewer ethical tensions might be possible.

Recommendation 2.1

FDA should adopt a consistent decision-making framework for regulatory actions across the lifecycle of all drugs that includes opportunities for input from patients and other stakeholders. This framework should be employed in making the initial drug approval decision and, in the postmarketing context, whenever new information that could affect the drug's benefit–risk profile emerges. The framework should include three stages:

Stage I: Define the public health question that requires a regulatory decision or agency response.
Stage II: Assess the drug's confirmed or potential benefits and risks by using a systematic process to evaluate and characterize existing evidence and any sources of disagreement about that evidence.
Stage III: Determine the appropriate regulatory response to the public health question specified in Stage I, including whether further research should be required, by integrating the evaluation of the evidence of benefits and risks from Stage II with legal and ethical considerations and input from stakeholders; communicate to the public the reasoning behind the decision; implement the regulatory response; and, particularly for difficult or controversial decisions (see Recommendation 2.5), evaluate the impact of the regulatory response.

Finding 2.2

No single, clear, comprehensive, and public document currently captures FDA's assessments of a drug's benefits and risks over the course of its lifecycle, nor does any documentation help to standardize FDA's decision-making processes or describe FDA's rationale for its regulatory actions. Capturing such information in a living document would formalize the lifecycle approach to drug regulation, improve regulatory oversight, and improve the transparency of FDA's decisions.

Recommendation 2.2
FDA should require and maintain, for each new drug and for already approved drugs for which questions about the benefit–risk profile are raised, a publicly available and understandable Benefit and Risk Assessment and Management Plan (BRAMP). For new drugs, the BRAMP document should be initiated during the drug-approval phase and updated over the lifecycle of the drug at pre-specified times in the postmarketing setting and whenever questions about the drug's benefit–risk profile arise. The document should include a description of: any public health questions raised during the drug's lifecycle; the benefit and risk assessment specific to each public health question; key stakeholder input specific to each question; any regulatory decisions or actions and the rationale for each decision, including requirements for postmarketing research or a risk evaluation and mitigation strategy (REMS); a schedule for future assessments of benefits and risks; and plans for and results of evaluating the effectiveness of any regulatory decisions or actions.

- In the *premarketing* phase, the drug sponsor should provide a summary of the drug's benefits and risks, any uncertainties in the evidence, and plans for decreasing those uncertainties. FDA should use that information as a starting point to develop the BRAMP document. FDA staff involved with the drug's premarketing application and staff with expertise and knowledge in postmarketing safety assessment should finalize the initial entry to the BRAMP document.
- In composing teams to monitor the safety of a drug and maintain its BRAMP in the *postmarketing* phase of the drug's lifecycle, FDA should consider the real or perceived confirmation bias of staff that played a significant role in approving the drug. This should be managed by ensuring that the leader of the postmarketing safety monitoring team is without the potential for such bias. The monitoring team should have expertise in surveillance, epidemiology, and the evaluation of safety data collected from different observational and clinical trial designs. The team should review and modify the BRAMP document at specified intervals throughout the lifecycle of the drug, including when new information warrants re-evaluation of the drug's benefit–risk profile.

Finding 2.3

In the premarketing setting, evidence is derived primarily from randomized controlled trials. In the postmarketing setting, however, evidence may be derived from surveillance, observational studies, patient registries, published and unpublished clinical trials, meta-analyses, and relevant case reports or series. Data sources, study designs, and analytic approaches for the postmarketing context are evolving rapidly. Given those differences, the expertise needed to evaluate and characterize the quality of evidence in the postmarketing setting is different from and broader than that needed in the premarketing setting.

Recommendation 2.3

In making determinations about appropriate regulatory decisions to be implemented in the postmarketing context, FDA should ensure that the full range of methodologic expertise is used to evaluate the strength of evidence of a drug's benefits and risks from a wide range of designs. For complex regulatory decisions, including decisions about requiring additional postmarketing research, such expertise should include, but not be limited to

- Clinical medicine and clinical practice, such as pharmacy.
- Biostatistics: Bayesian, frequentist, and causal inference methods.
- Epidemiology and pharmacoepidemiology.
- Clinical trials.

- Benefit–risk analysis.
- Research and public health ethics.
- Risk communication.

Finding 2.4

Section 901 of FDAAA[11] stipulates the purposes for which FDA has the authority to require postmarketing observational studies and RCTs, and 2011 FDA guidance for industry provides information on FDA's implementation of that section of FDAAA. Although FDA's decisions to require postmarketing research need to be made case by case, there are some identifiable conditions that are concordant with but more specific and detailed than those outlined in FDAAA and FDA guidance, which make information from additional postmarketing research important.

Recommendation 2.4

FDA should prospectively determine and publicly identify specific conditions, including drug characteristics and other features, that are associated with greater uncertainty about a drug's benefit–risk profile in the postmarketing setting. Under those identified conditions, FDA should require postmarketing research in a timely fashion unless there is a compelling reason not to, and should make public the rationale for requiring or not requiring postmarketing research in each case. Those premarketing and postmarketing conditions should include the following:

- A drug is approved when several surrogate endpoints provide conflicting evidence about the likely health outcomes associated with the drug.
- A first-in-class drug is approved on the basis of surrogate endpoints used in drugs of a different class.
- A drug is associated with safety signals from premarketing data or postmarketing surveillance when
  - there is a substantial public health concern,
  - a severe adverse event is seen, or
  - there is a strong biologic rationale for a particular adverse effect.
- A drug is expected to have a different benefit–risk profile in a subgroup or under real-world conditions.
- A drug is in a class for which a substantial safety signal has previously been identified.
- Evidence of a lack of benefit of a drug in the whole population or in identifiable subgroups emerges in the postmarketing setting.

---

[11]21 USC § 355(o) (2010).

Finding 2.5

Some FDA decisions in response to postmarketing public health questions are controversial or difficult. Complex instances tend to occur when FDA must make a decision despite scientific disagreement about the relevant evidence or when the likely effects of a given regulatory action are uncertain. These cases serve as important opportunities for FDA, external scientists, and the public to learn about the complexities of the decision-making process and the consequences of a regulatory decision, and for FDA to improve its processes and practices.

> **Recommendation 2.5**
> FDA should conduct after-action reviews of postmarketing drug-related decisions that are particularly controversial or difficult or when a major regulatory decision is made after marketing. Such a review should include an assessment of the decision-making process itself and the effects of the final decision on the public's health.

Finding 2.6

Surrogate endpoints are often relied on in the drug-approval process, and their use has been related to a number of high-profile drug-safety problems. The findings of postmarketing studies can be used to revise the approval process and improve the endpoints and methods used in it.

> **Recommendation 2.6**
> As part of a continuing effort to improve regulatory science, FDA should maintain and annually update a list of surrogate endpoints allowed for use in the approval of drugs, the rationale for their use, the postmarketing experience regarding their correlation with health outcomes of interest, and any revisions of approval requirements that may have been suggested by the results of the postmarketing studies. The list should accumulate the postmarketing experience of the successes and failures of various surrogates so that for each major drug class, the regulatory science related to approval methods can be modified and improved. FDA should also revise or develop guidance documents for the use of selected surrogate endpoints that, on the basis of postmarketing studies, appear to be inconsistently predictive of clinical outcomes.

Finding 3.1

Some of FDA's most difficult decisions are those in which experts disagree about how compelling is the evidence that informs the public health question. Understanding the nature and sources of those disagreements and their implications for FDA's decisions is key to improving the agency's decision-making process. For example, experts can disagree about the plausibility of a new risk (or decreased benefit) on the basis of different assessments of prior evidence, the quality of new data, the adequacy of confounding control in the relevant studies, the transportability of results, the appropriateness of the statistical analysis, the relevance of the new evidence to the public health question, how the evidence should be weighed and synthesized, or the threshold for regulatory actions.

Recommendation 3.1
FDA should use the framework for decision-making proposed in Recommendation 2.1 to ensure a thorough discussion and clear understanding of the sources of disagreement about the available evidence among all participants in the regulatory decision-making process. In the interest of transparency, FDA should use the BRAMP document proposed in Recommendation 2.2 to ensure that such disagreements and how they were resolved are documented and made public.

Finding 3.2

Such methods as Bayesian analyses or other approaches to integrating external relevant information with newly emerging information could provide decision-makers with useful quantitative assessments of evidence. An example would be sensitivity analyses of clinical-trial data that illustrate the influence of prior probabilities on estimates of probabilities that an intervention has unacceptable safety risks. These approaches can inform judgments, allow more rational decision-making, and permit input from multiple stakeholders and experts.

Recommendation 3.2
FDA should ensure that it has adequate expertise in Bayesian approaches, in combination with expertise in relevant frequentist and causal inference methods, to assess the probability that observed associations reflect actual causal effects, to incorporate multiple sources of uncertainty into the decision-making process, and to evaluate the sensitivity of those conclusions to different representations of external evidence. To facilitate the use of Bayesian approaches, FDA should develop a guidance document for the use of Bayesian methods for assessing a drug's benefits, risks, and benefit–risk profile.

Finding 3.3

Traditionally, the main criteria for evaluating a study are ones that contribute to its internal validity. A well-conducted RCT typically has higher internal validity than a well-conducted observational study. Results of observational studies, however, can have greater transportability if their participants are more similar to the target clinical population than to the participants in a clinical trial. In some circumstances, such as an evaluation of the association between a drug and an uncommon unexpected adverse event, observational studies may produce estimates closer to the actual risk in the general population than can be achieved in clinical trials. In assessing the relevance of study findings to a public health question, the transportability of the study results is as important as the determinants of its internal validity.

Recommendation 3.3
In assessing the benefits and risks associated with a drug in the postmarketing context, FDA should develop guidance and review processes that ensure that observational studies with high internal validity are given appropriate weight in the evaluation of drug harms and that transportability is given emphasis similar to that given bias and other errors in assessing the weight of evidence that a study provides to inform a public health question.

Finding 3.4

The principles of reproducible research are important for ensuring the integrity of postmarketing research used by FDA. Those principles include providing information on the provenance of data (from measurement to analytic dataset) and, when possible, making available properly annotated analytic datasets, study protocols (including statistical analysis plan) and their amendments, and statistical codes.

Recommendation 3.4
All analyses, whether conducted independently of FDA or by FDA staff, whose results are relied on for postmarketing regulatory decisions should use the principles of reproducible research when possible, subject to legal constraints. To that end, FDA should present data and analyses in a fashion that allows independent analysts either to reproduce the findings or to understand how FDA generated the results in sufficient detail to understand the strengths, weaknesses, and assumptions of the relevant analyses.

Finding 3.5

The ability of researchers in and outside FDA to analyze new information about the benefits and risks associated with a marketed drug and to design appropriate postmarketing research—including conducting individual-patient meta-analyses—is enhanced by access to data and analyses from all studies of the drug and others in the same drug class that were reported in the preapproval process. Although disclosure of such information is likely to advance the public's health, such disclosures raise concerns about the privacy of participants in the research that generated the information and may threaten industry interest in maintaining proprietary information, which is deemed important for innovation. New approaches to resolving this tension are needed.

Recommendation 3.5
FDA should establish and coordinate a working group, including industry and patient and consumer representatives, to find ways that appropriately balance public health, privacy, and proprietary interests to facilitate disclosure of data for trials and studies relevant to postmarketing research decisions.

Finding 3.6

The elements of the benefit–risk profile of a drug are best estimated by using all the available high-quality data, and meta-analysis is a useful tool for summarizing such data and evaluating heterogeneity. However, because the reporting of harms in published RCTs and observational studies is often poor or inconsistent and because there is often substantial publication bias in studies of drug risk, steps are needed to improve both the reporting of harms and the design of studies of harm. That can be done through prospective planning for selected meta-analyses and by monitoring compliance with the FDAAA requirement that summary trial results for all primary and secondary outcomes be published at ClinicalTrials.gov.

Recommendation 3.6
For drugs that are likely to have required postmarketing observational studies or trials, FDA should use the BRAMP document to specify potential public health questions of interest as early as possible; should prospectively recommend standards for uniform definition of key variables and complete ascertainment of events among studies or convene researchers in the field to suggest such standards and promote data-sharing; should prospectively plan meta-analyses of the data with reference to specified exposures, outcomes, comparators, and covariates; should conduct the meta-analyses of the data; and should make appropriate regulatory decisions in a timely fashion. FDA can also improve the validity of meta-analyses by monitoring and encouraging compliance with FDAAA requirements for reporting to ClinicalTrials.gov.

Finding 3.7

FDA produced a high-quality guidance document on the use of the noninferiority design for the study of efficacy. Increasingly, FDA is using the noninferiority design to evaluate drug safety endpoints as the primary outcomes in randomized trials. The use of noninferiority analyses to establish the acceptability of the benefit–risk profile of a drug can take the decision about how to balance the risks and benefits of two drugs out of the hands of regulators. Noninferiority trials also have the disadvantage of being biased toward equivalence when trial design or conduct is suboptimal; this is of particular concern when such trials are used to estimate risks.

Recommendation 3.7.1
FDA should develop a guidance document on the design and conduct of noninferiority postmarketing trials for the study of safety of a drug. The guidance should include discussion of criteria for choosing the standard therapy to be used in the active-treatment control arm; of methods for selecting a noninferiority margin in safety trials and ensuring high-quality trial conduct; of the optimal analytic methods, including Bayesian approaches; and of the interpretation of the findings in terms of the drug's benefit–risk profile.

Recommendation 3.7.2
FDA should closely scrutinize the design and conduct of any noninferiority safety studies for aspects that may inappropriately make the arms appear similar. FDA should use the observed-effect estimate and confidence interval as a basis for decision-making, not the binary noninferiority verdict.

Finding 4.1

A decision by FDA to require postmarketing research can put research participants at risk. It can also put patients and the public at risk by delaying a regulatory decision that might be protective of public health. Some conditions are necessary but not sufficient for an FDA decision to require postmarketing research to be ethical.

Recommendation 4.1.1
FDA should require postmarketing research only when (1) uncertainty about the benefit–risk balance is such that a responsible decision about the future regulatory status of the drug cannot be made on the basis of existing evidence; (2) it is expected that the research can be properly designed and implemented to reduce uncertainty about the benefit–risk profile to allow a responsible regulatory decision; (3) FDA has a plan for using the results of the research to make a regulatory decision in a timely fashion; and (4) the research can be conducted in a manner that provides sufficient protection of and respect for research participants.

Finding 4.2

For postmarketing investigations authorized under Section 901 of FDAAA,[12] FDA can require an RCT only if it is unable to obtain the data that it needs from an observational study or surveillance. Determining what kind of study will pro-

---

[12]21 USC § 355(o) (2010).

vide the information needed to answer FDA's public health question, however, is complex. In the postmarketing setting, both observational studies and RCTs have advantages and disadvantages. In some circumstances, the evidence provided by an observational study may be as good as or better for informing a public health question than the evidence provided by a feasible clinical trial; that is more likely to occur when the magnitude of the relative risk is large in contrast with the potential for confounding, which occurs with many drug harms. Observational studies also have a number of ethical and practical advantages over RCTs. In other circumstances, however, the evidence available from an observational study would not be able to provide the necessary additional information to help answer the public health question. Those instances are more likely to occur when the public health questions are related primarily to a drug's benefits.

Recommendation 4.2
When deciding which type of research to require in the postmarketing setting, FDA should carefully weigh the strengths of potential observational studies for evaluating risks and their ethical and practical advantages, including the timeframe within which the data are needed, against the limitations of potential observational studies for generating the data needed to answer the public health question. An RCT should be required only if FDA has concluded that an observational study could not provide the necessary information, that an RCT is likely to generate the information within the necessary timeframe, and that the necessary RCT is ethically acceptable.

Finding 4.3

When FDA requires a postmarketing RCT, the public health question is most likely to be properly addressed by a comparison of the target drug with the standard therapy for the condition involved—if there is a standard therapy. Such a trial would involve a "head-to-head" design, defined as a comparison of two active treatments that are indicated for the same patients who have the same condition. However, it is also important both scientifically and ethically for at least one clinically acceptable comparator in the required trial to have a well-defined benefit–risk profile.

Recommendation 4.3
If FDA requires a postmarketing RCT for an indication for which there is an accepted active treatment that would probably be used if access to the drug under study were restricted, the alternative treatment should be used as at least one comparator in the trial.

Finding 4.4

When deciding whether to require a postmarketing study, FDA must balance its ethical obligation to protect the public's health with its ethical obligation to protect research participants. In some instances, FDA may be faced with a decision to require an RCT that might expose participants to more net risk than they would probably face if decisions about their drug treatment were being made in the context of clinical practice or that offers no reasonable expectation of clinical benefit to participants although its results may benefit society. Requiring such a study may be ethically justifiable but only under special circumstances.

Recommendation 4.4

FDA should require a postmarketing RCT that might expose research participants to more risk or less net clinical benefit than they would probably face if decisions about their drug treatment were being made in the context of clinical practice only if a question of pressing public health significance is at stake, if no other design with a better benefit–risk balance for participants could supply the evidence needed for a responsible regulatory response to the question, and if special safeguards are in place to protect the rights and interests of the research participants. Those safeguards should include the determination by an appropriately constituted review committee that the additional risk is small enough for it to be ethical to ask people whether they are willing to accept it *solely* to contribute to the public good; the minimization of additional risk by careful study design and implementation of a robust monitoring plan throughout the study; the inclusion of special measures in the process of soliciting informed consent to confirm that patients understand and willingly accept that they are assuming an additional risk, beyond what they are likely to face in clinical practice, solely in the interest of the public good; and the implementation of processes to ensure that over the course of the trial participants are regularly informed of any changes in clinical practice or the medical literature relevant to assessments of the comparative benefits and risks associated with trial participation and (nonresearch) clinical management.

Finding 4.5

Although regulations governing human subjects research do not apply if an activity is considered public health practice, as is the case with the Sentinel system, it is often not possible to draw a clear or ethically relevant distinction between some kinds of FDA-required observational research and public health practice. It is important that FDA, in conjunction with the Office for Human Research Protections (OHRP), clarify whether its human subjects regulations (21 CFR 50) govern required postmarketing observational studies and, if so, how FDA will address and will expect IRBs to address any differences between 21 CFR 50 and other potentially applicable human subject regulations (45 CFR 46 Subpart A) in oversight and research-participant protection, including consent requirements, in different observational designs so that its regulations are not a barrier to what would otherwise be ethically acceptable observational designs. FDA also needs to determine how best to ensure that it is feasible for drug companies and their contractors to conduct the postmarketing observational studies that it requires, in view of the Health Insurance Portability and Accountability Act of 1996 and other potential constraints, while protecting the privacy of the people whose data are used. It is also likely that the desirability of linking datasets and of obtaining additional information from patients or otherwise needing access to some identifying information about patients will increase, whether studies are conducted under the auspices of FDA-supported surveillance systems, such as Sentinel and deemed public health practice, or conducted by manufacturers as required by FDA and interpreted at least by some to be research, raising additional ethical questions about the adequacy of data security, authorization of access to different datasets, and different research and public health purposes.

Recommendation 4.5.1
FDA, in conjunction with the Office for Human Research Protections (OHRP), should clarify whether its human subjects regulations (21 CFR 50) govern required postmarketing observational studies and, if so, how FDA will address and will expect IRBs to address any differences between 21 CFR 50 and other potentially applicable human subject regulations (45 CFR 46 Subpart A) in oversight and research-participant protection, including consent requirements.

Recommendation 4.5.2
To assure the public that surveillance and required observational studies can proceed with appropriate controls and protections, and to facilitate the conduct of ethically acceptable surveillance and required observational studies that are important to the public's health, FDA should form an independent body to advise FDA, on an as needed basis, on the ethics of postmarketing research and surveillance activities that it conducts or requires. This advisory body should be positioned to provide guidance on emerging ethical challenges, with particular focus on activities that are determined not to require IRB oversight.

Finding 4.6

FDA has an ethical obligation to ensure that the rights and interests of participants in the postmarketing research that it requires are properly protected. IRBs and data-monitoring committees (DMCs) can play a critical role in assisting FDA with this obligation, but these bodies require information and guidance from FDA to be effective in their research-participant protection responsibilities.

Recommendation 4.6

For all postmarketing research that it requires and that is subject to IRB or DMC oversight, FDA should provide each IRB (including centralized IRBs and multiple IRBs) and each DMC with the up-to-date BRAMP document for the study drug and sufficient information in writing for the IRB or DMC to provide appropriate oversight, including information about the public health question at issue, the specifics of the study design intended to address the question, design features that FDA views as necessary for the ethical justification of the study, and any changes in clinical practice or professional standards that arise over the course of the study that might affect the benefit–risk profile of a drug and influence a person's decision to participate or remain a participant in the study.

Finding 4.7

There are heightened informed consent concerns in the conduct of FDA-required RCTs in the postmarketing setting. FDA has an ethical responsibility to ensure that postmarketing clinical trials include appropriate informed consent processes and oversight.

Recommendation 4.7

FDA should issue guidance for interpreting disclosure and informed consent requirements in applicable federal regulations in the context of postmarketing RCTs that it requires, using the authorities granted to it in Section 901 of FDAAA[13] to help oversight bodies (such as IRBs) to ensure that such trials include a comprehensive informed consent process. The guidance should emphasize that, in addition to standard disclosure requirements, the following information of particular importance in the postmarketing setting should be communicated to research participants: why a new study of an approved drug is being required; salient risks posed by participation in required postmarketing research, including whether new information suggests that the drug under study may pose serious risks; and whether medical practice has shifted or is shifting away from prescribing the study drug. The guidance should make clear that participants must be informed of any substantial changes in clinical practice and professional standards over the course of the trial and informed of any new research findings relevant to their willingness to accept or to continue to accept the risks associated with the trial. And the guidance should identify the conditions under which consent processes should include measures to validate the adequacy of participants' understanding, not only the adequacy of the disclosures made to participants.

[13] 21 USC § 355(o) (2010).

Finding 4.8

During the last two decades, the volume of clinical trials conducted outside the United States has increased dramatically, and this has led to concerns about the quality, reliability, and transportability of research results and about the adequacy of protections for research participants. Those concerns apply as well to FDA-required postmarketing research that uses research sites outside the United States. FDA's Office of International Programs, through its Harmonization and Multilateral Relations Office, is tasked with the responsibility of coordinating and collaborating with other agencies and countries on international standards and harmonization issues and is therefore well positioned to address these concerns.

Recommendation 4.8
FDA should direct its Office of International Programs to include explicitly among its responsibilities working with counterpart agencies of other governments and with industry to resolve concerns about the ethics and quality of evidence in the conduct of FDA-required postmarketing research outside the United States.

1

Introduction

We are in the beginning of a new era for drug safety where protecting public health means that [the Food and Drug Administration's] responsibility doesn't end when we grant a product market approval; that is merely the first check point in ensuring safety.
—Dr. Margaret Hamburg, Commissioner, US Food and Drug Administration (FDA, 2011a).

An estimated 48 percent of the US population take at least one prescription drug[1] in a given month (Gu et al., 2010). Drugs provide great benefit to society by saving or improving lives. Antibiotics can cure infections, heart medications can decrease the risk of heart attacks, and drugs for multiple sclerosis can decrease the symptoms of the disease and improve patients' quality of life. At the same time, virtually all drugs have some unintended side effects, some of which are serious and can harm the people who take them. Budnitz et al. (2006) estimate that about 700,000 people are treated in US emergency rooms each year for severe adverse drug reactions, and about 120,000 require hospital admission. In a more recent study using data from 2007 through 2009, Budnitz et al. (2011) estimate that there are about "265,802 emergency department visits (95% confidence interval [CI], 184,040 to 347,563) for adverse drug events annually . . . among adults 65 years of age or older", of which 99,628 (95% CI, 55,531 to 143,724) required hospitalization.

The US Food and Drug Administration (FDA) is the agency responsible for ensuring that prescription drugs are safe and effective. FDA's approval of a drug for use in the United States is the result of a considered judgment based on available data and the agency's experience with such decisions that overall the potential benefits of the drug outweigh the risks to patients for whom the drug

[1]For simplicity, the committee uses the term *drugs* throughout this report, but similar considerations would apply to biologics. The committee's charge is related to the US Food and Drug Administration (FDA) regulation of the drug and biologics supply. When discussing FDA's regulatory authority and mission, therefore, the committee does not address FDA's roles related to other products, such as tobacco, medical devices, veterinary medicines, food, or animal feed.

is indicated. However, premarketing data used in approval applications are collected from studies that involve small numbers of participants[2]—often only a few hundred or a few thousand—over a relatively short period of time (IOM, 2007a), so not all risks associated with a drug are known at the time of approval. Warnings or restrictions may be added to the product label, or a drug may be removed from the market because unexpected or greater than expected morbidity or mortality is identified only after a drug enters widespread use. The discovery of new adverse events in the postmarketing setting is part of the normal, natural history of approved drugs. The timely identification of and response to drug-related risks are central to the mission of FDA.

Recent advances in information technology, including electronic health records, and changes in FDA laws, such as the Food and Drug Administration Amendments Act (FDAAA) of 2007,[3] provide the opportunity to improve the system for ensuring that drugs are safe and effective. Previous Institute of Medicine (IOM) reports have made recommendations about improving aspects of drug-related patient-safety issues to FDA, other federal agencies, and Congress (IOM, 2002, 2004, 2007a,b). However, no report has focused specifically on the ethical and scientific issues that arise in the postmarketing environment, including how these issues intersect with the authority of FDA to require manufacturers to conduct postmarketing research and how FDA should integrate that authority and evidence, into its regulatory decision-making. The present report addresses those issues in response to the committee's charge (see Box 1-1) and offers specific recommendations about the ethics and science of FDA required postmarketing research and about the decision-making process about approved drugs when safety issues arise.

THE EVOLUTION OF THE FOOD AND DRUG ADMINISTRATION'S RESPONSIBILITIES IN THE POSTMARKETING SETTING

Food and Drug Administration Authority Before 2007

FDA's regulatory authority has evolved over the last 100 years, often as a result of serious drug-related adverse events or deaths. Table 1-1 presents some milestones in FDA's regulatory history. The initial grant of authority to FDA's predecessor agency began in 1906 with the passage of the Pure Food and Drug Act,[4] which, for drugs, focused on misbranding and adulteration. Thirty years

[2]Throughout this report, the committee uses the term *participants* or *research participants* rather than *human subjects*. The committee recognizes that both terms have been used in policy discussions on this topic for decades and that neither term perfectly captures the nature of the relationship between the persons who are studied in research (who are both *subjects of* research and *participants in* research) and those who are conducting the research.

[3]Food and Drug Administration Amendments Act of 2007, PL No. 110-85, 121 Stat. 823 (2007).

[4]Pure Food and Drug Act of 1906, PL 59-384, 34 Stat. 768 (1906).

BOX 1-1
Charge to the Committee

The US Food and Drug Administration (FDA) has requested that the Institute of Medicine convene a committee to evaluate the scientific and ethical issues involved in conducting studies of the safety of approved drugs. Questions to be explored by a committee include

1. What are the ethical and informed consent issues that must be considered when designing randomized clinical trials to evaluate potential safety risks?
2. What are the strengths and weaknesses of various approaches, including observational studies, including patient registries, meta-analyses, including patient-level data meta-analyses, and randomized controlled trials, to generate evidence about safety questions?
3. Considering the speed, cost, and value of studies, what types of follow-up studies are appropriate to investigate different kinds of signals (detected pre-approval or postapproval) and in what temporal order?
4. Under what circumstances should head-to-head randomized clinical trials for safety be required?
5. How should FDA factor in different kinds of safety evidence in considering different kinds of regulatory actions?

later, after more than 100 deaths, many in children, caused by diethylene glycol in an elixir of sulfanilamide, the Food, Drug, and Cosmetic Act (FDCA)[5] was enacted (FDA, 2009a). Under the FDCA, a new drug could not enter into interstate commerce unless its sponsor filed a new-drug application (NDA) with FDA that contained convincing evidence from preclinical toxicity testing that the drug was safe for its intended uses (Daemmrich, 2004a; Marks, 1997a). A drug was to be evaluated *only* with regard to its toxicity; its sponsor was not required to provide FDA with evidence of effectiveness or benefits. FDA could, however, deem a drug misbranded "if its labeling is false or misleading".[6] Under those conditions, FDA had the authority to withdraw its approval of the drug and to prosecute the drug sponsor (Carpenter, 2010a; Daemmrich, 2004a; Grossman et al., 2007; Marks, 1997a).[7]

---

[5]Food, Drug, and Cosmetic Act, PL No. 75-717, 52 Stat. 1040 (1938).
[6]21 USC §§ 331(a), (b), (c), (k) (2010).
[7]21 USC § 331 (2010).

TABLE 1-1 Key Milestones in Food and Drug Administration History Related to Drug Safety and Drug Studies

Year	Milestone
1906	Pure Food and Drug Act passed
1938	Federal Food, Drug, and Cosmetic Act passed
1962	Kefauver–Harris Drug Amendments of 1962 passed
1981	Food and Drug Administration (FDA) and Department of Health and Human Services revise and promulgate separate regulations for protection of research participants
1987	Investigational-drug regulations revised to expand access to experimental drugs for patients who have serious diseases for which there are no alternative therapies
1991	Regulations published to accelerate the review of drugs for life-threatening diseases
1992	First Prescription Drug User Fee Act (PDUFA) passed
1992	FDA given the authority to require postmarketing trials for accelerated approvals
1993	Consolidation of several adverse-reaction reporting systems launched as MedWatch
1997	Food and Drug Administration Modernization Act reauthorizes PDUFA (PDUFA II)
2002	Public Health Security and Bioterrorism Preparedness and Response Act reauthorizes PDUFA (PDUFA III); some funds allocated for drug-safety activities
2003	Pediatric Research Equity Act allows FDA to require clinical research into possible pediatric applications for new drugs and biologic products
2005	Drug Safety Board formed[a]
2007	Food and Drug Administration Amendments Act passed; act reauthorizes PDUFA (PDUFA IV) and dedicates a greater portion of funds to drug safety[b]

[a]Consisting of FDA staff and representatives of the National Institutes of Health and the Department of Veterans Affairs. The board advises the FDA Center for Drug Evaluation and Research (CDER) on drug-safety issues and works with CDER in communicating safety information to health professionals and patients. The administrative action creating this body occurred after prominent drug-safety controversies (such as controversies about Cox-2 selective agents, such as Bextra and Vioxx). The board was later codified in FDAAA (121 Stat 938).
[b]PDUFA IV expires in September 2012. PDUFA V is under discussion. Abbreviations: FDA, Food and Drug Administration; FDAAA, Food and Drug Administration Amendments Act; PDUFA, Prescription Drug User Fee Act.
SOURCE: FDA (2009a).

The next major change in FDA's statutory authority occurred in the early 1960s. Thousands of children in a number of countries other than the United States were born with limb defects to mothers who had been administered thalidomide for morning sickness; FDA had prevented marketing of thalidomide in the United States (Carpenter, 2010b; Hilts, 2003a). Concerns about the implications of this tragedy prompted Congress to pass the Drug Amendments of 1962 (PL 87-781), often referred to as the Kefauver–Harris amendments. That legislation shifted the burden of proof for a drug from FDA proving harm to manufacturers proving safety and efficacy, and represented a major shift in FDA's role and authority. For the first time, a drug sponsor was required by statute to provide evidence of the effectiveness of a drug, codifying some of FDA's practices during the 1950s (Carpenter, 2010b). After enactment of the 1962 amendments, the randomized controlled trial (RCT) emerged as the gold standard for the adequate and well-controlled studies required to demonstrate efficacy (Marks, 1997b) and led to the current drug-approval process summarized in Box 1-2. The 1962 amendments emphasized FDA's role as the marketplace gatekeeper for new drugs. The Kefauver–Harris amendments also required pharmaceutical companies to keep records of "clinical experience",[8] which were later interpreted as a requirement to report adverse reactions and events. That requirement evolved into today's MedWatch program, a consolidation of several adverse-reaction reporting systems (available at http://www.fda.gov/Safety/MedWatch/default.htm).

Concerns emerged in the 1980s that the length and complexity of the drug-approval process were delaying the availability of new life-saving drugs, such as those to treat AIDS and cancer (Anderson, 1989; Carpenter, 2010c; Daemmrich, 2004a,b; Hilts, 2003b). Patient groups, regulators, pharmaceutical companies, and others argued that a lack of resources at FDA was slowing the drug-approval process and preventing important drugs from coming to market in a timely matter (FDA, 2011b). In response, Congress passed the Prescription Drug User Fee Act (PDUFA) of 1992,[9] whose aim was to increase the pace of drug review by increasing FDA's resources to expand its drug-review staff and capabilities. In exchange for sponsors paying user fees, FDA agreed to use the funds to meet scheduled review goals, and Congress guaranteed not to reduce FDA's appropriations to compensate for the user fees (Carpenter, 2010c). FDA also agreed that the increased funds from the PDUFA would "be dedicated towards expediting the drug development process and the process for the review of human drug applications".[10]

In an effort to decrease the approval time for selected life-saving drugs, FDA promulgated its accelerated approval regulations in 1992 (21 CFR pt. 314, subpt. H, often referred to simply as "Subpart H"). Under these regulations, FDA may approve new drugs that treat "serious or life threatening illnesses"[11] based on clinical trials that used surrogate endpoints[12] in assessing the drug's efficacy.[13] In 1997, Congress confirmed FDA's statutory authority to approve drugs under

---

[8]21 USC § 355(k) (2010).

[9]Prescription Drug User Fee Act of 1992, PL No. 102-571, 106 Stat. 4491 (1992).

The PDUFA was written to expire in 5 years, but later laws (PDUFA II through PDUFA IV) have ensured that the user fees continued. The current Congress is expected to approve another extension before October 1, 2012, when PDUFA IV user-fee authority expires.

[10]21 USC § 379g note (2010).

[11]21 CFR § 314.500 (2011).

[12]FDA defines a *surrogate endpoint* as a "biomarker intended to substitute for a clinical efficacy endpoint. Surrogate endpoints are expected to predict clinical benefit (or harm, or lack of benefit or harm)" (Atkinson et al., 2001; IOM, 2010a). In contrast, a "clinical endpoint is defined as a characteristic or variable that reflects how a patient feels, functions, or survives" (Atkinson et al., 2001; IOM, 2010a). For example, blood pressure might be used as a surrogate endpoint in tests of a drug that decreases the risk of a heart attack or stroke associated with hypertension. As another example, delay in progression to blast crisis—a phase in which immature granulocytes (white blood cells) rapidly proliferate in the chronic phase of chronic myelogenous leukemia—is used as a surrogate endpoint in studies used for evaluation and approval of drugs, but the true clinical benefit of the drug is long-term survival.

[13]21 CFR § 314.510 (2011).

BOX 1-2
Drug-Approval Process

The development of a candidate drug can begin with preclinical research and short-term animal testing by a drug sponsor. If a candidate drug shows therapeutic potential and low toxicity, the sponsor can submit an investigational new drug (IND) application to the US Food and Drug Administration (FDA), and agency oversight begins.[a] The IND should contain

- Manufacturing and chemical information about the drug.
- The results of any completed animal tests, toxicology studies, and any other preclinical tests that have been conducted.
- The protocols for Phase 1 human studies.
- The results of any human studies that the sponsor has conducted outside the United States; local institutional review boards must review Phase 1 protocols to ensure protection of reserach participants.

FDA then has 30 days to place a hold on the proposed human trials because of safety concerns. Without a hold, the sponsor can begin to test the compound in humans at 31 days. Long-term animal studies, including carcinogenicity and reproductive-toxicity studies, might occur simultaneously with human studies.

Phase 1 clinical trials test several increasing doses of a drug to assess toxicity and, to some degree, efficacy. In the absence of unacceptable toxicity, Phase 2 clinical investigations (which are conducted on a few dozen to several hundred patients who have the condition for which the drug is being developed) examine both efficacy and safety. Typically, two Phase 3 clinical trials, which can involve fewer than 100 patients or many thousands, are then conducted to evaluate the efficacy of the new product, usually in comparison with a placebo and sometimes in comparison with an already approved drug for the condition. Spon-

these conditions.[14] As a condition of the accelerated approval process, Subpart H also requires postmarketing clinical studies[15] to confirm the health benefits of the drug that were predicted on the basis of the surrogate endpoints; those trials are typically already underway at the time of approval. FDA also obtained a

[14]21 USC § 356(b)(2) (2010).

[15]Studies conducted after a drug has been approved for marketing are referred to as postmarketing, postapproval, or Phase 4 studies. For consistency the committee refers to such studies as *postmarketing studies*.

sors develop the study protocols, and trials are conducted under their auspices. FDA provides guidance documents for clinical trials, and the Office of New Drugs review team consults with the sponsor as trial protocols are developed, studies are conducted, and results are obtained. Sponsors are required to notify FDA of serious or unexpected adverse effects that are experienced by trial participants and are potentially attributable to the drug and any findings from animal tests that suggest an important risk for humans, including reports of mutagenicity, teratogenicity, or carcinogenicity.

After the completion of Phase 3 trials, the sponsor can submit a new drug application (NDA) for a chemical drug or a biologic license application for a biologic, which should include

- The chemical composition of the drug.
- The results of pharmacokinetic studies.
- The results of animal tests and clinical trials.
- Details of the manufacturing, processing, labeling, and packaging of the drug.

FDA will either approve the drug and send an "approval" letter to the sponsor with specified labeling and any postmarketing requirements or not approve the drug and send a "complete response" letter to the sponsor explaining why an application is not approved. FDA has a goal, in accordance with the Prescription Drug User Fee Act, of reviewing NDAs for standard approved drugs and for expedited approved drugs determined to be potentially breakthroughs or life-saving within a particular timeframe in accordance with the law.

[a]An investigational new drug application can be opened at any phase of drug testing. Given the global nature of drug development, it is not unusual for the first trial to be submitted to FDA to be a Phase 2 or 3 trial (FDA, 2003).

SOURCE: Modified from FDA (1998).

second authority to require postmarketing studies for approved drugs through the deferred-submission policy under the Pediatric Research Equity Act (PREA) of 2003,[16] which allows a drug to be approved for sale if sponsors agree to conduct the required trials in children after a drug enters the market.

[16]Pediatric Research Equity Act (PREA) of 2003, PL 108-155, 117 Stat. 1936 (2003). FDA initially published the pediatric rule in the *Federal Register* in 1998. After that rule was overturned in court because it went beyond FDA's regulatory authority, Congress passed PREA in 2003, giving FDA the necessary authority.

FDA began receiving more resources for postmarketing activities through the Public Health Security and Bioterrorism Preparedness and Response Act of 2002,[17] which included the PDUFA Amendments of 2002 (PDUFA III). Under this act, for the first time some user fees were allocated to postmarketing safety–related activities, for example, to support postmarketing surveillance of already-approved drugs and to allow risk-management oversight of newly approved drugs (2–3 years after approval). Furthermore, pharmaceutical companies could develop and submit a risk-minimization action plan (RiskMAP) with an NDA (FDA, 2005). RiskMAPs were plans intended for a small number of drugs that posed serious risks that warranted additional precautions beyond labeling to manage or limit the risks and ensure that the benefits[18] of the drugs outweighed their risks. For example, thalidomide was approved for use in the treatment of multiple myeloma and forms of leprosy and was accompanied by a RiskMAP[19] that outlined measures to prevent the risk of fetal exposure. As of February 2007, 30 drugs had been approved with RiskMAPs[20]; most plans contained only targeted education and outreach requirements (Office of Surveillance and Epidemiology, 2007; Shane, 2009).

The Institute of Medicine's 2007 Report

Despite those changes, the focus of FDA's authority and resources remained on the drug-approval process, with little oversight responsibility or authority related to drugs that had entered the market. High-profile withdrawals of some drugs within 5 years of their approval—such as troglitazone (Rezulin®, Resulin®, or Romozin®), cerivastatin (Baycol® or Lipobay®), rofecoxib (Vioxx®), and valdecoxib (Bextra®)—underscored concerns not only about FDA's ability to recognize and respond to safety signals in the postmarketing setting in a timely fashion but its ability to conduct appropriate oversight of approved drugs and to undertake appropriately targeted regulatory actions short of withdrawal. In 2006, FDA, the Centers for Medicare and Medicaid Services (CMS), the Agency for Healthcare Research and Quality (AHRQ), the National Institutes of Health (NIH), and the Department of Veterans Affairs asked the IOM to examine the US

---

[17]Public Health Security and Bioterrorism Preparedness and Response Act of 2002, PL 107-188, 1165 Stat. 594.

[18]When discussing the benefits and risks of a drug, like the term *risk*, the committee uses the term *benefits* in a probabilistic manner, that is, the potential or probability of benefits. To emphasize the importance of the benefit side of a drug's benefits and risks, the committee purposefully uses the phrase *benefit–risk* rather than the more traditional *risk–benefit*.

[19]FDA approved thalidomide in 1998 with a System for Thalidomide Education and Prescribing Safety (STEPS) oversight program that contained restrictions on use (see approval letter at http://www.accessdata.fda.gov/drugsatfda_docs/appletter/1998/20785ltr.pdf). The STEPS oversight program predates the establishment of RiskMAPs, but it was considered a RiskMAP after they were established.

[20]RiskMAPs were replaced with Risk Evaluation and Mitigation Strategies (REMS) following implementation of the FDAAA.

drug-safety system and to make recommendations to improve risk assessment, surveillance, and safe use of drugs (IOM, 2007a).

The 2007 IOM committee's report, *The Future of Drug Safety,* focused on how FDA's structure, organization, and scientific and regulatory activities should change to improve the monitoring and evaluation of drugs. The report concluded that "a transformed drug safety system has at its core a lifecycle approach to drug risk and benefit—not a new concept, but one that has been implemented, at best, in a limited and fragmented manner" (IOM, 2007a). The 2007 IOM committee recognized that changes were needed to implement such a safety system and made a number of recommendations, including (1) changes in the organization and culture of FDA to provide long-term stability and consistent direction for the agency and to increase the role of the Office of Surveillance and Epidemiology (OSE) in drug regulation; (2) an increase in funding for postmarketing activities in FDA; (3) improvements in FDA's information-technology infrastructure for monitoring drugs once they are approved, including development of public–private partnerships to gain access to and analyze data related to drug safety; (4) development by FDA of "a systematic approach to risk-benefit analysis for use throughout the FDA in the preapproval and postapproval settings"; (5) provision to FDA of new authority to require "postmarketing risk assessment and risk management programs as are needed to monitor and ensure safe use of drug products"[21]; (6) development and implementation by FDA of a high-quality, flexible system for the evaluation of postmarketing safety issues; and (7) the requirement for industry to register at NIH's ClinicalTrials.gov all Phase 2 through Phase 4 clinical trials (postmarketing trials) that are intended to be submitted to FDA.[22]

The Food and Drug Administration Amendments Act: The Food and Drug Administration's Increased Postmarketing Authority and Responsibility

In 2007, less than a year after that IOM report was published (IOM, 2007a), Congress passed FDAAA, which amended the FDCA to include many of the recommendations presented in the report. In addition to reauthorizing a higher level of prescription-drug user fees (PDUFA IV), Congress earmarked increased resources for postmarketing drug activities and included a number of substantial changes in FDA's regulatory authority. Described as "the most momentous shift

[21]The committee recommended that the risk-assessment and risk-management program could include the authority to require label changes, specific warnings or moratoriums on direct-to-consumer advertising for specific drugs, and restrictions on distribution of a specific drug, such as limiting distribution to particular facilities, pharmacists, or physicians with specific training or only after the performance of specific medical procedures (IOM, 2007a).

[22]FDA's responses to IOM's 2007 report can be found at http://www.fda.gov/Safety/SafetyofSpecificProducts/ucm184598.htm (accessed June 9, 2011).

in drug regulation in half a century" (Evans, 2010), FDAAA gave FDA expanded authority and responsibility in the postmarketing setting.

FDAAA increased requirements for registering clinical trials,[23] increased FDA's authority over the contents of direct-to-consumer advertising,[24] increased resources for FDA's premarketing and postmarketing activities related to drug risks,[25] gave FDA the authority to implement safety-labeling changes including class labeling,[26] and required that FDA increase the transparency of its information about drugs and improve its risk communication.[27] In addition—and most relevant to the present report—FDAAA provided FDA with the authority to require postmarketing studies in some circumstances[28] (see Box 1-3 for a discussion of the committee's terminology for postmarketing studies), provided FDA with the authority to require a risk evaluation and mitigation strategy (REMS),[29] and required that FDA develop an active surveillance system.[30] Those three elements are described in the subsections below; more details of other parts of FDAAA are presented in Appendix A.

Authority to Require Postmarketing Studies

Before FDAAA, most postmarketing studies were performed under voluntary written agreements between the sponsor and FDA called *postmarketing commitments* (PMCs), established at the time of drug approval (FDA, 2011c). FDA could *require* postmarketing studies or clinical trials in only two situations: in 21 CFR 314.510 and 21 CFR 601.4, for products that enter the marketplace as a consequence of accelerated approvals to demonstrate clinical benefit; and in PREA, for products that are approved based only on research with adult participants where postmarketing research is needed to assess their safety and efficacy of the drug in children.[31] A number of people have criticized the low completion rate of the postmarketing studies required by FDA through these mechanisms (Avorn, 2005; Carpenter, 2010d; GAO, 2008; Strom, 2006; Wood, 2006).[32]

FDAAA expanded FDA's authority to require sponsors of marketed drug and biologic products to conduct and report on postmarketing research studies.[33] A

[23]42 USC § 282(j) (2010).

[24]21 USC § 353b (2010).

[25]21 USC § 379g note (2010).

[26]21 USC § 355(o)(4) (2010).

[27]21 USC § 360bbb–6.

[28]21 USC § 355(o) (2010).

[29]21 USC § 355(p) (2010).

[30]21 USC § 355(k)(3) (2010).

[31]In the remainder of this report, when the committee discusses FDA-required studies, it is referring to studies FDA requires using its authorities in FDAAA, not those it requires using its authorities in 21 CFR 601 Subpart E or in PREA.

[32]As discussed below, however, at least part of the low completion rate has since been attributed to the tracking system.

[33]21 USC § 355(o) (2010).

BOX 1-3
Nomenclature for Postmarketing Studies

The Food and Drug Administration Amendments Act of 2007 differentiates between clinical trials and studies.[a] In response to that differentiation, FDA defines clinical trials and studies as follows (FDA, 2011d):

> "Clinical trials are any prospective investigations in which the applicant or investigator determines the method of assigning the drug product(s) or other interventions to one or more human subjects."
>
> "Studies are all other investigations, such as investigations with humans that are not clinical trials as defined above (e.g., observational epidemiological studies), animal studies, and laboratory experiments."

In this report, however, the committee uses the term *studies* in accordance with ordinary usage in the scientific literature as a parent or generic term that encompasses research projects of all types and regardless of design. Thus, as the committee uses the term, *studies* applies to both clinical trials and non-clinical trial investigations such as observational investigations. When referring specifically to either *observational designs* or *randomized controlled trial* (RCT) designs, the committee uses those specific terms.

[a]21 USC § 355(o)(3) (2010).

postmarketing requirement (PMR) is an FDA-required research study that a sponsor must conduct after a drug has been approved and is released to the market. Under FDAAA, a PMR can be required to

- Assess a known serious risk related to use of the drug.
- Assess signals of serious risk related to use of the drug.
- Identify an unexpected serious risk when available data indicate the potential of a serious risk.[34]

Within its definition of a *serious risk* of an adverse drug experience, FDAAA includes "any failure of expected pharmacological action of the drug" that results in serious medical consequences for the patient.[35] On the basis of that definition, Evans (2010) considers FDAAA to provide FDA with the authority to require a postmarketing study when emerging data or results suggest that patients are suffering serious harm because a drug is not performing as effectively as was expected at the time it was approved, either overall or in identifiable patient

[34]21 USC § 355(o)(3)(B) (2010).
[35]21 USC §§ 355-1(b)(1)(E), (b)(4), (b)(5) (2010).

BOX 1-4
Types of Studies for which the Food and Drug Administration Considers Postmarketing Requirements vs Postmarketing Commitments

The FDA recently issued guidance for industry on postmarketing studies that outlines the differences between postmarketing requirements (PMRs) and postmarketing commitments (PMCs) and provides examples of when it would require a PMR or request a PMC. In those guidelines, FDA provides the following examples of the kinds of studies that might be the subject of PMRs:

- "Observational pharmacoepidemiologic studies are generally studies designed to assess a serious risk associated with a drug exposure or to quantify risk or evaluate factors that affect the risk of serious toxicity, such as drug dose, timing of exposure, or patient characteristics. . . .
- "Meta-analyses may be designed to evaluate a safety endpoint by statistical analysis of data from completed studies or clinical trials. . . .
- "Clinical trials with a safety endpoint evaluated with prespecified assessments and adequately powered to analyze the serious risk. . . .
- "Studies or clinical trials designed to evaluate drug interactions or bioavailability when there are scientific data that indicate the potential for a serious safety risk."

A current example of a PMR is a current clinical trial that is assessing whether there is decreased survival with concomitant use of pani-

subgroups. The present committee considers providing FDA with that authority to be in the interest of the public's health. When questions arise about the health benefits of a drug, studies to document a drug's effectiveness may be as critical for ensuring that the benefit–risk profile of a drug remains favorable as studies that investigate its risks.

FDA can require a drug sponsor to conduct an observational study only when the information that FDA needs cannot be obtained from adverse-event or surveillance data,[36] including data from the Sentinel system (discussed below).[37] FDA's

[36]21 USC § 355(o)(3)(D)(i) (2010).
[37]21 USC § 355(k)(3) (2010).

tumumab (Vextibix®) and other chemotherapy for metastatic colorectal cancer (FDA, 2011d).

In contrast, the guidelines state that the following studies would generally not meet the statutory conditions for a PMR, and FDA would request them as a PMC:

- "Drug and biologic quality studies, including manufacturing, stability, and immunogenicity studies that do not have a primary safety endpoint. . . .
- "Pharmacoepidemiologic studies designed to examine the natural history of a disease or to estimate background rates for adverse events in a population not treated with the drug that is the subject of the marketing application. . . .
- "Studies and clinical trials conducted with vaccines, such as surveillance and observational pharmacoepidemiologic studies when data do not suggest a serious risk or signals of serious risk related to the use of the vaccine and when available data do not indicate the potential for serious risk", including studies to "evaluate long-term effectiveness or duration of response. . . .
- "Clinical trials in which the primary endpoint is related to further defining efficacy, designed to
  - evaluate long-term effectiveness or duration of response (that are not required under accelerated approval)
  - evaluate efficacy using a withdrawal design
  - evaluate efficacy in a subgroup".

SOURCE: FDA (2011c).

authority to require a clinical trial is further restricted to contexts in which the information that it needs cannot be obtained by requiring observational studies.[38]

In 2011, FDA issued guidance for industry that provides information on the implementation the section of FDAAA[39] that authorizes FDA to require certain postmarketing studies and trials (FDA, 2011c). The guidance outlines the differences between PMRs and PMCs and provides examples of PMRs and PMCs (see Box 1-4) (FDA, 2011c). In contrast to a PMR, a PMC that a sponsor agrees to in writing after approval of a product is typically designed to gather additional

[38]21 USC § 355(o)(3)(D)(ii) (2010).
[39]21 USC § 355(o) (2010).

information about product safety, efficacy, or optimal use. FDA has decided that such information is useful or important but is not a condition of approval.

FDA is required to track and monitor the progress of PMRs and PMCs to ensure that they are completed in a timely manner, and it reviews annual status reports submitted by sponsors. FDA has been criticized for not ensuring the initiation and completion of PMRs and PMCs; recent audits suggest, however, that although FDA system for tracking the progress of the studies was incomplete, most studies either had been completed or were under way. As of September 30, 2011, there were 675 PMRs and 369 PMCs open for drugs. Of those, 590 (87 percent) of the PMRs, and 295 (80 percent) of the PMCs were on schedule (FDA, 2012).

Risk Evaluation and Mitigation Strategies

As discussed above, PDUFA III in 2002 allowed drug sponsors to provide a RiskMAP for products that posed serious risks that outweighed their benefits when specific precautions could be implemented that would result in a favorable benefit–risk profile. Under FDAAA in 2007, REMS was introduced to replace the RiskMAP as part of a risk-management strategy intended to manage a known or serious risk posed by a drug or biologic product.[40] The possible elements of a REMS are listed in Box 1-5. FDAAA grants FDA the authority to require sponsors to submit a REMS before approval of a drug if it "determines that a [REMS] is necessary to ensure that the benefits of the drug outweigh the risks"[41] or after approval if FDA "becomes aware of new safety information and makes a determination that such a strategy is necessary to ensure that the benefits of the drug outweigh the risks of the drug".[42] As of March 1, 2012, there were 103 pharmaceutical products with active REMSs. Of those, 26 (25 percent) required only a medication guide; 39 (38 percent) required a communication plan, or a medication guide and communication plan; and 38 (37 percent) required elements to ensure safe use and other components (Center for Healthcare Supply Chain Research, 2012).[43]

Development of a Large-Scale Active Surveillance System

FDAAA mandated that FDA establish an active surveillance system for monitoring drugs by using large electronic databases belonging to health care information holders. An internal FDA task force had previously concluded that FDA's postmarketing surveillance would be improved by the agency having

[40]In general, products previously approved with a RiskMAP that had elements to ensure safe use were "deemed to have an approved REMS" (FDA, 2009b).

[41]21 USC §§ 355-1 (a)(2)(A) (2010).

[42]21 USC §§ 355-1 (a)(2)(A) (2010).

[43]The raw data are available on FDA's website: http://www.fda.gov/Drugs/DrugSafety/PostmarketDrugSafetyInformationforPatientsandProviders/ucm111350.htm (accessed June 9, 2011).

BOX 1-5
Potential Elements of a Risk Evaluation and Mitigation Strategy (REMS)

In addition to the required timetable for submission of assessments of the strategy, potential elements of the strategy are[a]

1. A medication guide[b] and, if helpful to mitigate a serious risk posed by the drug, a patient package insert.
2. A communication plan to health care providers that may include
   - Sending letters to health care providers.
   - "Disseminating information about the elements of the risk evaluation and mitigation strategy to encourage implementation by health care providers of components that apply to such health care providers, or to explain certain safety protocols (such as medical monitoring by periodic laboratory tests)".
   - "Disseminating information to health care providers through professional societies about any serious risks of the drug and any protocol to assure safe use".
3. Elements as are necessary to ensure safe use of the drug because of its inherent toxicity or potential harmfulness. The elements to ensure safe use shall include one or more goals to mitigate a specific serious risk listed in the labeling of the drug and, to mitigate such risk, may require that
   - Health-care providers who prescribe the drug have particular training or experience or are specially certified (the opportunity to obtain such training or certification with respect to the drug shall be available to any willing provider from a frontier area in a widely available training or certification method, including an online course or via mail, as approved by the secretary at reasonable cost to the provider).
   - Pharmacies, practitioners, or health care settings that dispense the drug are specially certified (the opportunity to obtain such certification shall be available to any willing provider from a frontier area).
   - The drug be dispensed to patients only in specific health care settings, such as hospitals.
   - The drug be dispensed to patients with evidence or other documentation of safe-use conditions, such as laboratory test results.
   - Each patient using the drug be subject to monitoring.
   - Each patient using the drug be enrolled in a registry.

---

[a] 21 USC §§ 355-1(e), (f).

[b] FDA can require a Medication Guide on its own or as part of a REMS. November 2011 FDA guidance states that "depending on the risks involved, FDA may approve a Medication Guide . . . without requiring a REMS when that alone is adequate to address the serious and significant public health concern" (FDA, 2011e).

"access to external healthcare databases" (FDA, 1999). Congress established goals and a timetable for the system, including a goal of the capacity to access data on 25 million patients by July 1, 2010, and 100 million patients by July 1, 2012.

That national electronic system, developed through the Sentinel Initiative, was launched by FDA in 2008 and has the aim of facilitating the development of active surveillance methods related to "signal detection, strengthening, and validation" (FDA, 2008; HHS, 2010; Platt et al., 2009, 2012; Robb et al., 2012). Sentinel will increase FDA's ability to track the benefit–risk profiles of drugs, biologics, medical devices, and other FDA regulated products and has the potential to decrease the time needed to identify and evaluate drug-related safety signals. Sentinel will be an active surveillance system and will complement the existing mandatory and voluntary reporting systems that FDA already has in place to track reports of adverse events linked to use of its regulated products. Sentinel will enable FDA to actively query diverse automated health care data holders—such as electronic health-record systems, administrative and insurance-claims databases, and registries—and to obtain the results of specific queries rapidly and securely (FDA, 2008). Sentinel is proceeding in stages, starting with a series of Mini-Sentinel projects to develop the individual parts of the system (HHS, 2010). The electronic data "will be accessed, maintained, and protected by the Sentinel System's data partners" (FDA, 2008). In such a structure, termed a *distributed system*, "data remain in their existing secure environments, rather than being consolidated into one database" (FDA, 2008). The Mini-Sentinel initiative also includes development of statistical and epidemiologic methods to improve the use of data from active surveillance (Cook et al., 2012; IOM, 2007a). Concurrently, the Observational Medical Outcomes Partnerships (OMOP), a "public–private partnership among the FDA, academia, data owners, and the pharmaceutical industry" is studying governance, data resource, and methodological issues with a national drug surveillance program (Stang et al., 2010). Those activities will facilitate the development and improvement of postmarketing surveillance systems.

FDA's Organizational Structure and the Postmarketing Setting

There are two offices within FDA's Center for Drug Evaluation and Research (CDER) of relevance to the postmarketing setting. The Office of New Drugs (OND) is responsible for "providing regulatory oversight for investigational studies during drug development and making decisions regarding marketing approval for new (innovator or non-generic) drugs" (FDA, 2011f), including decisions governing accelerated approvals. The Office of Surveillance and Epidemiology (OSE) is responsible for "postmarketing surveillance and risk assessment programs to identify adverse events that did not appear during the drug development process" (FDA, 2009c). IOM's 2007 drug safety report (IOM, 2007a) concluded that "the Office of Surveillance and Epidemiology . . . has not had a formal role in drug regulation—neither formal opportunities to learn from and participate in relevant aspects of the review process nor the authority to take action regarding postmarketing safety" (IOM, 2007a). The 2007 report noted that there existed interdisciplinary tension between the two offices, and the negative effect that tension has on anticipating and planning for postmarketing oversight of the benefit–risk profiles of drugs and recommended "that CDER appoint an OSE staff member to each New Drug Application review team and assign joint authority to the Office of New Drugs . . . and the Office of Surveillance and Epidemiology . . . for postapproval regulatory actions related to safety" (IOM, 2007a). Others have also described the tensions between OSE and OND (Carpenter, 2010d), and some researchers have commented on the need for independent drug safety review (Avorn, 2005; Strom, 2006; Wood et al., 1998).

Since the publication of the 2007 report (IOM, 2007a) and the passage of FDAAA, FDA has implemented a number of changes to increase the standing of the OSE and improve collaboration between OND and OSE on drug regulatory decisions. In January of 2008 FDA established its Equal Voice Initiative, an "operational philosophy and set of practices to ensure that each professional viewpoint has been fully expressed, understood, and brought into the decision-making process" (FDA, 2010a). In June 2009, OND and OSE signed a Memorandum of Agreement "on the management of significant safety issues associated with pending drug applications and approved drug products".[44] The document is designed to clarify the roles and responsibilities of OND and OSE, and it specifies that "OND and OSE views are to be given equal weight in determining how significant safety issues affecting drug products are resolved" (FDA, 2009d). OND has also established the positions of Deputy Director for Safety and Safety Regulatory Project Manager in each review division.

In 2009, GAO reported that the "OND retains the authority to decide whether to take regulatory action". It recommended that the FDA commissioner "develop a comprehensive plan to prepare OSE for the transfer of additional regulatory authorities from OND" (GAO, 2009). GAO indicated that such an approach is intended to improve the management and oversight of postmarketing studies. Consequently, an internal *Manual of Policies and Procedures* was developed

[44]"A significant safety issue for purposes of this memorandum of agreement is a safety issue that has the potential to lead to, for example: withdrawal of an approved drug from the market; withdrawal of an approved indication; limitations on a use in a specific population or subpopulation in the post-marketing setting; changes to the warnings, precautions, or contraindication sections of the labeling (including the addition of a boxed warning to the label); the establishment of, or changes to, the proprietary name/container label/labeling/packaging to reduce the likelihood of medication errors; the establishment or modification of a risk evaluation and mitigation strategy (REMS); addition or modification of a Medication Guide or other required Patient Package Insert that addresses a safety issue; the requirement that a sponsor conduct a post-marketing clinical trial; or the conduct of an observational pharmacoepidemiological study by the sponsor or FDA" (FDA, 2009d).

by FDA, effective September 16, 2010, that "provides the general guidance for incorporating the philosophy and practices of EV [Equal Voice] into CDER decision-making processes" (FDA, 2010a). FDA has also hired additional staff responsible for postmarketing monitoring of the benefit–risk profiles of drugs (FDA, 2009d), and increased the staff located within OSE and additional staff within OND responsible for evaluating and interpreting safety signals. The extent to which these changes have improved the communication and collaboration of OSE and OND with regard to postmarketing monitoring is unclear. A recent report by FDA's Science Board Subcommittee noted that tensions between the two offices remain (FDA Science Board Subcommittee, 2011). These issues have relevance to this report to the extent that they affect the effect or implementation of its recommendations designed to improve the quality of FDA decision-making in the postmarketing context.

THE CONTEXT OF THIS REPORT

The last 5 years have seen a major transformation in drug law and regulation. Before 2007, drug regulation emphasized primarily premarketing oversight. Although FDA could work with drug manufacturers to have drug labels changed, warnings and contraindications added, promotional materials modified, and restrictions added to distributions (Carpenter, 2010d), FDA had little statutory authority to manage the risks posed by drugs that had been approved for use other than to require a manufacturer to withdraw a drug from the market (CRS, 2008). FDAAA gave FDA expanded authorities and additional regulatory tools, such as the ability to require changes in a product label or to require the conduct of clinical trials or other studies in the postmarketing setting, all of which enable FDA to protect the health of the public better.

The authority to require postmarketing studies presents a new set of ethical and scientific questions for FDA to consider. Many of the new questions that FDA faces are illustrated by the Thiazolidinedione Intervention with Vitamin D Evaluation (TIDE) trial, in which the drug sponsor of a diabetes medication, rosiglitazone (Avandia®), was required by FDA to conduct a postmarketing clinical trial. TIDE was to be a "long-term controlled trial to assess the cardiovascular outcomes of patients treated with rosiglitazone, pioglitazone, and placebo (in addition to a other anti-diabetic background treatment)" (Jenkins, 2010). Key details of the research on rosiglitazone, including the TIDE trial, and its regulatory history are summarized in Box 1-6. The committee has identified a number of ethical and scientific questions that arise from the rosiglitazone case, and that might have led FDA to request this study, including

- *How should FDA respond when questions about the effectiveness of a drug that was approved on the basis of a surrogate endpoint arise in the postmarketing setting?* Rosiglitazone was approved on the basis of two surrogate endpoints—

blood glucose and glycated hemoglobin concentrations in diabetic patients—not on the basis of evidence on the effect of the drug on clinical outcomes.

- *How should FDA consider data from different types of studies when making its regulatory decisions?* In the case of rosiglitazone, FDA had to evaluate results from numerous studies, including clinical trials that used a variety of regimens, comparators, outcomes and dosing, and meta-analyses of data from these trials, and observational studies using administrative and outcomes data.
- *How should FDA's response to concerns about the safety of an approved drug be affected by the existence of a similar drug that is approved for the same indication?* In the setting of new safety concerns about rosiglitazone, FDA had to take into account that physicians and patients could choose to use pioglitazone, which is in the same drug class as rosiglitazone and approved for the same indication.
- *In the face of increasing concerns about potentially life-threatening risks, when is it ethically justifiable for FDA to require postmarketing clinical research?* Critics argued that enough was known about the risks of rosiglitazone to render TIDE trial unethical and unnecessary.
- *What role should FDA play in overseeing the postmarketing studies that it requires?* In the case of the TIDE trial, as has been customary, there was no expectation of an interaction between FDA and the trial's institutional review boards and data and safety monitoring board. The question going forward is whether there should be such interaction when FDA requires postmarketing research.
- *Are there relevant ethical differences between postmarketing trials that FDA requires sponsors to conduct and trials that sponsors conduct in anticipation of seeking FDA approval?* That so many physicians appeared to be taking their patients off rosiglitazone while other physicians and patients appeared to want to continue with the drug was a consideration that has no analogue in the premarketing context.
- *How should FDA make regulatory decisions when scientists disagree about the interpretation of the evidence?* There was disagreement among scientists both inside and outside FDA about how to interpret and respond to the evidence on rosiglitazone, including disagreements both between and within FDA's OND and OSE.

It is precisely those types of questions that are the subject of the present report, which was requested by FDA to help it to answer ethical and scientific challenges that arise from its new postmarketing authorities and responsibilities under FDAAA.

CHARGE TO THE COMMITTEE

In April 2010, FDA asked IOM to "convene a committee to evaluate the scientific and ethical issues involved in conducting studies of the safety of approved

BOX 1-6
Regulatory and Scientific History of Rosiglitazone

The Food and Drug Administration (FDA) approved rosiglitazone in 1999 on the basis of findings that indicated that it lowered blood glucose and glycated hemoglobin concentrations in diabetic patients. Concerns about adverse effects of rosiglitazone on lipids in the premarketing studies prompted FDA to ask the manufacturer to conduct a clinical trial to compare rosiglitazone with other diabetes drugs in the same class (A Diabetes Outcome Progression Trial) (FDA, 2007a). Major questions about the safety of rosiglitazone arose after a meta-analysis of the results of clinical trials showed an increased risk of cardiovascular events in people who took rosiglitazone (odds ratio [OR] for myocardial infarction, 1.43; 95% confidence interval [CI], 1.03–1.98; P = 0.03; OR for death of cardiovascular causes, 1.64; 95% CI, 0.98–2.74; P = 0.06) (Nissen and Wolski, 2007).

In July 2007, after publication of those results, an FDA advisory committee concluded that "the use of rosiglitazone for the treatment of type 2 diabetes was associated with a greater risk of myocardial is chemic events than placebo" and similar diabetes drugs (Rosen, 2007). Because of some limitations in the meta-analyses, however, the advisory committee voted that the drug should not be withdrawn from the market but "rather that label warnings and extensive educational efforts be instituted immediately", and it requested further studies (Rosen, 2007). In November 2007, FDA announced its decision that there was not "enough evidence to indicate that the risk of a heart attack or cardiac ischemia is higher for Avandia than other [t]ypes of diabetes treatment" and that it would allow rosiglitazone to remain on the market (FDA, 2007b,c). FDA, however, required the manufacturer to revise rosiglitazone's package insert to include a "boxed" warning regarding cardiovascular risk, to make a medication guide available to inform patients of the risk, and to conduct a long-term randomized controlled head-to-head clincal trial to evaluate the potential cardiovascular risk associated with rosiglitazone compared with an active control agent (that is, compared with another diabetes drug). Evidence from observational studies continued to appear in the literature as well.

By July 2008, the manufacturer had submitted the protocol for the Thiazolidinedione Intervention with Vitamin D Evaluation (TIDE)[a] trial to meet the third requirement, and the protocol had been approved by FDA.

Patient enrollment began in May 2009. Researchers not involved in the TIDE study, public health advocates, members of Congress, and some FDA staff, however, declared that there was already sufficient evidence that rosiglitazone was associated with an increased risk of cardiovascular events and questioned the ethics of requiring such a study (Bloomgarden, 2007).

A Senate Committee on Finance report in February 2010[b] reiterated many of those concerns about FDA's position on rosiglitazone. The Institute of Medicine committee's letter report was released on July 9, 2010. FDA's Endocrinologic and Metabolic Drugs Advisory Committee and Drug Safety and Risk Management Advisory Committee held a joint meeting on July 13–14, 2010, at which they voted on several possible approaches to responding to concerns about rosiglitazone. Although the advisory-committee members voted overwhelmingly to take some actions on rosiglitazone—such as to increase warnings, to restrict access, or to remove access—no consensus emerged as to which of those actions FDA should take. On July 21, 2010, FDA put the TIDE trial on partial clinical hold, thus barring the enrollment of new patients. On September 23, 2010, FDA discontinued the TIDE trial and placed severe restrictions on the continued availability of rosiglitazone (FDA, 2011g).[c]

---

[a]Rosiglitazone belongs to a class of drugs called thiazolidinediones that are used to treat diabetes mellitus type 2. The drug sponsor designed the Thiazolidinedione Intervention with Vitamin D Evaluation (TIDE) trial to evaluate "the cardiovascular effects of long-term treatment with rosiglitazone or pioglitazone when used as part of standard of care compared to similar standard of care without rosiglitazone or pioglitazone in patients with type 2 diabetes who have a history of or are at risk for cardiovascular disease" and "the effects of long-term supplementation of vitamin D on death and cancer" (NIH, 2011).

[b]The letter, dated February 18, 2010, from Senators Baucus and Grassley—the chair and ranking member, respectively, of the Senate Committee on Finance—is available at http://finance.senate.gov/newsroom/chairman/release/?id=bcf5aef6-9bc5-45ca-9cab-aadf5df135fa.

[c]FDA required the drug sponsor to issue a risk evaluation and mitigation strategy according to which "the drug will be available to patients not already taking it only if they are unable to achieve glycemic control using other medications and, in consultation with their health care professional, decide not to take pioglitazone [a diabetes medication in the same class of drugs] for medical reasons. Current users of rosiglitazone will be able to continue using the medication if they appear to be benefiting from it and they acknowledge that they understand [the risks associated with its use]. Doctors will have to attest to and document their patients' eligibility; patients will have to review statements describing the cardiovascular safety concerns" (Woodcock et al., 2011).

drugs". The five specific questions posed by FDA appear in Box 1-1. In response to FDA's request, IOM convened a committee of 12 members who have expertise in bioethics, biostatistics, clinical trials, epidemiology, health policy, law, patient safety, pharmacoepidemiology, and regulatory science.

FDA requested two reports: a letter report due in July 2010[45] and the present report. In its letter report, *Ethical Issues in Studying the Safety of Approved Drugs: A Letter Report* (see Appendix A), released on July 9, 2010, the committee addressed the first question of the committee's charge—related to the ethical and informed consent issues that must be considered in designing RCTs—by presenting a conceptual framework for analyzing the ethics of postmarketing RCTs required by FDA (Box 1-7) (IOM, 2010b). In this final report the committee addresses all five specific questions posed to the committee by FDA.

THE COMMITTEE'S APPROACH TO ITS CHARGE

The committee met in person six times, including two open information-gathering sessions at which representatives of FDA, AHRQ, NIH, other stakeholders, and researchers appeared (see Appendix B) to address the committee's broader charge.

The committee used the conceptual framework in its letter report (Box 1-7) (IOM, 2010b) as a starting point for this final report but conducted further research and deliberations related to its full charge. Several underpinnings of the conceptual framework and additional themes that emerged as the committee deliberated on its full charge shaped this report. These include an understanding of FDA's public health mission; the importance of adopting a lifecycle approach to drug safety and benefit–risk assessment (see Figure 1-1 for a schematic of a drug's lifecycle); FDA's ethical obligations in making regulatory decisions, including the centrality of transparency and communication of the decisions; and a commitment to using best practices in regulatory science[46] and high-quality evidence in regulatory decision-making.

Considerations of the Agency's Mission

FDA is a public health agency; its mission is to protect "public health by assuring the safety, effectiveness, and security of human and veterinary drugs, vaccines and other biological products" (FDA, 2011h). In making decisions about potential regulatory actions, therefore, FDA should consider their potential public

[45]FDA requested that the letter report be completed before a July 13–14, 2010, joint meeting of FDA's Endocrinologic and Metabolic Drugs Advisory Committee and Drug Safety and Risk Management Advisory Committee on rosiglitazone.

[46]FDA has defined regulatory science as "the development and use of new tools, standards and approaches to more efficiently develop products and to more effectively evaluate product safety, efficacy and quality" (FDA, 2010b).

BOX 1-7
Conceptual Framework from *Ethical Issues in Studying the Safety of Approved Drugs: A Letter Report* (IOM, 2010a) for Analyzing the Ethics of Postmarketing Randomized Clinical Trials Required by the Food and Drug Administration: Four Central Classes of Considerations and Recommendations

I. **The Public Health Context.** The Food and Drug Administration (FDA) should determine that there is a substantial public health question about the nature or acceptability of the risks, or the risk–benefit profile, of a marketed drug—a question that requires a policy decision from FDA.

II. **Regulatory Science and Public Accountability.** FDA should use regulatory-science principles and practices that include processes of public accountability and transparency to determine the need for a policy decision, the need for new knowledge to support a policy decision, and the policy decision based on the new knowledge.

III. **Design Considerations.** It is appropriate for FDA to require that a randomized controlled trial be conducted to provide additional evidence about an approved drug's efficacy and safety only when (i) uncertainty about the risk-benefit balance is such that a responsible policy decision cannot be made based either on the existing evidence or on evidence from new observational studies, and (ii) the trial is properly designed and implemented to reduce uncertainty about the benefit–risk balance sufficiently for a responsible policy decision to be made.

IV. **Additional Ethical Obligations to Trial Participants.** FDA should ensure that the trial will answer the public health question with a design that minimizes risks to trial participants and involves ongoing monitoring of risks. The risks should be judged to be acceptable by appropriate oversight bodies before and during the trial and by trial participants at enrollment and as appropriate during the trial. Specifically, FDA and appropriate oversight bodies should ensure that the trial includes a comprehensive and meaningful informed consent process that continues during the trial and that takes into account any substantial changes in clinical practice and professional standards and any new research findings relevant to a participant's willingness to accept the risks associated with the trial. The FDA and appropriate oversight bodies should ensure that those conducting the trial convey such changes to participants in a timely and understandable fashion.

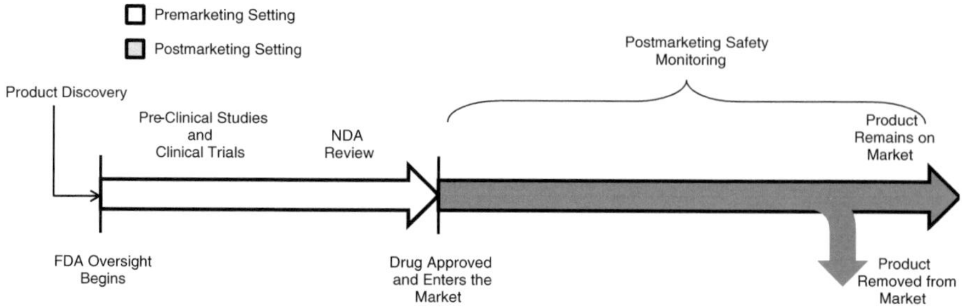

FIGURE 1-1 The lifecycle of a drug for a new molecular entity. After a product is discovered and the sponsor approaches FDA with the product as an investigational new drug, FDA oversight begins. After approved, FDA and the drug sponsor conduct postmarketing safety monitoring of the drug, which could include passive surveillance, active surveillance, observational studies, and randomized controlled studies. A product remains on the market until it is removed from the market either at FDA's request, FDA's withdrawal of marketing approval, or the company decides to no longer market it. FDA oversight of the drug continues for as long as the drug is on the market.

health consequences.[47] The committee emphasizes FDA's public health role, and the consequences of not protecting the public's health, throughout this report (Hamburg and Sharfstein, 2009).

FDA has a complex mission with obligations that sometimes conflict with one another. The committee recognizes that the effort to resolve those conflicts can complicate the agency's decisions but could only provide general guidance on how FDA may do it. In the premarketing context, FDA has to balance the effort to approve new drugs that could be beneficial to people with the effort to characterize potential harms, as well as benefits, and to make measured judgments about a new drug's benefit–risk profile with incomplete information. In the postmarketing context, new information requires that FDA continually re-examine its judgment about the benefit–risk profile and make regulatory decisions about the drug while being responsive to advocacy groups that are working from both sides of the issue. From an ethical standpoint, throughout the lifecycle of a drug, FDA has to balance its obligation to protect the public's health by having strong science on which to base regulatory decisions with its obligation to protect participants in research that it requires.

Such factors as the severity and prevalence of a disease or an adverse event, and the availability of effective alternative treatments necessarily affect FDA's regulatory decisions, including decisions about what postmarketing studies to require and how to use the information from different studies. Such decisions

[47]The committee views FDA's decisions as having public health consequences regardless of whether they affect a large population or a small group.

need to be made case by case, so the committee cannot provide a prescriptive formula for making them. Instead, the committee discusses principles that should be taken into account in decision-making, provides guidance on how to account for the factors, and offers a general framework for decision-making.

The FDA mission is to allow a drug to enter and remain on the market if, on the basis of its considered judgment, the benefits of the drug outweigh the risks that it poses; it is not charged with establishing, either for initial approval or for continued presence on the market, that a drug has the most favorable benefit–risk profile compared with other drugs for the same indication. FDA is one of many entities that influence the availability and safe use of drugs in the United States. Physicians and other health care providers, professional societies, pharmacies, and hospitals play crucial roles in ensuring that the expected benefits of a prescribed drug outweigh the risks in an individual patient. In addition, payers, such as medical insurance companies, take cost and the availability of alternative treatments into account and decide which drugs they will cover and at what level of reimbursement.

Government agencies are involved in sponsoring drug research, including an increasing focus on translational research in NIH and comparative-effectiveness research in AHRQ, CMS, and the Patient-Centered Outcomes Research Institute. Research sponsored or conducted by those agencies may inform FDA's evaluations of the benefits and risks associated with drugs. Moreover, the studies required by FDA may inform health care providers, payers, and other agencies and organizations in their drug-related decisions. The intersections of those roles require increased interactions among agencies; a number of initiatives indicate that the agencies recognize the need to coordinate their activities better. For example, FDA and NIH have established a collaborative initiative to move innovations to the public quickly (FDA, 2010b). The fact that the present report was financially supported by NIH and AHRQ, as well as FDA, illustrates the cooperation among the agencies. However, the committee's charge is related to FDA's role in regulating drugs, so it does not discuss the roles of other agencies and entities related to drugs.

A Lifecycle Approach to Safety and the Assessment of a Drug's Benefits and Risks

The committee starts with the assumption that ensuring the acceptability of the benefit–risk profile of a drug after it is approved for the US market is as important to FDA's public health mission as ensuring the acceptability of the benefit–risk profile before it is permitted to enter the market. A lifecycle approach to the regulatory oversight of drugs is therefore critical. The new authorities in FDAAA provide FDA with the tools to adopt a more comprehensive lifecycle approach than prior to FDAAA.

FDA assesses drug safety in relation to the drug benefits. For example, cancer chemotherapy drugs can cause serious adverse effects, including death, but are deemed adequately safe for their intended use because of the greater benefit of reducing cancer mortality risk. This report will use the word "safe" in this same sense, that is, that the magnitude and distribution of benefits and risks is acceptable for the intended use. The word "safety endpoint" will be used to describe the harms associated with a drug. "Risk" is the probability that those harms will be incurred. The committee will use an "efficacy" or "effectiveness" endpoint as the clinical outcome that a drug is intended to improve.

Major regulatory changes in a drug once it is on the market—such as changes in a drug's label, the addition of a boxed warning, or withdrawal of the drug—may appear to represent failures of the drug regulatory system (IOM, 2007a). It is important to recognize that the discovery of new information about a drug's adverse events or clinical effectiveness, if ascertained in a timely manner, is a normal and desirable part of the natural history or lifecycle of the drug. It is impossible to know everything about a drug at the point of approval. A responsible public health agency is structured to learn continually about the drugs that it approves with the expectation that what is known about a drug's benefits and risks will change over time. The timeliness of the identification of and response to new serious adverse events is an indication of a high-quality postmarketing system. The focus of this report thus responds to an expanded understanding of FDA as a public health agency whose approach to its mission is and should be shifting from a premarketing focus on efficacy and short-term harms, and a postmarketing focus on harms, to a continuous and integrated assessment of the benefit–risk profile of a drug throughout its market life.

Ethics and Decision-Making in the Food and Drug Administration

The committee's letter report focused heavily on FDA's ethical obligations to research participants. The present report continues that focus but broadens the discussion to include the ethical aspects of study design, how ethical considerations should be taken into account and integrated in FDA's decision-making framework, and how FDA can incorporate two key components of the ethics of public processes—stakeholder engagement and transparency—into its decision-making practices. The committee views ethical issues as inextricably intertwined with scientific and regulatory issues. Ethical issues are therefore discussed throughout this report.

Public engagement and transparency increase the likelihood that the perspectives of patients and consumers, who have knowledge different from those of technical experts, are included in the making of policy decisions. When including such perspectives, however, FDA should ensure that patient advocacy groups represent the views of patients rather than the views of commercial entities that provide funding to the organizations. The concerns and practical considerations voiced by other stakeholders, such as health care providers, payers, industry, and academe, are also important to include. Transparency and other public accountability processes may also increase the likelihood that the public will view regulatory and policy decisions, including a decision by FDA to require a sponsor to conduct postmarketing research or a decision to continue or discontinue a required postmarketing clinical trial, as fair and acceptable.[48]

Modern tools for risk communication and public engagement ensure that all stakeholders—including physicians, other health professionals, interested patients and their families, and members of the general public—understand the decision the agency is facing, including what is known about the benefits and risks associated with the therapy in question and the pertinent uncertainties. Uncertainties might pertain to the quantity and quality of evidence, the benefit–risk profile, or the effect of policy decisions on the health of the public. Engagement with stakeholders helps to explain the types of uncertainties at issue and how the agency is dealing with uncertainties in making its policy decisions and helps the agency to understand how those affected by its actions weigh benefits and risks.[49] Communication to stakeholders will be more important, and in some ways more complex, as FDA moves more toward a lifecycle approach to drug regulation. Education and outreach will help to ensure that the public understands the change in the regulation of a drug as part of the normal natural history of its lifecycle.

Regulatory Science and High-Quality Evidence

The committee was guided by the view that regulatory decision-making, including decisions that require the integration of postmarketing safety information, should be based on the best principles and practices for making policy decisions under conditions of uncertainty, such as appropriate processes for transparency in decision-making and public accountability. Those principles and practices, sometimes referred to as the emerging field of regulatory science, require that policy decisions reflect the best available scientific evidence and analytic techniques drawn from a wide array of disciplines and technical expertise, including decision science, behavioral economics, and cognitive psychology.

Accurately assessing the potential benefits of and risks posed by a drug requires the use of a wide variety of scientific data, including findings from clinical trials; epidemiologic and outcomes research, such as observational studies and meta-analyses; and postmarketing surveillance systems that detect and help to characterize adverse events. All sources of data—not only or primarily those

[48]FDA and those advising it should have access to all information relevant to a given public health question, whether or not the information is deemed proprietary or to constitute a trade secret. One source of tension in meeting acceptable standards of transparency with stakeholders is the management of public access to such information.

[49]The committee acknowledges that there are important challenges to implementing policy making and regulatory processes that balance scientific evidence and stakeholder input appropriately (Lomas, 2005).

obtained from clinical trials—have the potential to contribute to sound regulatory decision-making. The critical factors in determining how much weight to give to various data resources are the quality of the studies that generated them and their relevance to the public health questions at issue, not simply whether the studies were experimental or observational. The committee further recognizes the importance of toxicology studies—including molecular toxicology and animal studies—in both the premarketing and postmarketing setting, especially as genomic sciences progress. The committee, however, considered a review of pharmacologic, metabolic, or toxicologic studies as beyond the scope of its charge.

OVERVIEW OF THE REPORT

The transformation in FDA's authorities and responsibilities over the last five years provides FDA with valuable tools to help ensure that the benefits of a drug outweigh its risks throughout its lifecycle. Despite the challenges that this new era in postmarketing oversight brings, FDA should embrace the opportunities presented by FDAAA to protect the public's health. FDA has made policy and organizational changes, and has implemented new initiatives that are aimed at improving its oversight in the postmarketing setting. There are also indications in FDA's strategic plan and in negotiations for PDUFA V that FDA is moving further in the direction of strengthening its assessment of benefits and risks throughout a drug's lifecycle. The effects of these policies and initiatives, and even the full effect of the sweeping changes precipitated by FDAAA, will take several years to be completely realized. Those changes are promising, and they posed a challenge for the committee, which was dealing with a rapidly evolving FDA role in the postmarketing setting as this report was being written. The committee tried to make general, flexible recommendations that would be relevant in this changing landscape, and that could affect the course of these changes. The committee sees the present report and its recommendations as providing guidance to FDA as part of its evolving approach to drug oversight in which drug safety monitoring and regulatory action after drug approval is seen as increasingly important for protecting the health of the public.

Chapter 2 presents a broad framework for FDA's regulatory decision-making. The framework addresses the need for a clear explanation of the agency's decisions and organizational considerations that facilitate decision-making, and the committee recommends a process and formal documentation intended to help FDA assess the benefits and risks associated with a drug throughout its lifecycle. A major challenge for FDA is making decisions in the face of scientific disagreement about available evidence, and the implications of that evidence. Chapter 3 looks more closely at that particular challenge and discusses the nature of evidence and why scientists sometimes disagree about how to interpret and respond to evidence in a regulatory decision. Chapter 4 focuses on one of FDA's regulatory actions that were highlighted in the committee's charge (Box 1-1): the ability to require different types of postmarketing studies. That chapter discusses and makes recommendations about the circumstances under which different types of studies are ethically and scientifically justified. Chapter 5 summarizes the committee's findings by answering the specific questions in the committee's charge, and it reiterates the committee's recommendations.

A summary of key aspects of FDAAA, the agendas of the committee's public meetings, the committee's letter report, information on decision conferencing and multicriteria decision analysis, and biographies of the committee members are presented in Appendixes A, B, C, D, and E, respectively.

REFERENCES

Anderson, L. F. 1989. Cancer and aids groups push for changes in drug approval process. *Journal of the National Cancer Institute* 81(11):829-831.

Atkinson, A. J., W. A. Colburn, V. G. DeGruttola, D. L. DeMets, G. J. Downing, D. F. Hoth, J. A. Oates, C. C. Peck, R. T. Schooley, B. A. Spilker, J. Woodcock, and S. L. Zeger. 2001. Biomarkers and surrogate endpoints: Preferred definitions and conceptual framework. *Clinical Pharmacology & Therapeutics* 69(3):89-95.

Avorn, J. 2005. Navigating the third dimension. In *Powerful medicines: The benefits, risks, and costs of prescription drugs*. New York: Vintage Books.

Bloomgarden, Z. T. 2007. The Avandia debate. *Diabetes Care* 30(9):2401-2408.

Budnitz, D. S., D. A. Pollock, K. N. Weidenbach, A. B. Mendelsohn, T. J. Schroeder, and J. L. Annest. 2006. National surveillance of emergency department visits for outpatient adverse drug events. *JAMA* 296(15):1858-1866.

Budnitz, D. S., M. C. Lovegrove, N. Shehab, and C. L. Richards. 2011. Emergency hospitalizations for adverse drug events in older Americans. *New England Journal of Medicine* 365(21):2002-2012.

Carpenter, D. 2010a. Reputation and gatekeeping authority: The Federal Food, Drug and Cosmetic Act of 1938 and its aftermath. In *Reputation and power: Organizational image and pharmaceutical regulation at the FDA*. Princeton, NJ: Princeton University Press. Pp. 73-117.

Carpenter, D. 2010b. Reputation and power crystallized: Thalidomide, Frances Kelsey, and phased experiment, 1961-1966. In *Reputation and power: Organizational image and pharmaceutical regulation at the FDA*. Princeton, NJ: Princeton University Press. Pp. 228-297.

Carpenter, D. 2010c. Reputation and power contested: Emboldened audiences in cancer and AIDS, 1977-1992. In *Reputation and power: Organizational image and pharmaceutical regulation at the FDA*. Princeton, NJ: Princeton University Press. Pp. 393-464.

Carpenter, D. 2010d. The other side of the gate: Reputation, power, and post-market regulation. In *Reputation and power: Organizational image and pharmaceutical regulation at the FDA*. Cambridge, NY: Princeton University Press. Pp. 585-634.

Center for Healthcare Supply Chain Research. 2012. *The center publishes new report on Risk Evaluation and Mitigation Strategies (REMS)*. http://www.hcsupplychainresearch.org/projects/rems.asp (accessed April 2, 2012).

Cook, A. J., R. C. Tiwari, R. D. Wellman, S. R. Heckbert, L. Li, P. Heagerty, T. Marsh, and J. C. Nelson. 2012. Statistical approaches to group sequential monitoring of postmarket safety surveillance data: Current state of the art for use in the Mini-Sentinel pilot. *Pharmacoepidemiology Drug Safety* 21(Suppl 1):72-81.

CRS (Congressional Research Service). 2008. *Report to Congress: FDA Amendments Act of 2007 (P.L. 110-85)*. Washington, DC: Congressional Research Service.

Daemmrich, A. A. 2004a. Drug laws and therapeutic cultures. In *Pharmacopolitics: Drug regulation in the United States and Germany*. Chapel Hill, NC: The University of North Carolina Press.

Daemmrich, A. A. 2004b. Clincal trials as test and therapy, 1980-2000. In *Pharmacopolitics: Drug regulation in the United States and Germany*. Chapel Hill, NC: The University of North Carolina Press. Pp. 81-115.

Evans, B. 2010. Seven pillars of a new evidentiary paradigm: The Food, Drug, and Cosmetic Act enters the genomic era. *Notre Dame Law Review* 85(2):419-524. Pp. 19-47.

FDA (US Food and Drug Administration). 1998. *The CDER handbook*. Rockville, MD: Department of Health and Human Services.

FDA. 1999. *Managing the risks from medical product use: Creating a risk management framework. Report to the FDA commissioner from the Task Force on Risk Management.* Washington, DC: Department of Health and Human Services.

FDA. 2003. *Guidance for industry INDs for Phase 2 and Phase 3 studies. Chemistry, manufacturing, and controls information.* Washington, DC: Department of Health and Human Services.

FDA. 2005. *Guidance for industry: Development and use of Risk Minimization Action Plans.* Washington, DC: US Food and Drug Administration.

FDA. 2007a. *Advisory committee briefing document: Cardiovascular safety of rosiglitazone.* Washington, DC: US Food and Drug Administration.

FDA. 2007b. *FDA news release: FDA adds boxed warning for heart-related risks to anti-diabetes drug Avandia. Agency says drug to remain on market, while safety assessment continues*. http://www.fda.gov/NewsEvents/Newsroom/PressAnnouncements/2007/ucm109026.htm (accessed August 23, 2011).

FDA. 2007c. *Transcript of FDA press conference on the update to the existing box warning on Avandia. November 14, 2007.* http://www.fda.gov/NewsEvents/Newsroom/MediaTranscripts/ucm122244.htm (accessed August 23, 2011).

FDA. 2008. *The Sentinel Initiative.* Washington, DC: Department of Health and Human Services.

FDA. 2009a. *The history of drug regulation in the United States*. http://www.fda.gov/AboutFDA/WhatWeDo/History/FOrgsHistory/CDER/CenterforDrugEvaluationandResearchBrochureandChronology/ucm114470.htm (accessed September 9, 2011).

FDA. 2009b. *Guidance for industry format and content of proposed Risk Evaluation and Mitigation Strategies (REMS), REMS assessments, and proposed REMS modifications.* Washington, DC: Department of Health and Human Services.

FDA. 2009c. *Office of Surveillance and Epidemiology (OSE).* http://www.fda.gov/AboutFDA/CentersOffices/CDER/ucm106491.htm (accessed September 14, 2011).

FDA. 2009d. *Memorandum of agreement between the Office of New Drugs and the Office of Surveillance and Epidemiology in the Center for Drug Evaluation and Research.* Washington, DC: US Food and Drug Administration.

FDA. 2010a. *Initiatives (CDER).* http://www.fda.gov/AboutFDA/CentersOffices/CDER/WhatWeDo/Initiatives/default.htm#equalvoice (accessed April 15, 2011).

FDA. 2010b. *NIH and FDA announce collaborative initiative to fast-track innovations to the public.* http://www.fda.gov/NewsEvents/Newsroom/PressAnnouncements/ucm201706.htm (accessed August 23, 2011).

FDA. 2011a. *Strategic Priorities*, 2011-2015. Washington, DC: Food and Drug Administration.

FDA. 2011b. *FY 2010 performance report to the President and Congress for the Prescription Drug User Fee Act.* Washington, DC: Food and Drug Administration.

FDA. 2011c. *Guidance for industry postmarketing studies and clinical trials—implementation of section 505(o)(3) of the Federal Food, Drug, and Cosmetic Act.* Washington, DC: Department of Health and Human Services.

FDA. 2011d. *Postmarket requirements and commitments searchable database: Record for vectibix, NDA # 125147.* http://www.accessdata.fda.gov/scripts/cder/pmc/index.cfm?StartRow=6&StepSize=1&Paging=Yes (accessed April 24, 2011).

FDA. 2011e. *Guidance: Medication guides—distribution requirements and inclusion in Risk Evaluation and Mitigation Strategies (REMS).* Washington, DC: US Food and Drug Administration.

FDA. 2011f. *Office of New Drugs.* http://www.fda.gov/AboutFDA/CentersOffices/CDER/ucm184426.htm (accessed April 10, 2011).

FDA. 2011g. *FDA significantly restricts access to the diabetes drug Avandia.* http://www.fda.gov/Drugs/DrugSafety/PostmarketDrugSafetyInformationforPatientsandProviders/ucm226956.htm (accessed January 14, 2011).

FDA. 2011h. *FDA fundamentals. Do you know what FDA does?* http://www.fda.gov/aboutfda/transparency/basics/ucm192695.htm (accessed April 24, 2011).

FDA. 2012. Report on the performance of drug and biologics firms in conducting postmarketing requirements and commitments; availability. *Federal Register* 77(44):13339-13343.

FDA Science Board Subcommittee. 2011. *Review of the FDA/CDER pharmacovigilance program.* Washington, DC: US Food and Drug Administration.

GAO (Government Accountability Office). 2008. *FDA has begun to enhance its oversight of drugs approved on the basis of surrogate endpoints.* Washington, DC: Government Accountability Office.

GAO. 2009. *Drug safety: FDA has begun efforts to enhance postmarket safety, but additional actions are needed.* Washington, DC: Government Accountability Office.

Grossman, L. A., R. A. Merrill, and P. B. Hutt. 2007. *FDA jurisdiction: A matter of definition.* Washington College of Law Research Paper No. 2008-38. American University Washington College of Law.

Gu, Q., C. D. Dillon, and B. V. L. 2010. *Prescription drug use continues to increase: U.S. prescription drug data for 2007-2008.* Atlanta, GA: Centers for Disease Control and Prevention.

Hamburg, M. A., and J. M. Sharfstein. 2009. The FDA as a public health agency. *New England Journal of Medicine* 360(24):2493-2495.

HHS (US Department of Health and Human Services). 2010. *HIPAA Mini-Sentinel and Sentinel.* Washington, DC: Department of Health and Human Services.

Hilts, P. J. 2003a. Thalidomide. In *Protecting America's health.* New York: Alfred A. Knoff. Pp. 144-165.

Hilts, P. J. 2003b. The modern plague. In *Protecting America's health.* New York: Alfred A. Knoff. Pp. 236-254.

IOM (Institute of Medicine). 2002. *Responsible research: A systems approach to protecting research participants.* Washington, DC: The National Academies Press.

IOM. 2004. *Patient safety: Achieving a new standard for care.* Washington, DC: The National Academies Press.

IOM. 2007a. *The future of drug safety: Promoting and protecting the health of the public.* Washington, DC: The National Academies Press.

IOM. 2007b. *Understanding the benefits and risks of pharmaceuticals: Workshop summary.* Washington, DC: The National Academies Press.

IOM. 2010a. *Evaluation of biomarkers and surrogate endpoints in chronic disease.* Washington, DC: The National Academies Press.

IOM. 2010b. *Ethical issues in studying the safety of approved drugs: A letter report.* Washington, DC: The National Academies Press.

Jenkins, J. K. 2010. *Memorandum from John Jenkins to Janet Woodcock (dated September, 2010). Re: Recommendations for regulatory actions—rosiglitazone.* Washington, DC: Food and Drug Administration.

Lomas, J. 2005. Using research to inform healthcare managers' and policy makers' questions: From summative to interpretive synthesis. *Health Policy* 1(1):55-71.

Marks, H. M. 1997a. Playing it safe: The Federal Food, Drug and Cosmetic Act of 1938. In *The progress of experiment: Science and therapeutic reform in the United States, 1900-1990.* Cambridge, NY: Cambridge University Press. Pp. 136-163.

Marks, H. M. 1997b. Managing chance: Statistics and therapeutic experiments, 1950-1960. *The progress of experiment: Science and therapeutic reform in the United States, 1900-1990*. Cambridge, NY: Cambridge University Press. Pp. 71-97.

NIH (National Institutes of Health). 2011. *Thiazolidinedione Intervention with Vitamin D Evaluation (TIDE)*. http://clinicaltrials.gov/ct2/show/NCT00879970 (accessed April 25, 2011).

Nissen, S. E., and K. Wolski. 2007. Effect of rosiglitazone on the risk of myocardial infarction and death from cardiovascular causes. *New England Journal of Medicine* 356(24):2457-2471.

Office of Surveillance and Epidemiology. 2007. *An overview of RiskMAPs*. Washington, DC: US Food and Drug Administration.

Platt, R., M. Wilson, K. A. Chan, J. S. Benner, J. Marchibroda, and M. McClellan. 2009. The new Sentinel network—improving the evidence of medical-product safety. *New England Journal of Medicine* 361(7):645-647.

Platt, R., R. M. Carnahan, J. S. Brown, E. Chrischilles, L. H. Curtis, S. Hennessy, J. C. Nelson, J. A. Racoosin, M. Robb, S. Schneeweiss, S. Toh, and M. G. Weiner. 2012. The U.S. Food and Drug Administration's Mini-Sentinel program: Status and direction. *Pharmacoepidemiology and Drug Safety* 21(Suppl 1):1-8.

Robb, M. A., J. A. Racoosin, R. E. Sherman, T. P. Gross, R. Ball, M. E. Reichman, K. Midthun, and J. Woodcock. 2012. The U.S. Food and Drug Administration's Sentinel initiative: Expanding the horizons of medical product safety. *Pharmacoepidemiology and Drug Safety* 21(Suppl 1):9-11.

Rosen, C. J. 2007. The rosiglitazone story—lessons from an FDA advisory committee meeting. *New England Journal of Medincine* 357(9):844-846.

Shane, R. 2009. Risk Evaluation and Mitigation Strategies: Impact on patients, health care providers, and health systems. *American Journal of Health-System Pharmacy* 66(24 Suppl. 7):S6-S12.

Stang, P. E., P. B. Ryan, J. A. Racoosin, J. M. Overhage, A. G. Hartzema, C. Reich, E. Welebob, T. Scarnecchia, and J. Woodcock. 2010. Advancing the science for active surveillance: Rationale and design for the Observational Medical Outcomes Partnership. *Annals of Internal Medicine* 153(9):600-606.

Strom, B. L. 2006. How the U.S. drug safety system should be changed. *JAMA* 295(17):2072-2075.

Wood, A. J. 2006. A proposal for radical changes in the drug-approval process. *New England Journal of Medicine* 355(6):618-623.

Wood, A. J. J., C. M. Stein, and R. Woosley. 1998. Making medicines safer—the need for an independent drug safety board. *New England Journal of Medicine* 339(25):1851-1854.

Woodcock, J., R. E. Behrman, and G. J. Dal Pan. 2011. Role of postmarketing surveillance in contemporary medicine. *Annual Review of Medicine* 62(Feb):1-10.

2

Incorporating Benefit and Risk Assessment and Benefit–Risk Management into Food and Drug Administration Decision-Making

As part of its charge the committee was asked how the US Food and Drug Administration (FDA) should "factor in different kinds of safety evidence in considering different kinds of regulatory action". To respond to that question, the committee considered the relevance of different evidence to decisions about different potential regulatory actions, and how FDA should apply that evidence across the lifecycle of a drug. The committee concluded that there is no one answer to that question, because the evidence and circumstances surrounding each regulatory decision are different. Although decisions as to how to weigh evidence will always have to be made case by case, the committee provides a broad overall approach to guide the assessment of safety evidence and FDA decision-making. In this chapter, the committee highlights the importance of a lifecycle approach to FDA's regulatory decisions and proposes two mechanisms to facilitate adopting such an approach: a framework for decision-making and a document, referred to as a Benefit and Risk Assessment and Management Plan (BRAMP), to formalize the implementation of the lifecycle approach discussed in Chapter 1, and make FDA's decisions about each drug transparent. The framework is not intended as a one-time activity, but rather an activity that recurs when questions about the benefits or risks associated with a drug arise. The document is a record that tracks the experience of a drug across its lifecycle, to be updated whenever the framework is used to evaluate the benefits and risks associated with a drug.

EVALUATING BENEFIT AND RISK OVER A DRUG'S LIFECYCLE

FDA's decision to approve a drug for sale in the United States is based on a judgment that in view of the evidence from premarketing studies and clinical needs, it is, all things considered, in the interest of the public's health for the drug to enter the marketplace. In other words, the benefits of the drug outweigh its risks for the intended use and population. Although at the time of approval knowledge about efficacy from small, short-term clinical-trial populations is limited, far less is known about the drug's risks. Some adverse effects may be too rare to be identified in the small numbers of people who participate in premarketing studies. For example, although the premarketing clinical trials for a second-generation rotavirus vaccine involved relatively large numbers of research participants, the small, increased risk of intussusceptions with rotavirus vaccines was only identified in post-licensure safety monitoring (approximately 1 of every 51,000 to 68,000 vaccinated infants) (Greenberg, 2011; Patel et al., 2011). Other adverse events may have a latent period longer than the duration of premarketing trials or may occur in people who are unlike those who participated in the premarketing trials in relevant respects. For example, they may be less healthy, take other medications, or have comorbidities. Such patients are often excluded from or enrolled in small numbers in premarketing trials (Fung, 2001).

For several reasons, questions about the effectiveness of a drug in actual clinical practice may also remain at the time of approval (Borer et al., 2007; Hiatt, 2006; IOM, 2007a; Ray and Stein, 2006). Long drug exposure during the postmarketing period could lead to a loss of effectiveness as tolerance or resistance to the drug develops. The population taking an approved drug is likely to be more heterogeneous than the people who participated in premarketing clinical trials. The drug may not be as effective in the postmarketing general population as it was in the premarketing test population. Many factors can account for those differences, including differences in environmental factors, genetics, age, race, ethnicity, or sex; interactions with other drugs; comorbidities; and problems with drug adherence. For example, a person who has liver disease might not fully metabolize and activate a drug, leading to decreased clinical effectiveness. A drug approved on the basis of a surrogate endpoint might not be as effective in improving a clinical endpoint, for example tumor shrinkage may not correlate strongly with survival. Once a drug is allowed to enter the market, physicians are free to use it, on-label or off-label, for any indication, including those of which there may be little or no scientific evidence of effectiveness from premarketing trials.

In the remainder of this chapter, the committee outlines a three-stage framework for making regulatory decisions and how FDA could apply the framework as part of the lifecycle approach to drug safety discussed in Chapter 1. (See Box 2-1 for definitions of key terms used in this chapter.) The committee then proposes a BRAMP document as a mechanism for implementing a lifecycle approach to drug regulation and for making FDA's decisions transparent. Figure 2-1 shows how FDA can incorporate the framework and the BRAMP into a lifecycle approach to drug oversight. The chapter concludes by addressing the circumstance under which regulatory decisions should include requiring manufacturers to conduct postmarketing studies, a focus of the committee's charge (see

BOX 2-1
Key Definitions

Benefit assessment and risk assessment: The gathering and analyzing of information on the nature and magnitude of potential benefits and potential harms (risks) associated with a drug and the determination of the likelihood that those benefits and harms will occur.

Benefit–risk profile: An overall evaluation of the benefits and risks associated with a drug.

Benefit–risk management: The process of identifying, evaluating, selecting, and implementing actions to increase benefits and reduce risk to human health. The goal of benefit–risk management is scientifically sound, integrated actions that increase or maintain benefits and reduce or prevent risks while taking into account social, cultural, ethical, political, and legal considerations. "A good risk management decision emerges from a decision-making process that elicits the views of those affected by the decision, so that differing technical assessments, public values, knowledge, and perceptions are considered" (Presidential/Congressional Commission on Risk Assessment and Risk Management, 1997). The process of benefit–risk management should include not only information about current regulatory actions but plans for future evaluations and regulatory actions as part of the lifecycle process.

Uncertainty: Lack or incompleteness of information. Quantitative uncertainty analysis attempts to analyze and describe the degree to which a calculated value may differ from the true value; it sometimes uses probability distributions. Uncertainty depends on the quality, quantity, and relevance of data and on the reliability and relevance of models and assumptions.

Box 1-1; the question of which study designs FDA should require is addressed in Chapter 4).

THREE-STAGE FRAMEWORK FOR REGULATORY DECISION-MAKING

Overview and Rationale

Responding in a timely and appropriate way to safety signals from already-approved drugs is among the most important and challenging public health jobs that FDA must accomplish. Permitting a drug to stay on the market that is on

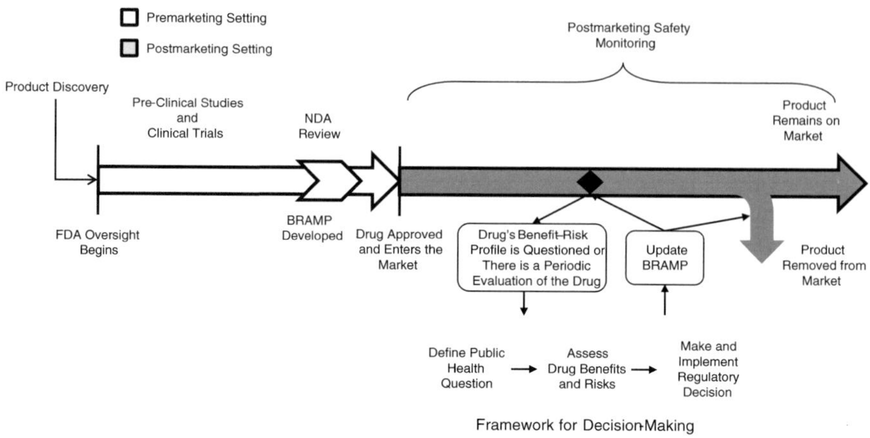

FIGURE 2-1 The lifecycle of a drug for a new molecular entity. After a product is discovered and the sponsor approaches FDA with the product as an investigational new drug, FDA oversight begins. During approval, the company submits information about the benefits, risks, and benefit–risk profile of the drug, and FDA develops a BRAMP. After approved, FDA and the drug sponsor conduct postmarketing safety monitoring of the drug, which could include passive surveillance, active surveillance, observational studies, and randomized controlled studies. If evidence arises that calls into question the benefit–risk profile of the drug, FDA uses the decision-making framework to review the new evidence in the context of existing evidence and the public health context of the drug, to make a regulatory decision about the drug. Depending on the decision, the drug will remain on the market, either with the same or different restrictions and conditions, or will be removed from the market. FDA updates the BRAMP document when it considers a regulatory decision for the drug, and when periodic evaluations occur over the drug's lifecycle. FDA oversight of the drug continues for as long as the drug is on the market.

balance harmful threatens public well-being,[1] but so too does limiting access to a drug whose benefits outweigh its harms. As discussed in Chapter 1, the Food and Drug Administration Amendments Act (FDAAA) of 2007[2] provides FDA with new tools and authorities to adopt a lifecycle approach to regulatory decision-making—an approach that FDA has endorsed (FDA, 2004). However, FDA has not yet taken full advantage of its new tools and authorities to implement a lifecycle approach in a systematic or comprehensive manner.

[1]There are instances where a drug is, on balance, harmful to the overall population but nevertheless provides a net benefit to a specific subgroup within the population. In those instances, the drug could remain on the market with restrictions to limit its use to those subgroups for whom the drug has a favorable benefit–risk profile.

[2]Food and Drug Administration Amendments Act of 2007, PL No. 110-85, 121 Stat. 823 (2007).

The assessment of benefits and risks and making management decisions in response to the assessment are not new challenges for FDA. The agency has a process in place for reviewing premarketing data on efficacy and risks, and making regulatory decisions about approving a drug on the basis of those data and other considerations. Similarly mature processes do not exist for evaluating a drug's benefits and risks in the postmarketing setting using FDA's authority in FDAAA, although in April, 2011 FDA issued guidance providing information for industry on how it would implement the section of FDAAA[3] that authorizes FDA to require postmarketing research. The link between benefit assessment, risk assessment, and FDA's regulatory decision-making has been criticized for failing to be explicit and transparent to external stakeholders (Asamoah and Sharfstein, 2010; Transparency Task Force et al., 2010).

Other US government agencies and organizations have a history of making decisions on the basis of formal assessments of risks. The US Environmental Protection Agency (EPA), for example, conducts formal chemical risk assessments to guide its decisions on allowable concentrations of chemicals in the environment (see for example EPA, 2005, 2009). The process used by EPA has evolved after publication of a number of reports outlining best practices for risk assessment and regulatory decision-making (NRC, 1983, 1989, 1996, 2009; Presidential/Congressional Commission on Risk Assessment and Risk Management, 1997). Characteristics of those best practices include the use of the best available scientific evidence, the involvement of parties that would be affected by the decision in the decision-making process, especially to incorporate the perspectives of patients and consumers in the process, and transparency in the process (NRC, 1989, 1996, 2009; Presidential/Congressional Commission on Risk Assessment and Risk Management, 1997). The 2009 National Research Council report *Science and Decisions: Advancing Risk Assessment* proposed that EPA use a formal three-phase framework when making its regulatory decisions (NRC, 2009, 2011). The framework includes a problem-formulation phase, a phase for the planning and conduct of the risk assessment, and a risk-management phase. A recent National Research Council report, *A Risk-Characterization Framework for Decision-Making at the Food and Drug Administration*, highlighted the 2009 framework and its general usefulness for FDA in its regulatory purview (NRC, 2011). It proposed a similar, three-step process for decision-making that involved identifying and defining the decision context, estimating or characterizing the public health consequences of each decision option, and using the completed characterization to compare decision options and to communicate their public health consequences within the agency, to decision-makers, and to the public. The report highlighted factors that are considered in FDA's decision-making, including scientific, social, and political factors, as well as the importance of the context of the decision to all steps of the decision-making process.

[3]21 USC § 355(o) (2010).

The need for a systematic process for drug-regulatory decisions has been discussed previously. The Pharmaceutical Research and Manufacturers of America's Benefit–Risk Action Team (BRAT)[4] discussed the need for a consistent framework for "transparent, rational and defensible decision-making that benefits patients, drug developers, and decision makers" (Coplan et al., 2011). The BRAT proposed a six-step framework for decision-making (Coplan et al., 2011). Health Canada and the European Medicines Agency have also discussed the need for a benefit–risk framework (CHMP, 2008; Health Canada, 2000).

In the present report, the committee adapts the framework from *Science and Decisions: Advancing Risk Assessment* specifically to FDA's postmarketing drug-regulatory setting to facilitate managing the benefits and risks associated with a drug throughout its lifecycle (see Figure 2-2). The framework should be used whenever FDA needs to make a regulatory decision about a drug; given its charge, the committee focuses on the use of the framework in the postmarketing setting where it could be used, for example, in choosing regulatory actions when the presence of a serious safety signal may precipitate or require consideration of a regulatory action. The adapted framework has three stages: define the public health question, assess the drug's benefits and risks, and make and implement the regulatory decision. Central to the framework is the need to elicit and incorporate the perspective of the patient.[5]

The three-stage framework is designed to be broadly applicable and assist the decision-maker in the exercise of sound judgment. It is intended to place reasonable demands on the limited resources of FDA given the volume of approved drugs, but to ensure that comprehensive evaluations of benefit and risk can be conducted when disagreements arise or when the public health effects may be substantial. FDA's decisions vary in their complexity (see Box 2-2). A recent NRC report noted that FDA's decision-making framework should be flexible enough to be applicable to the broad array of decisions FDA faces for its different regulatory purviews (NRC, 2011). That need for flexibility is equally true within the drug-regulatory setting. Although all three stages are necessary regardless of the complexity of the regulatory decision under consideration, the scope of each stage required to support sound policy decision-making will depend on the circumstances and available evidence. Many regulatory decisions will not require comprehensive evaluations at every stage, and efforts should be scaled accordingly.

A number of methods have been proposed for assessing benefits and risks, and for making regulatory decisions in response to these assessments. Some

---

[4]The Pharmaceutical Research and Manufacturers of America has transferred its Benefit–Risk Action Team (BRAT) framework to the Centre for Innovation in Regulatory Science "to further the program's technical development and broaden input from the scientific community" (PhRMA, 2012).

[5]FDA also recognizes the importance of the participation of patients, patient advocates, and health professional organizations in its regulatory decisions, and has established an office to facilitate such interactions (FDA, 2011a).

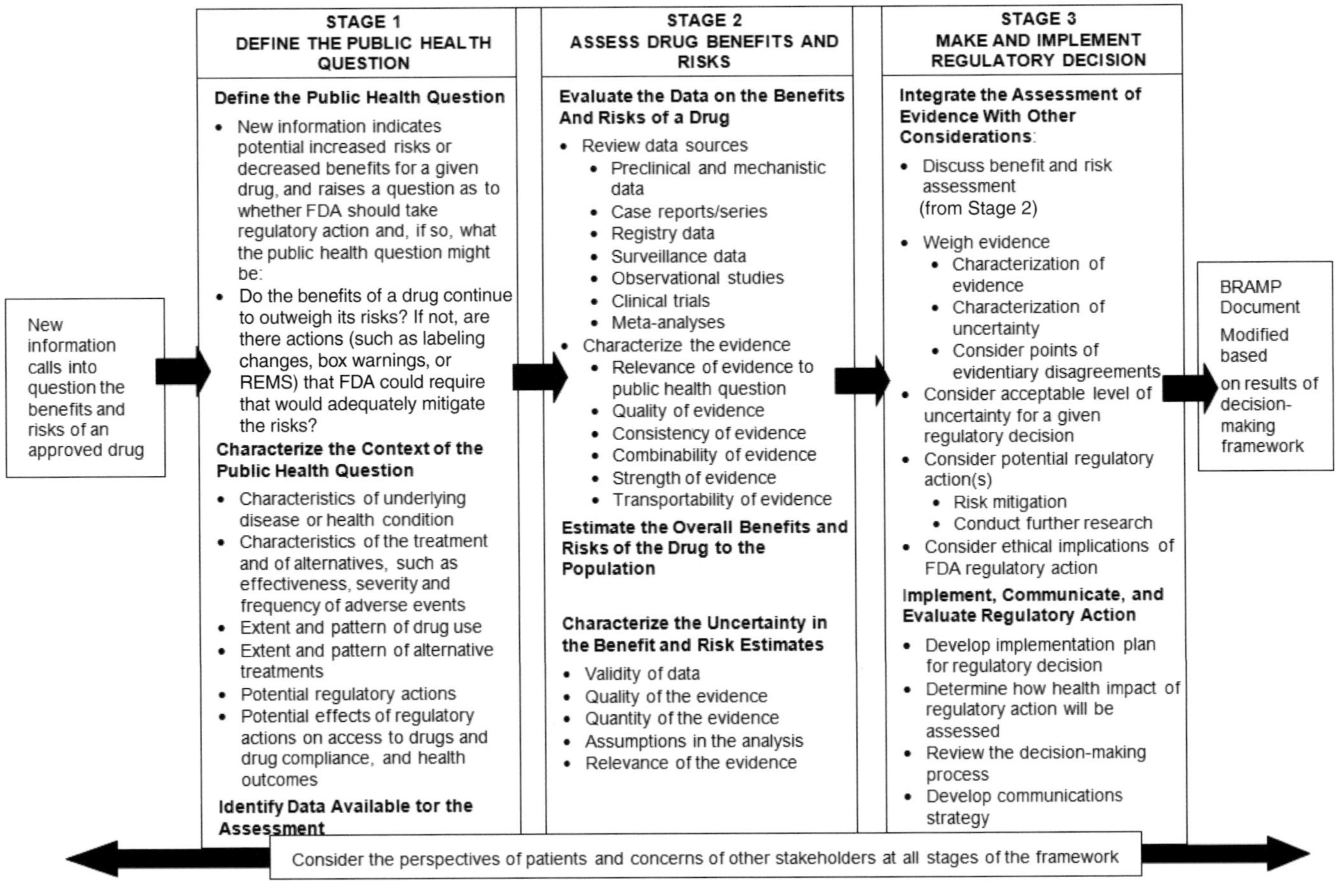

FIGURE 2-2 Three-stage framework for regulatory decision-making.
SOURCE: Modified from *Science and Decisions: Advancing Risk Assessment* (NRC, 2009).

BOX 2-2
Two Examples of the Diversity and Complexity of Food and Drug Administration (FDA) Decisions

FDA's decisions on drugs range from relatively easy decisions for which the science and the appropriate regulatory action are clear to ones for which the scientific evidence can be complex or contradictory and determining the appropriate regulatory action would benefit from input from many experts.

1. As an example of the former, the scientific evidence on the risk of liver problems associated with trovafloxacin (Trovan®), an antibiotic used for treatment for various infections, was clear soon after it was approved. Trovafloxacin was approved by FDA in December 1997 and became available to patients two months later (FDA, 1999). None of the 7,000 patients in the premarketing clinical trials experienced serious liver problems (hepatic failure, sometimes requiring liver transplantation, or death), but soon after entered the market, FDA began to receive reports of adverse events as early as two days after treatment; more serious adverse events (acute liver failure) occurred in patients after more than two weeks of treatment. Within seven months of approval, FDA had received more than 100 reports of patients' experiencing symptomatic and asymptomatic hepatic toxicity; some who sustained hepatic damage had to have transplants or died (FDA, 1999). In July of 1998, FDA worked with the drug sponsor to add further toxicity information on the medication label and package insert, informing physicians of the potential for hepatic toxicity. In addition, distribution of trovafloxacin was limited to inpatient facilities, patients receiving trovafloxacin had to have life-threatening or limb-threatening disease, and a physician must believe that the drug's benefits outweighed the risks it posed for a patient (FDA, 1999). In this example, once the drug was marketed, there was evidence of an association between trovafloxacin and severe, sometimes fatal adverse events. Other drugs that could be used effectively to treat for most infections were on the market. Given that evidence, FDA placed severe restrictions on the use of Trovan.
2. In contrast, when deciding about postmarketing regulatory decisions about aprotinin (Trasylol®), FDA was faced with conflicting scientific evidence about the risks associated with the drug. Aprotinin is a bovine-derived natural protease inhibitor that was approved by FDA in 1993 for use during coronary arterial bypass surgery to reduce blood loss and diminish the need for blood transfusions in surgical patients. From the time of its FDA approval through 2005, several studies and meta-analysis of results of randomized controlled trials supported

the efficacy of aprotinin for reducing the inflammatory response, the need for transfusions, and the risk of stroke, and it showed either no effect or a reduction in mortality, myocardial infarction, or renal failure risk (Henry et al., 2001; Levi et al., 1999; Sedrakyan et al., 2004). In early 2006, however, two observational studies further raised concerns about aprotinin's safety. Mangano et al. (2006) compared health outcomes related to the use of aprotinin (1,295 patients) with outcomes related to the use of two other hemostatic agents—aminocaproic acid (883 patients) and tranexamic acid (822 patients)—and results in 1,374 patients who did not receive a hemostatic agent. The study found that use of aprotinin doubled the risk of renal failure and was associated with higher rates of heart attacks and stroke than the use of other medications or no treatment. The study by Karkouti et al. (2006) used propensity scores and compared 449 of 586 patients who had received aprotinin during high–transfusion-risk surgery with 449 patents who received tranexamic acid; it determined that aprotinin may be associated with renal dysfunction. On the basis of the results of those two studies, FDA released a public health advisory for aprotinin in February 2006, detailing the results of the two observational studies and cautioning physicians to "consider limiting [aprotinin] use to those situations in which the clinical benefit of reduced blood loss is essential to medical management of the patient and outweighs the potential risks".

In late September 2006, after FDA held a public meeting of the Cardiovascular and Renal Drugs Advisory Committee, the drug sponsor disclosed preliminary findings from a new observational study that confirmed the findings of the previous observational studies. The new study, which was commissioned by the drug sponsor, reviewed hospital records of 67,000 patients who had undergone coronary bypass graft surgery. Preliminary study results found that the 30,000 patients who received aprotinin during surgery had an increased risk of death, renal failure, congestive heart failure, and stroke. Final study results, published in 2008, concluded that patients who received aprotinin had an estimated mortality 64% higher than patients who received aminocaproic acid (relative risk [RR], 1.64; 95% confidence interval [CI], 1.56–2.02) (Schneeweiss et al., 2008). Another advisory committee meeting was held, but the committee did not find the evidence compelling enough to recommend withdrawal of the product from the market, but did find it compelling enough to recommend a label change and that an RCT be

Continued

BOX 2-2 Continued

conducted (FDA, 2007a). Taking the preliminary data into account, FDA issued a new statement in September 2006, reiterating the cautions from the earlier health advisory and asking physicians to monitor patients for the occurrence of toxicity. In December 2006, FDA strengthened the safety warnings regarding aprotinin and added a warning that the drug increases the possible risk of renal damage. The advisory also included guidance for minimizing the risk.

In the meantime, the Blood Conservation Using Antifibrinolytics in a Randomized Trial (BART)—a multicenter, blinded, randomized, controlled study comparing aprotinin with two other antifibrinolytic agents (aminocaproic acid and tranexamic acid)—had begun to enroll patients in 2002. In October 2007, the study was halted early when preliminary results indicated a higher death rate seen in aprotinin-treated patients (RR, 1.53; 95% CI, 1.06–2.22) (Fergusson et al., 2008). In November, 2007, FDA announced that the sponsor agreed to an FDA-requested marketing suspension of aprotinin in February 2007, after preliminary results from the BART were released.

In May 2008, FDA announced that the drug sponsor would remove remaining stock of aprotinin from the market and limit access to aprotinin to investigational use. The special protocol allows the use of aprotinin for "certain patients who are at increased risk of blood loss or transfusions during coronary artery bypass surgery and who have no acceptable alternative therapy" (FDA, 2008a).

The differences in the complexity of these two examples illustrate FDA's need for a scalable framework for decision-making. Where the evidence is somewhat more clear-cut, such as the case of trovafloxacin, FDA could use the three stages of the framework, but the decision might not require as extensive weighing of the evidence, or engagement of stakeholders and external experts. Where the evidence is not as clear, where scientists might disagree about the value of different sources of evidence, or where requiring a randomized controlled trial is likely to be ethically controversial, such as in the case of aprotinin, each of the three stages might be more involved, with FDA eliciting external scientific advice, the perspectives of patients, and the concerns of other stakeholders.

---

[a]The committee uses these drugs as examples of the variability in FDA's decisions and its approach to safety signals, evidence, and regulatory decision-making. The committee is not commenting on, or drawing any conclusions about, the timing or nature of the regulatory decisions.

researchers and decision scientists have proposed the use of either decision-conferencing or multicriteria decision analysis for benefit-and-risk–based regulatory decision-making (see Appendix D for discussion) (NRC, 2011). The process of decision-conferencing or multicriteria decision analysis can increase transparency in regulatory decision-making, provide formal opportunities for input from stakeholders, and delineate the sources of disagreements among participants. Some of the methods, however, rely heavily on using a common metric, such as dollars saved, lives saved or quality-adjusted life-years, to quantify benefits and risks related to different endpoints and assigning numerical values to a number of subjective considerations, such as the importance of a given adverse event or a specific improvement in quality of life. Appendix C discusses the use of those processes as tools to elicit input into the decision-making process. They can be useful, and, in some cases, can provide informative results, but the committee emphasizes, as have others, that reducing benefits and risks to a common metric as the only output considered in a decision can sometimes lead to oversimplifying complex decisions, misunderstanding, and a lack of trust (NRC, 1989, 2011).

Consistent use by FDA of the proposed framework for decision-making would be valuable for several reasons. First, it would allow stakeholders to understand and anticipate key components of the process by which decisions are made. Second, it would emphasize the dynamic nature of benefit and risk assessments, particularly in the postmarketing setting, and the need for continual re-evaluation of decisions by an organization dedicated to protecting and promoting the public health. Third, it would provide an opportunity to consider the value of additional postmarketing studies (for example, through postmarketing requirements), to explore scientific and ethical issues with regard to the type of postmarketing studies under consideration, and to evaluate the potential effects of future regulatory decision-making. Fourth, use of a systematic approach for the routine re-evaluation of benefits, risks, and regulatory decisions could minimize long delays in decision-making or lack of transparency in the rationale for regulatory decisions may be minimized. It is important to note that while the need to change or modify a regulatory decision about a drug in the postmarketing context can sometimes be traced to errors in premarketing regulatory decision-making, often that is not the case. Rather, the ability to respond to the changing knowledge base regarding the benefit–risk balance is a valued characteristic of the agency that seeks to secure population benefits while mitigating harms, and modifications of regulatory decisions should be expected in the postmarketing phase and not regarded as reflecting a failure.

The following sections describe the three stages and the key elements for consideration in each stage. The three stages should not be interpreted as isolated activities, but as interconnected activities that inform each other and help to ensure that the characterization of risks or, in this case benefits and risks, is decision-driven, recognizes all significant concerns, includes both analysis and deliberations with input from the interested and affected parties, and is appropriate to the decision (NRC, 1996, 2011).

Stage I—Define the Public Health Question

In their 2009 commentary, Hamburg and Sharfstein defined in a broad outline the public health question that faces the agency (Hamburg and Sharfstein, 2009):

> A public health approach recognizes that the potential good of a new medical product or policy must be balanced against the potential harm. Some benefits are not worth the risk; some risks are worth taking. Key considerations are the severity of the illness at issue, the availability of alternative treatments or preventive interventions, and the current state of knowledge about individual responses.

In the postmarketing context, each regulatory decision is usually triggered by the receipt of new information about a drug's benefits, risks, or both. The new information may come to FDA in many ways, including routine surveillance initiated by FDA, reports of adverse events from physicians and manufacturers, and scientific studies published in the professional literature. Continuous monitoring of those sources of information is part of the lifecycle approach to FDA oversight. Stage I of the regulatory decision-making framework involves defining—each time that relevant new information about a drug emerges—the public health question that the new information raises. The broad public health question raised by new evidence of harms associated with a drug in the postmarketing setting, for instance, is whether any regulatory action is needed to ensure that the public's health is enhanced, and not unduly jeopardized, by a drug currently on the market.

The primary framing for this question is FDA's public health mission and responsibilities. Policy makers, regulators, and advisory-committee members need to determine the consequences of alternative regulatory actions on population health and target their efforts accordingly. All FDA regulatory decisions involve complex relationships between scientific evidence, regulatory authority, ethical values, and practical considerations. The public health question and the context within which it is being asked need to be clearly defined to ensure that all those relationships and the potential public health consequences of alternative actions, are properly considered from the onset of the decision-making process.

A first step in the decision-making framework is identifying the general public health question at issue and then making it more particular in response to specific characteristics of the drug and health problem at issue and the new information that has emerged. To make sure that the public health question defined in Stage I reflects a broad understanding of the public health interests at stake, it is important to elicit and take into account the perspectives of patients and the experiences of health-care providers, pharmacists, industry, and other stakeholders. A number of reports discuss the financial ties between some patient groups and the pharmaceutical industry (Abraham, 2010; Hemminki et al., 2010; Jones, 2008; Lofgren, 2004; Rothman et al., 2011). FDA should ensure that patient advocacy groups represent the views of patients rather than the views of commercial entities that provide funding to the organizations.

The major considerations that should be taken into account when specifying the public health question that underlies a regulatory decision are discussed below. The goal of the "public health question" is to ascertain what the public health impact would be of different regulatory responses triggered by new data pertaining to a drug's benefit–risk profile, not simply whether the use of the drug incurs unacceptable risk. This public health question contains all the components of a completely specified research question, which can be summarized under the acronym PICOTS: Population, Intervention, Comparison, Outcomes, Timing, and Setting (Brian Haynes, 2006; IOM, 2011a; Richardson et al., 1995; Straus et al., 2010). In the drug safety policy context, the population is those persons with a specified condition who currently take or might be eligible to take the drug, including information about relevant subgroups; the intervention is a regulatory action, with the predicted mix of treatments in the population induced by that action; the comparison is an alternative action (typically, the maintenance of current policies), with a projected population prevalence and pattern of treatments for the condition predicted to exist after that action; the outcomes are all the health outcomes deemed relevant to the policy decision, considered on the population level, due to both the drug and to the disease; the timing includes any time factors relevant to treatment (for example, chronic versus time-limited) or outcomes (immediate versus delayed); and the setting represents those contexts in which treatments for the condition are prescribed or administered.

It is important to note the difference between the elements of the question above and those concerning a simple drug treatment. For a single drug treatment, its effects can often be tested in a randomized controlled trial, where some research participants get the treatment and others do not. But there in fact is no single experiment that can be conducted to test directly the health effects of a given policy change, even if that involves market removal of a drug. Instead, the public health question must be addressed indirectly, piecing together a wide variety of facts and factors—both scientific and social—to estimate the likely population health impact of a policy intervention. Those factors are outlined in the following sections.

Characteristics of the Underlying Disease or Condition and of the Affected Population

Characteristics of the underlying disease or condition—such as its severity, duration, and natural history—are critical for specifying the public health question. A drug that improves quality of life or life expectancy of people who have advanced pancreatic cancer might continue to be acceptable even if new information suggests a high risk of a new, severe adverse event. Conversely, new information suggesting that a migraine drug poses a high risk of a severe adverse event would raise serious concerns about the drug's benefit–risk balance even if the drug were effective in controlling migraine attacks in many patients. Patient input may be crucial at this point (NRC, 2011). The value they put on the prevention of migraine attacks or other symptomatic conditions and how much risk of what type they are willing to accept for improvements in quality of life might be quite different than the values put explicitly or implicitly on outcomes by regulators. It is also important to keep in mind that patients will not all have the same values. Sicker patients, for example, might accept more frequent or severe side effects than patients whose illness or condition is well-controlled, and even patients with similar disease severity and therapeutic response might differ in their willingness to risk side effects.

The public health question cannot be properly specified without careful characterization of the population that is taking the drug and could take it in the future. Key considerations include the size of the population; whether it includes people who are in need of special protections, such as children and those with serious cognitive disabilities; whether it is made up largely of communities where there are substantial health disparities; and whether it is a population of mainly well or ill people.

Potential benefits beyond those to the people taking the drug should also be identified. Family and friends of patients benefit when drugs enhance the well being and functioning of those they love. For example, a marketed drug that improves the symptoms of dementia, other cognitive disabilities, or severe mental illnesses may have a direct effect on the quality of life of family members and other caregivers. Similarly, the benefits of a vaccine can extend far beyond the person vaccinated to others who might not be able to be vaccinated and more broadly to society.

Also relevant is whether the aim is prevention or treatment. Judgments about the acceptability of risks posed by such products as vaccines or drug therapies administered to healthy people to prevent them from becoming ill will be different from judgments about the acceptability of risks posed by drugs for treating those who are already ill.

Available Information About the Drug

To prepare for the formal assessment in Stage II of the quality of new and existing evidence about a drug's benefits and risks, it is important in Stage I to broadly identify what is understood about why the drug is given, how it is given, at what dose and how long, the variation in administration seen in the community with concomitant reasons, what monitoring or oversight is required for proper use, where it is given, and how the drug is experienced by patients, including benefits, harms and typical adherence. That understanding should be incorporated into the framing of the public health question. Additional characteristics related to safety include the severity, duration and reversibility of potential adverse events associated with the drug, whether it would be easy to mitigate or improve outcomes resulting from adverse events with close monitoring or other treatments, and whether estimates of efficacy are based on clinical endpoints or surrogate markers.

Availability of Alternative Treatments for the Disease or Condition

When deciding how to specify the public health question raised by new information about an approved drug, FDA should consider whether the drug is "first-in-class", and the benefits and risks of any alternative treatments, including whether there is a subgroup of patients in whom the other treatments do not appear to be effective. The willingness to restrict the use of rosiglitazone (Avandia®) in light of concerns about its risks was prompted in part by the availability in the market of a similar drug, pioglitazone, for the same indication that appeared to have a more favorable benefit–risk profile, although pioglitazone had not been on the market for as long as rosiglitazone.

Plausible Regulatory Actions and the Potential Effects of Alternative Regulatory Actions

It can be helpful in Stage I to narrow the public health question by specifying which regulatory actions are plausible candidates for a given situation. In some cases, a drug may already be subject to one or more of the regulatory actions, or it may already be clear that some options, such as withdrawal of the drug from the market, are inappropriate in a given context. Insofar as it is possible to narrow the range of plausible regulatory actions and thus the scope of the public health question, efforts in Stages II and III can be more focused. Potential options for postmarketing FDA regulatory action are defined by statute, implementing regulations, and judicial decisions. FDA's potential regulatory actions in the postmarketing setting expanded considerably with the passage of FDAAA (Kessler and Vladeck, 2008). Those regulatory actions are described in Chapter 1 and summarized in Box 2-3. The actions are not mutually exclusive; FDA can choose to use a single action or a mix of actions. For example, FDA could require both a Risk Evaluation and Mitigation Strategy (REMS) and a postmarketing study of a drug.

One important consideration is the extent to which alternative regulatory actions affect access to a drug, and whether any resultant restrictions in access would be desirable and fair. For example, the implementation or expansion of a REMS that only permits specially trained physicians to prescribe a drug or

BOX 2-3
Summary of Food and Drug Administration (FDA) Postmarketing Regulatory Actions and Authorities

No Change in Regulatory Action

FDA may determine that available evidence does not justify any change in regulatory action.

Changes in Labeling and Letters to Health Care Professionals

FDA may order changes in the labeling of approved prescription drugs and biologics to make patients and medical professionals aware of new safety information and recommendations concerning their safe use.[a] Manufacturers must submit their proposed labeling changes for FDA review. FDA has new enforcement tools to ensure timely and appropriate safety-labeling changes,[b] and may request that the manufacturer write an informational letter to health professionals indicating new label changes. FDA may also require boxed warnings if special problems are associated with a drug, particularly problems that may lead to death or serious injury.[c] Boxed warnings are intended to call special attention to the risks involved with a marketed drug.

Request that the Drug Sponsor Conduct a Postmarketing Study

FDA may request that a manufacturer enter into a postmarketing commitment (PMC) to conduct postmarketing studies (that is, Phase 4 trials) to characterize the safety and clinical effectiveness of an approved drug better. PMCs are not required.

Requirement that the Drug Sponsor Conduct a Postmarketing Study

FDA may require a manufacturer to conduct postmarketing studies (postmarketing requirements, PMRs). FDA may impose a PMR at any time in the lifecycle of a drug when (1) the need for a study is based on appropriate scientific data and (2) the adverse-event reporting and pharmacovigilance systems will not be sufficient to assess known or new signals of serious risk or the available data indicate the potential for unexpected serious risks.[d]

specially trained pharmacists to dispense it in rural communities where a short supply of such specially trained health professionals could have the effect of limiting drug availability in ways that are not intended.[6] In addition, removal of a warning label or of a REMS requirement could result in increased prescribing and

[6]Congress recognized this and tried to make it easier for "frontier" providers to participate in REMS training (21 USC § 355-1[a][f][3]).

Establishment or Modification of Risk Evaluation and Mitigation Strategies (REMS)

FDA may require, if new safety information concerning a drug arises, that the manufacturer submit a proposed REM that will ensure that the benefits of the drug will outweigh its risks.[e] FDA reviews and approves proposed REMSs to ensure their adequacy and compliance with statutory criteria. Failure to comply with an approved REMS can result in civil penalties and a removal of the drug from the market. Potential components of a REMS may be the inclusion of a medicine guide or patient package insert and limitation of an approved drug to a specific population, or a particular indication.

Withdrawal of an Approved Drug

FDA has the authority to withdraw approval of a marketed drug using several procedures, after due notice and opportunity for hearing to the manufacturer, if, among other things, new information shows that the drug has not been demonstrated to be either safe or effective.[f] FDA may also withdraw approval of a marketed drug if the new drug application contained false and misleading statements of material fact or if it is misbranded. It is relatively rare for FDA to remove an approved drug from the market entirely (McClellan, 2007). If a drug was granted accelerated approval for a serious or life-threatening disease, FDA has the authority to use an expedited procedure to remove it from the market if later clinical trials fail to confirm its expected clinical benefit or if the manufacturer did not satisfy its obligations for additional postmarketing studies.[g]

[a] 21 USC § 355(o)(4) (2010).
[b] 21 USC § 355(o)(4)(G) (2010).
[c] 21 CFR 201.57(e).
[d] 21 USC §§ 355(k), (o)(3) (2010).
[e] 21 USC § 355-1 (2010).
[f] 21 USC § 355(e) (2010).
[g] 21 USC § 356(b)(3); 21 CFR 314.500 et seq.

use of a drug, whereas a major label change could decrease the use of or compliance with a drug (see Box 2-4). For FDA to take proper account of unintended consequences of different regulatory actions in Stage III, it is important that, to the extent possible, FDA identify in Stage I of the decision-making process the potential consequences of a decision on the availability and utilization of a drug. Identifying those consequences at the onset of the process will help ensure that the affects of those consequences on the benefits and risks associated with dif-

BOX 2-4
Antiepileptic Drugs: An Example of Unintended Consequences Playing a Role in a Regulatory Decision[a]

Case reports of suicides or ideas of committing suicide, referred to as suicidality, resulting from the use of antiepileptic drugs triggered the US Food and Drug Administration (FDA) to ask drug sponsors to submit data from placebo-controlled trials for meta-analysis. FDA sent letters to sponsors requesting submission of clinical data on 11 antiepileptic drugs[b] from March 2005–January 2007 (FDA, 2008b). In all, FDA reviewed the data from 210 trials—199 placebo-controlled and 11 trials that used low-doses as the control. In total, the drug arms contained 27,863 patients and the placebo arms 16,029 patients (FDA, 2008c). FDA analyzed the data on patients who had epilepsy, psychiatric disorders, or other indications for four primary end points: completed suicide, attempted suicide, preparation toward suicide behavior, and suicidal ideation. Results from the meta-analysis, published in May 2008, indicated that a higher risk of suicidality occurred as early as 1 week after starting on antiepileptic treatment and continued for at least 24 weeks (FDA, 2008c). Overall, patients on treatments had a higher risk of experiencing a suicidal behavior or ideation event than placebo patients (odds ratio, 1.80; 95% confidence interval, 1.24, 2.66).

FDA issued an alert to physicians and other health care professionals of the increased risk of suicidal behavior or thoughts in patients taking antiepileptic drugs "to treat epilepsy, bipolar disorder, migraine headaches, and other conditions" (FDA, 2009a).

At a July 2008 joint meeting of FDA's Peripheral and Central Nervous System Drugs Advisory Committee and Psychopharmacologic Drugs Advisory Committee, the committees voted in favor of adding warnings to

ferent regulatory actions are assessed in Stage II of the process, and considered in the decisions made in Stage III of the process.

At the end of Stage I, FDA should have a clearly stated and carefully specified public health question that identifies the relevant regulatory actions under consideration. For example, as noted previously, when the decision-making process is initiated because of new evidence of harms associated with a drug, the general public health question is whether any regulatory action is needed to ensure that the approved drug or class of drug still has a favorable benefit–risk profile, and, if so, what those actions should be. By the end of the Stage I, the question should carefully articulate which regulatory actions might be needed to ensure that a given drug is still acceptable for a specified population with a prescribing information and requiring a medication guide for antiepileptic drugs but voted against adding a boxed warning to the drugs. The meeting included discussion of the potential for a decrease in prescriptions for and use of the drugs in the wake of a boxed warning, and the adverse effect on patient care such decreases might cause (FDA, 2008d).

On the basis of the meta-analysis results and the recommendations from the advisory committees, FDA required all sponsors of the class of antiepileptic drugs to include a warning label, not a boxed warning, and develop a medication guide informing patients of the possible increased risk of suicidal thoughts and behavior with the initiation of this class of drug. Health-care professionals were informed of the updated warning label "for antiepileptic drugs used to treat epilepsy, psychiatric disorders, and other conditions (e.g. migraine and neuropathic pain syndromes)" (FDA, 2008c). FDA also warned patients that suddenly stopping the use of antiepileptic drugs could cause serious problems.

The regulatory actions in connection with the antiepileptic class of drugs constitute an example of a complex regulatory decision that required balancing the risks posed by a drug and the unintended risks of imposing more stringent regulatory requirements, such as inclusion of a boxed warning about the association between the drugs and suicidality, were to be imposed.

---

[a]The committee uses this examples to illustrate the importance of considering all potential consequences of a regulatory decision. The committee is not commenting on, or drawing any conclusions about, the timing or nature of the regulatory decisions.

[b]The Food and Drug Administration requested clinical data on the following drugs: carbamazepine, felbamate, gabapentin, lamotrigine, levetiracetam, oxcarbazepine, pregabalin, tiagabine, topiramate, valproate, and zonisamide (FDA, 2008b). In 2009, clonazepam was added to the list of antiepileptic drugs associated with an increased risk of suicidality.

disease that has a characterized public health impact for which alternative interventions are or are not available. The specification of the public health question should have engaged patients and other stakeholders including clinicians, industry, and family members, and incorporate their perspectives when planning the benefit and risk assessments, and to identify their concerns, including practical considerations related to different regulatory actions.

Stage II—Assess Drug Benefits and Risks

In Stage II, scientific and technical experts—in conjunction with risk managers, policymakers, and regulators—evaluate the quality of evidence on both the benefits and the risks associated with an approved drug, including any new information that has triggered the need to consider regulatory action. The output of this stage includes estimates of the likelihood and magnitude of a drug's benefits and risks, and a characterization of the scientific evidence on which the estimates are based.

Evaluate the Data on the Benefits and Risks of a Drug

Evaluating a drug's benefits or harms on the population level is a two-step process. The first step involves scientific studies—usually controlled experiments—that aim to estimate the degree of difference in health outcomes under one treatment regimen versus another in a defined population. The second step is to use this and additional information to estimate the population impact of the drug's use in a given condition. This requires understanding population patterns of use, including dosage and co-treatments, and impact in more heterogeneous populations than might have been studied. This sometimes can be assessed in community-based studies or trials, but often must be evaluated by modeling the impact of a variety of disparate data sources pertaining to the above factors. These include surveillance data, observational studies, registry data, published and unpublished clinical trial data, and relevant case reports or series as appropriate. Information on structurally similar drugs and drugs in the same class may also be relevant and should be considered for inclusion.

The goal of the benefit assessment and risk assessment is to support FDA's decision-making. The assessments therefore should be designed with the public health question that needs to be answered and the array of regulatory actions in mind. The available evidence relevant to the public health question at issue, the expertise required to assess that evidence, and the additional evidentiary needs should be identified at the onset of the assessments. The evidence considered in benefit and risk assessments, at least initially, should be inclusive to avoid biasing their outcome.

The benefit-assessment and risk-assessment stage typically includes scientific judgments. For example, judgments are made about the strength of evidence on the basis of interpretations of the quality and applicability of individual studies, and about what constitutes a benefit or an adverse event. Those judgments can depend on a person's professional training, ethical values, and personal preferences. Such judgments are unavoidable but should be explicitly discussed among the participants in the assessment and documented to ensure transparency regarding the sources of the differences. Chapter 3 discusses the potential sources of disagreements in detail.

The expertise necessary for evaluating the quality of evidence and characterizing the evidence can differ substantially between the premarketing and postmarketing settings (GAO, 2009a). Given the rapidly evolving types of data sources, study designs, and analytic approaches used in the postmarketing setting (as described in Chapter 3), expertise in many fields is necessary for evaluating the quality of evidence for assumptions used in benefit and risk assessment.

Participants in the benefit-assessment and risk-assessment process should include, as appropriate, FDA policymakers, regulators, and scientists and external experts who have sufficient experience and expertise—including expertise in observational studies and clinical trials and in causal-inference methods—to evaluate for each study the quality of data sources, study-design elements, study conduct, data analyses, and interpretations of the results. The participants should also include persons with training and experience in clinical medicine, particularly in the specific specialties relevant to the disease in question and its potential adverse events, so that they can understand the clinical context within which medical care takes place. The people assessing the benefits and risks should have a comprehensive understanding of the public health question under consideration and of the potential implications of the assessments for regulatory decision-making.

To that end, there may be a need for capacity-building in FDA for it to be able to conduct, develop, and implement the benefit-assessment and risk-assessment process, including the elicitation of individual values and understanding of regulatory judgments about the different dimension of the decision-making process, and to have shared responsibility with industry for the development and oversight of benefit and risk management and planning documents of the sort described later in this chapter. If such resources are not yet fully available in FDA, FDA could build on its partnerships through federal collaborative initiatives, and public–private–nonprofit–academic partnerships. It could also build capacity through the centers-of-excellence models discussed in the Institute of Medicine regulatory science workshop summary (IOM, 2011b). Interactions and models of this kind can mitigate the issue of workforce constraints while providing FDA with access to requisite expertise. Appropriately managed interactions can also enhance transparency, minimize conflict of interest, and facilitate peer review. The overall decision, however, should rest with FDA.

Characterization of the Strength of Evidence

The estimates of the benefits and risks associated with a drug need to be characterized for regulatory decision-makers and stakeholders. The characterization should include a discussion of the nature of the evidence, including the types of studies that have been conducted (for example, observational studies and clinical trials), the quality of the studies, and the consistency of the findings among studies. Such a characterization will provide FDA's decision-makers and stakeholders with an indication of the confidence that they should place in the overall body of literature and in the benefit and risk estimates that are based on it. The characterization can be qualitative or, if sufficient data are available and the precision is warranted, the uncertainty in the benefit and risk assessments can be quantified.

The extent of the analysis of uncertainty and the complexity of the process used to incorporate expertise and perspectives will depend on the available evidence. If, for example, the available studies are of high quality and the results are consistent among studies, various experts are more likely to agree on the assessment of the risks and benefits and on the characterization of the evidence on which the assessment is based. As the quality and consistency of evidence decrease, disagreements are more likely, and more complex and formal processes may be helpful in clarifying and helping to resolve them.

A variety of approaches to characterization of the strength of evidence are possible and used by other US government agencies, foreign governments, and organizations (AHRQ, 2002; Miksad et al., 2009). Different approaches have their own strengths and limitations; some are simply qualitative assessments that provide categories of evidence, and others involve complex, quantitative methods for combining and statistically analyzing data from different studies. Chapter 3 further discusses the dimensions that contribute to the strength of evidence.

At the end of Stage II, FDA decision-makers should be provided with estimates of the likelihood and magnitude of the benefits and the risks of a drug, and a characterization of the scientific evidence on which those estimates are based. That characterization should include a summary of the data on which those estimates are based, the strengths and weaknesses of the data, the confidence in the evidence base, and any disagreements in the evaluation of the quality of the evidence (NRC, 2009, 2011).

Stage III—Make and Implement Regulatory Decisions

In the third stage of the framework, regulatory decisions are made and implemented. This stage involves synthesizing and integrating the estimates of benefits and risks and the quality of the evidence on which these are based (from Stage II) with the public health question (as specified in Stage I); deciding on the appropriate regulatory actions, including whether further study should be required; implementing the regulatory actions; and evaluating the effects of the regulatory actions.

Integrating the Assessment of the Evidence with Other Considerations

When making a regulatory decision, FDA should take into account not only the best available scientific evidence on a drug's benefits and risks but also a variety of legal, ethical, and practical considerations. A key benefit of distinguishing between Stage II from Stage III is the ability to disentangle technical scientific considerations from other factors relevant to decision-making (NRC, 2009, 2011; Presidential/Congressional Commission on Risk Assessment and Risk Management, 1997). That separation helps to ensure, for example, that there is clarity about the reasons behind a decision that is taken and about the sources of disagreements regarding the decision. For example, if the decision is that no new regulatory action is needed, it is important to know whether the decision reflects the scientific conclusion that the evidence associating the drug with a new adverse event is of poor quality or whether, on the basis of stakeholder input, FDA has judged the benefits of the drug to be so important that the newly discovered risk is acceptable. The various factors and their role in regulatory decision-making are discussed below.

Scientific Considerations

In Stage II of the framework, scientific and technical experts provide to regulators estimates of the benefits and risks associated with a drug and characterize the uncertainty in the estimates (NRC, 2009). Regulators should be given other relevant information that was identified in Stage I that also engages scientific assessments, in this case assessments of the public health and clinical effects of the drug and alternative regulatory actions. The information should include characteristics of the disease and of the adverse events, the availability of alternative treatments, and some features of the population affected (NRC, 2009).

Legal Considerations

Each postmarketing regulatory action has legal requirements that must be met before FDA may take it. Statutes and implementing regulations, as interpreted by US courts, define the requirements. Boxed warnings, for example, are "most likely to be based on observed serious reactions" (FDA, 2011b), but FDA can order a postmarketing requirement based on an indication of a potential serious health risk.[7] Most of the listed postmarketing regulatory actions also have procedural requirements—such as notice to the manufacturer and an administrative hearing with the right of judicial appeal[8]—that generally increase with the consequences of the regulatory action for stakeholders (Evans, 2010; FDA, 2012a).

FDA can be further constrained in choosing among regulatory actions by its precedent policies, and nonbinding guidance documents. There are many good reasons for FDA to maintain consistency and predictability in its regulatory actions. The perception of arbitrariness contributes to public mistrust and undermines compliance with decisions (FDA, 2011b; Transparency Task Force et al., 2010). FDA regulatory actions can be the subject of litigation because of their economic, political, and social consequences (Carpenter, 2010a; O'Reilly, 2008). Courts will largely defer to FDA's judgments about how to interpret the statutes that it is charged with administering. FDA decisions, however, can be overturned by the courts (O'Reilly, 2008).

Given the variety of factors involved, there is no single method for determining whether the relevant threshold for a particular regulatory action is satisfied. In some cases, there may be insufficient evidentiary certainty to support some kinds of regulatory actions. In others, the participants in the benefit–risk management

---

[7]21 USC § 355(o)(3)(B) (2010).

[8]For example, see 21 USC §§ 355(o)(3)(E), (F), and 355(o)(4)(B), (C), (D), (E), (F) (2010).

process may agree on the quality and degree of certainty of the overall evidence but disagree on whether that evidence satisfies legal or precedent thresholds for particular regulatory actions. Being clear on where the discrepancy originates is important for determining whether to pursue additional study through a postmarketing requirement and whether the evidence generated from the study would meet the threshold requirements for a particular regulatory action and result in a change in policy.

Ethical Considerations

Regulatory decision-making is an exercise in judgment by a person or leadership team in a position of authority, but the judgment is best made with the fullest possible understanding of the values and views of the relevant parties (NRC, 1994, 1996, 2009, 2011; Presidential/Congressional Commission on Risk Assessment and Risk Management, 1997). As has been discussed in the environmental regulatory context (NRC, 1996), people's values affect their preferences for health states, their perceptions of the benefit–risk balance of a drug, and their views regarding appropriate drug regulatory decisions. That is as true for policy makers, scientists, regulators, and industry executives as it is for patients, physicians, and health care managers. Among the key values relevant to drug decision-making are views about quality of life, risk tolerance, the appropriate role of government, and the overall objective of regulatory actions (NRC, 1996).

Patients' and physicians' preferences for health states reflect how they think about the value of prolonging life and about potential tradeoffs between prolonging life and preserving or maximizing quality of life. Some cancer patients and oncologists may feel disinclined to pursue chemotherapy regimens that hold out the prospect of extending life for a few weeks but involve burdensome side effects; others may wish to have access to such drugs notwithstanding their known harms and risks. Such differences in values are not restricted to life-threatening diseases. In February 2005, at an advisory-committee meeting on Vioxx®, a number of doctors representing arthritis patients urged FDA to leave Vioxx on the market because their patients, aware of the risks associated with the drug, were willing to accept the risks given the benefit of relieving the pain of arthritis (FDA, 2005a).

People's degree of risk tolerance affects not only their willingness to take a drug or have it on the market but also their willingness to tolerate uncertainty about the bases of regulatory decisions. More risk-averse people, for instance, might support regulatory action to remove a drug from the market on the basis of fairly modest evidence of a safety problem, whereas people with a higher risk tolerance would require a greater level of certainty about a safety problem before deeming such action acceptable.

Another important value is people's view of the appropriate exercise of regulatory authority in the limiting of access to therapies and the constraining of professional judgment and patient choice. Some stakeholders may emphasize the government's public-protection role, whereas others may feel that the free market and private decision-making by patients and their physicians should play a more prominent role in determining who has access to which drugs. Those views will drive stakeholders' perceptions of what postmarketing regulatory actions are appropriate in response to new information that emerges about a marketed drug.

An additional value concerns the overall purposes or objectives of regulatory decisions. Should decisions be made with the sole goal of maximizing the health and welfare of patients for whom the drug is indicated, or in some circumstances should decisions take into account the drug's effect on the well-being of family and other caretakers and on the health of others? Should the benefits and risks of a drug be weighted differently if they are experienced by particular population groups with special or unusual needs or whose health interests have not been well served historically?

The judgments of regulators and experts about alternative regulatory actions will necessarily reflect their own values about those issues, but they should also take into account the values of others, especially those most affected by their decisions, including principally patients and their families. It is important to recognize that there may be a wide array of values about, for example, quality of life and risk tolerance among patients and families. Particularly in contentious and high-stakes contexts, care should be taken throughout the decision-making process, especially in Stages I and III, to ensure that the full array of views is elicited (NRC, 1996). The values of patients and family members can give meaning to the scientific determinations that emerge from consideration of the evidence concerning a drug's benefit–risk balance. They may be helpful in pointing regulators toward a course of action in which the scientific assessment does not suggest a clear direction—for instance, when a drug is found to have both substantial benefits and substantial risks, when the benefits and risks are very different, or when there is considerable uncertainty about the benefit–risk balance. Explicitly describing the values that played a role in the decision-making process, whose values they were, and how they were elicited is critical for facilitating public understanding of how regulators reached a given decision (NRC, 1996).

The importance of seeking stakeholder participation in regulatory decision-making has been highlighted in many reports (NRC, 1996, 2009; Presidential/Congressional Commission on Risk Assessment and Risk Management, 1997). Recent examples of FDA decisions about regulatory actions in the postmarketing period also underscore how different the values and preferences of various stakeholder groups may be from one another and from those of FDA officials. Box 2-5 illustrates the importance of patient preferences in FDA decision-making using the examples of Tysabri® for patients with multiple sclerosis and Lotronex for patients with irritable bowel syndrome.

BOX 2-5
Natalizumab and Alosetron:
The Importance of Patient Perspective[a]

The cases of natalizumab (Tysabri®) and alosetron (Lotronex®) highlight the importance of patient preferences in FDA decision-making.

The US Food and Drug Administration (FDA) approved natalizumab—an intravenous monoclonal antibody approved for treatment for relapsing multiple sclerosis (MS)—for marketing in November 2004, under an accelerated approval, on the basis of "positive results to patients after one year of treatment" in two randomized, double-blind, placebo-controlled clinical trials (FDA, 2010a). Uncommon serious adverse events (such as pneumonia, rash, fever, depression, and gallstones) and common adverse events (such as urinary tract infections, headaches, and menstrual disorders) were seen in study participants. FDA approval was conditioned on the manufacturer's continuing clinical trials for one year after approval. Progressive multifocal leukoencephalopathy (PML), a serious adverse event, was reported in three clinical-trial participants three months after approval (February 2005)—nonfatal in two and fatal in one. The drug sponsor, with FDA's support, suspended the marketing of natalizumab, and FDA placed ongoing clinical trials on hold and issued a public health advisory informing patients and health-care providers to suspend its use (FDA, 2010b). At the time of the initial warnings about natalizumab, it was estimated that approximately 8,000 MS patients had taken natalizumab, 3,000 of whom were clinical-trial participants (FDA, 2005b).The drug sponsor further examined clinical-trial participants and convened a panel of medical and scientific experts to guide its activities. A year later, after extensive re-examination of clinical-trial participants, no additional cases of PML had been found.

In February 2006, FDA allowed the resumption of the clinical trial of natalizumab contingent on continued study of the risks associated with the drug. In March 2006, FDA held a meeting of its Peripheral and Central Nervous Systems Drug Advisory Committee regarding natalizumab (FDA, 2010b). MS patients testified at the advisory committee meeting as to how natalizumab greatly improved their quality of life. The committee "recommended a risk-minimization program" that included "mandatory patient registration and periodic follow-up to identify as early as possible any cases of PML that may occur, and to try to determine the reason the infection occurs" (FDA, 2010b). In response, the drug sponsor submitted a risk-management plan, called TOUCH, to ensure the safe use of natalizumab. In June 2006, FDA approved resumed marketing of natalizumab with the risk-management plan.

As of January 2010, 35 confirmed cases of PML had been reported to FDA (FDA, 2010b). Natalizumab remains on the market with a medication guide and with a new drug label that includes a table summarizing the rate of PML by number of infusions, PML risk, and information on the occurrence of immune reconstitution inflammatory syndrome, a condition that has been associated with natalizumab use in multiple sclerosis patients. Despite a well-defined risk of serious adverse effects, natalizumab remains on the market because preferences of some patients support the decision that the clinical benefits of natalizumab continue to outweigh its potential risks.

In February, 2000, FDA approved alosetron (Lotronex®) for "the treatment of irritable bowel syndrome [IBS] in women whose predominant bowel symptom is diarrhea" (FDA, 2000a). Approval was made on the basis of two clinical trials (a total of 1,273 women) in which "Lotronex was significantly more effective than placebo in providing relief from IBS pain and discomfort and in reducing the percentage of days with urgency" (FDA, 2000b). As of November 10, 2000, however, FDA had "reviewed a total of 70 cases of serious post-marketing adverse events, including 49 cases of ischemic colitis and 21 cases of severe constipation. Of these 70 cases, 34 resulted in hospitalizations without surgery, 10 resulted in surgical procedures and three resulted in death" and following discussion between FDA and the drug sponsor, the sponsor withdrew Lotronex® from the market in November, 2000 (FDA, 2000b).

After the withdrawal of Lotronex® from the market, FDA and the drug sponsor "received numerous emails, letters and telephone calls from patients who related how their IBS symptoms were not responsive to any therapy other than Lotronex®, and how their quality of life was adversely affected by its withdrawal" (FDA, 2002). FDA approved "a supplemental New Drug Application (sNDA) that allows restricted marketing of Lotronex® (alosetron hydrochloride), to treat only women with severe diarrhea-predominant irritable bowel syndrome (IBS). The approved sNDA for Lotronex® includes a risk management program to ensure patients and physicians are fully informed of risks and possible benefits of Lotronex®" (FDA, 2009a).

---

[a]The committee uses the regulatory history of these drugs to demonstrate the importance of considering the perspectives of the patients when FDA makes decisions. The committee is not commenting on, or drawing any conclusions about, the timing or nature of the regulatory decisions.

Considering stakeholder values in regulatory decisions requires a process for identifying key stakeholder groups and eliciting their views (see Appendix D for discussion of decision conferencing). Particularly for complex and controversial regulatory decisions, it may also require guidance from ethicists and others skilled at identifying sets of values from stakeholder and public comments and in methods for blending scientific and nonscientific considerations in decision-making. Careful analyses of the different reasons that underlie different stakeholders' and experts' views about which regulatory actions best advance the public health or the interests of particular patients can be instructive (NRC, 1996). To the extent that differences in the reasons reflect different technical interpretations of the relevant scientific findings, the results of a properly conducted Stage II should help reduce disagreements about appropriate regulatory policy. However, when the reasons differ because various stakeholders and technical experts use different values to attach meaning to the findings, such as how important it is to secure or avoid a particular benefit or risk, disagreements may be more difficult to bridge.

Practical Considerations

FDA should take into account a number of practical considerations when making its regulatory decisions. For example, it should be feasible to implement a restriction imposed by a REMS, any required medical testing should be affordable and accessible. As an illustration, the REMS for thalidomide contains specific certifications for health care providers prescribing and pharmacists dispensing thalidomide, and requirements for pregnancy testing (Celgene Corporation 2001), and is considered a successful REMS (IAF, 2010). In other instances, there may be substantial practical obstacles to the conduct of certain kinds of studies, limiting the extent to which they can be considered a viable regulatory option (Armitage et al., 2008; Ellenberg, 2011; GAO, 2009a; Hamburg, 2011). For example, experience from previous similar research may suggest that it will be difficult to accrue sufficient numbers of desired patients within the needed timeframe.

Deciding on a Regulatory Action

Regulatory decision-making is a qualitative process and necessitates judgments by regulators concerning the acceptability of the benefit–risk profile of a drug in light of relevant legal, ethical, and practical considerations (NRC, 1994, 1996, 2009, 2011; Presidential/Congressional Commission on Risk Assessment and Risk Management, 1997). Experts give decision-makers estimates of the benefits and risks associated with a drug—including the nature, magnitude, and likelihood of the risks and benefits—and a characterization of the confidence or uncertainty in the benefits and risks. The regulators' difficulty in reaching a decision will depend, in part, on the degree of uncertainty in the estimates of the benefits and risks and on the severity of the public health consequences if the wrong regulatory action is taken. Decisions are easiest when there is little uncertainty, the consequences of choosing regulatory alternatives are small, and there is broad agreement among most stakeholders and technical experts about the most appropriate regulatory action. Many of FDA's regulatory decisions are in that category. In those cases, the decision and its rationale should be apparent, and a complex and formal process for coming to that decision is probably neither necessary nor warranted.

Decisions are most difficult when there is large uncertainty in the scientific evidence, there is a potential for severe public health consequences if a wrong regulatory action is taken, and there is considerable disagreement among stakeholders and technical experts about what the right action should be. Difficult regulatory decisions should be identified and resolved in a more formal process. The key components of the decision-making stage when the situation is contentious should be

- Ensuring that the processes used to assess the data about benefits and risks, to determine data quality, and to elicit stakeholder preferences were adequate and that the regulatory decision-makers have the pertinent information from the processes.
- Determining and characterizing the social, political, ethical, and logistic factors that are affecting regulators' decision-making judgments.
- Determining the regulatory thresholds of evidence needed to justify alternative regulatory actions.
- Understanding the effect of regulatory actions, their effectiveness in improving the health of those who use the drug, the degree to which changes in assumptions about data or values affect the benefit–risk balance, and potential unintended consequences of the regulatory actions.
- Identifying the thresholds of evidence needed to justify alternative regulatory actions.
- Evaluating whether a postmarketing study (a postmarketing requirement or postmarketing commitment) would provide evidence sufficient to support changing a regulatory action.
- Understanding whether providers and patients are able to detect serious adverse events quickly, and particularly if an adverse event is reversible when the treatment is stopped. This information may be important for decision-makers as they consider whether the regulatory action they choose mitigates the risk to the population sufficiently. Such understanding might affect the regulatory actions under consideration. For example, a REMS might be considered to mitigate the risks posed by a drug that can cause a reversible adverse event that is easily detected.
- Assessing whether the time and resources needed to increase the level of evidence to justify a change in regulatory action are appropriate.

Sources of disagreement in FDA should be identified for each of those components so that, at a minimum, internal and external stakeholders will have a better understanding of key subjects of divergence and how the divergence might have led different decision-makers to recommend different regulatory actions. (See Chapter 3 for a discussion of potential sources of disagreement in FDA.)

Use of the framework that the committee proposes cannot eliminate disagreement about what regulatory actions are most appropriate, but it should enhance the likelihood that an appropriate decision is taken. Moreover, the framework can achieve the openness and transparency that are desired, foster a better understanding among stakeholders of how regulatory decisions are made, and enhance public trust and confidence (NRC, 1996, 2009, 2011)—all of which are consistent with FDA's goal of improved transparency (Hamburg and Sharfstein, 2009).

Communicating, Implementing, and Evaluating Regulatory Actions

Effective communication, including communication of risks, is an important aspect of regulatory decision-making and governance (Calman, 2002; Fischhoff, 2009, 2010; NRC, 1989, 1996; Pidgeon and Fischhoff, 2011). Although FDA has a long history of describing specific regulatory concerns for a wider scientific or general audience (Ellenberg et al., 1994; Siegel, 2002; Temple and Pledger, 1980), there has been a recent push for more communication about and greater transparency in FDA's regulatory decisions. FDAAA included a number of requirements for transparency,[9] and FDA has undertaken a number of initiatives in that regard (see Box 2-6). For example, FDA has improved transparency by posting review documents on Drugs@FDA and, in the case of Avandia and other drugs, posting memorandums outlining scientific disagreements among FDA scientists and the basis of the final decision. In addition, FDA scientists have recently written and published commentaries that explain their regulatory decisions and actions (Woodcock et al., 2010). Box 2-7, which discusses a published article by FDA staff explaining the rationale behind the agency's decision on dabigatran (Beasley et al., 2011), further illustrates efforts at increased transparency. FDA also recently published a guide, edited and authored by members of its Risk Communication Advisory Committee, that discusses the importance of and best practices in the communication of benefits and risks, including in the FDA context (FDA, 2011d). The committee commends FDA for those activities, but more needs to be done. For any particular drug, it remains difficult to find a clear, concise document that outlines the public health questions that have arisen over the drug's lifecycle that have prompted regulatory decisions; summarizes the benefit–risk assessment, including the evidence on which it was based; outlines the scientific, ethical, and practical considerations that influenced the decision; and describes plans to manage any potential or known risks associated with a

---

[9]21 USC § 360bbb–6 (2010).

BOX 2-6
Food and Drug Transparency Initiatives

The US Food and Drug Administration (FDA) has taken other actions to increase transparency not directly related to requirements under FDAAA. In 2009, FDA launched a transparency initiative. This initiative is proceeding in three phases: the first is intended to provide the public with information on how the agency works, the second on how FDA reaches decisions, and the third on how FDA can become more transparent to industry to foster a more cost-efficient regulatory process (FDA, 2012b).

In addition, FDA has published a series of perspectives and commentaries that describe agency policy positions and explain agency decisions about particular drugs. Communication of its regulatory decisions on rosiglitazone (Avandia®) is a good example. On September 23, 2010, FDA placed severe restrictions[a] on the availability of rosiglitazone and discontinued its approval of the Thiazolidine Intervention with Vitamin D Evaluation (TIDE) study that was planned to compare the benefit–risk balance of rosiglitazone and pioglitazone. European regulatory authorities that analyzed the same data reached a decision to suspend the marketing authorization of rosiglitazone. To explain the basis of its regulatory action, senior FDA officials published a commentary in the *New England Journal of Medicine* (Woodcock et al., 2010). Because there had been much controversy within FDA about the appropriate regulatory decision, the director of the Center for Drug Evaluation and Research took the unusual step of posting on the FDA website a memorandum, *Decision on continued marketing of rosiglitazone*, outlining how it weighed the available information and took the various internal recommendations into account (FDA, 2010c). That coordinated communication plan provided the public with a unique insight into the agency's decision-making process on a controversial topic.

---

[a]FDA required the drug sponsor to issue a Risk Evaluation Mitigation Strategy (REMS) according to which "the drug will be available to patients not already taking it only if they are unable to achieve glycemic control using other medications and, in consultation with their health care professional, decide not to take pioglitazone [a diabetes medication in the same class of drugs] for medical reasons. Current users of rosiglitazone will be able to continue using the medication if they appear to be benefiting from it and they acknowledge that they understand [the risks associated with the use of rosiglitazone]. Doctors will have to attest to and document their patients' eligibility; patients will have to review statements describing the cardiovascular safety concerns" (Woodcock et al., 2010).

BOX 2-7
Dabigatran: The Importance of Transparency in Food and Drug Administration (FDA) Decision-Making

The reaction to the approval of a higher dose rather than a lower dose of dabigatran (Pradaxa®) illustrates the importance of transparency in FDA's drug-approval process. The approval was seen as controversial and not understood by the public.

In October 2010, FDA approved a 150-mg twice-daily dose, but not a 110-mg twice-daily dose, of dabigatran, a direct thrombin inhibitor for stroke and embolism prevention for patients who have atrial fibrillation. Approval was based primarily on data from the Randomized Evaluation of Long-Term Anticoagulation Therapy trial, an active-control trial that compared the two doses of dabigatran to warfarin (Connolly et al., 2009). The trial followed 18,113 patients for a median of 2 years. The primary outcome measure was a composite of "time to first occurrence of stroke or systemic embolic event" and the secondary outcome measures were "time to first occurrence of stroke, [systemic embolic event] or all cause death" and "time to first occurrence of stroke, systemic embolic event, pulmonary embolism, myocardial infarction or vascular death". The 110-mg twice-daily dose was not inferior to warfarin, and the 150-mg twice-daily dose was superior. Bleeding complications and hemorrhagic stroke were more common in patients randomized to warfarin than to either dose of dabigatran. For the approved dose of 150 mg twice daily, ischemic strokes were less common in those randomized to dabigatran than in those randomized to warfarin (RR, 0.76; 95% CI, 0.60–0.98), but the risk of myocardial infarction was higher in those randomized to dabigatran (RR, 1.38; 95% CI, 1.00–1.91 for the 150-mg dose). An excess of serious coronary events was also noted in one of the ximelagatran trials (Fiessinger et al., 2005). The drug sponsor argued that dabigatran should be approved at both doses and that the 100-mg twice-daily dose should be available to people who were at risk for bleeding.

Seven months after FDA approved dabigatran, FDA staff published an article explaining its rationale for approving the 150-mg twice-daily dose, but not the 110-mg twice-daily dose, of dabigatran (Beasley et al., 2011). The article highlighted the underuse of warfarin, which was the only blood-thinner option for atrial-fibrillation patients, because of fear of bleeding, difficulties with its use, and the increased risks of strokes and disability. In the article, Beasley et al. (2011) explained that "both regimens would have been considered safe and effective if studied alone in comparison with warfarin, although the noninferiority finding for the 110-mg dose is somewhat less compelling. But given the clear differences

Continued

between the two doses, FDA's critical regulatory decision was whether to approve both strengths or only the higher strength". FDA reviewers were "unable to find any population for whom the availability of a lower dose would improve dabigatran's benefit–risk profile, and it appeared clear that most, if not all, patients should receive the higher dose." The article clearly articulated the rationale behind FDA's decision. In this benefit and risk analysis, FDA did not take into account the possibility that patients may vary in their risk aversion for one adverse event (bleeding) rather than another (stroke).[a]

Although the decision was criticized, when FDA communicated the rationale for the decision, it allowed clinicians, patients, and others to understand why FDA had made the decision. That better understanding could increase compliance with the recommended dose and improve public health.

[a]FDA recently issued a Drug Safety Communication on dabigatran through MedWatch related to reports of serious bleeding events. It stated that it is "working to determine whether the reports of bleeding in patients taking [dabigatran] are occurring more commonly than expected, based on observations in the large clinical trial that supported [its] approval" (FDA, 2011e).

drug or any evaluations of previous regulatory decisions. FDA review documents that are posted at Drugs@FDA contain much of that information, but critical documents are difficult to locate, and the key information is often difficult to find within documents.

In addition to improving transparency and effective communication of its decision-making processes and decisions, FDA policy makers should strive to continuously improve the efficiency and effectiveness with which they function. Evaluations should be conducted on a periodic basis to identify key facilitators of and barriers to timely regulatory action and potential improvements in the decision-making process. Such evaluations should also assess whether regulatory decisions are having the intended effects on drug use and health outcomes and whether unintended consequences are occurring. Much of the health care industry and other high-risk industries (such as aviation) have adopted such a learning approach to improve the quality of care and reduce preventable harm. FDA has an opportunity to learn from past and current decisions by fostering an organizational culture of continuous learning about decision-making processes that is consistent with the lifecycle approach. One goal of the Sentinel Initiative is to facilitate such evaluations. The public, industry, and regulators would all benefit if a learning process led to a systematic approach to regulatory decision-making that is flexible, timely, and consistent in its use.

The committee therefore recommends that the plan for implementation of the framework include a mechanism for reviewing the decision-making process through monitoring and evaluation, as outlined in *Science and Decisions: Advancing Risk Assessment* (NRC, 2009). Continuing evaluation of the benefit and risk assessment and management decisions is important for ensuring FDA's continued effectiveness, and the results of the evaluations would inform future improvements in the framework and in the underlying processes and timeliness of benefit and risk assessment and management.

As has been recommended to other agencies making risk-based decisions, FDA should specify which types of decisions will be evaluated, when the evaluations will be conducted, who will conduct them, and what the criteria for evaluations will be (Presidential/Congressional Commission on Risk Assessment and Risk Management, 1997). After-action reviews are of special importance for postmarketing drug-related decisions that are particularly controversial or difficult. FDA needs good outcome measures for the effects of its regulatory actions on public health, including whether the actions have the intended effect on drug use, such as an increase or decrease in prescriptions, and how they affect the occurrence of all relevant health outcomes, including adverse drug events, disease outcomes, and death. For instance, an intervention to reduce off-label use should actually reduce off-label use and thereby improve the health of the public. The importance of including a followup evaluation in Stage III of the framework is highlighted by empirical evidence on the utility of some postmarketing regulatory actions for addressing risks. For example, studies have demonstrated that providers and patients do not consistently heed safety labels, including even the most serious boxed warnings (IOM, 2007b; Lasser et al., 2006; Yu et al., 2011); in contrast, some boxed warnings have been associated with reductions in medication use and prescription (Bhatia et al., 2008). Those reductions might be appropriate or inappropriate, depending on the circumstances. The evaluations should be used to help to determine whether regulatory decisions should be revisited. All evaluations should consider whether and when it is appropriate to solicit stakeholder input.

BENEFIT AND RISK ASSESSMENT AND MANAGEMENT PLAN DOCUMENT

The three-stage decision-making framework recommended by the committee earlier in this chapter is not intended to be used only once, but rather whenever questions about the benefits or risks associated with a drug arise. In this section, the committee proposes the development of a document, akin to a technical support document, that would serve as a public record of the experience of a drug throughout its lifecycle, to be updated at regular points during its lifecycle, including whenever the framework is used to evaluate the drug's benefits and risks. The committee calls the document a Benefit and Risk Assessment and Management Plan, or BRAMP. Because the benefit–risk profile of a drug can change during its lifecycle, a BRAMP document serves as a living document that is updated when there is new safety or efficacy information or other information that affects the drug's benefit–risk profile. The committee does not anticipate that the BRAMP would document every postmarketing safety signal. Rather, the BRAMP document would be updated whenever FDA determines that new information about a drug warrants consideration of regulatory action to evaluate or manage the drug's benefit–risk profile, including consideration of whether to require the manufacturer to conduct postmarketing research.

A BRAMP document is intended to formalize and make concrete FDA's commitment to a lifecycle approach to drug oversight and benefit–risk management. It serves, in part, as a checklist that supports organizational adherence to the lifecycle approach. The BRAMP document will add to other FDA transparency initiatives discussed previously, increasing the transparency of FDA's decisions, and should foster collaboration between FDA and drug sponsors in the oversight of drugs and management of their risks. In addition to information about the stages of the decision-making framework whenever it is used, the BRAMP document should include a description of any boxed warnings, REMS, or other components of regulatory decisions, any future plans for managing or identifying risks, reassessing benefits and risks, and evaluating the effects of regulatory decisions. Details of the types of information that could be included in such a document are presented in Box 2-8 and discussed below.

Although FDA is responsible for making regulatory decisions about approved drugs, responsibility for ensuring that the benefits of a drug outweigh its risks is shared by FDA and the drug sponsor. For each new drug, therefore, responsibility for the initial development of some of the content that would go into the BRAMP document should rest with the drug sponsor; much of that material is already submitted as part of the documentation for approval, such as a summary and benefit and risk assessment, and any proposed postmarketing-study designs or REMS. FDA would use the company-submitted materials as a starting point for the BRAMP document and prepare the BRAMP document for posting on the agency's website within the same timeframe that is required for FDA to post documents related to new drug applications. FDA staff involved with the drug's premarketing application as well as staff with expertise and knowledge in postmarketing safety assessment should be responsible for describing the public health question, the process and outputs of the agency's benefit assessment and risk assessment, the rationale for the agency's regulatory decision, and the scientific, legal, ethical, and practical factors that went into the final decision to approve a drug. For example, if a drug was approved on the basis of a surrogate end point, that fact should be noted in the BRAMP document, as should any resulting pharmacovigilance or postmarketing commitments or requirements. Final approval of the BRAMP document would be FDA's responsibility.

Considerations for the oversight of drugs in the postmarketing setting are different from those in the premarketing setting. First, as discussed further in

BOX 2-8
Components of a Benefit–Risk Assessment and Management Plan Document

1. Public health question.
2. Summary of the benefit and risk assessment, including
   - Description of the process used to assess the benefits and risks, including how stakeholder input was sought and incorporated.
   - Summary of the available evidence used, the quality and uncertainty of the different studies, and the judgments made about the different studies, including how the studies were factored into decisions.
   - A characterization of the overall consistency and uncertainty of the body of evidence.
   - Explicit statements of the assumptions used in estimating benefits and risks.
   - Estimates of benefits and risks, including outputs of analyses.
   - Analyses of assessments sensitivity to the assumptions used and judgments made.
3. Regulatory actions and rationale, including
   - A statement of the regulatory decision, such as approval of a drug.
   - The rationale for the decision, including not only the final output of the benefit–risk assessment process but a description of any other factors that affected the decision, such as ethical issues, timeframe issues, the lack of an available treatment for a disease, or the risk posed by a drug in a specific population. It should also include a description of any value-of-information analysis, deci-

Chapter 4, the types of evidence likely to be available in the postmarketing setting are broader than those typically available premarketing. For example, data from surveillance and observational studies are much more likely to be available. In the postmarketing setting, therefore, expertise is needed in surveillance, epidemiology, and the evaluation of safety data collected from different observational studies, as well as clinical trial designs, biostatistics, medicine, pharmacology, risk communication, and ethics.

Second, research has demonstrated a tendency of individuals or groups to ignore or discount evidence that does not confirm a previous decision, and give more weight to evidence that confirms a previous decision; this tendency is often termed *confirmation bias* (Back et al., 2011; Jonas et al., 2001). Confirmation bias has been demonstrated for political (Strickland et al., 2011), medical (Mendel et

sion conferencing, or multiple-criteria decision analysis that was conducted

- Any actions that are meant to highlight or mitigate a drug's risks, including
  a. Labels or labeling changes.
  b. Boxed warnings.
  c. A Risk Evaluation and Mitigation Strategy.
- A description of any postmarketing surveillance, studies, or trial requirements or commitments including
  a. A description of any potential safety issues or effectiveness questions that are considered potential problems.
  b. The public health question and the uncertainties that need to be decreased to enable a regulatory decision.
  c. Details of the design of the study, including important human-subjects protections.
  d. Any other aspects of the studies that are required to be disclosed under the Food and Drug Administration Amendments Act (FDAAA).
  e. The timeframe and reporting requirements outlined in accordance with FDAAA.
  f. For clinical studies, the specific ClinicalTrials.gov URL where further information and results can be found.
- Schedule of future reviews, including
  a. A schedule for future benefit–risk assessments, with a given timeframe or, when there are potential safety or effectiveness issues, the events being detected.
  b. A plan to evaluate the effects of the regulatory decision on the public's health.

al., 2011), and risk evaluation decisions (Cox and Popken, 2008). Such confirmation bias could affect the interpretation of new evidence by FDA's drug approval staff after they have approved a drug. Along similar lines, Carpenter (Carpenter, 2010b) discusses criticisms of FDA for the "slowness and timidity with which they examine and question past decisions", the conflict between those within FDA "who approve drugs and those who monitor them after approval", and the effects on the reputation of FDA or offices within FDA when approval decisions are questioned or drugs are withdrawn.

Those two considerations suggest that postmarketing oversight should be done by FDA staff who have not been involved in premarketing, excluding all such staff would eliminate knowledge of the history of the drug, including the premarketing studies (IOM, 2007a). Seeking to balance breadth of expertise, management of confirmation bias, and continuity in knowledge of the drug, the committee suggests that the FDA team responsible for maintaining the BRAMP postmarketing should: (1) be led by FDA staff who did not play primary roles in the drug's approval process, (2) include continued input and involvement from representative staff involved in the premarketing setting, and (3) include membership with expertise in the areas listed above (surveillance, epidemiology, and the evaluation of safety data collected from different observational studies, as well as clinical trial designs, biostatistics, medicine, pharmacology, risk communication, and ethics).

Postmarketing updates or revisions to the BRAMP document would be needed throughout the lifecycle of the drug, including times when refined and validated safety signals or other issues arise that might affect the benefit–risk profile of an approved drug. Responsible staff—in consultation with others within FDA, with external experts as necessary, and with relevant stakeholders, including industry—should conduct periodic reviews of the BRAMP document, oversee audits and quality control as appropriate, review final reports of all studies included in the BRAMP document, and ensure that timely policy analysis and responses to any required studies occur and are recorded in the BRAMP document.

FDA currently posts a number of documents related to the approval of individual drugs at Drugs@FDA. The materials posted depend on the date of the approval; drugs approved more recently have a summary review document that contains many of the components of a BRAMP document. For example, the summary review for tesamorelin (Egrifta®) includes a description of the available evidence and a summary of the benefit and risk assessment (Center for Drug Evaluation and Research, 2010). The summary reviews, however, are prepared at the time of approval and apparently are not updated when new regulatory actions are considered, are not consistent among all drugs, and do not always include specific details about REMSs and postmarketing requirements. Having a single, living, publicly available summary document that contains the history of all regulatory actions related to a drug and a description of the rationale and support for the decisions is critical for improving FDA's ability to manage drugs in the postmarketing setting and to increase the transparency of FDA's regulatory decisions.

SPECIAL CONSIDERATIONS IN THE DECISION OF WHETHER TO REQUIRE A POSTMARKETING STUDY

Balancing the desire for more certainty about drug safety against the need for timely decisions is a key challenge in drug regulation. Regulators and policy makers must see themselves as managing uncertainty and delay, as well as managing risk (NRC, 2009). In this context, qualitative or quantitative assessments of the uncertainty of drug safety should be aligned with the regulatory requirements, the time pressure for managing a drug's benefits and risks generated by public health interests, and the ethical acceptability of conducting further research.

One of the regulatory actions available to FDA that can decrease uncertainty is a postmarketing requirement for research. Much of the committee's charge focuses on the scientific and ethical issues associated with postmarketing requirements, so the committee discusses requiring postmarketing research in more detail in this section. This section begins with a discussion of two specific circumstances under which FDA should give serious consideration to requiring a postmarketing requirement and should provide a public rationale if it decides *not* to do so. It then discusses one tool, value-of-information (VOI) analysis, which can help to determine whether additional information from a postmarketing requirement would help in decision-making.

General Ethical Considerations in a Food and Drug Administration Decision to Require a Postmarketing Study

The decision by FDA to require a postmarketing study is associated with particular ethical obligations for FDA, and requires an ethical justification. When FDA requires a study to be conducted, its decision may seem to be based on scientific or regulatory considerations alone. However, at its root, the decision to require research can also be viewed as fundamentally an ethical one. FDA must be confident that criteria for any regulatory action are satisfied not merely because the law allows or requires it but because of its mission to protect and promote public health—an ethical responsibility. The public has vested the agency with legal authority so that it can discharge that responsibility, agreeing to sacrifice some measure of liberty in exchange for the protection that FDA will provide and reposing trust in agency officials to discharge their mission responsibly.

When FDA imposes a postmarketing requirement, it is expressing not only scientific uncertainty about the benefits or harms of a drug but a judgment that the public health interests served by requiring additional research outweigh the burdens placed on pharmaceutical manufacturers and—more importantly, from an ethical standpoint—any risk of harm to or burdens on research participants. The burdens on pharmaceutical companies are the time and money involved in conducting the study, whereas the burdens on research participants may include inconvenience, loss of opportunities for more efficacious treatment, and physical or mental harm.

A related ethical consideration has to do with accountability for research harms. All research on human participants raises ethical questions about the rights and interests of participants and about accountability when participants experience research-related harms or indignities. When research is being conducted because of an FDA mandate, FDA bears a measure of ethical responsibility for any adverse outcomes that participants experience.

In Chapter 4, the committee discusses specific steps that FDA should take to increase the likelihood of adequate protection of the rights and interests of human participants who participate in the postmarketing research that it requires. In addition to its ethical responsibilities to human participants, there are pragmatic and political reasons for FDA to provide strong guidance and oversight of postmarketing studies that it requires, particularly clinical trials. Such studies will have the imprimatur of FDA because FDA ordered that the research be conducted, but without oversight there is no guarantee that it will satisfy minimum scientific standards or even that it will serve the policy purposes that led to the study mandate. FDA incurs a serious risk to its reputation if studies that it requires are judged to be flawed by the research community or an institutional review board (IRB). Alternatively, people may wrongly perceive that a poorly designed clinical trial is well designed and safe to participate in because FDA's "stamp" is on it. There is also a danger that investigators could use the fact that a study has been required by FDA to resist an IRB's proposed changes in study design. An IRB may assume that FDA has conducted a thorough review of the design of a required study whereas in reality it did not provide investigators with much guidance on design.

Each of those possibilities involves a breakdown in the quality-assurance system on which public trust in the clinical research enterprise depends. Furthermore, there is a danger that if FDA does not provide strong guidance on the design of research that it requires, it will not receive the kind of information that it needs to make a responsible policy decision. When FDA requires research to be conducted, it must not defer the question of study design to pharmaceutical companies or their academic collaborators but rather should participate actively in study design and monitoring to ensure that the research will serve the purposes for which it was ordered. When the tensions between FDA's mission to protect the public's health and its obligation to protect potential research participants appear particularly problematic, FDA may wish to seek the counsel of an independent advisory group before making final determinations about whether or what kinds of postmarketing research to require.

When FDA requires a postmarketing study, at a minimum, it should specify to drug sponsors and the public what information is needed to help reach an appropriate answer to the public health question that prompted the research. The type of study design needed to answer the question also should be specified, as should study endpoints and inclusion and exclusion criteria (see Chapter 4). That FDA should specify key aspects of study design is consistent with FDA's interpretation of FDAAA in its April, 2011 guidance document on postmarketing requirements: "the authority to require a responsible person to conduct a postapproval study or studies or clinical trial(s) of the drug includes the authority for FDA to describe the study or trial to be conducted, including how the study or trial is to be done and the population and indication. In other words, we can require a study or clinical trial that is well-designed and adequate to address the serious safety concern" (FDA, 2011f).

In addition to its obligation to ensure that a study will provide the requisite information, FDA has an obligation to ensure timely use of study findings in its regulatory decisions. Finally, in the case of clinical trials, FDA should articulate safety-monitoring schemes and any other design features that it views as necessary for the ethical justification of a trial, as the committee discusses in Chapter 4.

Specific Circumstances for Considering a Postmarketing Research Requirement

There is no absolute rule or algorithm as to when a postmarketing requirement should be required beyond the requirements in accelerated approvals and in the Pediatric Research Equity Act (PREA; see Chapter 1). In the information available during the approval process, there can be different indicators of the need for postmarketing research. After a drug is approved, there are many circumstances in which information could emerge that would suggest that, compared with the benefits and risks expected at the time of approval, either the benefits of a drug are smaller than expected or the risks posed by a drug are greater than expected.

FDA should prospectively determine and publicly identify the risk factors or conditions, including clinical drug characteristics, that are associated with greater uncertainty about the benefit–risk profile in both the premarketing and postmarketing settings. Given the conditions identified, FDA should require postmarketing research in a timely fashion unless there is a compelling reason not to and should make public the rationale for requiring or not requiring postmarketing research in each case. Value-of-information analyses (see Box 2-9), or at a minimum the conceptual framework that underlies them, can be a useful tool to help determine whether more research would improve the decision-making process.

The committee believes that the premarketing and postmarketing considerations should include the following:

- when information about several surrogate endpoints are available and they provide conflicting evidence about the likely health outcomes associated with a drug;
- when first-in-class drugs are evaluated on the basis of surrogate endpoints that are typically used to evaluate drugs in another class;
- when safety signals identified from premarketing data or postmarketing surveillance involve a substantial public health concern or a severe adverse event;
- when there is a strong biologic rationale for a particular adverse effect;

BOX 2-9
Value-of-Information Analysis

Value-of-information (VOI) analysis is a potentially useful tool for deciding whether further research is needed (Claxton et al., 2001; NRC, 2009). VOI helps determine whether or not it is worthwhile to collect additional information or conduct additional research, prior to making a decision (Ginnelly et al., 2005). The expected VOI is calculated by weighing the change in the potential net benefits to the population from the decisions from obtaining that information. If the information would not alter a regulatory decision, the VOI is zero (Ginnelly et al., 2005; Raiffa, 1968). Even if not formally applied, it provides a very helpful conceptual framework for deciding when and what types of research are needed by linking this determination to subsequent decision-making.

VOI analysis can be used to identify when and how a decision-maker's preferred option might be changed if the decision-maker were able to incorporate additional information into the decision (NRC, 2009). In other words, VOI analysis describes the relationship between the knowledge that might come from the considered source of information and its potential for improving decision outcomes, and it can help to establish a threshold for specific regulatory decisions. The analysis enables regulators, given the current state of knowledge, to evaluate the likely health benefits of various courses of action, including a decision to gather more information.

VOI analysis allows decision-makers to weigh the value of additional evidence against the potential risks posed by delaying a regulatory decision until the information is available (NRC, 2009). That assessment is an important part of the benefit–risk management decision-making process, it helps to determine whether to seek a postmarketing commitment (PMC) or postmarketing requirement (PMR).

VOI analysis has important limitations. It does not measure the scientific merit and broader utility of a study and therefore is not a substitute for the analysis of these issues. For the same reason, traditional VOI is helpful for determining *whether* to seek a PMC or require a PMR and less well suited to determine *which* types of studies are most appropriate for producing the evidence sought.

- when a drug is expected to have a different benefit–risk profile under real-world conditions or in specific patient groups;
- when a drug belongs to a class in which a substantial safety signal has previously been identified; and
- when evidence emerges in the postmarketing setting that suggests a lack of benefit.

The committee elaborates below on indications for requiring postmarketing research when drugs are approved on the basis of surrogate endpoints and when safety signals of concern are present in premarketing data.

Drugs Approved on the Basis of Surrogate Endpoints

Many drugs are approved on the basis of what are called surrogate endpoints, which FDA has defined as "a biomarker intended to substitute for a clinical endpoint", one that is "expected to predict clinical benefit (or harm, or lack of benefit) based on epidemiologic, therapeutic, pathophysiological or other scientific evidence" (Atkinson et al., 2001).[10] Examples include not only the measures of blood pressure, cholesterol, glucose or glycated hemoglobin (HbA1C), and serum chemistry but tumor shrinkage, electrocardiographic findings, pulmonary-function tests, and imaging studies, such as carotid ultrasonography to assess the arterial intimal–medial wall thickness as a measure of subclinical atherosclerosis.

Surrogate endpoints are commonly used in the approval of new drugs. Drugs that qualify for the accelerated approval mechanism require confirmatory postmarketing studies as a condition of approval, but about one-third of drugs that go through the traditional approval process are approved solely on the basis of evidence on surrogate endpoints (GAO, 2009b), which have been discussed extensively by scientists in and outside FDA (Fleming and DeMets, 1996; Prentice, 1989; Psaty et al., 1999; Temple, 1999). The primary advantage of surrogate-endpoint trials is the ability to evaluate drugs more quickly and in smaller studies than would be required for the demonstration of a reduction in the risk of major clinical events. In part because of the low sample size, information from trials that use surrogate endpoints remains incomplete with respect not only to uncommon risks but also to actual health benefits associated with the use of the drugs. Changes in a surrogate endpoint are sometimes poor predictors of changes in health outcomes (CAST, 1989). Surrogates for efficacy, moreover, are unlikely to capture information about off-target effects that may lead to adverse events. The 2009 Government Accountability Office (GAO) report *New Drug Approval: FDA Needs to Enhance Its Oversight of Drugs Approved on the Basis of Surrogate Endpoints* (GAO, 2009b) summarizes the matter well:

> While the use of surrogate endpoints can expedite the approval of drugs, reliance on these endpoints also introduces uncertainty regarding the risks and benefits of a drug because the clinical effectiveness is not directly measured. Thus their use can lead to the adoption of useless or even harmful therapies if the effect on a surrogate endpoint does not accurately predict whether treatments provide benefits to patients, or if the drug has a smaller than expected benefit and a larger than expected adverse effect.

---

[10]For a discussion of how to evaluate or validate surrogate endpoints see *Evaluation of Biomarkers and Surrogate Endpoints in Chronic Disease* (IOM, 2010).

FDA should consider requiring postmarketing requirements when

- Information about several surrogate endpoints is available and provides conflicting evidence about the likely health outcomes associated with a drug.
- First-in-class drugs are evaluated on the basis of surrogate endpoints that are typically used to evaluate drugs in another class.

Drugs approved on the basis of surrogate endpoints have on occasion been the subjects of postmarketing drug-safety problems. For instance, the premarketing studies of rosiglitazone demonstrated a reduction in fasting glucose and glycated hemoglobin (see Table 2-1). Using only glycated hemoglobin as the surrogate endpoint, one would have predicted a clinical benefit, such as a reduction in the risk of coronary disease (Selvin et al., 2004). However, rosiglitazone increased body weight and low-density lipoprotein (LDL) cholesterol (Law et al., 2003), a major risk factor for coronary disease. Indeed, LDL cholesterol is a traditional surrogate endpoint used in the approval of lipid-lowering drugs. On the basis of its effect on LDL cholesterol, the predicted effect of rosiglitazone on heart disease is not only larger than the effect predicted on the basis of glycated hemoglobin but in the opposite direction (Law et al., 2003). In an evaluation limited to surrogate endpoints, the adverse effects on lipids present a safety signal that requires additional evaluation.

The premarketing studies of the weight loss drug sibutramine also had mixed results (see Table 2-2). Compared with placebo, the use of the drug was associated with a weight loss of about 10 lb. Traditionally, weight loss is associated with a reduction in blood pressure (Wilson, 2008), but sibutramine, despite weight loss, increased blood pressure, which is an accepted surrogate endpoint in the evaluation of antihypertensive drugs (Temple, 1999). On the basis of its effect on blood pressure, the predicted effect of sibutramine on heart disease was not only larger than the effect size predicted on the basis of weight loss but in the opposite

TABLE 2-1 Rosiglitazone in Phase 3 Trials

Outcome	Placebo	4-mg rosiglitazone	8-mg rosiglitazone
Fasting glucose, mg/dL[a]	233	204	186
Glycated hemoglobin, %[a]	9.7	8.9	8.6
LDL cholesterol, mg/dL[b]	130	145	148
Weight change, kg median (25th, 75th percentile)	–0.9 (–2.8, 0.9)	1.0 (–0.9, 3.6)	3.1 (1.1, 5.8)

[a]Administered as once daily dose.
[b]Once daily and twice daily dosing groups combined.
Abbreviation: LDL, low-density lipoprotein.
SOURCE: Data from (FDA, 2007b).

TABLE 2-2 Sibutramine Trials

		Sibutramine		
	Placebo	10 mg	15 mg	20 mg
Weight loss, lb				
Study 1	2.0	9.7	12.1	13.6
Study 2	3.5	9.8	14.0	
Study 3	15.2		28.4	
Change in systolic blood pressure, mm HG				
Mean	–0.1		4.0	4.7
Early morning	–0.9		9.4	5.3
Change in diastolic blood pressure, mm Hg				
Mean	0.1		5.0	5.6
Early morning	–3.0		6.7	5.8

SOURCE: Data from FDA (2008e).

direction. Given evidence on surrogate endpoints pointing in opposite directions (Law et al., 2009), it is not possible to predict the drug's effect on actual health outcomes reliably. The Sibutramine Cardiovascular Outcomes Trial (SCOUT), which demonstrated an increased risk of major cardiovascular events (James et al., 2010), led to the withdrawal of sibutramine on October 8, 2010.

Torcetrapib, a cholesterol ester transfer protein (CETP) inhibitor, presents a case in which two surrogate endpoints that were available during the premarketing evaluation pointed in opposite directions and there was no validated surrogate endpoint for a first-in-class drug (see Box 2-10 for details of studies). In Phase 2 trials, torcetrapib raised high-density lipoprotein (HDL) cholesterol, possibly reducing cardiovascular risk, but increased blood pressure, possibly increasing cardiovascular risk. As a condition of approval, FDA required a large Phase 3 outcome trial for approval; this trial was stopped early because torcetrapib increased the risk of cardiovascular events and death. An increase in HDL cholesterol remains a surrogate endpoint that lacks support for use in future trials. These examples suggest that FDA should track the experience with a variety of surrogates.

A serious study-design bias may arise from the use of a surrogate endpoint during drug approval to infer or predict its effects on actual health outcomes. This bias, when present, is detected almost exclusively in the postmarketing setting, sometimes by observational studies but more frequently by randomized trials. The findings from these studies provide critical information about the reliability and the validity of surrogate endpoints that are likely to be used for the approval of future medications. As an essential element of the lifecycle approach to improving regulatory science at FDA, the ability to refine, enhance and improve the surrogate endpoints used for future drug approvals represents an effort to protect the health of the public and prevent the adverse events occasioned by faulty or flawed inferences on the basis of trial results from surrogate endpoints that turn

BOX 2-10
Torcetrapib

Low concentrations of HDL cholesterol, the "good cholesterol", are associated with an increased risk of cardiovascular events. Torcetrapib, an inhibitor of CETP, raised HDL cholesterol in a 4-week crossover study that included 19 participants (Brousseau et al., 2004). In another study of 1,188 participants who had coronary disease and who were taking atorvastatin (Lipitor®), torcetrapib was compared with placebo for the primary outcome of coronary atherosclerosis or atheroma volume as assessed by coronary intravascular ultrasonography (Nissen and Wolski, 2007). The increase in HDL cholesterol associated with torcetrapib was pronounced (see table below), and LDL was significantly decreased. There was no significant change in the primary outcome of atheroma volume, and torcetrapib was associated with a small increase in the risk of cardiovascular events (relative risk, 1.07; 95% confidence interval, 0.85–1.34). Both systolic and diastolic blood pressures were increased significantly by torcetrapib. FDA required the conduct of a large outcome trial for drug approval (Barter et al., 2007), but it was stopped early because torcetrapib increased the risk of cardiovascular events and death.

Torcetrapib Trial

	Atorvastatin	Atorvastatin plus Torcetrapib	p
Cholesterol			
HDL, % change	–2.2	+58.6	<0.001
LDL, % change	+6.6	–13.3	<0.001
Atheroma volume, % change	0.19	0.12	0.72
Change in blood pressure			
Systolic, mm Hg	2.0	6.5	<0.001
Diastolic, mm Hg	0.8	2.8	<0.001
Change in composite of all cardiovascular events (%)	19.6	21.0	0.55

Abbreviations: CETP, cholesterylester transfer protein; FDA, Food and Drug Administration; HDL, high-density lipoprotein; LDL, low-density lipoprotein.

SOURCE: Data from Nissen et al. (2007).

out to be "biased," poor predictors of actual health outcomes that are important to patients. Since FDAAA specifies "failure of expected pharmacological action" as a safety issue, improving methods to predict drug effectiveness in the postmarketing context can be regarded as part of FDA's drug safety responsibility.

The opportunity for surrogate-endpoint bias occurs often. According to a GAO report (GAO, 2009b) between January 1, 1998, and June 30, 2008, about one-third (69 of 204) new molecular entities approved under the traditional approval process were approved on the basis of surrogate endpoints. The GAO report notes that "according to FDA officials, they do not have specific criteria for determining when they will accept a surrogate endpoint as a valid substitute for a clinical endpoint, and such decisions are made on a case-by-case basis" (GAO, 2009b). During the GAO review, the "FDA planned to develop a comprehensive inventory of all surrogate endpoints used to approve new drugs, including those under the traditional process. FDA officials told us [the GAO] that they were able to compile a partial list of such endpoints, but due to other competing priorities, this inventory was never completed" (GAO, 2009b).

Based in part on the experience with rosiglitazone, FDA revised its guidance for the approval of anti-diabetic medications (FDA, 2008f). Phase 2 and 3 trials are now required to include an evaluation of cardiovascular events by an independent cardiovascular endpoints committee, and the sponsor is expected to perform a meta-analysis of the data from these studies. The upper limit of the two-sided 95 percent confidence interval for the association with cardiovascular events now influences not only the decision about drug approval but also the requirements for postmarketing trials. This guidance represents an excellent example of the lifecycle approach to methods. Postmarketing experience and research helped to shape and improve the methods by which future medications in the same class will be evaluated.

Like the guidance on anti-diabetic therapies, the guidance on drug-induced liver injury incorporates experience from postmarketing studies to improve the use of surrogate endpoints for safety in future drug evaluations (FDA, 2009c). These models can and should be replicated and documented. For instance, the postmarketing study findings for sibutramine may suggest ways of improving the surrogate marker methods for evaluating weight loss drugs during the premarketing setting (James et al., 2010); and the postmarketing study findings for ezetimibe (Kastelein et al., 2008; Rossebo et al., 2008) and fenofibrate (Tonkin and Chen, 2010) may suggest ways of improving these methods for evaluating lipid-lowering drugs.

Drugs About Which Premarketing Data Yield Safety Signals

Although not all safety signals that are seen in premarketing trials will require postmarketing studies, there are some circumstances in which they should be considered. One is when there is a substantial public health concern, as occurred in the case of the H1N1 vaccine (DeStefano and Tokars, 2010; Steel-Fisher et al., 2010). Another is when a severe adverse event is seen, and a third is when there is a strong biologic rationale for a particular adverse effect. Rofecoxib (Vioxx®) is a nonsteroidal anti-inflammatory drug (NSAID) that primarily inhibits the cyclo-oxygenase-2 (COX-2) enzyme. Rofecoxib was evaluated in 58 premarketing studies that included 5,771 patients, 3,629 of whom received rofecoxib for 1 day or more. Writing in May 1999, the medical officer reviewing rofecoxib noted "there is a theoretical concern that patients chronically treated with a COX-2 selective inhibitor may be at higher risk for thromboembolic cardiovascular adverse experiences than patients treated with COX-1/COX-2 inhibitors (conventional NSAIDs), due to the lack of effect of COX-1 inhibition on platelet function".[11] The same reviewer noted that "there was a . . . higher incidence of ischemic/thromboembolic events (angina, myocardial infarction, CVA, TIA) in patients taking rofecoxib when compared with patients taking placebo. . . . In 6 weeks [sic] studies there was one event in the placebo group (0.2%) and a total of 12 events (approximately 1%) in the rofecoxib group."[12] The summary goes on to say that "with the available data, it is impossible to answer with complete certainty whether the risk of cardiovascular and thromboembolic events is increased in patients on rofecoxib. A larger database will be needed to answer this and other safety questions."[13]

After approval for marketing, the manufacturer conducted the Vioxx GI Outcomes Research (VIGOR) trial, seeking to demonstrate that rofecoxib would be associated with fewer serious gastrointestinal complications, such as perforations and major bleeds, than naproxen (Bombardier et al., 2000). Cardiovascular events were "not specified in the study design" although data on them apparently were collected and "assessed for a future meta-analysis" (Bombardier et al., 2000). Later, a colonic polyp prevention trial that was also designed to look at thrombolytic events (the Adenomatous Polyp Prevention on Vioxx [APPROVe] trial) demonstrated an increased risk of such events with rofecoxib; the study was stopped, and the manufacturer voluntarily withdrew rofecoxib from the market. Had the VIGOR trial been designed to evaluate both the gastrointestinal benefits and the thromboembolic adverse events because of the safety signal in premarketing studies and the biologic rationale for such effects, more complete information about the benefit–risk profile of rofecoxib might have been available much sooner. (Interestingly, VIGOR was conducted at twice the daily recommended chronic dose, which underscores the importance of being attentive to dose levels both for benefits and risk contrasts [Bombardier et al., 2000].) Postmarketing observational studies of rofecoxib also provided safety information (see discussion in Box 4-1).

[11] Villalba ML. FDA Medical Officer Review of VIOXX (rofecoxib), Part 7, NDA 21-042 (capsules) and NDA 21-052 (oral solution) available through Drugs@FDA (accessed February 19, 2011), p. 104.

[12] Villalba ML. FDA Medical Officer Review of VIOXX (rofecoxib), Part 7, NDA 21-042 (capsules) and NDA 21-052 (oral solution) available through Drugs@FDA (accessed February 19, 2011), p.104.

[13] Villalba ML. FDA Medical Officer Review of VIOXX (rofecoxib), Part 7, NDA 21-042 (capsules) and NDA 21-052 (oral solution) available through Drugs@FDA (accessed February 19, 2011), p.105.

SUMMARY

At the time a drug is approved, uncertainties about its benefits and risks necessarily remain. Adequate protection of the public's health requires a lifecycle approach to the management of the benefit–risk profile of drugs, including an increasing role for postmarketing surveillance and required postmarketing research. The three-stage decision-making framework and BRAMP document presented in this chapter provide guidance to FDA on how to respond to new information about a drug's benefits and risks as experience with the drug grows. The framework and BRAMP document, with its division of oversight responsibility between FDA offices, are mechanisms for incorporating sound science, ethical considerations, high-quality benefit and risk assessments, and the principles and practices of regulatory science, including public accountability and transparency, into FDA's decision-making processes and oversight practices.

FINDINGS AND RECOMMENDATIONS

Finding 2.1

FDA's current approach to drug oversight in the postmarketing setting is not sufficiently systematic and does not ensure consistent assessment of benefits and risks associated with a drug over its lifecycle. Use of a standardized regulatory decision-making framework that is flexible enough to adapt to decisions of different complexity could make FDA's decision-making process more predictable, transparent, and active, allowing FDA to better anticipate postmarketing research needs and to plan for such research early when more design options with fewer ethical tensions might be possible.

Recommendation 2.1
FDA should adopt a consistent decision-making framework for regulatory actions across the lifecycle of all drugs that includes opportunities for input from patients and other stakeholders. This framework should be employed in making the initial drug approval decision and, in the postmarketing context, whenever new information that could affect the drug's benefit–risk profile emerges. The framework should include three stages:

***Stage I:* Define the public health question that requires a regulatory decision or agency response.**
***Stage II:* Assess the drug's confirmed or potential benefits and risks by using a systematic process to evaluate and characterize existing evidence and any sources of disagreement about that evidence.**
***Stage III:* Determine the appropriate regulatory response to the public health question specified in Stage I, including whether further research should be**

required, by integrating the evaluation of the evidence of benefits and risks from Stage II with legal and ethical considerations and input from stakeholders; communicate to the public the reasoning behind the decision; implement the regulatory response; and, particularly for difficult or controversial decisions (see Recommendation 2.5), evaluate the impact of the regulatory response.

Finding 2.2

No single, clear, comprehensive, and public document currently captures FDA's assessments of a drug's benefits and risks over the course of its lifecycle, nor does any documentation help to standardize FDA's decision-making processes or describe FDA's rationale for its regulatory actions. Capturing such information in a living document would formalize the lifecycle approach to drug regulation, improve regulatory oversight, and improve the transparency of FDA's decisions.

Recommendation 2.2
FDA should require and maintain, for each new drug and for already approved drugs for which questions about the benefit–risk profile are raised, a publicly available and understandable Benefit and Risk Assessment and Management Plan (BRAMP). For new drugs, the BRAMP document should be initiated during the drug-approval phase and updated over the lifecycle of the drug at pre-specified times in the postmarketing setting and whenever questions about the drug's benefit–risk profile arise. The document should include a description of: any public health questions raised during the drug's lifecycle; the benefit and risk assessment specific to each public health question; key stakeholder input specific to each question; any regulatory decisions or actions and the rationale for each decision, including requirements for postmarketing research or a risk evaluation and mitigation strategy (REMS); a schedule for future assessments of benefits and risks; and plans for and results of evaluating the effectiveness of any regulatory decisions or actions.

- In the *premarketing* phase, the drug sponsor should provide a summary of the drug's benefits and risks, any uncertainties in the evidence, and plans for decreasing those uncertainties. FDA should use that information as a starting point to develop the BRAMP document. FDA staff involved with the drug's premarketing application and staff with expertise and knowledge in postmarketing safety assessment should finalize the initial entry to the BRAMP document.
- In composing teams to monitor the safety of a drug and maintain its BRAMP in the *postmarketing* phase of the drug's lifecycle, FDA should

consider the real or perceived confirmation bias of staff that played a significant role in approving the drug. This should be managed by ensuring that the leader of the postmarketing safety monitoring team is without the potential for such bias. The monitoring team should have expertise in surveillance, epidemiology, and the evaluation of safety data collected from different observational and clinical trial designs. The team should review and modify the BRAMP document at specified intervals throughout the lifecycle of the drug, including when new information warrants re-evaluation of the drug's benefit–risk profile.

Finding 2.3

In the premarketing setting, evidence is derived primarily from randomized controlled trials. In the postmarketing setting, however, evidence may be derived from surveillance, observational studies, patient registries, published and unpublished clinical trials, meta-analyses, and relevant case reports or series. Data sources, study designs, and analytic approaches for the postmarketing context are evolving rapidly. Given those differences, the expertise needed to evaluate and characterize the quality of evidence in the postmarketing setting is different from and broader than that needed in the premarketing setting.

Recommendation 2.3
In making determinations about appropriate regulatory decisions to be implemented in the postmarketing context, FDA should ensure that the full range of methodologic expertise is used to evaluate the strength of evidence of a drug's benefits and risks from a wide range of designs. For complex regulatory decisions, including decisions about requiring additional postmarketing research, such expertise should include, but not be limited to

- Clinical medicine and clinical practice, such as pharmacy.
- Biostatistics: Bayesian, frequentist, and causal inference methods.
- Epidemiology and pharmacoepidemiology.
- Clinical trials.
- Benefit–risk analysis.
- Research and public health ethics.
- Risk communication.

Finding 2.4

Section 901 of FDAAA[14] stipulates the purposes for which FDA has the authority to require postmarketing observational studies and RCTs, and 2011 FDA guid-

[14] 21 USC § 355(o) (2010).

ance for industry provides information on FDA's implementation of that section of FDAAA. Although FDA's decisions to require postmarketing research need to be made case by case, there are some identifiable conditions that are concordant with but more specific and detailed than those outlined in FDAAA and FDA guidance, which make information from additional postmarketing research important.

Recommendation 2.4

FDA should prospectively determine and publicly identify specific conditions, including drug characteristics and other features, that are associated with greater uncertainty about a drug's benefit–risk profile in the postmarketing setting. Under those identified conditions, FDA should require postmarketing research in a timely fashion unless there is a compelling reason not to, and should make public the rationale for requiring or not requiring postmarketing research in each case. Those premarketing and postmarketing conditions should include the following

- **A drug is approved when several surrogate endpoints provide conflicting evidence about the likely health outcomes associated with the drug.**
- **A first-in-class drug is approved on the basis of surrogate endpoints used in drugs of a different class.**
- **A drug is associated with safety signals from premarketing data or postmarketing surveillance when**
  - **there is a substantial public health concern,**
  - **a severe adverse event is seen, or**
  - **there is a strong biologic rationale for a particular adverse effect.**
- **A drug is expected to have a different benefit–risk profile in a subgroup or under real-world conditions.**
- **A drug is in a class for which a substantial safety signal has previously been identified.**
- **Evidence of a lack of benefit of a drug in the whole population or in identifiable subgroups emerges in the postmarketing setting.**

Finding 2.5

Some FDA decisions in response to postmarketing public health questions are controversial or difficult. Complex instances tend to occur when FDA must make a decision despite scientific disagreement about the relevant evidence or when the likely effects of a given regulatory action are uncertain. These cases serve as important opportunities for FDA, external scientists, and the public to learn about the complexities of the decision-making process and the consequences of a regulatory decision, and for FDA to improve its processes and practices.

Recommendation 2.5

FDA should conduct after-action reviews of postmarketing drug-related decisions that are particularly controversial or difficult or when a major regulatory decision is made after marketing. Such a review should include an assessment of the decision-making process itself and the effects of the final decision on the public's health.

Finding 2.6

Surrogate endpoints are often relied on in the drug-approval process, and their use has been related to a number of high-profile drug-safety problems. The findings of postmarketing studies can be used to revise the approval process and improve the endpoints and methods used in it.

Recommendation 2.6

As part of a continuing effort to improve regulatory science, FDA should maintain and annually update a list of surrogate endpoints allowed for use in the approval of drugs, the rationale for their use, the postmarketing experience regarding their correlation with health outcomes of interest, and any revisions of approval requirements that may have been suggested by the results of the postmarketing studies. The list should accumulate the postmarketing experience of the successes and failures of various surrogates so that for each major drug class, the regulatory science related to approval methods can be modified and improved. FDA should also revise or develop guidance documents for the use of selected surrogate endpoints that, on the basis of postmarketing studies, appear to be inconsistently predictive of clinical outcomes.

REFERENCES

Abraham, J. 2010. Pharmaceuticalization of Society in context: Theoretical, empirical and health dimensions. *Sociology* 44(4):603-622.

AHRQ (Agency for Healthcare Research and Quality). 2002. *Systems to rate the strength of scientific evidence*. Washington, DC: Department of Health and Human Services.

Armitage, J., R. Souhami, L. Friedman, L. Hilbrich, J. Holland, L. H. Muhlbaier, J. Shannon, and A. Van Nie. 2008. The impact of privacy and confidentiality laws on the conduct of clinical trials. *Clinical Trials* 5(1):70-74.

Asamoah, A. M., and J. M. Sharfstein. 2010. Transparency at the Food and Drug Administration. *New England Journal of Medicine* 362(25):2341-2343.

Atkinson, A. J., W. A. Colburn, V. G. DeGruttola, D. L. DeMets, G. J. Downing, D. F. Hoth, J. A. Oates, C. C. Peck, R. T. Schooley, B. A. Spilker, J. Woodcock, and S. L. Zeger. 2001. Biomarkers and surrogate endpoints: Preferred definitions and conceptual framework. *Clinical Pharmacology & Therapeutics* 69(3):89-95.

Back, E. A., P. Esaiasson, M. Gilljam, O. Svenson, and T. Lindholm. 2011. Post-decision consolidation in large group decision-making. *Scandinavian Journal of Psychology* 52(4):320-328.

Barter, P. J., M. Caulfield, M. Eriksson, S. M. Grundy, J. J. Kastelein, M. Komajda, J. Lopez-Sendon, L. Mosca, J. C. Tardif, D. D. Waters, C. L. Shear, J. H. Revkin, K. A. Buhr, M. R. Fisher, A. R. Tall, and B. Brewer. 2007. Effects of torcetrapib in patients at high risk for coronary events. *New England Journal of Medicine* 357(21):2109-2122.

Beasley, B. N., E. F. Unger, and R. Temple. 2011. Anticoagulant options—why the FDA approved a higher but not a lower dose of dabigatran. *New England Journal of Medicine* 364(19):1788-1790.

Bhatia, S. K., A. J. Rezac, B. Vitiello, M. A. Sitorius, B. A. Buehler, and C. J. Kratochvil. 2008. Antidepressant prescribing practices for the treatment of children and adolescents. *Journal of Child and Adolescent Psychopharmacology* 18(1):70-80.

Bombardier, C., L. Laine, A. Reicin, D. Shapiro, R. Burgos-Vargas, B. Davis, R. Day, M. B. Ferraz, C. J. Hawkey, M. C. Hochberg, T. K. Kvien, and T. J. Schnitzer. 2000. Comparison of upper gastrointestinal toxicity of rofecoxib and naproxen in patients with rheumatoid arthritis. VIGOR study group. *New England Journal of Medicine* 343(21):1520-1528.

Borer, J. S., H. Pouleur, E. Abadie, F. Follath, J. Wittes, M. A. Pfeffer, B. Pitt, and F. Zannad. 2007. Cardiovascular safety of drugs not intended for cardiovascular use: Need for a new conceptual basis for assessment and approval. *European Heart Journal* 28(15):1904-1909.

Brian Haynes, R. 2006. Forming research questions. *Journal of Clinical Epidemiology* 59(9):881-886.

Brousseau, M. E., E. J. Schaefer, M. L. Wolfe, L. T. Bloedon, A. G. Digenio, R. W. Clark, J. P. Mancuso, and D. J. Rader. 2004. Effects of an inhibitor of cholesteryl ester transfer protein on HDL cholesterol. *New England Journal of Medicine* 350(15):1505-1515.

Calman, K. C. 2002. Communication of risk: Choice, consent, and trust. *Lancet* 360(9327):166-168.

Carpenter, D. 2010a. Reputation and power institutionalized: Scientific networks, congressional hearings, and judicial affirmation, 1963-1986. In *Reputation and power: Organizational image and pharmaceutical regulation at the FDA.* Cambridge, NY: Princeton University Press.

Carpenter, D. 2010b. The other side of the gate: Reputation, power, and post-market regulation. In *Reputation and power: Organizational image and pharmaceutical regulation at the FDA.* Cambridge, NY: Princeton University Press.

CAST (The Cardiac Arrhythmia Suppression Trial Investigators). 1989. Preliminary report: Effect of encainide and flecainide on mortality in a randomized trial of arrhythmia suppression after myocardial infarction. *New England Journal of Medicine* 321(6):406-412.

Celgene Corporation 2001. *Thalomid REMS.* http://www.fda.gov/downloads/Drugs/DrugSafety/PostmarketDrugSafetyInformationforPatientsandProviders/UCM222649.pdf],%20and%20is%20considered%20a%20successful%20REMS (accessed December 12, 2011).

Center for Drug Evaluation and Research. 2010. *Division director review: Summary review. Application number 22-505.* Washington, DC: Food and Drug Administration.

CHMP (Committee for Medical Products for Human Use). 2008. *Reflection paper on benefit-risk assessment methods in the context of the evaluation of marketing authorization applications of medicinal products for human use.* London, UK: European Medicines Agency.

Claxton, K., P. J. Neumann, S. Araki, and M. C. Weinstein. 2001. Bayesian value-of-information analysis. *International Journal of Technology Assessment in Health Care* 17(10):38-55.

Connolly, S. J., M. D. Ezekowitz, S. Yusuf, J. Eikelboom, J. Oldgren, A. Parekh, J. Pogue, P. A. Reilly, E. Themeles, J. Varrone, S. Wang, M. Alings, D. Xavier, J. Zhu, R. Diaz, B. S. Lewis, H. Darius, H. C. Diener, C. D. Joyner, and L. Wallentin. 2009. Dabigatran versus warfarin in patients with atrial fibrillation. *New England Journal of Medicine* 361(12):1139-1151.

Coplan, P. M., R. A. Noel, B. S. Levitan, J. Ferguson, and F. Mussen. 2011. Development of a framework for enhancing the transparency, reproducibility and communication of the benefit-risk balance of medicines. *Clinical Pharmacology & Therapeutics* 89(2):312-315.

Cox, L. A., Jr., and D. A. Popken. 2008. Overcoming confirmation bias in causal attribution: A case study of antibiotic resistance risks. *Risk Analysis* 28(5):1155-1172.

DeStefano, F., and J. Tokars. 2010. H1N1 vaccine safety monitoring: Beyond background rates. *Lancet* 375(9721):1146-1147.

Ellenberg, S. S. 2011. Accelerated approval of oncology drugs: Can we do better? *Journal of the National Cancer Institute* 103(8):616-617.

Ellenberg, S. S., J. S. Epstein, J. C. Fratantoni, D. Scott, and K. C. Zoon. 1994. A trial of RSV immune globulin in infants and young children: The FDA's view. *New England Journal of Medicine* 331(3):203-205.

EPA (US Environmental Protection Agency). 2005. *Human health risk assessment protocol for hazardous waste combustion facilities, support materials.* http://www.epa.gov/osw/hazard/tsd/td/combust/riskvol.htm (accessed December 12, 2010).

EPA. 2009. *General guidance on risk management programs for chemical accident prevention (40 CFR Part 68).* Washington, DC: Environmental Protection Agency.

Evans, B. 2010. Seven pillars of a new evidentiary paradigm: The Food, Drug, and Cosmetic Act enters the genomic era. *Notre Dame Law Review* 85(2):419-524.

FDA (US Food and Drug Administration). 1999. *Food and Drug Administration 09 June 1999 Trovan (trovafloxacin/alatrofloxacin mesylate).* http://www.fda.gov/drugs/drugsafety/postmarketdrugsafetyinformationforpatientsandproviders/drugsafetyinformationforheathcareprofessionals/publichealthadvisories/ucm053103 (accessed June 6, 2011).

FDA. 2000a. *Drugs@FDA: Lotronex (alosteron hydrochloride). 02/09/2000 Approval Letter.* http://www.accessdata.fda.gov/scripts/cder/drugsatfda/index.cfm?fuseaction=Search.DrugDetails (accessed March 7, 2012).

FDA. 2000b. *Questions and answers about Lotronex.* http://www.fda.gov/Drugs/DrugSafety/PostmarketDrugSafetyInformationforPatientsandProviders/ucm110887.htm (accessed March 7, 2012).

FDA. 2002. *Questions and answers about Lotronex.* http://www.fda.gov/Drugs/DrugSafety/PostmarketDrugSafetyInformationforPatientsandProviders/ucm110859.htm (accessed March 7, 2012).

FDA. 2004. *Pharmaceutical cGMPs for the 21st century—a risk-based approach (final report).* Washington, DC: Department of Health and Human Services.

FDA. 2005a. *Joint meeting of the Arthritis Advisory Committee and the Drug Safety and Risk Management Advisory Committee.* Paper read at Joint Meeting of the Arthritis Advisory Committee and the Drug Safety and Risk Management Advisory Committee, Hilton Gaithersburg.

FDA. 2005b. *FDA news release: FDA issues public health advisory on Tysabri, a new drug for MS.* http://www.fda.gov/NewsEvents/Newsroom/PressAnnouncements/2005/ucm108413.htm (accessed July 7, 2011).

FDA. 2007a. *Transcript of FDA press conference on Trasylol. November 5, 2007.* http://www.fda.gov/NewsEvents/Newsroom/MediaTranscripts/ucm122244.htm (accessed August 23, 2011).

FDA. 2007b. *Avandia (rosiglitazone maleate) label revision. Supplement number 028, 08/14/2007.* http://www.accessdata.fda.gov/drugsatfda_docs/label/2007/021071s028lbl.pdf (accessed March 17, 2012).

FDA. 2008a. *Manufacturer removes remaining stocks of Trasylol: Access limited to investigational use.* http://www.fda.gov/NewsEvents/Newsroom/PressAnnouncements/2008/ucm116895.htm (accessed March 20, 2012).

FDA. 2008b. FDA alerts health care providers to risk of suicidal thoughts and behavior with antiepileptic medications. http://www.fda.gov/Drugs/DrugSafety/PostmarketDrugSafetyInformationforPatientsandProviders/ucm100200.htm (accessed June 15, 2011).

FDA. 2008c. *Statistical review and evaluation: Antiepileptic drugs and suicidality.* Washington, DC: Department of Health and Human Services.

FDA. 2008d. *Transcript. Joint meeting of the Peripheral and Central Nervous System Drugs Advisory Committee (PCNS) and the Psychopharmacologic Drugs Advisory Committee (PDAC).* Beltsville, MD: Department of Health and Human Services.

FDA. 2008e. *Meridia (sibutramine hydrochloride monohydrate) label revision. Supplement number 030, 05/29/2008.* http://www.fda.gov/downloads/Drugs/DrugSafety/PublicHealthAdvisories/UCM130745.pdf (accessed March 7, 2012).

FDA. 2008f. *Guidance for industry. Diabetes mellitus—evaluating cardiovascular risk in new antidiabetic therapies to treat type 2 diabetes.* Washington, DC: Department of Health and Human Services.

FDA. 2009a. *Suicidal behavior and ideation and antiepileptic drugs.* http://www.fda.gov/Safety/MedWatch/SafetyInformation/SafetyAlertsforHumanMedicalProducts/ucm074939.htm (accessed January 24, 2012).

FDA. 2009b. Lotronex (alosetron hydrochloride) information. http://www.fda.gov/Drugs/DrugSafety/PostmarketDrugSafetyInformationforPatientsandProviders/ucm110450.htm (accessed March 2012).

FDA. 2009c. *Guidance for industry: Drug-induced liver injury. Premarketing clinical evaluation.* Washington, DC: Department of Health and Human Services.

FDA. 2010a. *Natalizumab (marketed as Tysabri) questions and answers.* http://www.fda.gov/Drugs/DrugSafety/PostmarketDrugSafetyInformationforPatientsandProviders/ucm107202.htm (accessed March 20, 2012).

FDA. 2010b. *FDA drug safety communication: Risk of progressive multifocal leukoencephalopathy (PML) with the use of Tysabri (natalizumab).* http://www.fda.gov/Drugs/DrugSafety/PostmarketDrugSafetyInformationforPatientsandProviders/ucm199872.htm#_Ref252346632 (accessed March 20, 2012).

FDA. 2010c. *Decision on continued marketing of rosiglitazone (Avandia, Avandamet, Avandaryl).* http://www.fda.gov/downloads/Drugs/DrugSafety/PostmarketDrugSafetyInformationforPatientsandProviders/UCM226959.pdf (accessed March 20, 2012).

FDA. 2011a. *Office of Special Health Issues.* http://www.fda.gov/AboutFDA/CentersOffices/OC/OfficeofExternalAffairs/OfficeofSpecialHealthIssues/default.htm (accessed February 18, 2012).

FDA. 2011b. *Guidance for industry warnings and precautions, contradictions, and boxed warning sections of labeling for human prescription drug and biological products-content and format.* Washington, DC: US Food and Drug Administration.

FDA. 2011c. *Driving biomedical innovation: Initiatives for improving products for patients.* Washington, DC: US Food and Drug Administration.

FDA. 2011d. *Communicating risks and benefits: An evidence-based user's guide.* Edited by B. Fischhoff, N. Brewer and J. S. Downs. Washington, DC: Department of Health and Human Services.

FDA. 2011e. *FDA drug safety communication: Safety review of post-market reports of serious bleeding events with the anticoagulant Pradaxa (dabigatran etexilate mesylate).* http://www.fda.gov/Drugs/DrugSafety/ucm282724.htm#sa (accessed March 7, 2012).

FDA. 2011f. *Guidance for industry postmarketing studies and clinical trials—implementation of section 505(o)(3) of the Federal Food, Drug, and Cosmetic Act.* Washington, DC: Department of Health and Human Services.

FDA. 2012a. *PDUFA reauthorization performance goals and procedures fiscal years 2013 through 2017.* Washington, DC: US Food and Drug Administration.

FDA. 2012b. *FDA transparency initiative.* http://www.fda.gov/AboutFDA/Transparency/TransparencyInitiative/default.htm (accessed March 20, 2012).

Fergusson, D. A., P. C. Hebert, C. D. Mazer, S. Fremes, C. MacAdams, J. M. Murkin, K. Teoh, P. C. Duke, R. Arellano, M. A. Blajchman, J. S. Bussieres, D. Cote, J. Karski, R. Martineau, J. A. Robblee, M. Rodger, G. Wells, J. Clinch, and R. Pretorius. 2008. A comparison of aprotinin and lysine analogues in high-risk cardiac surgery. *New England Journal of Medicine* 358(22):2319-2331.

Fiessinger, J. N., M. V. Huisman, B. L. Davidson, H. Bounameaux, C. W. Francis, H. Eriksson, T. Lundstrom, S. D. Berkowitz, P. Nystrom, M. Thorsen, and J. S. Ginsberg. 2005. Ximelagatran vs low-molecular-weight heparin and warfarin for the treatment of deep vein thrombosis: A randomized trial. *JAMA* 293(6):681-689.

Fischhoff, B. 2009. Risk perception and communication. In *Oxford textbook of public health*. Fifth ed., edited by R. Detels, R. Beaglehole, M. A. Lansang and M. Gulliford. Oxford: Oxford University Press. Pp. 940-952.

Fischhoff, B. 2010. Judgment and decision making. *Wiley Interdisciplinary Reviews: Cognitive Science* 1(5):724-735.

Fleming, T. R., and D. L. DeMets. 1996. Surrogate end points in clinical trials: Are we being misled? *Annals of Internal Medicine* 125(7):605-613.

Fung, M. 2001. Evaluation of the characteristics of safety withdrawal of prescription drugs from worldwide pharmaceutical markets—1960 to 1999. *Drug Information Journal* 35(1):293-317.

GAO (Government Accountability Office). 2009a. *Drug safety: FDA has begun efforts to enhance postmarket safety, but additional actions are needed.* Washington, DC: Government Accountability Office.

GAO. 2009b. *New drug approval: FDA needs to enhance its oversight of drugs approved on the basis of surrogate endpoints.* Washington, DC: Government Accountability Office.

Ginnelly, L., K. Claxton, M. J. Sculpher, and S. Golder. 2005. Using value of information analysis to inform publicly funded research priorities. *Applied Health Economics and Health Policy* 4(1):37-46.

Greenberg, H. B. 2011. Rotavirus vaccination and intussusception—act two. *New England Journal of Medicine* 364(24):2354-2355.

Hamburg, M. A. 2011. Commentary: The growing role of epidemiology in drug safety regulation. *Epidemiology* 22(5):622-624.

Hamburg, M. A., and J. M. Sharfstein. 2009. The FDA as a public health agency. *New England Journal of Medicine* 360(24):2493-2495.

Health Canada. 2000. *Health Canada decision-making framework for identifying, assessing, and managing health risks.* Ottawa: Health Canada.

Hemminki, E., H. K. Toiviainen, and L. Vuorenkoski. 2010. Co-operation between patient organizations and the drug industry in Finland. *Social Science & Medicine* 70(8):1171-1175.

Henry, D. A., A. J. Moxey, P. A. Carless, D. O'Connell, B. McClelland, K. M. Henderson, K. Sly, A. Laupacis, and D. Fergusson. 2001. Anti-fibrinolytic use for minimising perioperative allogeneic blood transfusion. *Cochrane Database System Review*(1): CD001886.

Hiatt, W. R. 2006. Observational studies of drug safety—aprotinin and the absence of transparency. *New England Journal of Medicine* 355(21):2171-2173.

IAF (Institute for Alternative Futures). 2010. *Optimal futures for Risk Evlauation and Mitigation Strategies (REMS)—workshop report.* Alexandria, VA: Institute for Alternative Futures and Society for Women's Health Research.

IOM (Institute of Medicine). 2007a. *The future of drug safety: Promoting and protecting the health of the public.* Washington, DC: The National Academies Press.

IOM. 2007b. *Understanding the benefits and risks of pharmaceuticals: Workshop summary.* Washington, DC: The National Academies Press.

IOM. 2010. *Evaluation of biomarkers and surrogate endpoints in chronic disease*. Washington, DC: The National Academies Press.

IOM. 2011a. *Finding what works in health care: Standards for systematic reviews*. Washington, DC: The National Academies Press.

IOM. 2011b. *Advancing regulatory science for medical countermeasure development: Workshop summary.* Washington, DC: The National Academies Press.

James, W. P., I. D. Caterson, W. Coutinho, N. Finer, L. F. Van Gaal, A. P. Maggioni, C. Torp-Pedersen, A. M. Sharma, G. M. Shepherd, R. A. Rode, and C. L. Renz. 2010. Effect of sibutramine on cardiovascular outcomes in overweight and obese subjects. *New England Journal of Medicine* 363(10):905-917.

Jonas, E., S. Schulz-Hardt, D. Frey, and N. Thelen. 2001. Confirmation bias in sequential information search after preliminary decisions: An expansion of dissonance theoretical research on selective exposure to information. *Journal of Personality and Social Psychology* 80(4):557-571.

Jones, K. 2008. In whose interest? Relationships between health consumer groups and the pharmaceutical industry in the UK. *Sociology of Health & Illness* 30(6):929-943.

Karkouti, K., W. S. Beattie, K. M. Dattilo, S. A. McCluskey, M. Ghannam, A. Hamdy, D. N. Wijeysundera, L. Fedorko, and T. M. Yau. 2006. A propensity score case-control comparison of aprotinin and tranexamic acid in high-transfusion-risk cardiac surgery. *Transfusion* 46(3):327-338.

Kastelein, J. J. P., F. Akdim, E. S. G. Stroes, A. H. Zwinderman, M. L. Bots, A. F. H. Stalenhoef, F. L. J. Visseren, E. J. G. Sijbrands, M. D. Trip, E. A. Stein, D. Gaudet, R. Duivenvoorden, E. P. Veltri, A. D. Marais, and E. de Groot. 2008. Simvastatin with or without ezetimibe in familial hypercholesterolemia. *New England Journal of Medicine* 358(14):1431-1443.

Kessler, D. A., and D. C. Vladeck. 2008. A critical examination of the FDA's efforts to preempt failure-to-warn claims. *Georgetown Law Journal* 96:1-47.

Lasser, K. E., D. L. Seger, D. T. Yu, A. S. Karson, J. M. Fiskio, A. C. Seger, N. R. Shah, T. K. Gandhi, J. M. Rothschild, and D. W. Bates. 2006. Adherence to black box warnings for prescription medications in outpatients. *Archives of Internal Medicine* 166(3):338-344.

Law, M. R., N. J. Wald, and A. R. Rudnicka. 2003. Quantifying effect of statins on low density lipoprotein cholesterol, ischaemic heart disease, and stroke: Systematic review and meta-analysis. *BMJ* 326(7404):1423.

Law, M. R., J. K. Morris, and N. J. Wald. 2009. Use of blood pressure lowering drugs in the prevention of cardiovascular disease: Meta-analysis of 147 randomised trials in the context of expectations from prospective epidemiological studies. *BMJ* 338:1245-1261.

Levi, M., M. E. Cromheecke, E. de Jonge, M. H. Prins, B. J. de Mol, E. Briet, and H. R. Buller. 1999. Pharmacological strategies to decrease excessive blood loss in cardiac surgery: A meta-analysis of clinically relevant endpoints. *Lancet* 354(9194):1940-1947.

Lofgren, H. 2004. Pharmaceuticals and the consumer movement: the ambivalences of 'patient power'. *Australian Health Review* 28(2):228-237.

Mangano, D. T., I. C. Tudor, and C. Dietzel. 2006. The risk associated with aprotinin in cardiac surgery. *New England Journal of Medicine* 354(4):353-365.

McClellan, M. 2007. Drug safety reform at the FDA—Pendulum swing or systematic improvement? *New England Journal of Medicine* 356:1700-1702.

Mendel, R., E. Traut-Mattausch, E. Jonas, S. Leucht, J. M. Kane, K. Maino, W. Kissling, and J. Hamann. 2011. Confirmation bias: Why psychiatrists stick to wrong preliminary diagnoses. *Psychological Medicine* 41:2651-2659.

Miksad, R. A., M. Gonen, T. J. Lynch, and T. G. Roberts, Jr. 2009. Interpreting trial results in light of conflicting evidence: A Bayesian analysis of adjuvant chemotherapy for non-small-cell lung cancer. *Journal of Clinical Oncology* 27(13):2245-2252.

Nissen, S. E., and K. Wolski. 2007. Effect of rosiglitazone on the risk of myocardial infarction and death from cardiovascular causes. *New England Journal of Medicine* 356(24):2457-2471.

Nissen, S. E., J. C. Tardif, S. J. Nicholls, J. H. Revkin, C. L. Shear, W. T. Duggan, W. Ruzyllo, W. B. Bachinsky, G. P. Lasala, and E. M. Tuzcu. 2007. Effect of torcetrapib on the progression of coronary atherosclerosis. *New England Journal of Medicine* 356(13):1304-1316.

NRC (National Research Council). 1983. *Risk assessment in the federal government: Managing the process*. Washington, DC: National Academy Press.

NRC. 1989. *Improving risk communication*. Washington, DC: National Academy Press.

NRC. 1994. *Science and judgment in risk assessment*. Washington, DC: National Academy Press.

NRC. 1996. *Understanding risk: Informing decisions in a democratic society*. Washington, DC: National Academy Press.

NRC. 2009. *Science and decisions: Advancing risk assessment*. Washington, DC: The National Academies Press.

NRC. 2011. *A risk-characterization framework for decision-making at the Food and Drug Administration*. Washington, DC: The National Academies Press.

O'Reilly, J. T. 2008. Losing deference in the FDA's second century: Judicial review, politics, and a diminished legacy of expertise. *Cornell Law Rev* 93(5):939-980.

Patel, M. M., V. R. López-Collada, M. M. Bulhões, L. H. De Oliveira, A. B. Márquez, B. Flannery, M. Esparza-Aguilar, E. I. Montenegro Renoiner, M. E. Luna-Cruz, H. K. Sato, L. d. C. Hernández-Hernández, G. Toledo-Cortina, M. Cerón-Rodríguez, N. Osnaya-Romero, M. Martínez-Alcazar, R. G. Aguinaga-Villasenor, A. Plascencia-Hernández, F. Fojaco-González, G. Hernández-Peredo Rezk, S. F. Gutierrez-Ramírez, R. Dorame-Castillo, R. Tinajero-Pizano, B. Mercado-Villegas, M. R. Barbosa, E. M. C. Maluf, L. B. Ferreira, F. M. de Carvalho, A. R. dos Santos, E. D. Cesar, M. E. P. de Oliveira, C. L. Osterno Silva, M. de los Angeles Cortes, C. Ruiz Matus, J. Tate, P. Gargiullo, and U. D. Parashar. 2011. Intussusception risk and health benefits of rotavirus vaccination in Mexico and Brazil. *New England Journal of Medicine* 364(24):2283-2292.

PhRMA (Pharmaceutical Research and Manufacturers of America). 2012. *PhRMA transitions management of benefit-risk action team framework to CIRS*. http://www.phrma.org/media/releases/phrma-transitions-management-benefit-risk-action-team-framework-cirs (accessed February 18, 2012).

Pidgeon, N., and B. Fischhoff. 2011. The role of social and decision sciences in communicating uncertain climate risks. *Nature Climate Change* 1:35-41.

Prentice, R. L. 1989. Surrogate endpoints in clinical trials: Definition and operational criteria. *Statistics in Medicine* 8(4):431-440.

Presidential/Congressional Commission on Risk Assessment and Risk Management. 1997. *Risk assessment and risk management in regulatory decision-making. Final report. Volume 2*. http://www.riskworld.com/Nreports/1997/risk-rpt/volume2/pdf/v2epa.PDF (accessed September 15, 2008).

Psaty, B. M., N. S. Weiss, C. D. Furberg, T. D. Koepsell, D. S. Sisčovick, F. R. Rosendaal, N. L. Smith, S. R. Heckbert, R. C. Kaplan, D. Lin, T. R. Fleming, and E. H. Wagner. 1999. Surrogate end points, health outcomes, and the drug-approval process for the treatment of risk factors for cardiovascular disease. *JAMA* 282(8):786-790.

Raiffa, H. 1968. Decision analysis. In *Tools for making acute risk decisions: With chemical process safety applications*. Hoboken, NJ: John Wiley & Sons, Inc.

Ray, W. A., and C. M. Stein. 2006. Reform of drug regulation—beyond an independent drug-safety board. *New England Journal of Medicine* 354(2):194-201.

Richardson, W. S., M. C. Wilson, J. Nishikawa, and R. S. Hayward. 1995. The well-built clinical question: A key to evidence-based decisions. *ACP Journal Club* 123(3):A12-13.

Rossebo, A. B., T. R. Pedersen, K. Boman, P. Brudi, J. B. Chambers, K. Egstrup, E. Gerdts, C. Gohlke-Bärwolf, I. Holme, Y. A. Kesäniemi, W. Malbecq, C. A. Nienaber, S. Ray, T. Skjærpe, K. Wachtell, and R. Willenheimer. 2008. Intensive lipid lowering with simvastatin and ezetimibe in aortic stenosis. *New England Journal of Medicine* 359(13):1343-1356.

Rothman, S. M., V. H. Raveis, A. Friedman, and D. J. Rothman. 2011. Health advocacy organizations and the pharmaceutical industry: an analysis of disclosure practices. *American Journal of Public Health* 101(4):602-609.

Schneeweiss, S., J. D. Seeger, J. Landon, and A. M. Walker. 2008. Aprotinin during coronary-artery bypass grafting and risk of death. *New England Journal of Medicine* 358(8):771-783.

Sedrakyan, A., T. Treasure, and J. A. Elefteriades. 2004. Effect of aprotinin on clinical outcomes in coronary artery bypass graft surgery: A systematic review and meta-analysis of randomized clinical trials. *The Journal of Thoracic and Cardiovascular Surgery* 128(3):442-448.

Selvin, E., S. Marinopoulos, G. Berkenblit, T. Rami, F. L. Brancati, N. R. Powe, and S. H. Golden. 2004. Meta-analysis: Glycosylated hemoglobin and cardiovascular disease in diabetes mellitus. *Annals of Internal Medicine* 141(6):421-431.

Siegel, J. P. 2002. Assessing the use of activated protein C in the treatment of severe sepsis. *New England Journal of Medicine* 347(13):1030-1034.

Steel-Fisher, G. K., R. J. Blendon, M. M. Bekheit, and K. Lubell. 2010. The public's response to the 2009 H1N1 influenza pandemic. *New England Journal of Medicine* 362(22):e65(1)-e65(6).

Straus, S. E., P. Paul Glasziou, W. S. W. Scott Richardson, and R. B. R. Brian Haynes. 2010. *Evidence-based medicine: How to practice and teach it, 4th edition*. Edinburgh: Churchill Livingstone.

Strickland, A. A., C. S. Taber, and M. Lodge. 2011. Motivated reasoning and public opinion. *Journal of Health Politics, Policy and Law* 36(6):935-944.

Temple, R. 1999. Are surrogate markers adequate to assess cardiovascular disease drugs? *JAMA* 282(8):790-795.

Temple, R., and G. W. Pledger. 1980. The FDA's critique of the anturane reinfarction trial. *New England Journal of Medicine* 303(25):1488-1492.

Tonkin, A. M., and L. Chen. 2010. Effects of combination lipid therapy in the management of patients with type 2 diabetes mellitus in the Action to Control Cardiovascular Risk in Diabetes (ACCORD) trial. *Circulation* 122(8):850-852.

Transparency Task Force, HHS, and FDA. 2010. *FDA transparency initiative: Draft proposals for public comments regarding disclosure policies of the U.S. Food and Drug Administration.* Washington, DC: Department of Health and Human Services.

Wilson, P. W. 2008. Cardiovascular risk assessment—where are we going? *Preventive Cardiology* 11(3):183-184.

Woodcock, J., J. M. Sharfstein, and M. Hamburg. 2010. Regulatory action on rosiglitazone by the U.S. Food and Drug Administration. *New England Journal of Medicine* 363(16):1489-1491.

Yu, D. T., D. L. Seger, K. E. Lasser, A. S. Karson, J. M. Fiskio, A. C. Seger, and D. W. Bates. 2011. Impact of implementing alerts about medication black-box warnings in electronic health records. *Pharmacoepidemiology and Drug Safety* 20(2):192-202.

3

Evidence and Decision-Making

In Chapter 2, the committee recommends a framework for the US Food and Drug Administration (FDA) regulatory decision-making process in which scientific evidence plays a critical role, together with other factors including ethical considerations and the perspectives of patients and other stakeholders. This chapter focuses on the evaluation of the scientific evidence and on how FDA should use evidence in its decisions. Just as courts determine when evidence is admissible and which standard of proof to apply in a given case, scientific evidence must be evaluated for its quality and applicability to the public health question that is the focus of regulatory decision-making. FDA needs to base its decisions on the best available scientific evidence related to that question. Different people, however, can interpret and judge scientific evidence in various ways. Decisions in which there is disagreement among experts about what decisions are best supported by a given body of evidence are among the most difficult that FDA must make. For these decisions to properly incorporate all the relevant uncertainties and values, the regulators need to understand the bases of the various judgments that the experts are making. As has been shown in many difficult cases that FDA has had to decide, evidence does not speak for itself.

This chapter will categorize and discuss the sources of technical disagreements between experts about the kinds of data that FDA typically deals with. It will start with a short primer on approaches to statistical inference, with an introduction to Bayesian methods, followed by a discussion of the distinctions between scientific data and evidence. It then discusses why scientists sometimes disagree about the evidence of a drug's benefits and risks and how their disagreements may affect regulatory decision-making.

STATISTICAL INFERENCE AND DECISION-MAKING

Evidence

Although the terms *data* and *evidence* are often used interchangeably, *data* is not a synonym for *evidence*. The *Compact Oxford English Dictionary* defines *data* as "facts and statistics collected together for reference or analysis" and *evidence* as "the available body of facts or information indicating whether a belief or proposition is true" (Oxford Dictionaries, 2011). The difference is whether or not the information is being used to draw scientific conclusions about a specific proposition. In the context of a drug study, the "proposition" is a hypothesis about a drug effect, often stated in the form of a scientific question, such as "Do broad-spectrum antibiotics increase the risk of colitis"? In the broader context of FDA's regulatory decisions, the proposition may be implicit in the public health question that prompts the need for a regulatory decision, such as, "Does the risk of colitis caused by broad-spectrum antibiotics outweigh their benefits to the public's health"? In this way, evidence is defined with respect to the questions developed in the first step of the decision-making framework described in Chapter 2.

Statistical methods help to ascertain the "strength of the evidence" supporting a given hypothesis by measuring the degree to which the data support one hypothesis rather than the other. The evidence in turn affects the likelihood that either hypothesis is true. The most common scientific hypothesis in the realm of drug evaluation is the "null hypothesis"—that in a given treated population, the drug has *no effect* relative to a comparator treatment. For the concept of evidence to have meaning, however, there must be at least one other hypothesis under consideration, such as that the drug has *some* effect.

A small change in the scientific hypotheses being compared can change the strength of the evidence provided by a given set of data. For example, if the question above changed from whether broad-spectrum antibiotics produce *any* increase in the risk of colitis to whether broad-spectrum antibiotics produce a *clinically important* increase in the risk of colitis—say, an increase of more than 10 percent—the strength of the evidence provided by the same data could change. Where one observer might see a four percent increase in risk as strong evidence of *some* excess risk, another could regard it as strong evidence against a 10 percent increase in risk.[1] Agreement on the strength of the evidence therefore requires agreement on the hypotheses being contrasted and on the public health questions that gives rise to them.

[1]Confusion can result from use of the word *significant* to describe an effect that is both statistically significant and clinically relevant; the latter is often termed clinically significant. The two uses should remain separate.

Inference

Good science, together with proper statistics, has a dual role. The first role is to decrease uncertainty about which hypotheses are true; the second is to properly measure the remaining uncertainty. These are carried out in part through a process called statistical inference. Statistical inference involves the process of summarizing data, estimating the uncertainty around the summary, and using the summary to reach conclusions about the underlying truth that gave rise to the data.

The two main approaches to statistical inference are the standard "frequentist" approach and the Bayesian approach. Each has distinctive strengths and weaknesses when used as bases for decision-making; including both approaches in the technical and conceptual toolbox can be extraordinarily important in making proper decisions in the face of complex evidence and substantial uncertainty. The frequentist approach to statistical inference is familiar to medical researchers and is the basis for most FDA rules and guidance. The Bayesian approach is less widely used and understood, however, it has many attractive properties that can both elucidate the reasons for disagreements, and provide an analytic model for decision-making. This model allows decision-makers to combine the chance of being wrong about risks and benefits, together with the seriousness of those errors, to support optimal decisions.

The frequentist approach employs such measures as P values, confidence intervals, and type I and II errors, as well as practices such as hypothesis-testing. Evidence against a specified hypothesis is measured with a P value. P values are typically used within a hypothesis-testing paradigm that declares results "statistically significant" or "not significant", with the threshold for significance usually being a P value less than 0.05. By convention, type I (false-positive) error rates in individual studies are set in the design stage at 5 percent or lower, and type II (false-negative) rates at 20 percent or below (Gordis, 2004).

In the colitis example, if the null hypothesis posits that broad-spectrum antibiotics do not increase the risk of colitis, a P value less than 0.05 would lead one to reject that null hypothesis and conclude that broad-spectrum antibiotics *do* increase the risk of colitis. The range of that elevation statistically consistent with the evidence would be captured by the confidence interval. If the P value exceeded 0.05, several conclusions could be supported, depending on the location and width of the confidence interval; either that a clinically negligible effect is likely, or that the study cannot rule out either a null or clinically important effect and thus is inconclusive. In the drug-approval setting, the FDA regulatory threshold of "substantial evidence"[2] for effectiveness is generally defined as two well controlled trials that have achieved statistical significance on an agreed upon endpoint, although there can be exceptions (Carpenter, 2010; Garrison et al., 2010).

---

[2]21 USC § 355(d) (2010).

Hypothesis-testing provides a yes-or-no verdict that is useful for regulatory purposes, and its value has been demonstrated over time, both procedurally and inferentially. Its emphasis on pre-specification of endpoints, study procedures and analytic plans has regulatory and often inferential benefits. But hypothesis tests, P values, and confidence intervals do not provide decision-makers with an important measure—the probability that a hypothesis is right or wrong. In settings where a difficult balancing of various decisional consequences must be made in the face of uncertainty about both the presence and magnitude of benefits and risks, the probability that a given hypothesis is true plays a central role. The failure to assign a degree of certainty to a conclusion is a weakness of the frequentist approach when it is used for regulatory decisions (Berry et al., 1992; Etzioni and Kadane, 1995; IOM, 2008; Parmigiani, 2002).

In contrast, the Bayesian approach to inference allows a calculation on the basis of results from an experiment of how likely a hypothesis is to be true or false. However, this calculation is premised on an estimated probability that a hypothesis is true prior to the conduct of the experiment, a probability that is not uniquely scientifically defined and about which scientists can differ. Both in spite of this and because of this, Bayesian approaches can be very useful complements to traditional frequentist analyses, and can yield insights into the reasons why scientists disagree, a topic that will be discussed in more depth later in this chapter.

The use of Bayesian approaches is not new to FDA. FDA's Center for Devices and Radiological Health (CDRH) has published guidance for the use of Bayesian statistics in medical device clinical trials (FDA, 2010a) and FDA has used Bayesian approaches in regulatory decisions. A 2004 FDA workshop on the use of Bayesian methods for regulatory decision-making included extensive discussion by FDA scientists, as well as Center for Drug Evaluation and Research (CDER) and CDRH leadership, of ways in which Bayesian approaches could enhance the science of premarketing approval.[3] Campbell (2011), director of the CDRH Biostatistics division, discussed the uses of Bayesian methods for FDA decision-making, and presented 17 requests for premarketing approval submitted to and approved by the CDRH for medical devices that used Bayesian methods. Although Bayesian methods have been little used by CDER, Berry (2006) discusses how a Bayesian meta-analysis served as the basis for a CDER approval of Pravigard™ Pac (co-packaged pravastin and buffered aspirin) to lower the risk of cardiovascular events. Bayesian sensitivity analyses were used to help evaluate the literature investigating the possible association between antidepressants and suicidal outcomes (Laughren, 2006; Levenson and Holland, 2006), elaborated later in Kaizar (2006). Finally, FDA staff has recently proposed Bayesian methodology for analysis of safety endpoints in clinical trials (McEvoy et al., 2012).

[3]Published papers from the workshop are available in the August 2005 issue of *Clinical Trials* (2:271-378).

The Bayesian approach does not use a P value to measure evidence; rather, it uses an index called the Bayes factor (Goodman, 1999; Kass and Raftery, 1995). The Bayes factor encodes mathematically the principle presented earlier—that the role of evidence is to help adjudicate between two or more competing hypotheses. The Bayes factor modifies the probability of whether a hypothesis is true. Decision-makers can then use that probability to characterize the likelihood that their decisions will be wrong. In its simplest form, Bayes theorem can be defined in the following equation (Goodman, 1999; Kass and Raftery, 1995):

The odds that a hypothesis is true after new evidence	=	**The odds that a hypothesis is true before new evidence**	×	**The strength of new evidence (the Bayes factor)**

The Bayes factor is sometimes regarded as the "weight of the evidence" comparing how strongly the data support one hypothesis (or combination of hypotheses) to another (Good, 1950; Kass and Raftery, 1995). Most important is the role that the Bayes factor plays in Bayes theorem; it modifies the probability that a given hypothesis is true. This concept that a hypothesis has a certain "truth probability" has no counterpart in standard frequentist approaches.

There is not a one-to-one relationship between P values and Bayes factors, because the magnitude of an observed effect and the prior probabilities of hypotheses also can affect the Bayes factor calculation itself. But in most common statistical situations, there exists a strongest possible Bayes factor, and that can be defined as a function of the observed P value. That relationship can be used to calculate the maximum chance that the non-null hypothesis is true as a function of the P value and a prior probability (Goodman, 2001; Royall, 1997).

Assume that the null hypothesis is that a given drug does not cause a given harm, and that the alternative hypothesis is that it does elevate the risk of that harm. Table 3-1 shows how a given P value (translated into the strongest Bayes factor) alters the probability of the hypothesis of harm, defining the null hypothesis as stating that a given drug does not harm, and the alternative hypothesis is that it does elevate the risk of that harm. For example, if a new randomized controlled trial (RCT) yields a P value of 0.03 for a newly reported adverse effect of a drug and there was deemed to be only a 1 percent chance before the RCT of that unsuspected adverse effect being caused by the drug, the new evidence increases the chance of the causal relationship to at most 10 percent (see Table 3-1). A regulatory decision predicated on the harm being real would therefore be wrong more than 90 percent of the time.

Without a formal Bayesian interpretation, that high probability of error would not be apparent from any standard analysis. Using conventional measures, such a study might report that "a previously unreported association of tinnitus was observed with the drug, OR [odds ratio] = 3.5, 95% CI [confidence interval] 1.1 to 11.1. P = 0.03". This statement does not actually indicate how likely it is

TABLE 3-1 Maximum Change in the Probability of a Drug Effect as a Function of P Value and Bayes Factor, Calculated by Using Bayes' Theorem

P Value in New Study	Strongest Bayes Factor	Strength of Evidence[a]	Prior Probability of an Effect, %[b]	Maximum Probability After the New Study, %
0.10	0.26	Weak	1	2.5
			25	46
			50	79
			83	95
0.05	0.15	Moderate	1	6
			25	69
			50	87
			76	95
0.03	0.10	Moderately Strong	1	10
			25	78
			50	81
			67	95
0.01	0.04	Strong	1	21
			25	90
			40	95
			50	96.5
0.001	0.005	Very Strong	1	75
			8	95
			25	99
			50	99.5

[a]The qualitative descriptor of the strength of the evidence is made on the basis of the quantitative change in the probability of truth of a null-null drug effect.
[b]The prior truth probabilities of 1%, 25%, or 50% are arbitrarily chosen to span a wide range of strength of prior evidence. The shaded prior probability illustrates the minimum prior probability required to provide a 95% probability of a drug effect after observing a result with the reported P value.
SOURCE: Modified from Goodman (1999).

that the drug actually raises the risk of tinnitus. For that, a prior probability is needed, and the Bayes factor. If the mechanism or some preliminary observations justified a 25 percent prior chance of a harmful effect, the same evidence would raise that to at most a 78 percent chance of harm—that is, at least a 22 percent chance that the drug does *not* cause that harm. Table 3-1 shows that after observing P = 0.03 for an elevated risk of harm, in order to be 95 percent certain that this elevation was true, the prior probability of a risk elevation would have to have been at least 67 percent before the study. That might be the case if there was an established mechanism for the adverse effect, if other drugs in the same class were known to produce this effect, or if a prior study showed the same effect.

In practice, however, there exist no conventions or empirical data to determine exactly how to assign such prior probabilities, although the elicitation of prior probabilities from experts has been much studied (Chaloner, 1996; Kadane and Wolfson, 1998). FDA incorporated the notion of a prior informally in its incorporation of "biologic plausibility" into decision-making of how to respond to drug safety signals that arise in the course of pharmacovigilance, in March 2012 draft guidance (FDA, 2012):

> CDER will consider whether there is a biologically plausible explanation for the association of the drug and the safety signal, based on what is known from systems biology and the drug's pharmacology. The more biologically plausible a risk is, the greater consideration will be made to classifying a safety issue as a priority.

As demonstrated in the above paragraph, biologic plausibility and other forms of external evidence are currently accommodated qualitatively; Bayesian approaches allows that to be done quantitatively, providing a formal structure by which both prior evidence and other sources of information (for example, on common mechanisms underlying different harms, or their relationship to disease processes) should affect decisions.

This discussion illustrates a number of important issues

- Given new evidence, the probability that a drug will be harmful can vary widely depending on the strength of the prior or external information, represented as a prior probability distribution.
- The chance that a drug will be harmful, based on P values for a harmful effect in the borderline significant range (0.01–0.05), is often far lower than is suspected, unless there are fairly strong reasons to believe in the harm before the study.
- The Bayesian approach allows the calculation of intermediate levels of certainty (for example, less than 95 percent) that might be sufficient for regulatory action, particularly for drug harms.
- Without agreed-upon conventions or empirical bases for assigning prior probabilities, the prior probabilities derived from a given body of evidence will differ among scientists, resulting in different conclusions from the same data.

The probability that a given harm will be caused by a drug is a key attribute in regulatory decision-making. How sure regulators must be to take a given action varies according to the consequences of decisions. In some cases, 95 percent certainty might be needed, in others 75 percent, and in still others less than 50 percent. The Bayesian approach provides numbers that feed into that judgment (Kadane, 2005).

Despite these advantages, one of the weaknesses of Bayesian calculations is that there is no unique way to assign a prior probability to the strength of external evidence, particularly if that evidence is difficult to quantify, such as biologic plausibility. Although it may be impossible to assess subtle differences in prior probability, even crude distinctions can be helpful, such as whether the prior evidence justifies probability ranges of 1–5 percent, 15–50 percent, 60–80 percent, or 90+ percent. Such categorizations often provide fine enough discrimination to be useful for decision-making. In the absence of agreement on prior probabilities, "non-informative" prior distributions can be used that rely almost exclusively on the observed data, and sensitivity analyses with different kinds of prior probabilities from different decision-makers can be conducted (Emerson et al., 2007; Greenhouse and Waserman, 1995). At a minimum, these prior probabilities should be elicited and their evidential bases made explicit so that this potential source of disagreement can be better understood, and perhaps diminished.

The difference between Bayesian and frequentist approaches can go well beyond the incorporation of prior evidence, extending to more complex aspects of how the analytic problem is structured and analyzed. Madigan et al. (2010) provide a comprehensive suite of Bayesian methods to analyze safety signals arising from a broad range of study designs likely to be employed in the post-marketing setting.

WHY SCIENTISTS DISAGREE

When new information arises that puts into question a drug's benefits and risks, FDA's decision-makers often face sharp disagreements among scientists over how to interpret that information in the context of pre-existing information and over what regulatory action, if any, should be taken in response to the new information. Such disagreements are often unavoidable, and moving forward with appropriate decision-making is difficult if the underlying reasons for them are unknown or misunderstood. The committee identified a number of reasons for the disagreements about scientific evidence that occur among scientists. Those reasons, which are listed in Box 3-1, are discussed below.

Different Prior Beliefs About the Existence of an Effect

People's beliefs about the plausibility of an effect of a drug are determined, in part, by their knowledge and interpretation of prior evidence about the drug's benefits and risks (Eraker et al., 1984). That knowledge shapes their responses to new evidence. Prior evidence can come directly from earlier clinical studies of the drug's effects, from studies of drugs in the same class that demonstrate the effect, and from information about the drug's mechanism of action. Newly observed evidence might be interpreted as resulting in a higher chance that a drug is harmful if earlier studies have also demonstrated the harm. If other drugs in the same class have been associated with a particular adverse effect, the drug has a higher prior probability of causing that effect than a drug in a class whose mem-

BOX 3-1
Why Scientists Disagree About the Strength of Evidence Supporting Drug Safety

Prior Evidence

1. Different weights given to pre-existing mechanistic or empirical evidence supporting a given benefit or risk.

Quality of the New Study

2. Different views about the reliability of the data sources.
3. Different confidence in the design's ability to eliminate the effect of factors unrelated to drug exposure.
4. Different views on the appropriateness of statistical models.

Relevance of the New Evidence to the Public Health Question

5. Different views of the hypotheses needing evaluation.
6. Different assessments of the transportability of results.

Synthesizing the Evidence

7. Different ideas about how to weigh and combine all the available evidence from disparate sources relevant to the public health question.

Appropriate Regulatory Response to the Body of Evidence

8. Different opinions among scientists regarding the thresholds of certainty to justify concern or regulatory action, which can affect how they view the evidence

bers have not produced such an effect. If a drug has a mechanism of action that has been implicated in a particular adverse effect, it has a higher prior probability of causing that effect than a drug for which such a mechanism is implausible. For example, the prior probability that a topical steroid would produce significant internal injury would be very low because what is known about the absorption, metabolism, and physiologic actions of topical steroids makes it difficult to imagine how such an injury could occur, but the prior probability of an adverse dermatologic effect would be much higher.

Evidential bases of prior probability can take two forms: an assessment of the evidence supporting the mechanistic explanation of a proposed effect and the cumulative weight of previous empirical studies. Marciniak, in the FDA Office of New Drugs (OND) Division of Cardiovascular and Renal Products discussed mechanism directly in a letter that was provided for a July 2010 FDA Advisory Committee meeting related to Avandia (Marciniak, 2010):

> Others have speculated that rosiglitazone could increase MI [myocardial infarction] rates through its effects upon lipids or by the same mechanism whereby it increases HF [heart failure] rates. There are no clinical studies establishing these mechanisms. We propose that there is a third mechanism for which there is some evidence from clinical studies. The third possible mechanism is the following: The Avandia label states that "In vitro data demonstrate that rosiglitazone is predominantly metabolized by Cytochrome® P450 (CYP) isoenzyme 2C8, with CYP2C9 contributing as a minor pathway." The published literature suggests that rosiglitazone may also function as an inhibitor of CYP2C8 . . . . Allelic variants of the CYP2C9 gene have been associated in epidemiological studies with increased risk of myocardial infarction and atherosclerosis. . . . Recently, CYP2C8 variants has also been associated with increased risk of MI. . . . CYP2C9 and 2C8 catalyze the metabolism of arachidonic acid to vasoactive substances, providing one potential mechanism for affecting cardiac disease. Interference with cigarette toxin metabolism is another. . . . Rosiglitazone effects upon CYP2C8 and CYP2C9 could be the mechanism for its CV adverse effects. Regardless, there are several possible mechanisms for CV toxicity of rosiglitazone.

The above paragraph describes a mechanism that is fairly speculative, as labeled. There is no suggestion or claim that such a mechanism would definitely or even probably produce adverse cardiovascular effects. Rather, this particular exposition is exploratory and aimed at establishing that such an effect is possible rather than probable. Those who have a good understanding of this particular set of pathways might interpret the explanation differently and establish a different starting point for the probability of such an effect. It is unlikely, though, that on the basis of such evidence general consensus could be garnered for a high prior probability of effect.

Mechanistic explanations generally provide weak evidence when they are offered post hoc to support an observed result. They carry more weight when they are proposed before such an effect is observed. Misbin (2007) raised questions about the safety of rosiglitazone on the basis of its effects on body weight and lipids—both well-established risk factors for cardiovascular disease—long before any risk of myocardial infarction (MI) was seen in any studies.

Another, more subtle way in which mechanistic considerations can affect inferences is in the choice of endpoints, as illustrated in discussions by Marciniak, from the FDA Office of New Drugs (OND) Division of Cardiovascular and Renal Products, of the wisdom of combining silent and clinical MIs into a single endpoint (Marciniak, 2010):

> There is additional evidence from RECORD [the Rosiglitazone Evaluated for Cardiac Outcomes and Regulation of Glycemia in Diabetes trial] that the MI risk for rosiglitazone is real rather than a random variation:
>
>> We prospectively excluded silent MIs from our primary analysis because we had concerns that silent MIs might represent a different disease mechanism than symptomatic MIs, e.g., could they represent

gradual necrosis from diabetic microvascular disease rather than an acute event with coronary thrombosis in an epicardial coronary artery?

Whether or not silent and clinical MIs should be combined—a critical decision in assessing the evidence—is framed here as contingent on whether or not they represent different manifestations of the same pathophysiologic process. What is important to recognize is that the numbers arising from an analysis that excludes silent MIs are only as credible as the underlying mechanistic explanation. This example shows how a mechanistic explanation can affect the analyses, especially exploratory analysis, even if it is not explicitly invoked as an evidential basis of a claim.

Even if two scientists agree about what evidence new data provides, if they have different assessments of the strength of prior evidence they might disagree about the probability of a higher drug risk. Such a disagreement might appear outwardly to be about the new evidence when in fact the disagreement is about the prior probability. That phenomenon is captured quantitatively by Bayes theorem, as previously noted (Fisher, 1999), which can use sensitivity analyses with different priors to illustrate the plausible range of chances that the drug induces unacceptable safety risks.

Quality of the New Study

Standard approaches to evaluating evidence rely on the use of evidence hierarchies, which traditionally emphasize the type of study design as the main determinant of evidential quality; an example is the US Preventive Services Task Force guidance (AHRQ, 2008). Many scientists judge a study on the basis of its type of design above all other considerations. The type of study design, however, is only one of the factors that should be taken into account in assessing the quality of a study and thereby the quality of the evidence from the study. In addition to the type of study, such other aspects as the source and reliability of the data, study conduct, whether there are missing or misclassified data, and data analyses influence the quality of the evidence generated by a study. Some of these reflected in the Grading of Recommendations Assessment, Development and Evaluation (GRADE) approach to evidence assessment (Guyatt et al., 2008). Those factors and their role in disagreements among scientists are discussed below.

Different Views about the Reliability of the Data Source

Most evidence hierarchies assume that data in a study are generated for research purposes and that outcome measures are specified in advance. Much postmarketing research about a drug's benefits and risks, however, whether an RCT or an observational study, depends at least in part on data gathered with systems developed for other purposes. For example, billing data that happen to include diagnoses or RCTs that were designed to assess outcomes other than safety-related outcomes could be used in the postmarketing setting. One source of disagreement among scientists is the reliability of the data sources that are used for a study.

Data are gathered and captured electronically in many settings and provide important evidence about exposures, covariates, and outcomes. A number of health-monitoring systems or (linked) databases are or could be used for drug- or vaccine-safety investigation, including the Adverse Event Reporting System (AERS), Sentinel, Vaccine Safety Datalink, Post-licensure Rapid Immunization Safety Monitoring, the Health Maintenance Organization (HMO) Research Network, health plan records, data from the Centers for Medicare and Medicaid Services (CMS) and the Department of Veterans Affairs (VA), disease registries, pharmacy records and prescriber databases, hospital administrative databases, and cohort studies.

Concerns related to reliability include concerns about the measurement quality, completeness, and accuracy of the data. The conduct of high-quality studies using electronic data requires local knowledge about how care is delivered, how the computerized systems operate, and how they change. Problems with data quality affect the quality of evidence, decreasing precision and increasing bias in a study. (Formal definitions of bias and precision are presented later in this chapter.) Some of the issues are discussed below.

The quality of databases is variable. In the case of the AERS database, for instance, reporting of adverse events is incomplete, and the quality of the information about the adverse events that are reported may be poor. There is no information about the denominators, such as the number of people taking a drug, which is necessary for estimating event rates. Despite their limitations, however, a database of adverse-event reports can provide sufficient evidence of a drug's harm, especially when the reported harm is rare, unrelated to the indication for using the drug, and distinctive enough for most of or all the reports to be attributed to the drug. More than half the 36 drugs withdrawn from the US market since 1956 were withdrawn on the basis of safety evidence from case reports like those included in AERS (Saunders et al., 2010). For example, after a request by FDA, the manufacturer of the statin cerivastatin (Baycol®) withdrew it from the market because of the number of reports of rhabdomyolysis (a breakdown of muscle fibers that can result in kidney failure) (Furberg and Pitt, 2001; Lanctot and Naranjo, 1995; Staffa et al., 2002). The number of reports of that adverse event occurred at more than 50 times the frequency associated with other drugs in the same class and was unrelated to the indication for cerivastatin therapy (Staffa et al., 2002).

When databases are used for dual purposes, changes for one purpose may affect the quality of data used for the other. Hospitals, health plans, and other sources of care often change computerized systems, typically to optimize them for administrative purposes. With each of those changes, the quality of the data and their ability to capture events, exposures, or covariates for investigations of drug safety can change as well. Estimates of the reliability and validity of various methods and approaches may not stay accurate when the underlying systems change. Therefore, if data are to be used for drug safety research, continuing quality-control analyses are essential.

Considerations Regarding Data on Drug Exposures

Closed systems of care, such as health plans, tend to provide the most complete information on medical care. The denominators of membership are known, and entry into and exit from the cohort of patients can be reasonably well defined, allowing calculation of the risk of adverse events. Health insurance databases are likely to capture most drug exposures and serious adverse events requiring medical care, although the complete ascertainment of outcomes may require the use of multiple administrative files.

Computerized pharmacy files are likely to provide more complete and accurate information about drug use than medical records or patient surveys. Information about the date of a prescription, the number of days of supply, and the refill date for a chronic-disease medication often permit an assessment of drug exposure during a specific time window, assuming that the patient is taking the medication.[4] Computerized drug data will provide less reliable and valid estimates of exposure to medications that are used as needed and medications that are available over the counter. Drug-use information might be missing for inpatient medications, medications received from family members or friends, and medications purchased outside the system of care.

Considerations for Data on Outcomes

Problems arise in efforts to capture information about events of interest. The more disparate the sources of care, the more dangerous it is to rely on a single administrative data source for the conduct of a study. In the setting of health plans that own hospitals, inpatient diagnostic codes are generally available in administrative records, but codes for out-of-plan hospitalizations (such as a hospitalization that occurs when a patient is away from home) might not be available unless billing records include sufficient diagnostic information. Similarly, medical records of veterans might be complete in the VA's data systems for hospitalizations in the VA system of hospitals but might lack information on hospitalizations in non-VA hospitals or on drugs prescribed by non-VA providers.

Whether the data come from a single source or multiple sources, the diagnostic codes used in the administrative files are subject to error. For instance, a hospital discharge diagnosis of hypertension has been associated with a decreased risk of in-hospital death even though hypertension is a risk factor for adverse

[4]Except for drugs that may have resale value on the street, patients typically do not refill prescriptions for drugs that they are not taking (Lau et al., 1997).

cardiovascular outcomes, including death (Jencks et al., 1988). That paradoxical finding arises from the fact that there are fewer discharge diagnoses on fatal hospitalizations and such diagnoses as hypertension tend to be omitted; as a result, patients discharged alive will probably have more discharge diagnoses than those who died during their hospitalization. In one study, a comparison between hospital discharge diagnoses and six major cardiovascular events adjudicated according to accepted diagnostic criteria revealed levels of agreement between 44 percent and 86 percent (Ives et al., 1995). Diagnostic coding matters for reimbursement, so some diagnoses, such as heart failure, appear with surprising frequency in the absence of evidence (Psaty et al., 1999). In a recent study of the association between opioid use and fracture risk, only 67 percent of fractures identified with administrative diagnostic or X-ray data were actually incident fractures (Saunders et al., 2010). Agreements between death-certificate causes of death and adjudicated deaths based on medical records, interviews with witnesses, questionnaires to physicians, and autopsies are only modest—coronary heart disease: kappa statistic, 0.61, 95% CI, 0.58–0.64; death from stroke: kappa statistic, 0.59, 95% CI, 0.54–0.64 (Ives et al., 2009).

Diagnostic codes can also change. The International Classification of Diseases codes are used worldwide and provide consistency in information on effects, but the codes are periodically updated, and the updates can affect health data both within a study over time and in comparisons among different studies. In addition, nonstandard definitions of endpoints, economic incentives for listing particular diagnoses, and insufficient detail about key variables of interest can affect data quality.

Data Quality in Primary Research

Issues about data quality can arise in research even when data-gathering and quality control are parts of the design. The problem occurs particularly in the classification of cause-specific events. Questions and disputes over the extent and possible effect of data-quality issues arose in the discussion of the RECORD trial with respect to rosiglitazone-related risks. The questions included whether events were properly adjudicated and recorded and whether events were missed, whether followup was sufficient, whether handling of withdrawals was appropriate, how disagreements were settled, whether unclear or incomplete case-report forms were handled properly, and whether cotreatments were recorded. Below are comments bearing on some of those issues and noting the role of judgment in assessing the likely effects of the problems (Marciniak, 2010):

> Our assignments regarding bias involve varying levels of subjectivity. While we believe we have strong, documented justifications for some assignments, such as our unacceptable handling [of] cases, for other assignments our judgment calls are not unquestionable. For this reason we have provide[d] copies of the relevant case report forms (CRFs—redacted for personal and institutional identifiers) for a selection of problem cases in Appendix 1. We have also provided short sum-

> maries of many of the other problem cases in Appendix 3 and short summaries of all cases for which we made a different CV death, MI, or stroke assignment than GSK in Appendices 5-7. . . .
>
> Our review of the trial conduct appears to confirm that, as the protocol issues suggest, biases did arise in RECORD. The trial conduct issues reinforce our belief that RECORD can not provide any reassurances regarding rosiglitazone CV safety.

In contrast, Ellis Unger, deputy director of the Office of New Drug-I in OND, disagreed with the judgments made by Marciniak (in the OND Division of Cardiovascular and Renal Products) (Unger, 2010):

> For the upper bound of the 95% CI for the relative risk of death to exceed 1.2, there would need to have been a differential of approximately 16 deaths between subjects lost to follow-up in the rosiglitazone and control groups. . . .
>
> Such striking imbalances may be plausible, but they seem highly unlikely. I disagree, therefore, with Dr. Marciniak's interpretation of all-cause mortality. I deem the results of RECORD to be reassuring with respect to all-cause mortality, an endpoint essentially unaffected by ascertainment bias in an open-label study.
>
> There may be some merit in re-adjudicating MIs in RECORD; however, there are reasons why diagnostic criteria are strictly defined and enshrined in the protocol, reasons why adjudication committees are actually committees (i.e., more than a single individual), and reasons why scrupulous blinding is essential for these committees to perform their duties correctly.
>
> My view of MIs in RECORD is that the findings are neither reassuring nor concerning. I am not surprised that, using modified criteria, Dr. Marciniak was able to increase the number of MIs by 18%; I am somewhat concerned that nearly all of them were in the rosiglitazone group.

What is particularly important to note about these disputes is that they have a direct connection with the estimated quantitative risk and its attendant uncertainty. However, such disputes cannot always be settled by reviewing records or by repeating procedures. They typically involve some degree of missing information whose potential impact can be assessed only with sensitivity analyses. How much the various assumptions should be allowed to vary in those analyses is a matter of judgment. So data-quality issues can have a central, sometimes irresolvable role in creating disagreement among scientists about numerical results; at best, the plausible range of estimates that would be consistent with their qualitative disagreement can be calculated with sensitivity analyses.

Confidence in a Design's Ability to Eliminate Bias

The science of drug safety concerns questions of causal, not just statistical, relationships. That is, the important drug safety question is whether drug exposure actually *causes* an adverse outcome, not simply whether such an outcome occurs more frequently in people who choose to take the drug. Whether or not an observed increase in risk is likely to be causally related to drug exposure depends on a variety of non-statistical judgments about the design of the study, the analytic methods, and the underlying biologic mechanisms. Those judgments focus on whether something other than the drug itself could be causing the increase in risks—or in benefits. If the evidence pointing to such a relationship has been generated by a well-designed, well-conducted clinical trial in which drug treatment has been randomly assigned and there is adequate size and time for adverse effects to appear, confidence is typically fairly high that the difference in drug exposure is the cause of any differences in benefits or risks. However, if deviations from initial randomization occur (such as that caused by dropouts, missing data, or poor adherence), the conclusion of causality will rest heavily on judgments about the appropriateness of analytic procedures, the plausibility of alternative causes given the study designs, and knowledge of drug action and the natural history of disease. These issues assume even greater prominence in the analysis of observational studies. Those considerations are not always objectively quantifiable and can be the subject of disagreement and debate among scientists.

Two main determinants of the inherent quality of a study are *precision* and *bias* (Figure 3-1). Precision is the magnitude of variability in an estimated benefit or risk that can be ascribed to the play of chance. It is the only determinant that

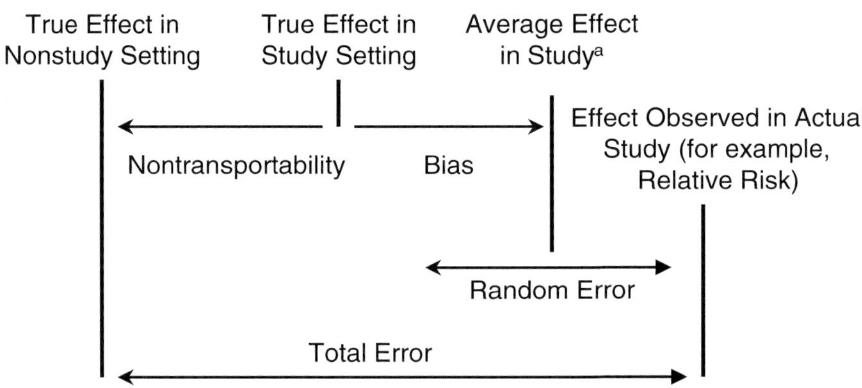

FIGURE 3-1 Illustration of the contributions of different types of errors to the average effect of a drug in a study, the true effect of a drug in a study setting, and the true effect of a drug in nonstudy settings. The total error is the difference between the effect of a drug observed in the study and the true effect of the drug in nonstudy settings. If the bias is large, the confidence interval around the average effect in a study (represented as the random error) will not include the true effect in the study setting.

[a]The average effect in the study is a hypothetical value that would be seen if the study were conducted multiple times.

has a clearly quantifiable effect on the strength of evidence. The confidence limits or intervals around an estimate of benefits or risks are a quantitative indication of the precision of a study. The more precise a result, the stronger the evidence it will provide for one hypothesis versus another. In practice, study sample size is the prime determinant of precision—a large study produces an estimate of benefits or risks that has a small confidence interval, indicating high precision.

Bias is the difference between the average effect of many hypothetical repetitions of a given study and the true effect in the population being studied. If the study draws research participants randomly from a target population (that is, the population likely to be prescribed the drug), the quality of evidence is determined, in part, by the degree of bias in the results. Unlike precision, bias cannot be eliminated by increasing sample size; only proper design or analysis can control or eliminate it. The presence of bias is not apparent in the numerical results of a study; it can only be discerned from close examination of the design and conduct of the study, and even then it may not be evident. A study without bias is said to have high internal validity. The three main types of bias that affect the internal validity of a study are confounding, selection bias, and information bias, which are described in Box 3-2.

Confidence in the Transportability of Results

The Concept of Transportability

A study estimate of the benefit or risk associated with a drug can deviate from the results that patients would actually experience in wider clinical practice if the study participants were not representative of the wider target population. That disparity can occur when a study is conducted in hospitalized patients but the results are used to estimate the risks in outpatients or when a study is conducted in patients who do not have comorbidities or cotreatments but the drug will be used in patients who have both. The *transportability*[5] of study results, also known as external validity or generalizability of a study, is determined by the difference between the effect seen in the people studied and those in the wider target population.

The concept of transportability captures what is at stake in the traditional efficacy-versus-effectiveness distinction (Gordis, 2004). Traditionally, efficacy is a measurement of the beneficial effect of the drug with respect to a specific endpoint of interest under conditions that are optimized to favor an accurate assessment of the drug's benefits and risks. Effectiveness is a measurement of the beneficial effects of a drug as it is used in the less controlled conditions of

[5]The term *transportability* is used in this report, rather than *external validity* or *generalizability*, because the committee thinks that it better reflects a nonbinary characteristic. Different effects can occur in a variety of settings, and study results may be transportable to some populations or settings but not others, so transportability may not be a simple binary property.

BOX 3-2
Explanations of the Three Main Types of Bias

Confounding

Confounding occurs when the populations compared in a study differ in important predictors of the outcome being studied other than an exposure of interest (such as exposure to a drug), that is, when another risk factor is associated with both the exposure and the outcome of interest and is a cause of the outcome. For instance, a disease state may affect both the use of a drug and the clinical outcome of interest.

Selection Bias

Selection bias results when the exposure affects participation ("selection") in the study or analysis and selection is associated with the outcome of interest. For example, if the use of a drug increases both the risk of harm and the probability that people using the drug will drop out of the study and be lost to follow-up, the risk of harm is likely to be underestimated because the people whose data are used in estimating the incidence of the adverse event (that is, those not lost to follow-up) are less likely to have experienced the harm simply because they remained in the study.

Other types of selection bias that affect estimates in randomized controlled trials and observational studies include missing data and non-response bias, healthy-worker bias, and self-selection bias (Hernán and Robins, 2012). Although the terms *selection bias* and *confounding* are sometimes used interchangeably outside epidemiology, it is valuable to use the terms to refer to the two different types of bias (see Figure 3-1).

Information Bias

Information bias, caused by certain patterns of measurement error, occurs when "the association between treatment and outcome is weakened or strengthened as a result of the process by which the study data are measured" (Hernán and Robins, 2012). Errors in measuring and classifying exposures, outcomes, and confounders can influence the strength and direction of effect estimates.

clinical practice. However, neither efficacy nor effectiveness is an absolute concept, and their distinction is less clear than commonly supposed. For example, a double-blind RCT conducted in one country might produce an estimate of a drug's efficacy under conditions that might be optimal for that country but not relevant or applicable to the United States. There is no one unique set of "real-world conditions"—estimates of a drug's effectiveness may vary among many populations and settings. The appropriate and informative question about a study is not whether it is "generalizable" in the binary sense, but to which populations and settings its results are transportable, to what degree, and what the determinants of that transportability are.

Nontransportability is caused by different distributions of "effect-modifiers" in the study and target settings (Hernán and Robins, 2012). For example, if women are more likely than men to experience an adverse effect as a result of taking a drug, sex would be an effect-modifier. Effect-modifiers may include characteristics of the patients (such as severity of disease or comorbidities), nonadherence, cotreatments, and cointerventions, such as the monitoring that typically takes place in clinical trials. For example, the risk of an adverse effect may be lower in a study in which patients are closely monitored than in a setting in which such monitoring is not part of clinical care. Variations in dosage and administration of the treatment may also present different or additional risks relative to those identified in the trial (Weiss et al., 2008).

It is important to note that the scale upon which the effect-modification is measured is important. The public health question typically depends on the degree of additional absolute risk incurred by drug exposure. If two populations are at different baseline risk for an adverse effect, a relative risk of 2 will be more dangerous for the high-risk group than those at low initial risk. This will not show up as effect-modification on the multiplicative scale, which is most often used in epidemiology, but it will be effect modification on the additive scale, the scale relevant to public health decisions. So if multiplicative models are being used for analysis, close attention must be paid to the variation in baseline risks from one population to another when transportability is assessed.

The assessed risks in a given population can differ according to how an adverse effect is elicited from the patient. Studies that depend on passive reporting of adverse events versus those that ask patients about specific adverse events can affect the reported frequency several-fold (Bent et al., 2006; Ioannidis et al., 2006).

Assessing the transportability of the results of any study requires clinical, pathophysiologic, and epidemiologic knowledge of the factors that can change a drug's benefits or harms and of how the factors are distributed in the study and in community settings. RCTs often do not have adequate power to detect such effect-modifiers statistically, and relevant effect-modifiers (such as co-treatments) may be absent or unmeasured. In the absence of such information, conducting a study in the community setting is the best way to obtain direct knowledge about a drug's effect in routine clinical practice. In the absence of high-quality information from a community-based setting, disputes about transportability—the relevance of study information to the public health context—can be among the most difficult to resolve because the empirical evidence base may be thin and claims based on clinical experience or claimed knowledge of biologic mechanisms hard to adjudicate. The experience with the RECORD trial shows the complexity of this issue; some criticisms of the RECORD trial arose because of weaknesses that could be partly attributed to the attempt to conduct it in pragmatic fashion in a community setting.

Transportability is not typically treated as a formal source of error and is not taken into account in traditional evidence hierarchies, which focus almost exclusively on precision and bias. But using a public health perspective requires that the focus be on the effects of a drug as it is used in the general population. For that, transportability is a key consideration. From the perspective of FDA's decisions, therefore, transportability should be treated as a potential source of error, with bias and imprecision, as displayed graphically in Figure 3-1. That approach leads to treating the transportability of study results as a formal contributor to the relevance of evidence for a given decision, rather than as a minor qualifier.

Issues related to transportability were raised repeatedly (using the more familiar term *generalizability*) in the FDA briefing document for the rosiglitazone hearings. One of FDA's statistical reviewers questioned the relevance of research done with the UK General Practice Research Database (GPRD) (Yap, 2010):

> While the GPRD database captures information for a large number of subjects, the generalizability of these data to the U.S. population might be difficult given varying prescribing practices, risk factors, and medical practices.

Critiquing a study that used a multistate Medicaid database, the FDA statistical reviewer stated (Yap, 2010):

> Cohort eligibility required that a patient have at least one inpatient claim. This led to a huge reduction in cohort size from approximately 307,000 individuals to approximately 95,000. In addition, the cohort was restricted to patients receiving Medicaid services. Findings from this restrictive cohort might not be generalizable to the intended population. . . . The diabetes population studied comprises mostly older and generally sicker patients thus raising concerns of generalizability of results to healthier and younger diabetic populations.

Finally, the transportability of another study was criticized for having been done in Canada (Yap, 2010):

> The population studied comprises patients aged 65 or older residing in Quebec, Canada. Therefore, the results reported in the publication cannot be generalized to a population of patients below 65 years of age. In addition, results might not be fully generalizable to non-Canadian population given varying baseline characteristics and differences in access to care.

In the text above, the evidential basis for claiming nontransportability is unclear at best, and therefore difficult to adjudicate. Such assertions may be reasonable, but whether they should be accepted and how much they should affect the assessment of a study require more detailed explanation of why the differences noted would be expected to modify the drug effect and by how much. For example, is it literally true that evidence derived from people over 65 years old cannot be applied to those who are younger? What is the evidence for that claim, and how big is that effect? What if the target population had an age range of 60–64 years? Those are the kinds of questions that must be asked because differences between the study and target populations will always exist, even if the differences are only between past and future members of the same community.

In summary, if the "true effect of a drug" is defined in public health terms as its benefit–risk profile when it is used in medical practice in the general population of patients for whom the drug is used, or on a subset of the population, all three sources of error—bias, imprecision, and nontransportability—must be considered as contributing equally to the relevance of evidence generated by studies. Claims of nontransportability should be supported with evidence that the differences between settings or populations would be expected to introduce different effects that are clinically meaningful.

Randomized Controlled Trials Versus Observational Studies

Observational studies are a major source of evidence related to drug safety and are playing an increasing role in FDA's oversight of drug safety (Hamburg, 2011). Such designs play a relatively minor role in establishing drug efficacy in the preapproval stage in FDA, where RCTs are regarded as fulfilling the statutory requirement of "adequate and well-controlled" studies to support a marketing claim. However, as discussed in this section, the relative value and quality of evidence from the two classes of designs can be quite different in connection with efficacy vs safety endpoints.

The different quality attributed to evidence from observational and randomized designs was a central aspect of the rosiglitazone debate. It is often stated that ORs less than 2, and certainly less than 1.5, cannot be reliably regarded as different from unity if they are generated by an observational study. That claim is based on a sense that there are unknowable and uncontrollable biases in all observational studies that are not discernable or controllable even with close examination of study details. The issue is described in the following passage from the Avandia memorandum from Dal Pan, director of the FDA Office of Surveillance and Epidemiology (Dal Pan, 2010), in which this viewpoint is contested:

> The results of the observational studies strengthen the concern over the risks of rosiglitazone, especially when compared to pioglitazone. Observational drug safety studies are often criticized because they lack the experimental design rigor of a controlled clinical trial. Specifically, there is often concern that patients who are prescribed a particular medicine are different from those who are prescribed an alternative treatment, in ways that may be correlated with the outcome of

interest. This phenomenon is known as channeling bias, and is often a concern when measures of relative risk are below 2.0, when the effect of unmeasured confounders could account for the observed findings. While this concern is generally valid, it should not be automatically invoked to dismiss the results of observational studies in which the measure of relative risk is below 2.0. Data from the CMS observational study, for example, indicate that rosiglitazone and pioglitazone recipients were similar with regard to multiple cardiac and non-cardiac factors, a finding that suggests minimal channeling bias. Furthermore, the risk estimates from the observational studies are generally similar to those from the meta-analyses of clinical trials. Thus, dismissing the results of the observational studies simply because the observed measures of risk may be due to channeling bias may not be appropriate.

Traditional evidence hierarchies that rely on the type of study design to classify evidence generally focus on the strengths and weaknesses of those designs with respect to the evaluation of therapeutic efficacy (Barton et al., 2007; Owens et al., 2010). Study designs are ranked according to their capacity to generate unbiased evidence about efficacy endpoints, and considerations of transportability are given no weight.

The RCT design, in theory, produces the highest confidence that observed differences are caused by drug exposure, not by ancillary characteristics that might be associated with drug exposure. Such ancillary characteristics are known as confounders. In the context of a perfectly designed and conducted RCT—one without patient dropout, missing data, or nonadherence—causal inference effectively becomes statistical inference. That is, there is confidence that any quantitative differences between groups in the endpoints evaluated were due to the randomized intervention. The likelihood that a statistical hypothesis about association is true becomes equivalent to the likelihood that a hypothesis about causality is true.

As conduct deviates from ideal design, however, the certainty about a causal hypothesis decreases with the decreasing certainty that the design or analysis has adequately "controlled" for other causal factors. Such deviations include patient dropout, crossover between treatment arms, loss to followup, missing data, non-adherence to treatment, differential cotreatment, and differential measurement (Dal Pan, 2010). Those aspects of study design and conduct must be assessed to determine the evidential value of an RCT, especially if oversight of the study might have been complicated by its being conducted at multiple, overseas sites (Frank et al., 2008; GAO, 2010a, 2010b; Greene et al., 2006; Manion et al., 2009). Observational studies are affected by similar issues, with biases induced by treatment selection in place of those caused by deviation from treatment assignment.

Various characteristics of safety endpoints, with other constraints, may favor the strength of observational evidence over evidence from RCTs in generating valid and reliable evidence needed for benefit–risk assessments in the postmarketing setting. In a standard RCT, participants are randomly assigned to different treatment arms. The groups are then compared for observed risks of developing a particular health outcome, such as myocardial infarction. The most important property of an RCT is that—in large samples—the baseline distribution of risk factors, both known and unknown, is expected to be equal among groups. Under a number of assumptions—including complete event ascertainment, no differential loss to followup, and perfect treatment compliance—the estimate of the drug's efficacy is unbiased and provides high confidence that any observed association between the drug and the efficacy endpoint is due to the drug.

Observational studies of efficacy, in contrast, are often subject to a variety of biases, the most common of which is known as confounding by indication (Vandenbroucke and Psaty, 2008). Confounding by indication, also known as "channeling bias", occurs when treatment assignment is based on a risk factor for an outcome. In clinical medicine, patients are typically treated to improve their chances of a beneficial outcome. That makes it difficult to separate the effect of the drug itself from that of the patient's condition that led to the drug's use, that is, the drug's indication. When physicians treat some patients differently for reasons related to their risk for various outcomes, confounding by indication is likely. For example, if sicker patients choose medical care for a given condition more often than surgery because they are afraid that they will not survive the operation and if sicker patients are more likely to die whether or not they receive surgery, observational studies of surgical versus medical care will show that surgery is safer than medical care even if they are equally efficacious.

Confounding by contraindication is the corresponding concern in studies that evaluate safety endpoints, although it is not as common as confounding by indication. If an adverse effect of a drug is known, physicians might avoid prescribing it for patients who are at higher risk for that effect (for example, the use of nonsteroidal anti-inflammatory drugs and GI bleeding, or the use of aspirin and anticoagulants together). If the use of the drug increases the risk of a particular adverse effect and patients who were at higher risk for that effect avoid taking the drug, the results will be biased toward the hypothesis of no effect. The findings of such a study may mistakenly indicate that the use of the drug does not increase the risk of the adverse event or, worse, that it prevents it. Such a treatment approach is in the patient's best interest, but it makes observational studies of the harms associated with drugs difficult to conduct well. Confounding by contraindication, however, is not a major concern in studies of unexpected adverse events. If the risk itself or the factors that affect it are unknown, treatment cannot be based on avoidance of the risks (Golder et al., 2011); although it could be based on correlates of those unknown risks (for example, age, disease severity).

Empirical evidence suggests that the findings of observational studies of harms can be similar to the findings of RCTs for the same drugs and harms (Vandenbroucke, 2006). In a recent study of safety outcomes, Golder et al. (2011) compared the results of meta-analyses of RCTs with the results of meta-analyses of observational studies. Their meta-analysis of the meta-analyses included 58 drug–adverse event comparisons. The ratio of ORs was used as the method of comparison, and the RCTs were associated with only a slightly higher estimate of risk (ratio of odds ratio, 1.03; 95% CI, 0.93–1.15). Of the 58 comparisons, 64 percent agreed completely (same direction and same level of significance), although some of the studies had low statistical power. This large meta-analysis provides empirical support for the claim that in large samples, observational studies can yield findings on adverse events that are similar to those of RCTs. However, more empirical research is needed into the factors that determine concordance between observational and randomized studies of harms.

A number of features of safety endpoints and the postmarketing context strengthen the role of observational studies in generating valid and reliable evidence needed to answer public health questions of interest. Differences in the frequency of efficacy and safety endpoints and the timescale on which they occur affect comparative judgments about the quality of evidence generated by RCTs and observational studies. Adverse effects resulting from the use of a drug may be severe but rare, and the sample size of preapproval RCTs, or achievable postmarketing RCTs, may be insufficient to detect rare or delayed outcomes. Preapproval RCTs are also likely to miss adverse effects resulting from chronic use or those arising after a long latent period, whereas observational studies, particularly those based on existing data, can typically provide longer followup. Observational studies based on data sources collected from large populations with long follow up can often report a greater number of adverse events than typical RCTs. However, any design with long followup, whether it is concurrent or nonconcurrent, needs to be scrutinized very carefully for the extent and pattern of missing data; over time, the problems with selective retention or reporting can be substantial in all designs.

A second way in which the strength of evidence from an RCT for safety can be weakened is when the adverse effects are unknown or unforeseeable. Such endpoints by definition cannot be pre-specified (Claxton et al., 2005). It has been shown that quality and consistency of the reports and measurements of non-specified endpoints is often poor (Lilford et al., 2003; Thomas and Petersen, 2003). This problem will affect prospective observational studies as well, but it nevertheless can narrow the internal validity gap between randomized and nonrandomized designs.

Potential confounders of efficacy endpoints may differ from confounders of safety endpoints; if only the former are measured, effect estimates of safety endpoints may not be appropriately adjusted for confounders (see for example Camm et al., 2011). This is likely to affect observational studies more than RCTs, whose results will typically require less adjustment, if any, depending on the extent and patterns of deviations from randomization and degree and determinants of missing information.

Finally, as noted previously, the transportability of evidence from observational studies to populations of interest may be superior to that of evidence produced by an RCT. Because RCTs often restrict eligibility to patients for whom the anticipated benefit is thought to outweigh (known) drug risks, RCTs are incapable of detecting adverse events that may arise only in the populations excluded from the trial, which are often characterized by a wider array of comorbidities, different disease severity, concomitant treatments, or other risk factors (such as age, sex, low socioeconomic status, poor monitoring of dose, adherence, or outcomes) that may modify the effects of treatment. Observational studies can include people who are more representative of those who receive the treatment of interest in the general population and in diverse care settings. Thus, less restrictive eligibility criteria typically used in observational studies can increase the transportability of the resulting effect estimates.

The eligibility criteria for observational studies, however, are sometimes restricted in an attempt to limit the magnitude of confounding (Psaty and Siscovick, 2010). For example, consider an observational study to compare cardiovascular risk in initiators vs noninitiators of statin therapy in a particular population. Suppose that all patients in that population who have LDL cholesterol greater than 4.9 mmol/L already receive statin therapy. The observational study should exclude current users and thus restrict participation to patients who have LDL cholesterol less than 4.9 mmol/L; otherwise, it would be difficult to adjust the effect estimate for confounding by concentration of LDL cholesterol. The desire for increased transportability in observational studies should be tempered by the need to ensure internal validity.

There is no study in which all measurements are perfectly reliable or in which many judgments have not already been made before study data are analyzed. In studies of drug safety, there is a long documented history of underreporting, selective reporting, or misclassification of harms (Ioannidis and Lau, 2001; Lilford et al., 2003; Talbot and Walker, 2004). Missing data are common in such studies, and the validity of statistical methods to account for missing data rests on assumptions that often cannot be confirmed by using the data. Data quality affects not only estimates of harms themselves but also the measurement of other risk factors for those harms, such as cotreatments, comorbidities, and patient-specific characteristics. It is often critical to understand the exact operational procedures by which harms were identified and reported and other key data recorded if one is to judge properly whether data on harms reported in a study are reliable. That degree of detailed operational knowledge is often not available to those outside the study, or, if the extent of that knowledge differs among scientists, their assessments of the reliability of any ensuing inferences may differ as well.

Disagreements About the Choice of Statistical Analysis

Judgments about the most appropriate statistical model for a given study depend on many implicit and often unverifiable assumptions, both statistical and biologic, and scientists often disagree on the most appropriate statistical methods. Different ways of coding the same data can change their probability. For example, dichotomizing a continuous variable or combining harms of different severities can lead to vastly different estimates of effect size. The probability can depend heavily on how issues of multiplicity (that is, testing statistically for multiple endpoints) are treated. If researchers evaluate many adverse events statistically and only a few are observed to have increased risks, the strength of evidence of those adverse events depends on whether the "data" are treated as all the comparisons taken together or as each taken separately for the specific adverse events whose risks seem to be increased. Sometimes this problem is handled through multiplicity adjustments, but there is no ideal or universally agreed-on solution for knowing how much the analytic strategy should depend on patterns seen after the data have been observed.

Decision-makers cannot be expected to be expert in the many technical issues involved in statistical modeling (see Chapter 2 for more discussion of needed expertise for decision-making). The intricacies and nuances of statistical modeling highlight the importance of having inputs from several statisticians or others with deep technical understanding, just as the input from multiple scientists familiar with the content is routine. Data do not always speak for themselves—they speak through the filter of statistical models—and getting input from multiple experts in statistical analysis and modeling can be critical in understanding the extent to which the models being used are introducing clarity or distortion.

A further source of disagreements about statistical analyses is whether to analyze the data from a study according to the intention to treat (ITT) perspective or "as treated". Assuming that all confounders are identified and well measured, the simplest approach to compare two treatments is an analysis that follows the ITT principle. In RCTs, an ITT analysis measures the effect of being assigned to a treatment; when all research participants initiate the treatment, an ITT analysis measures the effect of treatment assignment. For ITT analyses of large RCTs, only data on each individual's treatment assignment and outcome are needed (Hernán and Hernandez-Diaz, 2012).

The observational analogue to ITT analysis needs to adjust for potential confounders. An observational ITT estimate will have only a causal interpretation as the effect of treatment initiation if all confounders have been appropriately identified, measured, and included in the analysis. Adjustment methods include stratification, outcome regression, standardization, matching, restriction, inverse-probability (IP) weighting, and g-estimation (Hernán and Robins, 2006).

Instrumental-variable approaches can also be used to estimate the effect of treatment initiation in observational studies (Hernán and Robins, 2006). An "instrumental-variable" is a variable on which exposure, but not the outcome, depend. In an RCT, the "instrument" is the randomization itself, which determines drug treatment but by itself has no relationship with the outcome. "Natural experiments" often have an embedded instrument that causes groups to be treated or exposed in different ways unrelated to the group characteristics. The most common instrument is geography, that is, different regions of the country (or care settings) that use different treatment regimens for essentially equivalent patients. The instrumental variable method, however, relies on strong assumptions, the primary one being the validity of the instrument itself, and these always have to be examined closely.

When people drop out of a study or are otherwise lost to followup, their outcomes cannot be ascertained. As a result, regardless of whether the study is an observational study or an RCT, the ITT effect cannot be calculated directly. Loss to followup forces investigators to make untestable assumptions about why people were lost to followup. If one assumes that the people lost and not lost to followup are perfectly comparable, one would restrict the ITT analysis to participants on whom there was complete followup. A safer approach is to adjust for measured predictors of loss to followup that also predict the outcome (NRC, 2010). Such adjustments can be appropriately achieved with longitudinal outcome models by regression if the factors are non–time-varying or by inverse probability weighting otherwise.

The magnitude of the ITT effect depends on the type and patterns of nonadherence, which may vary among studies, whether they are observational studies or RCTs. Dependence of the ITT effect on nonadherence makes the effect particularly unfit for safety and noninferiority studies. One alternative to estimating the ITT effect is estimating the effect of treatment if all participants had adhered to the intended treatment regimen. In RCTs, that approach would estimate the effect of treatment if no one had deviated from the protocol. Such an effect is sometimes referred to as the effect of continuous treatment. To estimate the effect of continuous treatment, whether in observational studies or in RCTs, one needs to compare groups of people according to the treatment they actually received rather than the treatment to which they were assigned (an as-treated analysis) and make untestable assumptions about the time-varying reasons why people adhere or do not adhere to treatment. Specifically, valid estimation of the effect of continuous treatment requires that all time-varying factors that predict both adherence to treatment and the outcome of interest be measured reasonably well.

In RCTs, as-treated comparisons ignore the randomization assignment and therefore involve comparisons of groups that are not necessarily balanced with respect to prognostic factors. As-treated estimates can be confounded in RCTs. The problem with using ITT in safety analyses was noted in the FDA Avandia briefing documents (Graham and Gelperin, 2010a):

> The primary analysis for RECORD was intention-to-treat (ITT), which is generally accepted as the preferred analytic method for trials conducted to show

> efficacy. It is conservative in that poor study execution or inadequate follow-up will serve to make it more difficult to show a difference from the null. For purposes of safety, where a safety concern has been raised and is under evaluation, the ITT approach is protective of the drug at the potential expense of patient safety. Patients who drop out of a study and for whom outcomes might not be counted, and patients who stop the drug and hence are probably not at the same risk of a cardiovascular event off the drug as they were while on it, will bias the estimated event rates towards the null under an ITT approach. In studies for safety, the preferred analytic approach is on-treatment.

The assertion above that the on-treatment approach is preferred for safety analyses shows how difficult it is to assess such studies. Both the ITT and on-treatment approaches introduce a degree of bias related to the effect, and on-treatment analyses are not the only alternative to ITT; these are situations in which causal inference methods are most appropriate (Ten Have et al., 2008).

Another difficulty is that the predictors of adherence may be affected by whether a patient took treatment earlier in the followup. In that setting, a simple as-treated analysis with standard adjustment (regression) may be biased, and adjustment via IP weighting or g-estimation is required (Toh and Hernán, 2008). Those methods can be used to estimate the effect of dynamic treatment regimens (for example, take treatment A until toxicity appears, and then switch to treatment B). Instrumental-variable estimation can also be used to estimate the effect of continuous treatment. Unlike all other methods, instrumental-variable estimation does not require measurement of the joint predictors of adherence and the outcome. It is less controversial for RCTs, because the randomized assignment is a known instrument, than for observational studies, in which it must be justified (Gelfand and Mallick, 1995).

In summary, when dealing with observational or RCT data involving loss to followup and nonadherence, all analytic approaches rely on untestable assumptions, which may influence effect estimates in unknown ways. One way to assess the sensitivity of effect estimates to such assumptions is to conduct both ITT analysis to estimate the effect of treatment assignment (with and without adjustment for loss to followup) and analyses adjusted for adherence to estimate the effect of continuous treatment (via the statistical approaches mentioned). Many approaches, most notably ITT, that are deemed conservative when used for efficacy determinations can be anticonservative when used for safety analyses in that statistical signals of drug harm can be missed.

Relevance of New Evidence to the Public Health Question

In evaluating the evidence that a study provides in support of a regulatory decision, it is important to consider the relevance of the study to the public health question that motivates the decision. This section discusses aspects of a study and analysis that affect the relevance of a study to the public health question.

The relevance of a study to a regulatory decision depends on the hypotheses that the study is designed to test and on how suitable the hypotheses are for providing evidence about the public health question of interest. The questions "Does a given drug cause excess harm"? and "Does a given drug cause benefits"? seem straightforward, but need to be refined further to become testable scientific hypotheses. A testable scientific hypothesis must specify the intervention or exposure, the study population, the setting, the comparator, and the outcomes. It is rare that two studies pose the scientific question, explicitly or implicitly, in exactly the same way. For example, if studies are investigating adverse cardiovascular effects, one study could define the adverse-event endpoint as a myocardial infarction or death, and another might develop a composite endpoint that includes those plus unstable angina, hospitalization, and stroke. With all such endpoints measured in a given study, there might be disagreement about whether or how they should be combined into a composite endpoint. The timing of the adverse event relative to the drug exposure might also be an issue; the relevant time window might vary among studies, reflecting disagreement among scientists. Such disagreements are often manifested as arguments among scientists about whether particular aspects of study design are "right" or "wrong". A better way to frame the disagreement, however, is that the different studies address different questions. The real issues, with respect to regulatory decision-making, are what the most important questions are from the standpoint of the regulatory decision. Are the questions that the study addresses similar enough to the public health questions of interest?

Trial interpretation is most profoundly affected by the underlying hypothesis in the case of "noninferiority" trials. Superiority trials for efficacy are the most familiar type of design used in the drug-approval process (Erik, 2007). The objective of a superiority trial is to generate evidence that a particular drug is superior to a comparator, which is often a placebo but could be an active treatment (Lesaffre, 2008). The incentives for high-quality design and conduct in such studies are strong because a poorly conducted study can bias the result toward a finding of no difference. Because of their incentives for scrupulous study conduct and clear interpretation, superiority trials are generally preferred for establishing efficacy.

However, when well-evaluated therapies are accepted as effective for a serious indication or condition, it can be difficult or impossible to withhold them or difficult for a new treatment to exceed them appreciably in efficacy. Therefore, a commonly used approach to the evaluation of efficacy is the noninferiority design, which attempts to show that the new experimental therapy is not worse than the standard therapy by a particular margin. The margin needs to be small enough for it to be assumed that the new therapy is still superior to placebo even if a placebo treatment is not included in the study (Fleming et al., 2011).

The FDA draft guidance on noninferiority studies, praised by the Government Accountability Office (2010c), calls the design and conduct of such trials a "formidable challenge" (FDA, 2010b). Fleming (2008) lists three conditions that permit reliable estimates of the efficacy of an experimental therapy in an active-control noninferiority trial: the effect estimates of the standard therapy that is used as the active control should be of substantial magnitude, precisely estimated, and relevant to the setting of the current trial. From 2002–2009, noninferiority designs were used in 43 (25 percent) of 175 new drug applications (NDAs) for new molecular entities; more than half of the 43 NDAs which used noninferiority designs were for antibiotics, other drug classes for which they were used included anticoagulants (GAO, 2010c).

Recently FDA has begun to use the noninferiority trial design for the study of safety. For instance, the PRECISION (Prospective Randomized Evaluation of Celecoxib Integrated Safety vs Ibuprofen or Naproxen) trial is randomizing 20,000 patients who have osteoarthritis or rheumatoid arthritis to receive celecoxib, ibuprofen, or naproxen (Becker et al., 2009). The TIDE (Thiazolidinedione Intervention with Vitamin D Evaluation) trial is another example (Juurlink, 2010). FDA has also required a series of noninferiority safety trials of long-acting beta-agonists (Chowdhury and Dal Pan, 2010).

Noninferiority studies are particularly problematic for evaluating safety endpoints (Fleming, 2008; Kaul and Diamond, 2006, 2007). Low-quality study conduct, such as poor compliance with treatment regimens, usually biases a superiority trial toward a finding of "no difference" between treatments—a conservative bias for efficacy studies (Temple and Ellenberg, 2000). In contrast, the bias for safety studies evaluating noninferiority among treatments is anticonservative: a more dangerous drug could be incorrectly deemed to be as "equally safe" or "equally effective" relative to its comparator. Furthermore, a choice of "noninferiority margin" that is large will result in a finding that two treatments are "equally safe" even if their risks are substantially different (Fleming, 2008).

The most critical shortcoming of the noninferiority trial for safety is its fundamental logic. In the efficacy realm, a "noninferiority" verdict can imply some degree of efficacy vs placebo because the observed effect is clearly within the efficacy margin. But in the safety realm, there is no such margin, and the logic is different. A "noninferiority" verdict connotes that the degree of possible inferiority in safety, which by itself might not be acceptable, is not so great as to outweigh the drug's benefit in some other domain, such as convenience or tolerability. It therefore has embedded within it an implicit benefit–risk calculus. The noninferiority margin encodes the degree of extra risk that is considered acceptable for the drug's purported benefits. Whether the drug actually has such benefits or whether that degree of risk increase is indeed what should be deemed acceptable may not have been directly addressed in setting the noninferiority margin. Setting that margin is a process that is best conducted by individuals without conflict of interest and who have the requisite scientific and regulatory expertise; noninferiority trials can take decision-making out of the hands of regulators and embed the assessment of the benefit–risk balance within the logic and mathematics of the noninferiority analysis. That approach is undesirable in that sound public policy requires that regulators make explicit and transparent assessments of the acceptability of a drug's benefit–risk balance. The problem was noted with respect to the RECORD trial of rosiglitazone; it was stated in the FDA briefing document that "the non-inferiority design, with a clinically excessive margin of 20 percent also contributes to masking rosiglitazone risk" (FDA, 2010c). In other words, the noninferiority verdict can encode unacceptable benefit–risk tradeoffs in the statistical verdict and the noninferiority margin.

The solution to this is twofold. First, all noninferiority trials must pay close attention to both design and conduct to ensure that they do not bias results toward an equivalence, or noninferiority, finding. Noninferiority margins should be established or reviewed by non-conflicted groups with regulatory, ethics and scientific expertise. Second, and potentially more important, the binary "noninferiority" verdict of such trials should not dominate the regulatory decision-making process. Rather, the estimated difference between the treatments being compared, together with their uncertainty, should be taken as the relevant result, and regulatory decisions should be based directly on that. If the trials are combined in a meta-analysis, that is the information that is used. This is also a domain in which Bayesian approaches can be helpful which can be used to calculate the probability that either the risk or the benefit–risk margin is within an acceptable range (Kaul and Diamond, 2006).

Different Criteria for Weighing or Synthesizing Evidence Among Studies

Meta-analysis is a method of combining the results from various RCTs or observational studies. Meta-analysis synthesizes information quantitatively and provides an opportunity to evaluate the consistency of findings among studies. Heterogeneity among RCTs can also be quantified, and its sources can be evaluated and sometimes identified (Thompson and Sharp, 1999). The method of meta-analysis is an observational study design, and the units of analysis are the studies or RCTs included in the meta-analysis. Key features of high-quality meta-analyses resemble those of other observational studies and include prespecified hypotheses, entry criteria, sampling frames, data collection, and high-quality measures of exposures and outcomes. The appropriate methods of analysis require that within-trial comparisons be preserved and that when estimates based on different trials are combined, each one be weighted by their precision, that is, more precise estimates are given a larger weight.

The data from meta-analyses can be incorporated into analyses that characterize the overall benefit–risk profile of a drug. Meta-analyses can also be used to identify and validate the possibility that one group may respond to a medication differently from another group. If groups do differ in their response in important ways, the benefit–risk profiles in the groups can be estimated separately as well.

Traditionally, many meta-analyses have used published study results. The published studies of an intervention may have included a variety of populations; the intervention may vary among studies; and, even though the outcomes may have been similar, the definitions of endpoints and elements used in a composite primary outcome may have varied from one study to another. The potential sources of heterogeneity include not only the intervention (timing, drug, dose, and duration) and the outcome (timing, type, methods of ascertainment, and validation) but study quality (concealment of randomization, crossovers, noncompliance, and blinding), patients (severity of illness, age sex, ethnicity, and setting), and the presence of cointerventions. How different is "too different" to combine is ultimately an issue of scientific judgment and one for which the reasons and supporting data must be provided. In Chapter 2, suggestions are made for how FDA can play a role in minimizing this heterogeneity to facilitate valid evidence synthesis.

Meta-analysis of RCTs for safety outcomes have difficulties if the studies originally focused on efficacy outcomes. It has long been recognized that the reporting of harms in RCTs is poor (Ioannidis and Lau, 2001), and the Consolidated Standards of Reporting Trials (CONSORT, http://www.consort-statement.org), has been expanded to facilitate their proper reporting (Ioannidis et al., 2004). Problems that afflict the primary reporting of risk outcomes inevitably affect meta-analyses. That those problems continue and are encountered by FDA was documented in a 2011 report by FDA scientists that outlined the challenges of using meta-analysis to study drug risk (Hammad et al., 2011). The problems included:

- High and differential patient dropout.
- Unblinded studies or failure of blinding.
- Inconsistent definitions and selective gathering or reporting of adverse events.
- Failure to document compliance and to measure actual drug exposure.
- Followup too short to detect important adverse events.
- Populations too homogeneous to identify important adverse events or interactions.
- Publication and reporting bias.
- Qualitative or quantitative heterogeneity.
- Incomplete and biased reporting of group results.
- Combining studies of drug "classes", obscuring critical within-class differences.
- Relevance of unpublished data (particularly relevant to FDA), such as discordance between data accessible by FDA and other information published on the same studies.
- Effects of use of different statistical models on results, particularly if data are sparse, as they often are in the case of uncommon safety outcomes.

What the above list indicates is that the meta-analysis of safety outcomes, even from RCTs, is generally less reliable than meta-analysis of efficacy outcomes. That view was reflected in the filings of FDA in relation to rosiglitazone. Jenkins, director of OND, stated in a memorandum (2010) that

> in weighing the available data for rosiglitazone the primary signals of concern arise from meta-analyses of controlled clinical trials that were not designed to rigorously collect CV outcome data and observational studies. Data from these sources provided risk estimates of a magnitude that fall well short of what has traditionally been considered a level that would support scientific and regulatory inferences, even in the face of nominal statistical significance.

Meta-analyses of observational studies have a somewhat different but no less important suite of problems. If the observational studies are designed to address risk, meta-analyses may improve the capacity to identify and characterize the potential harms associated with a drug (Golder et al., 2011). But if there is substantial risk of confounding, meta-analysis will not eliminate bias by pooling results. The potential of each study for confounding must be evaluated before it is included in a meta-analysis. Finally, both publication bias and reporting bias in observational studies can be severe, particularly if they were not designed to capture a specific adverse event (Chan et al., 2004).

Meta-analyses for drug safety can provoke intense disagreement among experts because of uncertainty about the completeness and quality of reporting—either of the risks or the studies themselves—and because of the many judgments that need to be made about whether to combine, which studies to combine and how to account for the many sources of heterogeneity and bias that can affect individual and collective trial estimates. Meta-analysis for safety is less straightforward than that for efficacy, and judgments made in meta-analyses conducted by different investigators on the same drug-safety question may result in different conclusions.

To set the stage for high-quality future evaluations of a drug's benefits and risks, FDA could lay the groundwork for future meta-analyses performed by themselves or others. While meta-analysis is often a retrospective effort to combine evidence already gathered, steps can be taken before studies are done to facilitate meaningful data synthesis later, avoiding some of the problems of meta-analyses noted earlier. FDA is well positioned to take these steps to improve the reliability of meta-analyses for risk outcomes in the postmarketing context. For risk outcomes of concern identified in the premarketing phase or as part of the postmarketing lifecycle review of drug safety, FDA can include in the benefit and risk assessment management plan key design characteristics to raise the quality, completeness, and consistency of adverse-event gathering and reporting.

The core element of the approach described above is a prospective plan for conducting meta-analyses related to key questions of benefits and harms. A "prospective meta-analysis" of RCTs is designed with consistent approaches to defining, capturing, and reporting adverse events to ensure the validity of later meta-analyses of the trials. Prospective meta-analyses have been designed and published (for example, Baigent et al., 2005; Psaty et al., 2009; Reade et al., 2010), and the method continues to be refined (PMA [Cochrane Prospective Meta-Analysis Methods Group], 2010). There are FDA precedents for this; plans have been described to combine data from the noninferiority safety studies required for the long-acting beta-agonists used to treat asthma (Chowdhury et al., 2011). On the basis of its rosiglitazone experience, FDA revised its guidance for the approval of diabetes medications, which now includes a requirement for prospective meta-analysis (FDA, 2008).

Prospectively planned meta-analysis can reduce the heterogeneity among studies. In the observational setting of genome-wide association studies (Psaty et al., 2009), many consortia develop prospective analytic plans; work to harmonize the outcomes, exposures, and covariates; and use meta-analysis to combine association results from many studies. The coordinated, prospectively planned meta-analyses of the genetics consortia have provided results that are as efficient as and virtually identical with those of a cohort-adjusted pooled analysis of individual-patient data (Lin and Zeng, 2010).

FDA can play a similar role in facilitating the performance of meta-analyses that use individual patient data (IPD), potentially greatly enhancing the value of this kind of evidence synthesis. IPD meta-analysis is a form of data pooling in which the analyst has access to the original data of a study instead of merely the summary effect estimates and can thus adjust for covariates and investigate group effects with stronger confounding control than possible with study-level summaries, and can adjust better for design differences between studies (Cooper and Patall, 2009; Fisher et al., 2011; Jones et al., 2009; Kufner et al., 2011). IPD meta-analyses are superior to retrospective meta-analyses that use published results of those same studies, but it is often difficult to gain access to IPD for all studies. Even if IPD can be obtained, their value is low if key variables are not defined or coded similarly among studies. The most successful IPD meta-analyses are ones that are planned prospectively and in which researchers agree a priori on data definitions and standards and on data-sharing—a process that has also been called collaborative meta-analysis (Darby et al., 2011; Davies et al., 2011). For drugs identified before marketing as requiring special scrutiny postmarketing for concerns about the benefit–risk profile, an alternative to sponsoring a single large postmarketing safety study would be for FDA, as part of the approval process or shortly after drug approval, to convene a meeting of researchers in the relevant field to agree on standardized outcome and key variable definitions, data standards, and agreements and procedures for data-sharing, with the aim of making postmarketing IPD meta-analyses for benefit and risk possible and maximally informative. That would also diminish the selective reporting and publication that have demonstrably impaired the quality of some meta-analyses (Turner et al., 2008); 26 of the 42 studies that Nissen and Wolski (2007) used in their meta-analysis of rosiglitazone risk were unpublished at the time.

Different Thresholds for Regulatory Action

Even if scientists are not the final policy makers, they often have opinions about what regulatory decision should be made. This can shade their assessment of the strength of the evidence, particularly when that assessment involves many qualitative judgments about adequacy of confounding control, relevance of differences among studies, and the like. Even if they assess the evidence similarly, differences in their recommendations may be due to differences in their views about what level of certainty, measured in a Bayesian fashion, is sufficient for various decisions.

Standard approaches to statistical inference do not provide tools for assessing intermediate levels of certainty (for example, 70 percent certain), although steps to prevent drug harm may be justified even when only moderate certainty about that harm exists, depending on the degree of the drug benefit and magnitude and seriousness of the harm. Statistical significance, therefore, is not always sufficiently nuanced for such policy decisions.

It is also important to note that in the postmarketing setting FDA has a number of regulatory options. As discussed in Chapter 2, the options might require differing weights of scientific evidence, and therefore of certainty. For example, all other things being equal, a higher standard of evidence is required for withdrawal of a drug than for requiring a labeling change. Different opinions about what the regulatory outcome should be are evident in the testimony of scientists in the rosiglitazone case. The following is a series of exchanges in the Avandia memos and hearings that reflect such differences.

Graham and Gelperin, in the FDA Office of Surveillance and Epidemiology, in their presentation to a July 13–14, 2010, joint meeting of FDA's Endocrinologic and Metabolic Drugs Advisory Committee and Drug Safety and Risk Management Advisory Committee on rosiglitazone (Graham and Gelperin, 2010b), noted that

- The cost of a wrong decision is not symmetric.
  - If rosiglitazone increases cardiovascular risk, [a] wrong decision will cost thousands of lives.
  - If rosiglitazone doesn't increase cardiovascular risk, [a] wrong decision causes no real patient harm.

Parks (2010), director of the Division of Metabolism and Endocrinology Products, stated in a memorandum:

> Although I have argued . . . that each of the data sources does not provide sufficient evidence for me to conclude risks outweighing benefits for rosiglitazone

to recommend its withdrawal, I believe the data sources meet the regulatory requirements to modify safety labeling for this drug.

Parks (2010) further stated:

Some might ask why I don't just recommend the drug's withdrawal given that the safety signal is sufficient enough to justify its relegation to second-line or even last-option therapy. After all, withdrawal would effectively eliminate any chances for the drug to continue to do harm. While I cannot dispute that fact, I believe withdrawal of rosiglitazone in the setting of scientific uncertainty is an inappropriate display of FDA's authority to make a decision for all healthcare providers because of concern that these trained professionals can not reasonably decide on or take responsibility for the use of this drug. I am also concerned that such an action would set an unsettling precedent for future regulatory decisions or may be referenced in legal challenges to the FDA to withdraw other drugs based on meta-analyses and observational studies of similar uncertainty for drug risk.

Jenkins (2010), in OND, stated in a memorandum:

In my view the available data for ischemic CV risk of rosiglitazone, while concerning, do not rise to the level that would support a regulatory conclusion that the benefits of the drug as a treatment for Type 2 diabetes no longer outweigh its risks, which is the statutory finding FDA must reach to withdraw approval of a drug. Such decisions as this require a careful balance between placing the threshold for action too high or too low. If the threshold for action is placed too high there is greater protection against actions based on false positive results, but there is also a greater risk that patients will be subjected to undue harm by continued availability of a harmful drug. On the other hand, if the threshold for action is placed too low there is a greater chance of actions based on false positive results with the unintended consequence that physicians and patients do not have access to a safe and effective drug.

One aspect that is both interesting and admirable about those statements is that there is a reasonably clear separation between what is deemed the strength of the evidence, the degree of attendant uncertainty, and the thresholds for regulatory action. That is often not the case; an action may be portrayed as an inevitable consequence of a particular analytic result (such as statistical significance) and thereby produce pressures to distort the evidential base itself. However, what is absent here is a formal quantification of the uncertainty alluded to.

IMPLICATIONS FOR REGULATORY DECISIONS: THE IMPORTANCE OF UNDERSTANDING THE SOURCES OF DISAGREEMENTS

The preceding section discussed eight broad reasons why scientists can look at the same data and disagree about the credibility of a conclusion that a drug is beneficial or harmful (see Box 3-1). There are few normative guidelines for the many issues raised in this chapter; all have to be judged in context. If the underlying reasons for disagreements are not properly expressed or elicited, however, it will be difficult to reach a consensus on the appropriate regulatory action. Quite often, a debate about one issue (such as what is an appropriate harm endpoint to consider) transmutes into debate about another (such as whether the relationships are statistically significant or what statistical model to use). To permit informed and productive discussions about potential regulatory actions or design choices, the nature of scientific differences must be identified and explicitly stated. Scientists' views on the reasons must be explicit and documented to determine the underlying source of disagreements and to work to resolve them. For example, scientists' views on a number of questions should be made clear to decision-makers to provide them with the context of the opinions. Clear answers to such questions should also be made available to all stakeholders to facilitate understanding of the sources of potential disagreements and the rationale behind a decision.

Those considerations often are unarticulated and are expressed in the form of disagreements about factors far afield from the actual differences. That lack of clarity makes it extraordinarily difficult for the involved scientists and decision-makers to understand the reasons for the disagreements, adjudicate them, and make decisions. Understanding the root causes of scientific disagreement about the harms of a drug is one of the most difficult and important tasks facing a decision-maker, but it is a necessary precondition for proper regulatory decisions. The three-stage decision-making process and the Benefit and Risk Assessment Management Plan (BRAMP) document recommended by the committee in Chapter 2 provide FDA with a formal mechanism for ensuring that scientists' views and reasoning are elicited and made publicly available.

REPRODUCIBLE RESEARCH, DATA SHARING, AND TRANSPARENCY

In addition to direct elicitation of the reasons for disagreements, which were well outlined in the rosiglitazone case, adherence to principles of reproducible research—an emerging set of standards or principles for presentation of complex and scientific findings—would be of substantial help to FDA in enforcing a transparency standard for all results on which regulatory decisions will be made. Principles of reproducible research have been outlined for epidemiologic research (Peng et al., 2006), clinical research (Laine et al., 2007), and molecular biology (Baggerly, 2010; Carey and Stodden, 2010), and are increasingly embraced as standards to facilitate the post-publication peer review of all biomedical research.

In the ideal reproducible research, analyses are presented in such a way that the reader of results can understand most of or all the process that occurred from the gathering of the data to the reporting of specific analyses. At a minimum, that requires provision of study protocols with statistical-analysis plans, statistical code, and information about how decisions were made to produce the analytic dataset from the raw measured data. Optimally, it involves some form of data-sharing. Such data sharing permitted the reanalysis of the RECORD trial that was presented to FDA in the rosiglitazone case. The review revealed that innumerable discrepancies and judgment calls frequently occurred in the original study—from defining a clinical event to the choice of analytic method—and those discrepancies and judgments affected the weight that the results were given in the regulatory decision-making process. For critical research that is to be the basis of regulatory decisions, which can be primary studies like RECORD or can be meta-analyses, standards should be developed within FDA to adhere to reproducible research principles so that the basis of the many judgments can be examined and adjudicated by scientists and regulators when disputes over data interpretation and its implications arise.

Going a step beyond reproducibility, FDA is well-positioned to help assure the accurate public reporting of risk information submitted to it as part of the premarketing approval process. These are often, but not always, published after approval and included in postmarketing safety assessments. FDA scientists themselves have identified the discordance of published data from that submitted to FDA as a problem for the validity of postmarketing safety meta-analyses (Hammad et al., 2011), and there are numerous examples of under or delayed reporting of harms that had been previously reported to regulatory authorities (for example, Carragee et al., 2011; Lee et al., 2008; Melander et al., 2003; Vedula et al., 2009). FDAAA addressed this problem by requiring that all clinical trials submitted for new drug approval or for new labeling be registered at inception at ClinicalTrials.gov, and that the summary results of all pre-specified outcomes be posted within one year of drug approval for new drugs, or three years for new indications (Miller, 2010; Wood, 2009). However, recently reported evidence has shown that compliance with this aspect of FDAAA has been low (Law et al., 2011). In addition, the FDA policy on the reporting of studies submitted for non-approved drugs has not been settled (Miller, 2010). Finally, publishing summary results is not equivalent to sharing primary data, which allows for re-analyses. New approaches are needed to facilitate the publication of safety data submitted to FDA for approved drugs, and to find ways to release similar data for drugs that are disapproved, but whose information might be extremely valuable for the interpretation of safety information from approved drugs in the same class.

FINDINGS AND RECOMMENDATIONS

Finding 3.1

Some of FDA's most difficult decisions are those in which experts disagree about how compelling the evidence that informs the public health question is. Understanding the nature and sources of those disagreements and their implications for

FDA's decisions is key to improving the agency's decision-making process. For example, experts can disagree about the plausibility of a new risk (or decreased benefit) on the basis of different assessments of prior evidence, the quality of new data, the adequacy of confounding control in the relevant studies, the transportability of results, the appropriateness of the statistical analysis, the relevance of the new evidence to the public health question, how the evidence should be weighed and synthesized, or the threshold for regulatory actions.

Recommendation 3.1
FDA should use the framework for decision-making proposed in Recommendation 2.1 to ensure a thorough discussion and clear understanding of the sources of disagreement about the available evidence among all participants in the regulatory decision-making process. In the interest of transparency, FDA should use the BRAMP document proposed in Recommendation 2.2 to ensure that such disagreements and how they were resolved are documented and made public.

Finding 3.2

Such methods as Bayesian analyses or other approaches to integrating external relevant information with newly emerging information could provide decision-makers with useful quantitative assessments of evidence. An example would be sensitivity analyses of clinical-trial data that illustrate the influence of prior probabilities on estimates of probabilities that an intervention has unacceptable safety risks. These approaches can inform judgments, allow more rational decision-making, and permit input from multiple stakeholders and experts.

Recommendation 3.2
FDA should ensure that it has adequate expertise in Bayesian approaches, in combination with expertise in relevant frequentist and causal inference methods, to assess the probability that observed associations reflect actual causal effects, to incorporate multiple sources of uncertainty into the decision-making process, and to evaluate the sensitivity of those conclusions to different representations of external evidence. To facilitate the use of Bayesian approaches, FDA should develop a guidance document for the use of Bayesian methods for assessing a drug's benefits, risks, and benefit–risk profile.

Finding 3.3

Traditionally, the main criteria for evaluating a study are ones that contribute to its internal validity. A well-conducted RCT typically has higher internal validity than a well-conducted observational study. Results of observational studies, however, can have greater transportability if their participants are more similar to the target clinical population than to the participants in a clinical trial. In some circumstances, such as an evaluation of the association between a drug and an uncommon unexpected adverse event, observational studies may produce estimates closer to the actual risk in the general population than can be achieved in clinical trials. In assessing the relevance of study findings to a public health question, the transportability of the study results is as important as the determinants of its internal validity.

Recommendation 3.3
In assessing the benefits and risks associated with a drug in the postmarketing context, FDA should develop guidance and review processes that ensure that observational studies with high internal validity are given appropriate weight in the evaluation of drug harms and that transportability is given emphasis similar to that given bias and other errors in assessing the weight of evidence that a study provides to inform a public health question.

Finding 3.4

The principles of reproducible research are important for ensuring the integrity of postmarketing research used by FDA. Those principles include providing information on the provenance of data (from measurement to analytic dataset) and, when possible, making available properly annotated analytic datasets, study protocols (including statistical analysis plan) and their amendments, and statistical codes.

Recommendation 3.4
All analyses, whether conducted independently of FDA or by FDA staff, whose results are relied on for postmarketing regulatory decisions should use the principles of reproducible research when possible, subject to legal constraints. To that end, FDA should present data and analyses in a fashion that allows independent analysts either to reproduce the findings or to understand how FDA generated the results in sufficient detail to understand the strengths, weaknesses, and assumptions of the relevant analyses.

Finding 3.5

The ability of researchers in and outside FDA to analyze new information about the benefits and risks associated with a marketed drug and to design appropriate postmarketing research—including conducting individual-patient meta-analyses—is enhanced by access to data and analyses from all studies of the drug and others in the same drug class that were reported in the preapproval process. Although disclosure of such information is likely to advance the public's health, such disclosures raise concerns about the privacy of participants in the research that generated the information and may threaten industry interest in maintaining proprietary information, which is deemed important for innovation. New approaches to resolving this tension are needed.

Recommendation 3.5
FDA should establish and coordinate a working group, including industry and patient and consumer representatives, to find ways that appropriately balance public health, privacy, and proprietary interests to facilitate disclosure of data for trials and studies relevant to postmarketing research decisions.

Finding 3.6

The elements of the benefit–risk profile of a drug are best estimated by using all the available high-quality data, and meta-analysis is a useful tool for summarizing such data and evaluating heterogeneity. However, because the reporting of harms in published RCTs and observational studies is often poor or inconsistent and because there is often substantial publication bias in studies of drug risk, steps are needed to improve both the reporting of harms and the design of studies of harm. That can be done through prospective planning for selected meta-analyses and by monitoring compliance with the FDAAA requirement that summary trial results for all primary and secondary outcomes be published at ClinicalTrials.gov.

Recommendation 3.6
For drugs that are likely to have required postmarketing observational studies or trials, FDA should use the BRAMP to specify potential public health questions of interest as early as possible; should prospectively recommend standards for uniform definition of key variables and complete ascertainment of events among studies or convene researchers in the field to suggest such standards and promote data-sharing; should prospectively plan meta-analyses of the data with reference to specified exposures, outcomes, comparators, and covariates; should conduct the meta-analyses of the data; and should make appropriate regulatory decisions in a timely fashion. FDA can also improve the validity of meta-analyses by monitoring and encouraging compliance with FDAAA requirements for reporting to ClinicalTrials.gov.

Finding 3.7

FDA produced a high-quality guidance document on the use of the noninferiority design for the study of efficacy. Increasingly, FDA is using the noninferiority design to evaluate drug-safety endpoints as the primary outcomes in randomized trials. The use of noninferiority analyses to establish the acceptability of the benefit–risk profile of a drug can take the decision about how to balance the risks and benefits of two drugs out of the hands of regulators. Noninferiority trials also have the disadvantage of being biased toward equivalence when trial design or conduct is suboptimal; this is of particular concern when such trials are used to estimate risks.

Recommendation 3.7.1
FDA should develop a guidance document on the design and conduct of noninferiority postmarketing trials for the study of safety of a drug. The guidance should include discussion of criteria for choosing the standard therapy to be used in the active-treatment control arm; of methods for selecting a noninferiority margin in safety trials and ensuring high-quality trial conduct; of the optimal analytic methods, including Bayesian approaches; and of the interpretation of the findings in terms of the drug's benefit–risk profile.

Recommendation 3.7.2
FDA should closely scrutinize the design and conduct of any noninferiority safety studies for aspects that may inappropriately make the arms appear similar. FDA should use the observed-effect estimate and confidence interval as a basis for decision-making, not the binary noninferiority verdict.

REFERENCES

AHRQ (Agency for Healthcare Research and Quality). 2008. *U.S. Preventive Services Task Force procedure manual.* Washington, DC: Department of Health and Human Services.

Baggerly, K. 2010. Disclose all data in publications. *Nature* 467(7314):401.

Baigent, C., A. Keech, P. M. Kearney, and L. Blackwell. 2005. Efficacy and safety of cholesterol-lowering treatment: Prospective meta-analysis of data from 90,056 participants in 14 randomised trials of statins. *Lancet* 366(9493):1267-1278.

Barton, M. B., T. Miller, T. Wolff, D. Petitti, M. LeFevre, G. Sawaya, B. Yawn, J. Guirguis-Blake, N. Calonge, R. Harris, and U.S. Preventive Services Task Force. 2007. How to read the new recommendation statement: Methods update from the U.S. Preventive Services Task Force. *Annals of Internal Medicine* 147(2):123-127.

Becker, M. C., T. H. Wang, L. Wisniewski, K. Wolski, P. Libby, T. F. Lüscher, J. S. Borer, A. M. Mascette, M. E. Husni, D. H. Solomon, D. Y. Graham, N. D. Yeomans, H. Krum, F. Ruschitzka, A. M. Lincoff, and S. E. Nissen. 2009. Rationale, design, and governance of Prospective Randomized Evaluation of Celecoxib Integrated Safety versus Ibuprofen or Naproxen (PRECISION), a cardiovascular end point trial of nonsteroidal antiinflammatory agents in patients with arthritis. *American Heart Journal* 157(4):606-612.

Bent, S., A. Padula, and A. L. Avins. 2006. Brief communication: Better ways to question patients about adverse medical events: A randomized, controlled trial. *Annals of Internal Medicine* 144(4):257-261.

Berry, D. A. 2006. Bayesian clinical trials. *Nature Reviews Drug Discovery* 5(1):27-36.

Berry, D. A., M. C. Wolff, and D. Sack. 1992. Public health decision making: A sequential vaccine trial. In *Bayesian statistics*, edited by J. Bernardo, J. Berger, A. Dawid and A. Smith. Oxford, UK: Oxford University Press. Pp. 79-96.

Camm, A. J., A. Capucci, S. H. Hohnloser, C. Torp-Pedersen, I. C. Van Gelder, B. Mangal, and G. Beatch. 2011. A randomized active-controlled study comparing the efficacy and safety of vernakalant to amiodarone in recent-onset atrial fibrillation. *Journal of the American College of Cardiology* 57(3):313-321.

Campbell, G. 2011. Bayesian statistics in medical devices: Innovation sparked by the FDA. *Journal of Biopharmaceutical Statistics* 21(5):871-887.

Carey, V. J., and V. Stodden. 2010. Reproducible research concepts and tools for cancer bioinformatics. In *Biomedical informatics for cancer research,* edited by M. F. Ochs, J. T. Casagrande and R. V. Davuluri. Springer US. Pp. 149-175.

Carpenter, D. 2010. Reputation and power institutionalized: Scientific networks, congressional hearings, and judicial affirmation, 1963-1986. In *Reputation and power: Organizational image and pharmaceutical regulation at the FDA*. Cambridge, NY: Princeton University Press. Pp. 298-392.

Carragee, E. J., E. L. Hurwitz, and B. K. Weiner. 2011. A critical review of recombinant human bone morphogenetic protein-2 trials in spinal surgery: Emerging safety concerns and lessons learned. *Spine Journal* 11(6):471-491.

Chaloner, K. 1996. Elicitation of prior distributions. In *Bayesian biostatistics*, edited by D. A. Berry and D. K. Stangl. New York: Marcel Dekker.

Chan, A.-W., A. Hróbjartsson, M. T. Haahr, P. C. Gøtzsche, and D. G. Altman. 2004. Empirical evidence for selective reporting of outcomes in randomized trials. *JAMA* 291(20):2457-2465.

Chowdhury, B. A., and G. Dal Pan. 2010. The FDA and safe use of long-acting beta-agonists in the treatment of asthma. *New England Journal of Medicine* 362(13):1169-1171.

Chowdhury, B. A., S. M. Seymour, and M. S. Levenson. 2011. Assessing the safety of adding LABAs to inhaled corticosteroids for treating asthma. *New England Journal of Medicine* 364(26):2473-2475.

Claxton, K., J. T. Cohen, and P. J. Neumann. 2005. When is evidence sufficient? *Health Affairs* 24(1):93-101.

Cooper, H., and E. A. Patall. 2009. The relative benefits of meta-analysis conducted with individual participant data versus aggregated data. *Psychological Methods* 14(2):165-176.

Dal Pan, G. J. 2010. *Memorandum from Gerald Dal Pan to Janet Woodcock (dated September 12, 2010). Re: Recommendations for regulatory action for rosiglitazone and rosiglitazone-containing products (NDA 21-071, supplement 035, incoming submission dated August 25, 2009).* Washington, DC: Department of Health and Human Services.

Darby, S., P. McGale, C. Correa, C. Taylor, R. Arriagada, M. Clarke, D. Cutter, C. Davies, M. Ewertz, J. Godwin, R. Gray, L. Pierce, T. Whelan, Y. Wang, and R. Peto. 2011. Effect of radiotherapy after breast-conserving surgery on 10-year recurrence and 15-year breast cancer death: Meta-analysis of individual patient data for 10,801 women in 17 randomised trials. *Lancet* 378(9804):1707-1716.

Davies, C., J. Godwin, R. Gray, M. Clarke, D. Cutter, S. Darby, P. McGale, H. C. Pan, C. Taylor, Y. C. Wang, M. Dowsett, J. Ingle, and R. Peto. 2011. Relevance of breast cancer hormone receptors and other factors to the efficacy of adjuvant tamoxifen: Patient-level meta-analysis of randomised trials. *Lancet* 378(9793):771-784.

Emerson, S. S., J. M. Kittelson, and D. L. Gillen. 2007. Bayesian evaluation of group sequential clinical trial designs. *Statistics in Medicine* 26(7):1431-1449.

Eraker, S. A., J. P. Kirscht, and M. H. Becker. 1984. Understanding and improving patient compliance. *Annals of Internal Medicine* 100(2):258.

Erik, C. 2007. Methodology of superiority vs. equivalence trials and non-inferiority trials. *Journal of Hepatology* 46(5):947-954.

Etzioni, R. D., and J. B. Kadane. 1995. Bayesian statistical methods in public health and medicine. *Annual Review of Public Health* 16(1):23-41.

FDA (US Food and Drug Administration). 2008. *Guidance for industry. Diabetes mellitus—evaluating cardiovascular risk in new antidiabetic therapies to treat type 2 diabetes.* Washington, DC: Department of Health and Human Services.

FDA. 2010a. *Guidance for industry and FDA staff: Guidance for the use of Bayesian statistics in medical device clinical trials.* Rockville, MD: Department of Health and Human Services.

FDA. 2010b. *Guidance for industry: Non-inferiority clinical trials, draft guidance.* Washington, DC: Department of Health and Human Services.
FDA. 2010c. *FDA briefing document. Advisory committee meeting for NDA 21071: Avandia (rosiglitazone maleate tablet).* Silver Spring, MD: Department of Health and Human Services.
FDA. 2012. *Classifying significant postmarketing drug safety issues: Draft guidance.* Washington, DC: Department of Health and Human Services.
Fisher, D. J., A. J. Copas, J. F. Tierney, and M. K. B. Parmar. 2011. A critical review of methods for the assessment of patient-level interactions in individual participant data meta-analysis of randomized trials, and guidance for practitioners. *Journal of Clinical Epidemiology* 64(9):949-967.
Fisher, L. D. 1999. Carvedilol and the Food and Drug Administration (FDA) approval process: The FDA paradigm and reflections on hypothesis testing. *Controlled Clinical Trials* 20(1):16-39.
Fleming, T. R. 2008. Current issues in non-inferiority trials. *Statistics in Medicine* 27(3):317-332.
Fleming, T.R., K. Odem-Davis, M. Rothmann, and Y. Li Shen. 2011. Some essential considerations in the design and conduct of non-inferiority trials. *Clinical Trials* 8:432-439.
Frank, E., G. B. Cassano, P. Rucci, A. Fagiolini, L. Maggi, H. C. Kraemer, D. J. Kupfer, B. Pollock, R. Bies, V. Nimgaonkar, P. Pilkonis, M. K. Shear, W. K. Thompson, V. J. Grochocinski, P. Scocco, J. Buttenfield, and R. N. Forgione. 2008. Addressing the challenges of a cross-national investigation: Lessons from the Pittsburgh-PISA study of treatment-relevant phenotypes of unipolar depression. *Clinical Trials* 5(3):253-261.
Furberg, C. D., and B. Pitt. 2001. Commentary: Withdrawl of cerivastatin from the world market. *Current Controlled Trials in Cardiovascular Medicine* 2(5):205-207.
GAO (Government Accountability Office). 2010a. *Drug safety: FDA has conducted more foreign inspections and begun to improve its information on foreign establishments, but more progress is needed.* Washington, DC: Government Accountability Office.
GAO. 2010b. *Food and Drug Administration: Overseas offices have taken steps to help ensure import safety, but more long-term planning is needed.* Washington, DC: Government Accountability Office.
GAO. 2010c. *New drug approval: FDA's consideration of evidence from certain clinical trials.* Washington, DC: Government Accountability Office.
Garrison, L. P., Jr., P. J. Neumann, P. Radensky, and S. D. Walcoff. 2010. A flexible approach to evidentiary standards for comparative effectiveness research. *Health Affairs* 29(10):1812-1817.
Gelfand, A. E., and B. K. Mallick. 1995. Bayesian analysis of proportional hazards models built from monotone functions. *Biometrics* 51(3):843-852.
Golder, S., Y. K. Loke, and M. Bland. 2011. Meta-analyses of adverse effects data derived from randomised controlled trials as compared to observational studies: Methodological overview. *PLoS Med* 8(5):e1001026.
Good, I. J. 1950. *Probability and the weighting of evidence.* London, UK: Charles Griffin & Co.
Goodman, S. N. 1999. Toward evidence-based medical statistics. 2: The Bayes factor. *Annals of Internal Medicine* 130(12):1005-1013.
Goodman, S. N. 2001. Of P-values and Bayes: A modest proposal. *Epidemiology* 12(3):295-297.
Gordis, L. 2004. *Epidemiology.* Third ed. Philadelphia, PA: Elsevier Inc.
Graham, D. J., and K. Gelperin. 2010a. Memorandum to Mary Parks regarding comments on RECORD, TIDE, and the benefit-risk assessment of rosiglitazone vs. pioglitazone. In *FDA Briefing Document Advisory Committee Meeting for NDA 21071: Avandia (rosiglitazone maleate) tablet: July 13 and 14, 2010.* Washington, DC: Department of Health and Human Services.
Graham, D. J., and K. Gelperin. 2010b. *TIDE and benefit-risk considerations.* http://www.fda.gov/downloads/AdvisoryCommittees/CommitteesMeetingMaterials/Drugs/EndocrinologicandMetabolicDrugsAdvisoryCommittee/UCM224732.pdf (accessed October 11, 2011).
Greene, B. M., A. M. Geiger, E. L. Harris, A. Altschuler, L. Nekhlyudov, M. B. Barton, S. J. Rolnick, J. G. Elmore, and S. Fletcher. 2006. Impact of IRB requirements on a multicenter survey of prophylactic mastectomy outcomes. *Annals of Epidemiology* 16(4):275-278.

Greenhouse, J. B., and L. Waserman. 1995. Robust Bayesian methods for monitoring clinical trials. *Statistics in Medicine* 14(12):1379-1391.

Guyatt, G. H., A. D. Oxman, G. E. Vist, R. Kunz, Y. Falck-Ytter, P. Alonso-Coello, and H. J. Schunemann. 2008. GRADE: An emerging consensus on rating quality of evidence and strength of recommendations. *BMJ* 336(7650):924-926.

Hamburg, M. A. 2011. Commentary: The growing role of epidemiology in drug safety regulation. *Epidemiology* 22(5):622-624.

Hammad, T. A., S. P. Pinheiro, and G. A. Neyarapally. 2011b. Secondary use of randomized controlled trials to evaluate drug safety: A review of methodological considerations. *Clinical Trials* 8(5):559-570.

Hernán, M. A., and S. Hernandez-Diaz. 2012. Beyond the intention-to-treat in comparative effectiveness research. *Clinical Trials* 9(1):48-55.

Hernán, M. A., and C. Robins. 2012. *Causal inference*. New York: Chapman & Hall/CRC.

Hernán, M. A., and J. M. Robins. 2006. Instruments for causal inference: An epidemiologist's dream? *Epidemiology* 17(4):360-372.

Ioannidis, J. P. A., and J. Lau. 2001. Completeness of safety reporting in randomized trials: An evaluation of 7 medical areas. *JAMA* 285(4):437-443.

Ioannidis, J. P. A., S. J. W. Evans, P. C. Gøtzsche, R. T. O'Neill, D. G. Altman, K. Schulz, and D. Moher. 2004. Better reporting of harms in randomized trials: An extension of the consort statement. *Annals of Internal Medicine* 141(10):781-788.

Ioannidis, J. P., C. D. Mulrow, and S. N. Goodman. 2006. Adverse events: The more you search, the more you find. *Annals of Internal Medicine* 144(4):298-300.

IOM (Institute of Medicine). 2008. *Improving the presumptive disability decision-making process for veterans*. Washington, DC: The National Academies Press.

Ives, D. G., A. L. Fitzpatrick, D. E. Bild, B. M. Psaty, L. H. Kuller, P. M. Crowley, R. G. Cruise, and S. Theroux. 1995. Surveillance and ascertainment of cardiovascular events: The Cardiovascular Health Study. *Annals of Epidemiology* 5(4):278-285.

Ives, D. G., P. Samuel, B. M. Psaty, and L. H. Kuller. 2009. Agreement between nosologist and cardiovascular health study review of deaths: Implications of coding differences. *Journal of the American Geriatrics Society* 57(1):133-139.

Jencks, S. F., D. K. Williams, and T. L. Kay. 1988. Assessing hospital-associated deaths from discharge data. *JAMA* 260(15):2240-2246.

Jenkins, J. K. 2010. *Memorandum from John Jenkins to Janet Woodcock (dated September, 2010). Re: Recommendations for regulatory actions—Rosiglitazone.* Washington, DC: US Food and Drug Administration.

Jones, A. P., R. D. Riley, P. R. Williamson, and A. Whitehead. 2009. Meta-analysis of individual patient data versus aggregate data from longitudinal clinical trials. *Clinical Trials* 6(1): 16-27.

Juurlink, D. N. 2010. Rosiglitazone and the case for safety over certainty. *JAMA* 304(4):469-471.

Kadane, J. B. 2005. Bayesian methods for health-related decision making. *Statistics in Medicine* 24(4):563-567.

Kadane, J., and L. J. Wolfson. 1998. Experiences in elicitation. *Journal of the Royal Statistical Society: Series D (The Statistician)* 47(1):3-19.

Kaizar, E. E., J. B. Greenhouse, H. Seltman, and K. Kelleher. 2006. Do antidepressants cause suicidality in children? A Bayesian meta-analysis. *Clinical Trials* 3(2):73-90; discussion 91-98.

Kass, R. E., and A. E. Raftery. 1995. Bayes factors. *Journal of the American Statistical Association* 90(430):773-795.

Kaul, S., and G. A. Diamond. 2006. Good enough: A primer on the analysis and interpretation of noninferiority trials. *Annals of Internal Medicine* 145(1):62-69.

Kaul, S., and G. A. Diamond. 2007. Making sense of noninferiority: A clinical and statistical perspective on its application to cardiovascular clinical trials. *Progress in Cardiovascular Diseases* 49(4):284-299.

Kufner, S., A. de Waha, F. Tomai, S.-W. Park, S.-W. Lee, D.-S. Lim, M. H. Kim, A. M. Galloe, M. Maeng, C. Briguori, A. Dibra, A. Schömig, and A. Kastrati. 2011. A meta-analysis of specifically designed randomized trials of sirolimus-eluting versus paclitaxel-eluting stents in diabetic patients with coronary artery disease. *American Heart Journal* 162(4):740-747.

Laine, C., S. N. Goodman, M. E. Griswold, and H. C. Sox. 2007. Reproducible research: Moving toward research the public can really trust. *Annals of Internal Medicine* 146(6):450-453.

Lanctot, K. L., and C. A. Naranjo. 1995. Comparison of the Bayesian approach and a simple algorithm for assessment of adverse drug events. *Clinical Pharmacology & Therapeutics* 58(6):692-698.

Lau, H. S., A. de Boer, K. S. Beuning, and A. Porsius. 1997. Validation of pharmacy records in drug exposure assessment. *Journal of Clinical Epidemiology* 50(5):619-625.

Laughren, T. P. 2006. *Overview for December 13 meeting of psychopharmacologic drugs advisory committee (PDAC)*.

Law, M. R., Y. Kawasumi, and S. G. Morgan. 2011. Despite law, fewer than one in eight completed studies of drugs and biologics are reported on time on ClinicalTrials.gov. *Health Affairs* 30(12):2338-2345.

Lee, K., P. Bacchetti, and I. Sim. 2008. Publication of clinical trials supporting successful new drug applications: A literature analysis. *PLoS Medicine* 5(9):e191.

Lesaffre, E. 2008. Superiority, equivalence, and non-inferiority trials. *Bulletin of the NYU Hospital for Joint Diseases* 66(2):150-154.

Levenson, M., and C. Holland. 2006. *Slide presentation: Antidepressants and suicidality in adults: Statistical evaluation*. http://www.fda.gov/ohrms/dockets/ac/06/slides/2006-4272s1-04-FDA_files/frame.htm (accessed April 6, 2012).

Lilford, R. J., M. A. Mohammed, D. Braunholtz, and T. P. Hofer. 2003. The measurement of active errors: Methodological issues. *Quality and Safety in Health Care* 12(Suppl 2):ii8-ii12.

Lin, D. Y., and D. Zeng. 2010. Meta-analysis of genome-wide association studies: No efficiency gain in using individual participant data. *Genetic Epidemiology* 34(1):60-66.

Madigan, D., P. Ryan, S. E. Simpson, and I. Zorych. 2010. Bayesian methods in pharmacovigilance. In *Bayesian statistics 9*, edited by J. M. Bernardo, M. J. Bayarri, J. O. Berger, A. P. Dawid, D. Heckerman, A. F. M. Smith and M. West. Oxford, UK: Oxford University Press.

Manion, F., R. Robbins, W. Weems, and R. Crowley. 2009. Security and privacy requirements for a multi-institutional cancer research data grid: An interview-based study. *BMC Medical Informatics and Decision Making* 9(1):31.

Marciniak, T. A. 2010. Memorandum from Thomas Marciniak to Jena Weber (dated June 14, 2010) regarding cardiovascular events in RECORD, NDA 21-071/s-035. In *FDA Briefing Document Advisory Committee Meeting for NDA 21071: Avandia (rosiglitazone maleate) tablet: July 13 and 14, 2010*. Washington, DC: Department of Health and Human Services.

McEvoy, B., R. R. Nandy, and R. C. Tiwari. 2012. *Applications of Bayesian model selection criteria for clinical safety data (abstract, ASA joint statistical meetings)*. http://www.amstat.org/meetings/jsm/2012/onlineprogram/AbstractDetails.cfm?abstractid=305627 (accessed April 5, 2012).

Melander, H., J. Ahlqvist-Rastad, G. Meijer, and B. Beermann. 2003. Evidence b(i)ased medicine—selective reporting from studies sponsored by pharmaceutical industry: Review of studies in new drug applications. *BMJ* 326(7400):1171-1173.

Miller, J. D. 2010. Registering clinical trial results: The next step. *JAMA* 303(8):773-774.

Misbin, R. I. 2007. Lessons from the Avandia controversy: A new paradigm for the development of drugs to treat type 2 diabetes. *Diabetes Care* 30(12):3141-3144.

Nissen, S. E., and K. Wolski. 2007. Effect of rosiglitazone on the risk of myocardial infarction and death from cardiovascular causes. *New England Journal of Medicine* 356(24):2457-2471.

NRC (National Research Council). 2010. *The prevention and treatment of missing data in clinical trials. Panel on handling missing data in clinical trials*. Washington, DC: The National Academies Press.

Owens, D. K., K. N. Lohr, D. Atkins, J. R. Treadwell, J. T. Reston, E. B. Bass, S. Chang, and M. Helfand. 2010. AHRQ series paper 5: Grading the strength of a body of evidence when comparing medical interventions-Agency for Healthcare Research and Quality and the Effective Health-care Program. *Journal of Clinical Epidemiology* 63(5):513-523.

Oxford Dictionaries. 2011. *Oxford English Dictionary online*. Oxford University Press.

Parks, M. H. 2010. *Memorandum from Mary Parks to Curtis Rosebraugh (dated August 19, 2010). Re: Recommendations on marketing status of Avandia (rosiglitazone maleate) and the required post-marketing trial, Thiazolidinedione Intervention and Vitamin D Evaluation (TIDE) following the July 13 and 14, 2010 Public Advisory Committee Meeting.* Silver Spring, MD: US Food and Drug Administration.

Parmigiani, G. 2002. *Modeling in medical decision making: A Bayesian approach (statistics in practice)*. New York: Wiley.

Peng, R. D., F. Dominici, and S. L. Zeger. 2006. Reproducible epidemiologic research. *American Journal of Epidemiology* 163(9):783-789.

PMA (Cochrane Prospective Meta-Analysis Methods Group). 2010. *Welcome: The prospective meta-analysis methods group*. http://pma.cochrane.org/ (accessed December 12, 2011).

Psaty, B. M., and D. S. Siscovick. 2010. Minimizing bias due to confounding by indication in comparative effectiveness research: The importance of restriction. *JAMA* 304(8):897-898.

Psaty, B. M., R. Boineau, L. H. Kuller, and R. V. Luepker. 1999. The potential costs of upcoding for heart failure in the United States. *The American Journal of Cardiology* 84(1):108-109.

Psaty, B. M., C. J. O'Donnell, V. Gudnason, K. L. Lunetta, A. R. Folsom, J. I. Rotter, A. G. Uitterlinden, T. B. Harris, J. C. M. Witteman, E. Boerwinkle, and (on behalf of the CHARGE Consortium). 2009. Cohorts for Heart and Aging Research in Genomic Epidemiology (CHARGE) consortium. *Circulation: Cardiovascular Genetics* 2(1):73-80.

Reade, M., A. Delaney, M. Bailey, D. Harrison, D. Yealy, P. Jones, K. Rowan, R. Bellomo, and D. Angus. 2010. Prospective meta-analysis using individual patient data in intensive care medicine. *Intensive Care Medicine* 36(1):11-21.

Royall, R. M. 1997. *Statistical evidence: A likelihood paradigm*. London, UK: Chapman & Hall.

Saunders, K., K. Dunn, J. Merrill, M. Sullivan, C. Weisner, J. Braden, B. Psaty, and M. Von Korff. 2010. Relationship of opioid use and dosage levels to fractures in older chronic pain patients. *Journal of General Internal Medicine* 25(4):310-315.

Staffa, J. A., J. Chang, and L. Green. 2002. Cerivastatin and reports of fatal rhabdomyolysis. *New England Journal of Medicine* 346(7):539-540.

Talbot, J. C. C., and P. Walker. 2004. *Stephens' detection of new adverse drug reactions*. 5th ed. West Sussex, England: John Wiley & Sons Ltd.

Temple, R., and S. S. Ellenberg. 2000. Placebo-controlled trials and active-control trials in the evaluation of new treatments. Part 1: Ethical and scientific issues. *Annals of Internal Medicine* 133(6):455-463.

Ten Have, T. R., S. L. Normand, S. M. Marcus, C. H. Brown, P. Lavori, and N. Duan. 2008. Intent-to-treat vs. non-intent-to-treat analyses under treatment non-adherence in mental health randomized trials. *Psychiatrics Annals* 38(12):772-783.

Thomas, E. J., and L. A. Petersen. 2003. Measuring errors and adverse events in health care. *Journal of General Internal Medicine* 18(1):61-67.

Thompson, S. G., and S. J. Sharp. 1999. Explaining heterogeneity in meta-analysis: A comparison of methods. *Statistics in Medicine* 18:2693-2708.

Toh, S., and M. A. Hernán. 2008. Causal inference from longitudinal studies with baseline randomization. *International Journal of Biostatistics* 4(1):Article22.

Turner, E. H., A. M. Matthews, E. Linardatos, R. A. Tell, and R. Rosenthal. 2008. Selective publication of antidepressant trials and its influence on apparent efficacy. *New England Journal of Medicine* 358(3):252-260.

Unger, E. 2010. Memorandum to the file regarding NDA: 21-071; suppl 35, 36, 37 Avandia (rosiglitazone). In *FDA Briefing Document: Advisory Committee Meeting for NDA 21071: Avandia (rosiglitazone maleate) tablet: July 13 and 14, 2010*. Washington, DC: Department of Health and Human Services.

Vandenbroucke, J. P. 2006. What is the best evidence for determining harms of medical treatment? *Canadian Medical Association Journal* 174(5):645-646.

Vandenbroucke, J. P., and B. M. Psaty. 2008. Benefits and risks of drug treatments: How to combine the best evidence on benefits with the best data about adverse effects. *JAMA* 300(20):2417-2419.

Vedula, S. S., L. Bero, R. W. Scherer, and K. Dickersin. 2009. Outcome reporting in industry-sponsored trials of gabapentin for off-label use. *New England Journal of Medicine* 361(20):1963-1971.

Weiss, N. S., T. D. Koepsell, and B. M. Psaty. 2008. Generalizability of the results of randomized trials. *Archives of Internal Medicine* 168(2):133-135.

Wood, A. J. J. 2009. Progress and deficiencies in the registration of clinical trials. *New England Journal of Medicine* 360(8):824-830.

Yap, J. S. 2010. Statistical review and evaluation: Clinical studies NDA 21-071/35 and 21-073. In *FDA Briefing Document Advisory Committee Meeting for NDA 21071: Avandia (rosiglitazone maleate) tablet: July 13 and 14, 2010*. Washington, DC: Department of Health and Human Services.

4

Selection and Oversight of Required Postmarketing Studies

In keeping with a commitment to a lifecycle approach to benefit–risk management, Chapter 2 offered recommendations related to how the US Food and Drug Administration (FDA) should decide among multiple regulatory actions when conducting periodic assessments of the benefit–risk profiles of marketed drugs. Deciding which regulatory action to pursue takes on particular importance when new information about a benefit–risk profile emerges. The present chapter focuses on one of FDA's possible regulatory actions: to require that the manufacturer conduct postmarketing research.[1] It assumes that FDA has determined that it is appropriate to require postmarketing research.[2] The committee recommends that FDA use the framework presented in Chapter 2 to make this determination. However, regardless of how the decision is reached, this chapter provides guidance to FDA in deciding what types[3] of study designs should be required and in meeting its ethical responsibilities in making that determination and in providing

[1]The committee includes clinical trials, observational studies, and meta-analyses in the terms *study* and *research*. That is in contrast with the Food and Drug Administration Amendments Act (FDAAA) of 2007, in which *study* is used to refer to "all investigations other than clinical trials". FDAAA defines a clinical trial as "any prospective investigation in which the sponsor or investigator determines the method of assigning the investigational product or other interventions to human subject(s)".

[2]This judgment by FDA presupposes that it has already determined that it cannot get the information it needs from additional surveillance activities, such as using Sentinel.

[3]It is important to note that FDA could require multiple investigations or a staged approach, in which it could start by requiring an observational study and then require a randomized controlled trial if the observational one does not produce sufficient evidence for decision-making. Because FDA could require multiple postmarketing studies in response to concerns about a particular drug, the committee refers to the "types" of research design that FDA might require. Use of the plural does not mean that FDA would never require a single investigation of some type.

oversight once research is under way. This chapter thus expands the committee's responses to Questions 1, 3, and 4 of its charge (see Box 1-1).

The chapter begins with a discussion of relevant features of the complex postmarketing context that bear on the selection of the types of designs to require. It then puts forward two sets of considerations that frame the decision problem more specifically: the scientific and practical criteria for assessing the advantages and disadvantages of alternative research designs and the statutory conditions and ethical preferences that often favor observational designs over randomized controlled trials (RCTs) in the postmarketing setting. It then identifies the conditions under which it is acceptable for FDA to require each. The committee then discusses factors that affect choosing among types of observational studies and RCTs, once it has been decided to require an observational design, an RCT design, or both. That discussion is followed by an analysis of the ethical considerations that should guide the design and conduct of postmarketing research, including issues related to informed consent and safety monitoring, and FDA's ethical obligations in the postmarketing setting.

THE POSTMARKETING CONTEXT

Because concerns about a drug's benefit–risk profile can emerge throughout a drug's lifecycle, the decision by FDA to require a manufacturer to conduct postmarketing research can occur when the drug is first approved or at any time thereafter.

In the premarketing setting, the RCT is the standard for providing the efficacy data used by FDA to make approval decisions, although occasionally less-well-controlled designs have been accepted if the effect is of sufficient magnitude. In contrast, population-based observational designs, which require drug use in larger clinical populations, play no role in approval decisions unless approval in other countries has provided opportunity for observational study. Over the years, the agency has amassed considerable expertise in the design and interpretation of RCTs and in the ethics of randomizing research participants to receive unapproved, investigational drugs. For example, FDA has provided guidance documents on good clinical practice, institutional review boards, and informed consent (FDA, 2011a), and FDA officials have opined on when it is ethically acceptable to use placebos, rather than active comparators, to evaluate an investigational drug (Ellenberg and Temple, 2000; FDA, 2001; Temple and Ellenberg, 2000).

FDA has less experience in undertaking comprehensive assessments of the ethical and scientific issues arising in the postmarketing context, which differs from the premarketing context in several relevant respects. For example, in the premarketing context, a drug's manufacturer sponsors all the research with the investigational drug and generally uses randomized controlled designs developed in consultation with FDA (after Phase 1 and early Phase 2 studies); in contrast, in the postmarketing setting, FDA may be responding to new information about a drug whose benefit–risk profile has been or is being studied by multiple investigators, supported by various funders, using a variety of observational and RCT designs. FDA's decision about what kinds of studies it should require to assess a drug's benefit–risk profile after the drug is on the market may depend heavily on its critical assessment of the evolving evidence base and the evidential gaps that may remain. Because in the postmarketing setting patients may have been taking a drug for many years and others will continue to be prescribed the drug, FDA has the option of requiring observational studies that use existing or routinely collected patient information, an alternative that is not available in the premarketing context. Another difference between the premarketing and postmarketing contexts is that after marketing FDA can require both observational studies and RCTs, either simultaneously or sequentially. Although in the premarketing setting FDA can require multiple research designs and studies, its process typically is to pursue the sequence and progression of research from Phase 1 to Phase 3.

In the premarketing setting for a new molecular entity, access to the investigational drug by patients is possible only through participation in research conducted to satisfy FDA premarketing requirements or through a few other selected avenues that are also controlled by FDA, such as expanded access through "compassionate use" (FDA, 2011b). In the postmarketing setting, physicians are free to prescribe a drug to any patient for whom they think it medically appropriate. In most cases, if a doctor and a patient decide that it is in the patient's medical best interests to take the drug, the patient does not have to enter a research study required by FDA to have access to it.

In the premarketing context, FDA regulators and the manufacturer typically focus on the drug's benefit–risk relationship compared with a placebo and use active comparators less often, typically when it is either ethically or methodologically necessary, such as to evaluate assay sensitivity. In the postmarketing context, concerns about a drug's benefit–risk profile are more likely to involve comparisons with other active treatments. For example, although at the time of approval and for some time thereafter a drug that poses serious risks may have a favorable benefit–risk profile, the acceptability of its profile may come into question when a new drug becomes available and appears to offer comparable benefits with less severe risks.

In the case of Avandia® (rosiglitazone), the presence in the marketplace of the clinical alternative pioglitazone, a similar drug with a purportedly more acceptable benefit–risk profile, affected the public controversy and FDA's response to it. Although the remit of FDA is not to ensure that the drug supply contains only the comparatively "best" drugs for an indication, it has a duty to the public's health to remove or restrict from the supply drugs that pose unacceptable risks in relation to benefit. In this respect, FDA's responsibility to ensure that drugs continue to have a favorable benefit–risk profile may on occasion move the focus of required postmarketing research more toward comparative-effectiveness research or comparative-safety research, which entails the scientific and ethical challenges of doing research in the context of "regular" clinical practice. The public health question at issue in the postmarketing setting is typically what the effect will be of a regulatory decision to limit the use of or withdraw a drug from the market. To answer that question, studies must include the comparators that are most likely to be used in lieu of the drug.

As a public health agency, FDA has ethical obligations both to protect the public from unsafe drugs and to safeguard the rights and interests of research participants who participate in the research that supports the agency's decisions about drug benefits and risks. In both the premarketing and postmarketing contexts, FDA must balance those potentially competing obligations. Difficult choices must be confronted when a study design that seems to offer the greatest potential for obtaining knowledge relevant to the public health question also involves the greatest burden on and risks to research participants.

In the postmarketing setting, there may be circumstances in which it is ethically acceptable to ask patients to participate in research that exposes them to possible risks that are not likely to be outweighed by the prospect of clinical benefit to them, and that are readily avoidable if they use treatment options that are available outside research participation. Although the risks to research participants are required to be "reasonable in relation to anticipated benefits of the research to subjects and society", there is substantial consensus in both domestic regulatory and other guidance documents that various ways of balancing benefit and risk can be ethically justified.

An RCT that might expose research participants to more net risk than they would probably face in regular clinical practice or that offers participants no reasonable expectation of clinical benefit may be justifiable if a question of pressing public health importance is at stake, no other design with a better benefit–risk balance for participants could supply the evidence needed for a responsible regulatory response to that question, FDA uses the findings of the research in formulating its regulatory response, and special safeguards are in place to protect the rights and interests of the research participants. The safeguards should include (1) the determination by an appropriately constituted review committee that the additional net risk is small enough for it to be ethical to ask people whether they are willing to accept the risk *solely* to contribute to the public good, (2) the additional net risk has been minimized by careful study design and implementation of a robust monitoring plan throughout the study, (3) special measures will be taken in the process of soliciting informed consent to confirm that patients understand and willingly accept that they are assuming a net risk beyond what they are likely to face in clinical practice solely in the interest of the public good, and (4) processes will be implemented to ensure that over the course of the trial participants are regularly informed of any changes in clinical practice or the medical literature relevant to assessments of the comparative benefits and risks associated with trial participation and non–research-related clinical management.

Given the complexity of the postmarketing background against which the determination of the types of studies to require must be made, the committee recognizes that there is no simple formula for making such decisions. Instead, it recommends that FDA use two sets of criteria to guide its decisions: general criteria for assessing the advantages and disadvantages of alternative research designs, and the statutory conditions and ethical preferences that favor observational designs over RCTs in the postmarketing setting.

REQUIRING OBSERVATIONAL STUDIES AND RANDOMIZED CONTROLLED TRIALS

General Criteria in Selection of Required Postmarketing Studies

In theory, and assuming that there is no public health need to obtain relevant evidence quickly, an ideal RCT would almost always provide the evidence that regulators need to identify the best regulatory response to the public health question of interest. The design of such an ideal hypothetical trial would be structured to be responsive to the scientific uncertainties that underlie the public health question that is the focus of the regulatory decision. For example, it would use standard therapy or placebo as the comparator, depending on which choice best suits the public health question; it would include patients who have severe disease if the public health question is about those patients; it would have a long duration if that was of interest from a public health standpoint; and so on. It would be designed to secure the best level of adherence that is achievable in a real-world setting. The hypothetical trial would also be designed to minimize bias, nontransportability, and random error.

In practice, however, a number of constraints can make the ideal trial infeasible. Ethical obligations to obtain informed consent mean that the patients in the trial are restricted to those willing to participate, which may not be representative of the source population in important respects, such as risk status. It may be difficult to recruit sufficient numbers of willing patients. Adherence may not reach the maximum achievable. Patients can withdraw from a trial at any time, potentially losing outcome information. Information from studies published while the trial is going on may affect the willingness of patients or physicians to continue. All such departures from the ideal hypothetical trial contribute to imprecision, bias, and nontransportability of results.

The challenge then is to design and conduct a postmarketing study or collection of studies that comes as close as possible to emulating the ideal hypothetical trial while accommodating important ethical and practical considerations. Depending on the circumstances, the type of study design that best approximates the ideal hypothetical trial may be an RCT, but it also may be an observational study, based either on existing data, or prospective data, with a protocol similar to an RCT, except for patient assignment. Deciding which design is better structured to generate the evidence needed to answer the public health question turns on a number of considerations, including

- how strong the safety signal is that motivates the design, and whether it primarily involves an elevation in risk, a decrease in benefit, or both, for either the general population or a definable subgroup.
- time-urgency of the regulatory response.
- how large the change in risks or benefits must be, on both relative and absolute scales, to justify a regulatory response.
- the potential for and likely magnitude of confounding.
- the quality of data to be used in any given design on drug exposure, outcomes, confounders and effect modifiers.
- how study design, conduct or context are likely to affect the transportability of the study results.
- the logistical requirements of a design, including cost, data access, patient availability, and other determinants of feasibility.
- ethical dimensions, consent, confidentiality, and study oversight.

The first consideration is whether resolution of the public health question requires new evidence primarily on a drug's benefits, its risks, or on both. In some cases, the benefit–risk profile is close enough to an unacceptable threshold that obtaining high-quality evidence on both in the same population, in the same study is critical for resolving the public health question. Questions about clinical benefit can arise either because original approval was on the basis of surrogate endpoints, or because a group is subsequently found in whom reduced or absent benefit is suspected. The latter situation falls under a "failure of expected pharmacological action of the drug", which constitutes an adverse drug experience under FDAAA.[4] These situations favor conduct of a large, high-quality RCT with a sufficient followup period to assess longer-term outcomes of interest and sufficient power to detect a risk elevation of public health importance. But if the benefits of a drug are well-characterized and a concern emerges about a new risk, there can be advantages to a broader range of designs, contingent on the other considerations listed.

Combination strategies can be optimal for assessing both benefits and risks (Vandenbroucke and Psaty, 2008). The time interval over which the harms or benefits occur also will affect design. The latent period of some adverse effects (such as cancer) may be too long to ascertain prospectively, requiring retrospective designs examining patients in whom these outcomes that have already occurred. Observational designs that rely on electronic health records or claims data can be used to assessing such risks, whereas small, short-term RCTs can be used to

[4]FDAAA (PL 110-8521) §§ 901(b), 905(a) (2007), USC §§ 355-1(b)(1)(E), (b)(4), and (b)(5) (2010).

assess certain benefits detectable in that time frame, for example, symptom relief, physiologic effects, or biomarker effects.

Second, timeliness is an important practical consideration in deciding among study designs. If a signal is of a serious, unexpected adverse event that gains public notice, the need to take action quickly can be paramount, requiring designs such as case-control studies or case-series with population controls or those based on administrative data, with potential for confounding. At the time of approval, large observational studies may not be feasible until a sufficiently large number of patients start to use the drug. As time passes, however, and more patients are using the drug, such studies become feasible. At that point, experimental studies may take more time to conduct than do observational studies that use existing data sources (such as a health-plan database). In some cases, the decision to require an RCT necessitates a tradeoff between a delay in generating high-quality evidence and a more rapid return of findings that are potentially confounded. As previously noted, the best approach may be a combination strategy in which a range of different observational study types are initiated, with a postmarketing trial required only if the required observational research does not adequately clarify the concern.

Third and fourth are the issues of the magnitude of effect that is being sought, either with respect to benefit or harm, and how this magnitude compares to the expected or plausible degree of confounding. Very large relative increases in the background rate, such as the almost 1,000-fold increase in progressive multifocal leukoencephalopathy with natalizumab treatment in patients with multiple sclerosis or Crohn's Disease (Drazen, 2005; Kleinschmidt-DeMasters and Tyler, 2005; Langer-Gould et al., 2005; Van Assche et al., 2005), or the greater than ten-fold increase in intussusception seen with rotavirus vaccine, are likely beyond the bounds of anything that can be explained through imbalances on other risk factors for those outcomes, that is confounders. In the setting of large relative risks for an adverse event, designs with quite weak control of confounding, like those that compare the number of cases arising from an exposed population to an expected number based on background population rates, might be sufficient for public policy purposes. On the other hand, relative risks of 1.20 to 2.0, within the reach of plausible confounding (depending on case-specific considerations), might require designs with substantial confounding control, such as an RCT or an observational study with a very strong instrumental variable, mimicking randomization. The degree of plausible confounding due to known factors can be modeled, as can be the strength of confounding due to unknown or unmeasured confounders that would be sufficient to create (or obscure) a relationship of a given magnitude (Greenland, 2005).

Another issue when considering the magnitude of effect that must be detectable by a given design is what degree of increase would be relevant to the policy decision. An increase of a rare effect, or one not designated as a "serious adverse event", might not be sufficient to outweigh a drug's benefit. A design is needed that is sufficient to detect a policy-relevant increase in that outcome, which again might justify an observational design with weak confounding control if the policy-relevant effect is large, or a stronger design if the effect is small relative to the potential for confounding. If the event, like myocardial infarction, or serious asthma exacerbations, has a high background rate in the population, then relatively small relative increases (for example, 20 percent to 30 percent) in that rate could raise the absolute risk in the population sufficiently to offset the drug's benefit. In choosing designs for the postmarketing assessment of either benefit or risk, the key considerations then become how large an effect in either benefit or risk is necessary to be of policy relevance.

Fifth is the quality of available data, discussed in Chapter 3. If existing data are of sufficient completeness and quality, it may be possible to provide the evidence that regulators need through an observational design based on that data. With the advance of sophisticated electronic medical records in integrated health care systems that capture patient data accurately and efficiently, and analytic techniques that allow greater approximation of inferences generally reserved for randomized designs, the likelihood that observational studies based on existing data will on occasion be able to provide high-quality evidence about postmarketing risks and, in some cases, postmarketing benefit increases. Indeed, with those developments and the advent of the Sentinel initiative and the Observational Medical Outcomes Partnership (OMOP), observational research is likely to play a larger role in postmarketing risk research, whether conducted by manufacturers as required by FDA or conducted by FDA directly or through FDA contractors (Reskin, 2007; Stang et al., 2010). Even as data sources continue to improve, however, Evans (2012) points out that drug companies and the academic researchers and research firms with which they contract may face challenges accessing data needed for large-scale observational studies held by health care systems, insurance companies, and the like. Such entities are subject to the Privacy Rule and the Administrative Simplification Rule[5] developed in response to the Health Insurance Portability and Accountability Act of 1996 (HIPAA; PL 104-191) which sets strict limits on their ability to release the information in their databases to others (see below for further discussion).

Sixth is the likely transportability of results from a given study. The target population at risk must be defined, and the achievable design measured against its relevance for that population. For example, the public health question may be whether the drug has an acceptable benefit–risk profile in high-risk patients, but the RCT that is deemed feasible may need to exclude some people at high risk for either ethical or practical reasons (for example, patients who have severe disease that may be difficult to enroll and keep under observation). Another factor that often differs between controlled trials and observational studies of community practice is the degree of monitoring or expertise involved in care. If proper use

[5]45 CFR Parts 160 and 164, Subparts A and E.

of a drug, like warfarin, involves close monitoring of drug levels or drug effects (for example, coagulation measures), then the hazards posed by the drug from non-optimal monitoring in non-investigational settings may not be replicable in designs in which the patient is prospectively followed.

Seventh is whether a given design is feasible, with the key factors being patient availability, data availability, cost, and other logistical factors. Some observational studies require only a review of existing data and thus do not require the direct participation of patients or clinicians, but do require this data to be adequate to address the question. With respect to patient availability, there needs to be a sufficient sample of comparable patients both taking and not taking the drug to detect a safety signal of a given magnitude. To the extent that an RCT excludes patients with particular conditions from participation, the pool of people eligible for the study decreases, and it may be challenging to enroll sufficient numbers of participants. Observational studies, either prospective or based on existing data, can typically involve more patients, but this must be assessed against the potential for confounding, selection bias, and measurement error. The act of consent or extensive pre-screening can reduce the pool of patients for both observational studies and RCTs, but the need to agree to randomization in the latter case often reduces that enrollment yet further.

Finally, are ethical dimensions in study design, including consent, confidentiality, and study oversight. Discussions of these elements follow in subsequent sections.

The Presumption in Favor of Observational Designs

FDAAA provides FDA with a starting point for decisions about which type of postmarketing studies to require. FDAAA specifies that in the postmarketing setting FDA may require an RCT only when sufficient information cannot be obtained from an observational study. Specifically, the law states that "[t]he Secretary may not require the responsible person to conduct a study under this paragraph, unless the Secretary makes a determination that the reports under subsection (k)(1) and the active postmarket risk identification and analysis system as available under subsection (k)(3) will not be sufficient to meet the purposes set forth in subparagraph (B)", and that "[t]he Secretary may not require the responsible person to conduct a clinical trial under this paragraph, unless the Secretary makes a determination that a postapproval study or studies will not be sufficient to meet the purposes set forth in subparagraph (B)".[6,7] Thus, the statute explicitly specifies a priority for observational study designs. The committee notes that

[6]21 USC § 355(o)(3)(D)(i), (ii).

[7]The reports referred to in subsection (k)(1) are from the drug sponsor's records of "data relating to clinical experience and other data or information". FDA's Sentinel system is the "active postmarket risk identification and analysis system as available under subsection (k)(3)" of FDAAA.

FDAAA does not provide an explanation for the particular design hierarchy that it imposes on FDA's authority to require manufacturers to conduct postmarketing studies. Clinical trials are generally more expensive and complicated to conduct than observational studies and so are more burdensome for manufacturers. A common view in the ethics of research is that observational studies are also less burdensome for research participants (FDA, 2010a).

All observational studies of a drug's benefits and risks, however, are not equal in their ethical implications. Some observational studies ask patients to respond to surveys or to use special devices that monitor adherence to drug regimens; others impose no burdens on patients and rely only on information available in health records. It is not the case that observational studies are necessarily less risky to patients than randomized designs. Some observational studies impose no clinical risks on patients beyond what they would experience in ordinary clinical care, but that is also true of some RCTs.

However, studies that alter the clinical experience of participants with regard to how their medical condition will be diagnosed or treated generally require more justification and greater protections and oversight than studies that do not. That is so not because they *necessarily* impose more risks on research participants or because they *necessarily* offer participants less in the way of offsetting clinical benefits, but because research that alters the clinical experience of patients in such ways also is likely to alter the norms and expectations of the clinical encounter. Most notably, in the traditional clinical context, treatment choices are made with the intent of bringing about the best outcome for the patient that is commensurate with the patient's values and priorities. That is, they are driven by the patient's and the physician's assessment of that patient's interests. In contrast, treatment assignment in clinical RCTs is determined randomly. Although maximizing benefits and minimizing risks to the particular patients participating in a trial remain goals, these considerations do not determine treatment assignment. Rather, in many trials, both the array of available therapeutic options and the method by which research participants are assigned to them are driven by scientific objectives—that is, the need to obtain a valid answer to a scientific question.

Patients are sometimes better off if they receive their medical care through participation in research that modifies their clinical experience than if they receive it through standard medical practice, even if the modification includes randomization of treatment, that is, there are collateral benefits to participating in a study (King, 2000). In some studies, research-related alterations in clinical management may redound to participants' clinical benefit. In the premarketing context, research participation in a clinical trial may be the only way patients can secure access to a promising new intervention. Although the outcome is uncertain, randomization to the experimental arm of a clinical trial may—if the investigational therapy proves efficacious, safe, and well-tolerated—result in improved health compared with what is likely under standard care. Participation in premarketing clinical trials can be especially attractive for patients who have few if any clinical options.

In the postmarketing context, the potential advantage of access to a promising experimental intervention is less relevant; unless distribution of the drug is restricted—for example, by a risk evaluation and mitigation strategy—or patients have financial barriers to access, the drug is available for physicians to prescribe in standard practice and thus for patients to use. Recruitment of research participants can be more problematic when the intervention or drug is available outside the trial (Campbell et al., 2004). One possible explanation is that patients are not interested in the uncertainty that randomization introduces when they already have unimpeded access to the treatment option that they prefer. The principal health advantage of research participation to patients in the postmarketing context, when FDA has required research in response to a safety signal, is the prospect that research participation may offer them regular or extra clinical monitoring. However, clinical monitoring may in the end involve more burden than benefit.

The relative merits of RCTs and observational studies in the postmarketing context are thus more nuanced than the statutory conditions prioritizing observational designs stipulated in FDAAA, which, for example, does not distinguish between observational studies that impose burdens or additional risks on patients and observational studies that do not. Nonetheless, because RCTs alter a particularly salient feature of a patient's clinical experience in the postmarketing context, the committee believes that the *general* requirement established by FDAAA in favor of observational research is ethically justifiable and consonant with FDA's ethical obligations to research participants in the postmarketing context.

Circumstances Justifying the Requirement of Observational Studies and RCTs

The circumstances under which FDA is justified in requiring a manufacturer to conduct a postmarketing *observational study* are those in which

- uncertainty about the benefit–risk balance is such that a responsible decision about the future regulatory status of the drug cannot be made on the basis of existing evidence or evidence that can be obtained by existing surveillance activities.
- it is expected that an observational study can be properly designed and implemented to reduce uncertainty about the benefit–risk balance sufficiently to inform a responsible regulatory decision.
- FDA will use the results of the observational study in making the regulatory decision in a timely fashion.
- the observational study can be carried out in a manner that provides sufficient protection of and respect for research participants.

It should be emphasized that it would be unethical for FDA not to require an RCT in a context in which only an RCT can provide the kind of evidence needed to inform the regulatory decision on a public health question. FDAAA permits FDA to require an RCT in such cases. When the primary public health concern is about a drug's risks, observational designs can often provide evidence of sufficient quality for regulatory decision-making. However, if the adverse event of concern can be pre-specified, is expected to occur frequently and soon after initiation of drug treatment, and the relative risk is moderate, RCTs may be more appropriate (Golder et al., 2011). In such cases, the quality of evidence produced by RCTs may be superior to that obtainable with observational studies,[8] and, depending on the public health question and relevant ethical and practical considerations, the additional quality may be of sufficient regulatory importance to justify FDA's requiring an RCT.

In addition, if evidence emerges that a marketed drug is not producing the intended effect—that is, it is not producing the clinical benefit that it was approved to produce—FDAAA allows FDA to require a study to re-evaluate the drug's benefit–risk profile. Because the focus would be on the drug's benefits, it is less likely that observational studies would provide evidence of sufficient quality to answer the public health question, given concerns about confounding and potential limitations in the ability to control for these concerns. RCTs are likely to be needed to aid decision-making when the primary concern in the postmarketing context is a drug's intended effects or its effectiveness.

Thus, FDA is sometimes ethically justified in requiring a postmarketing RCT using its authorities in FDAAA.[9] The circumstances under which FDA is justified in requiring a manufacturer to conduct a postmarketing RCT are those in which

- uncertainty about the benefit–risk balance is such that a responsible decision about the future regulatory status of the drug cannot be made on the basis of existing evidence or evidence that could be obtained from new observational studies.
- it is expected that an RCT can be properly designed and implemented to reduce uncertainty about the benefit–risk balance sufficiently to inform a responsible regulatory decision.
- FDA will use trial results in the making of the regulatory decision in a timely fashion.
- the RCT can be carried out in a manner that provides sufficient protection of and respect for research participants.

Whether this last, independent condition is satisfied hinges on such issues as the ability to obtain meaningful informed consent, whether the risks to research

[8]Basic design variations of RCTs are described in Strom (2005).

[9]21 USC § 355(o) (2010).

participants in the trial can be justified, the presence of a robust safety-monitoring plan and other mechanisms for minimizing risk and harm to participants, and the equitable selection of participants.

Determining whether the other conditions are satisfied entails a thorough assessment of the evidence available and potentially available from observational studies. That assessment would be expected to address a number of questions, such as the following:

- What are the limitations of the available evidence and the studies that provided it, and how important are these limitations?
- Have possible uses of all existing data pertaining to the public health question been adequately explored?
- What new information could FDA reasonably expect to obtain from new observational studies?
- Would unacceptably large knowledge gaps or levels of uncertainty remain if FDA relied on observational studies or required additional observational studies to be conducted?

That determination also requires assessment of the likelihood that an RCT can provide the missing information with such questions as these:

- Is it likely that a sufficient number of the eligible research participants could be recruited?
- Is the expected timeframe of such a study to return information sufficient to inform FDA's policy decision?
- Would an appropriately designed RCT entail serious practicability issues?

DESIGN, ANALYTIC, AND ETHICAL CONSIDERATIONS IN SELECTING SPECIFIC OBSERVATIONAL AND RCT DESIGNS TO REQUIRE

Observational Studies

The determination by FDA that the additional evidence it needs to resolve a public health question can be obtained with observational studies presupposes that FDA has already identified a specific type of observational design that is both capable of generating the needed data and can be feasibly and ethically implemented. The success of an observational study in generating valid and reliable evidence requires access to sufficient high-quality data on the interventions compared, the outcomes of interest, and potential confounders to allow researchers to use analytic techniques that can approximate randomization to intervention assignment and preserve the study's implications for causal inference.

As a general rule, observational studies should be designed so that the start of the clinical interventions to be compared coincides with the start of followup. Studies with followup observation that begins after the initiation of drug treatment may be affected by selection bias. If the drug affects the early risk of developing the outcome, then cases that occurred between the initiation of the drug and the initiation of followup will be disproportionately excluded from the treated group (Danaei et al., 2012; Hernán et al., 2008; Robins et al., 2007). Also, including people who are already taking the drug is problematic if the drug alters risk factors for the outcome of interest and thus makes controlling for potential confounders difficult. Controlling for potential confounders may result in adjusting for variables on the causal pathway and result in a false conclusion that there is no association between the drug and the outcome of interest (that is, a false-negative conclusion), but not adjusting for them may lead to confounding and biased estimates of the drug's effect (Fisher, 1996).

One design to emulate the ideal hypothetical trial is the prospective cohort study in which a sample of persons (a cohort) is followed to see whether they develop the outcomes of interest. Like a clinical trial, these studies should have pre-specified protocols, endpoints, analytic plans, and procedures in place to ensure timely recruitment, adequate and uniform follow-up, ascertainment and adjudication of endpoints, and other steps to ensure data quality. Data on exposure (that is, drug treatment) and other covariates of interest are collected at baseline before the initiation of treatment and, depending on the specific design, may continue to be collected throughout the study. Patients are monitored throughout the defined risk period to determine whether and when they experience the event of interest. The data are analyzed to estimate the effect of the exposure on the outcome of interest among groups defined by exposure status.

Case–control and case–cohort designs may also be used to generate data on the endpoint of interest to the regulatory decision but use only a sample of persons in the cohort. Rather than selecting patients on the basis of the exposure of interest and observing whether they develop the outcome of interest, case–control designs select persons on the basis of whether they have experienced the outcome of interest and then select controls—persons who have not experienced the outcome of interest—to compare their past exposures (such as use of a particular drug). One potential weakness of such designs, if drug exposure is obtained, for example, by patient self report, is that the knowledge of the outcome is potentially known, and, therefore, can bias the ascertainment of the exposure. Steps must be taken to assure this does not occur.

Case–control and case–cohort designs are especially helpful when the measurement of a key variable is difficult or expensive, when health outcomes in an administrative claims database need to be validated against actual medical records, when the outcome is too rare to study prospectively, or when additional data collection is required to measure confounders. In those settings, case–control designs may be more efficient for emulating the hypothetical RCT by reducing the logistical burden of sampling and generating data. Box 4-1 provides an example of an observational case–control study that uses electronic health care records that detected an increased risk of an adverse outcome associated with the use of a drug.

Selecting the appropriate comparison group is key in the design of observational studies. In an RCT, randomization is used to ensure an equal distribution of measured and unmeasured risk factors in large samples, and this reduces the

BOX 4-1
Rofecoxib and Coronary Heart Disease: An Observational Study

A nested case–control study was conducted with computer records from the database of an integrated managed-care organization to evaluate the risk of acute myocardial infarction (MI) and sudden cardiac death among users of rofecoxib and users of celecoxib and nonselective nonsteroidal anti-inflammatory drugs (NSAIDs) (Graham et al., 2005).[a] The study population comprised people who filled at least one prescription for rofecoxib, celecoxib, or a nonselective NSAID between January 1, 1999, and December 31, 2001; who met medical eligibility criteria; and who had at least 12 months of health-plan coverage before their entry into the cohort, which allowed the researchers to obtain data on potential risk factors for serious coronary arterial disease. The exposure status of cases and controls was classified on the basis of the number of pills dispensed, and ascertainment of outcomes was validated through studies of computerized hospital and laboratory data. A telephone survey of a "random sample of controls currently exposed to celecoxib, ibuprofen, naproxen, or rofecoxib, or controls with remote exposure to a NSAID" was used to assess potential confounding by variables that were not included in the computer database (such as use of over-the-counter NSAIDs, smoking, and family history of MI). The results of this observational study provided strong high-quality evidence that supported the hypothesis that the use of rofecoxib increases the risk of serious coronary heart disease compared with celecoxib and other NSAIDS. In fact, at a March 2007 Food and Drug Administration–organized, public meeting on the Sentinel system, Dr. Richard Platt discussed the potential of a system such as Sentinel, if it has enough sets of records, detecting a signal for myocardial infarctions within months of rofecoxib entering the market (FDA, 2007). Well-designed observational studies can provide evidence of sufficient quality for regulatory decision-making and may be completed in much less time than a randomized controlled trial.

[a]Clinical trials of rofecoxib are discussed in Chapter 2.

possibility of confounding. Through the selection of an appropriate comparison group, observational studies can emulate the hypothetical RCT and limit confounding by attempting to achieve a similar distribution of known risk factors between groups.

Observational cohort designs that come the closest to emulating an RCT are those that can build into their design a feature or "instrument" that mimics randomization. This instrument must be highly correlated with the receipt of treatment, but not by itself related to the outcome. In this way, treatment assignment can mathematically resemble the flip of a coin, determining treatment assignment but with no relation to the outcome. The most common "instrument" is practice location, when there is variation in the use of a particular drug that is a function of local practice patterns but that has little to do with the kinds of patients seen. When such an instrument exists, "instrumental variable" methods of analysis can produce results quite similar to randomized controlled trials (Hernán and Robins, 2006; Mcclellan et al., 1994). The validity of the assumptions underlying the claim for a given instrument, however, must be closely scrutinized; those assumptions typically cannot be tested empirically.

The choice of a comparison group can also affect measurement error. Some new drugs, especially ones that are first in their class (that is, the first drug in a given class to be used), may make the selection of a comparator difficult. For example, patients who are first to use a newly approved drug are likely to differ in many ways from patients who are using traditional and previously approved therapies. For example, they may have better insurance coverage or the ability otherwise to afford expensive new medications. Or they may not be doing well on previously approved therapies or may have physicians who are early adopters of new interventions. Such differences may influence the identification or ascertainment of health outcomes of interest.

Case reports or series are usually ranked near the bottom in traditional evidence hierarchies and are useful for generating hypotheses about features such as latency period, drug-drug interactions and susceptible populations, (Concato et al., 2000; Stolberg et al., 2004), but, for the most part, do not emulate the hypothetical RCT in relevant respects. However, they may in some cases be able to provide critical information about especially risky endpoints. As noted previously, an adverse effect may be so unusual and so rare in the untreated population that there is little need for a well-defined comparison group. Many drug-safety problems, such as drug-induced liver injury, are identified and confirmed by using little more than reported occurrence rates in exposed patients and general information about population rates of the adverse effect.

High-quality observational research can provide sufficient evidence to ground a well-reasoned regulatory decision; in some cases, such research can provide more relevant and timely evidence than any feasible RCT.

Observational studies of harm outcomes have some advantages over RCTs. In the case of some safety signals, additional analysis of the adverse-event reporting data with relative reporting rates (comparing observed to expected numbers of adverse event reports) may be the quickest method of obtaining additional information. For other signals, simple analyses of administrative data may be the best step; for still others, analytic epidemiologic efforts or designs that involve direct contact with patients may be required.

Choosing among observational designs requires that risks to research participation be reasonable in relation to a study's expected benefits and that the risks be kept to a minimum. In observational study designs that rely exclusively on existing data, the major risk to participants typically is breach of confidentiality. Ethical concerns about such studies are tractable as long as the study protocol includes adequate provisions for data security and confidentiality that are closely adhered to by the investigators and research staff. Observational studies that involve collection of new data directly from participants raise further ethical issues related to the burden on participants. Such burdens may range from inconvenience and loss of time associated with the completion of questionnaires and interviews to physical risks associated with medical tests that are done purely for research purposes. Selecting an observational design that involves an increased burden on research participants over designs that involve a smaller burden requires a determination that the additional benefit outweighs the increased burden.

While often methodologically superior to studies that use existing data, an FDA-required postmarketing observational study that requires the collection of new data—such as a study for which followup begins at the same time as the start of the clinical intervention—can raise ethical issues that are parallel in some respects to the issues raised by an RCT, assuming both are initiated at the same time in the drug's lifecycle. In both cases, some patients are starting to take a drug about which FDA is sufficiently concerned to require research. In the case of the observational study, the decision to take the drug is made by the treating physician in consultation with the patient; FDA plays no direct role in that decision. In the case of the RCT, the patient is randomly assigned to take the drug in a trial that FDA has required be conducted. As a consequence, FDA arguably has different ethical obligations to patients in the RCT than it has to patients in the prospective observational study. That said, from the standpoint of the rights and interests of patient participants, it is not possible to determine in the abstract if it is preferable for FDA to require a prospective observational study or an RCT. The answer to that question will depend on the specifics of the situation, including the nature and severity of the concern that prompted FDA to require research, the state of the relevant evidence, and current clinical practice patterns with regard to the drug and any alternative treatments. It is important to emphasize, however, that if FDA already had decided that the available evidence was sufficient to warrant a regulatory action to restrict access to the drug, it would not be requiring research.

Nevertheless, in such circumstances, there may be ethical advantages to FDA's requiring an observational design that is retrospective in the sense that patients have already been exposed to the drug of interest or its comparator, with the outcome already having occurred. Although physicians may continue to prescribe the drug, the success of the research does not depend on their doing so. Moreover, assuming that the public health question of interest can be adequately addressed, a retrospective design may allow FDA to better honor its ethical obligations to the public by allowing it to make a more rapid determination as to whether any new regulatory action is needed to protect the public's health. The ability of such designs to provide the information FDA requires for regulatory action rests, in turn, not only on the availability of high quality of data but also on access to that data. Access is itself a function of ethical considerations related to privacy and authorization, a tension that the committee recognizes is likely to occur increasingly and in different forms; a structure to provide guidance on ethical challenges as they emerge over time could help FDA resolve such tensions, particularly for activities that are not or may not be subject to Institutional Review Board (IRB) review.

Randomized Controlled Trials

If FDA determines that the evidence that it needs to resolve a public health question includes data obtainable only with an RCT, it must then determine which type of RCT to require. Just as in the selection of observational studies, FDA should consider which RCT would best approximate the ideal hypothetical trial, subject to ethical, legal, and practical constraints.

As with observational studies, the choice of a comparator for a drug is an important element in the design of an RCT. If in current clinical practice there is no alternative treatment to the drug whose performance is to be studied, placebo-controlled trials or trials that involve standard care (such as symptom management) are the main options.[10] Placebo-controlled trials have routinely satisfied FDA's criterion of "adequate and well-controlled studies" for the purpose of drug approval.

If an effective treatment is available for the same indication, an active-controlled design (a head-to-head trial, defined as a comparison of two active treatments indicated for the same patients with the same conditions) is often preferred on both ethical and public health grounds; in the postmarketing setting, there may be additional scientific reasons for considering an active-controlled design. As noted previously, the public health question at issue in most postmarketing regulatory decisions is whether the health of the public would on balance be better if the drug in question were removed from the market or its use were limited. Under either scenario, medical practice would presumably shift to alternative interventions, perhaps nonpharmacologic, if no drug for the same indica-

[10]One difference between placebo-controlled studies and studies that use standard care is that blinding is possible in the former but typically not in the latter.

tion existed. In that situation, at least one arm of any postmarketing study should include the most likely alternative treatment. That does not mean that FDA must act to restrict use of the drug of concern if it proves inferior to its active control on either effectiveness or safety; to do so could constitute too fine a regulation of medical practice. Many drugs remain on the market when they have been superseded by newer therapies that have superior benefit–risk profiles. Sometimes these drugs are preferred by a subset of patients who have different perspectives on which risks are most important to avoid or minimize. But such comparisons would provide the needed evidence for a regulatory decision, including whether the availability of the inferior therapy constitutes a true public health risk because its benefit–risk profile is judged to be unacceptable.

The primary rationale for the use of the active-controlled design in the regulatory setting is sometimes an ethical one. The ethics of placebo-controlled trials have been discussed at length in the literature (Castro, 2007; CHMP, 2011; Emanuel and Miller, 2001; Halpern et al., 2002; Lurie and Wolfe, 1998; Miller and Rosenstein, 2002; Temple and Ellenberg, 2000). There is a longstanding view that it is unethical to conduct a placebo-controlled trial if an effective treatment that prevents or treats a serious or life-threatening condition is available. It may be ethically acceptable for FDA to require a placebo-controlled postmarketing trial even if an alternative treatment is available under some specific circumstances—such as studies of interventions intended to provide symptomatic relief for minor, self-limiting conditions—if the trial can answer the public health question. In addition, placebos are often used in short-term trials to evaluate surrogate endpoints, such as blood pressure or lipid profiles.

One RCT design that can be implemented most easily early after the introduction of a drug is a cluster randomized design, when regions, practices, or hospitals are randomized to use that drug for specified indications. This is more difficult but still possible once the drug is in wide use (Hennessy et al., 2010; Mazor et al., 2007; Platt et al., 2010). Cluster randomized designs combine some of the features and advantages of observational and randomized designs in being easier to implement randomization and enroll large populations, capturing many of the characteristics of care in community settings, and retaining advantages of randomization, but being somewhat more susceptible to confounding and having lower precision than an individually randomized RCT of equal size.

THE FOOD AND DRUG ADMINISTRATION'S ETHICAL OBLIGATIONS REGARDING THE CONDUCT AND OVERSIGHT OF REQUIRED POSTMARKETING STUDIES

As noted by the National Bioethics Advisory Commission, two principal mechanisms of protecting research participants are *independent peer review*, such as that provided by IRBs, and *voluntary informed consent* (National Bioethics Advisory Commission, 2001 #3514; National Bioethics Advisory Commission,

2001 #3514). To those can be added *safety monitoring* during the course of the research, which can be particularly important in the postmarketing context if concerns about risk have already been raised. This section addresses FDA's duties to ensure that the postmarketing research it requires is conducted ethically; it explores FDA's responsibilities with respect to each of the mechanisms of protection, including FDA's role in the ethical oversight of such research.

Informed Consent Issues in the Postmarketing Setting

One component of FDA's obligation to ensure that required postmarketing research is conducted ethically focuses on securing the voluntary informed consent of research participants. An important goal of the general requirement that research participants provide voluntary informed consent is to verify that they have freely agreed to participate on the basis of an accurate understanding of the research purpose and procedures, its potential benefits and risks, and the alternatives to participation. It is a basic principle of research ethics that participants who would be placed at risk in human research should receive an understandable, unbiased, accurate, and appropriate disclosure of the potential benefits and risks attached to study participation (DHEW, 1979; ICH, 1996). The general requirements for disclosure have been codified and described in federal regulations[11] and are now well-understood by IRBs and investigators, particularly for premarketing studies. However, a few issues are worth noting when considering the application of informed consent requirements to studies of already marketed drugs.

Observational Designs

One key issue is that the ethical obligation to obtain prior informed consent is not applicable to all required postmarketing research; some observational designs are in many relevant respects similar to activities that are not considered to be research, or research with human participants. Surveillance and other activities undertaken by FDA to monitor for and pursue the benefits and risks of marketed drugs, including the activities of Sentinel (McGraw et al., 2012; Rosati et al., 2010), have been determined by relevant federal offices to be public health practice, and not research. A number of human-subjects research regulations, including those requiring informed consent, do not apply if an activity is considered public health practice. It is often impossible, however, to draw a clear or ethically relevant distinction between some kinds of observational research that FDA could require manufacturers to conduct and FDA activities that are classified as public health practice. For example, if FDA were to require a postmarketing

[11] See, for example, the eight basic elements and six *additional* disclosures that FDA requires be presented to research subjects, at 21 CFR 50.25(a)(b). The same categories are found at 45 CFR 46.116(a)(b).

observational study that entailed only secondary use of de-identified data, as is the current practice in the Sentinel Initiative, requiring the consent of participants for that study but not for a Sentinel activity would be difficult to defend.

Nowhere is it clearly stated whether FDA's human subjects regulations (21 CFR 50 and 56), rather than the Common Rule (45 CFR 46 Subpart A), are the operative regulations for FDA-required, postmarketing observational studies. FDA's 2011 guidance to industry-related postmarketing requirements states that "[a]pplicants conducting postmarketing studies and clinical trials must continue to comply with . . . Health and Human Services (HHS) and FDA human subject protection regulations at 45 CFR part 46 and 21 CFR parts 50 and 56 when applicable", but it is not clear whether FDA's definition of "clinical investigations" includes any types of observational studies. It is also not clear whether in 21 CFR 50—which appears to have been designed with clinical trials in mind—observational studies are subjected to more, less or different requirements for review and consent than would be applicable under the Common Rule. For example, unlike the Common Rule, FDA's human subjects regulation does not appear to permit exceptions to the informed consent requirement. Thus, even if HIPAA is not a significant obstacle to drug companies securing access to health information without prior consent for required postmarketing observational research, which Evans (2012) maintains is unlikely, FDA's human subjects regulations might still impose informed consent requirements, making the conduct of at least some kinds of observational studies infeasible. Whether the barrier is HIPAA, FDA human subjects regulations, or both, as Evans (2012) argues, the end result might be restriction, if not elimination, of the role of at least some required observational studies from the arsenal of FDA's responses to safety signals. That outcome would likely be ethically and scientifically unacceptable, and counter to the interests of the public's health.

Going forward, it is important that FDA clarify whether its human subjects regulations govern required postmarketing observational studies, and, if so, how FDA will address and will expect IRBs to address any differences in oversight and research participant protections, including consent requirements, for different observational designs between 21 CFR 50 and 45 CFR 46 so that its regulations are not a bar to what would otherwise be ethically acceptable observational designs. FDA also will need to determine how best to ensure that required postmarketing observational studies can be feasibly conducted, in view of HIPAA and other potential constraints, while still protecting the privacy of the people whose data are used.

Moreover, it is likely that the use of large data sets to pursue concerns about the benefits and risks of marketed drugs will only increase, whether conducted under the auspices of FDA-supported surveillance systems like Sentinel and deemed public health practice, or, assuming the aforementioned issues can be addressed, conducted by manufacturers as required by FDA and interpreted by at least some to be research. It is also likely that the desirability of linking data sets and of obtaining additional information from patients or otherwise needing access to some identifying information about patients will increase over time, raising additional ethical questions about the adequacy of data security practices, authorization for access to different data sets and different research and public health purposes, and beyond. In order to assure the public that surveillance and required observational studies are conducted with appropriate controls and protections, an independent advisory body should be formed by FDA. In the near term, this body should advise FDA on how to resolve the challenges of human subjects regulatory oversight and access to health data for required postmarketing observational studies. Going forward, this body will be needed to advise FDA on the ethics of the postmarketing research and surveillance activities involving large data sets that it conducts or requires, including, for example, activities that raise questions about re-identification of data or of linking to new or existing identifiable information.

Randomized Controlled Trials

Although there is commentary defending the conduct of some clinical trials without prior express consent (Faden et al., 2011; Largent et al., 2011; Truog et al., 1999), the dominant view in research ethics is that clinical trials are paradigmatic of the sorts of study designs that must involve informed consent. Informed consent obligations may be especially salient in the context of required *postmarketing* trials because patients may be asked to submit to a drug regimen where a safety signal has prompted concerns about risk, and possibly about the acceptability of the drug's benefit–risk profile.

Investigators, IRBs, and FDA should ensure that several kinds of disclosure are made in the informed consent process. First, it is important to provide information about why a new study is required. This may be particularly true for persons already taking the drug who may undergo a change in regimen as a result of study participation. Prospective research participants need to understand why additional research is important even though the drug that they are taking was found by FDA to have a favorable benefit–risk profile on the basis of existing evidence. They also need to understand why, since the study is prompted by concerns about risk or the drug's benefit–risk profile, it is still considered to be ethically acceptable to ask them to consider participating in the study. To convey that information, the informed consent process may involve providing general information about how experts view the relative benefits and risks associated with the different medications to be administered in the study, as well as the important public health question driving the need to conduct the study, and the societal benefit that is expected to result from the study. In addition, provisions may need to be made to ensure adequate discussion of how well patients' existing treatment is working for them.

Second, special care may be needed to ensure that prospective participants understand the risks posed by study participation in the postmarketing context. When a substantial amount of information indicating that a drug to be studied may involve serious risks has already accumulated, there are heightened obligations to ensure that potential research participants understand the risks posed by study enrollment. Those obligations may include special efforts to communicate complex risk information clearly and to establish that research participants understand what the risks mean to them. The emphasis given to risk information in the consent process should increase with the severity of risk and the level of confidence about the causal association between the drug and the adverse outcome. At a minimum, risks that should be disclosed should include any boxed warnings, the "major statement" currently listed in direct-to-consumer advertisements, any adverse-event findings of an FDA advisory committee, and a summary of evidence from published peer-reviewed studies.

Communicating complicated risk information and research findings to potential research participants poses challenges to investigators, IRB, and participants. To fulfill the ethical obligation to obtain informed consent, research participants should understand what is being asked of them, including the benefits (if any) and risks, and not merely be given information (Faden and Beauchamp, 1986). It can be difficult for potential participants to understand the nature, purpose and risks of clinical research. For example, it is well established that some research participants in clinical trials have difficulty understanding the role that randomization plays in their care and believe that treatment decisions are being determined solely based on what is in their medical best interests even when they are not (Appelbaum et al., 1987; Joffe et al., 2001; Kodish et al., 2004; Wendler, 2009). At the very least, a "kitchen sink" approach to consent-form drafting, in which voluminous information is included with little attempt to distill it into a short format that is useful to potential participants, should be avoided. Research participants are likely to be overwhelmed by a long and complex form and unable to weigh conflicting study findings or findings about different types of risk. That is particularly true of people who have low levels of health literacy or educational attainment. Special efforts should be made to ensure that they understand the study information. For example, there is a growing set of additional resources (such as decision aids, videos, and interactive electronic presentations) to supplement written materials that may enhance potential research participants' understanding of complex clinical information. Although evidence about the effectiveness of techniques designed to improve and document understanding by potential research participants is mixed (Kass and Taylor, 2008), such interventions as engaging in additional personal conversations with potential participants (Flory and Emanuel, 2004; Kass and Taylor, 2008; Lindegger et al., 2006) and asking them to explain the study to a friend (Lindegger et al., 2006) have been shown to be helpful.

Whatever efforts are used to communicate with potential research participants, it is important that they include information that is useful to participants about where the weight of the evidence falls with regard to serious risks and the level of confidence that experts have in drawing conclusions about the risks. A statement that "some studies have found that the drug causes X, whereas other studies have not" may be true but misleading if nearly all well-designed studies have reached the same conclusion and there is little or no reliable evidence on the other side.

Third, in addition to considerations of benefits and risks, people who are considering participation in research need to know how the care that they will receive in a protocol may differ from the care that they would ordinarily receive. Thus, information about "Alternatives to Participation" should convey the current standard of care for the health condition that the study drug targets. That is particularly crucial in cases in which medical practice has shifted away from prescribing the study drug because accumulating evidence from passive surveillance, observational studies, and small trials or meta-analyses suggests that another therapy is as effective and has a more favorable risk profile. A statement that if a potential participant does not enroll in the trial, he or she is more likely to have a different drug prescribed should be communicated in this situation. If clinical practice continues to shift during the trial period, the statement should be strengthened; researchers have an ethical obligation to disclose all new developments that may affect a person's willingness to continue to participate in a research study.

The Thiazolidinedione Intervention with Vitamin D Evaluation (TIDE) study provides an example of a consent form that did not satisfy those disclosure requirements.[12] Graham and Gelperin (2010) outlined a number of concerns with that form at the July 13, 2010, Joint Meeting of the Endocrinologic and Metabolic Drugs Advisory Committee and the Drug Safety and Risk Management Advisory Committee, including a misleading study title and the absence of a clear statement of purpose. The committee agrees that the TIDE consent form is inadequate in several key respects—most notably, in not providing information about the issues discussed above—and should not have been approved by an IRB or ethics review board: it is too long, too complex, too confusing, poorly organized, lacks clear explanations of the purpose and procedures to be followed, and excludes or renders opaque important information that a reasonable person might need to have prior to deciding whether to participate. The committee outlines its concerns, in addition to those of Graham and Gelperin (2010), in Box 4-2.

Comprehensive informed consent processes can help to ensure that trial participants understand the potential consequences of study participation in addition to what they are contributing to the advancement of public health in the regulatory arena. They cannot, however, serve as an exclusive or sufficient ethi-

[12]The Thiazolidinedione Intervention with Vitamin D Evaluation (TIDE) study informed consent form is available at http://www.circare.org/consents/Avandia-TIDE-trial_consentform.pdf (accessed March 3, 2012).

BOX 4-2
The Committee's Concerns with Informed Consent in the Thiazolidinedione Intervention with Vitamin D Evaluation (TIDE) Trial[a,b]

1. Study Title

- The study title does not provide an accurate description of the study. It describes the study as a cardiovascular endpoint trial without referring to cardiovascular disease, and it does not mention that rosiglitazone is the primary source of cardiovascular concern in the study.

2. Discussion of the Purpose of the Study

- There is no clear statement of the purpose of the study, and the emphasis in the consent form is shifted away from the cardiovascular risks by the extent of discussion of other aspects of the study. For example, acute myocardial infarction is mentioned only 5 times, whereas cancer and Vitamin D are mentioned 4 and 18 times, respectively.
- Multiple unrelated potential side effects are lumped together (for example, it refers to heart attack, stroke, death, broken bone, and cancers as "diseases").
- Rosiglitazone and pioglitazone are discussed together, which could be interpreted to mean that current evidence suggests that they pose the same risks. There is no clear statement indicating that Food and Drug Administration (FDA) is not concerned about cardiovascular effects with pioglitazone.
- The form does not highlight that the association between vitamin D and cancer was weak.
- It is not made clear that the inclusion of a Vitamin D arm in the study is not relevant to the reason study was required (that is, concerns about the adverse cardiovascular effects of rosiglitazone), and the discussion about Vitamin D and cancer introduces confusion and could be distracting.
- There is no mention that the purpose of the trial was to establish whether or not there is harm definitively, and the wording does not make clear that there is conflicting evidence about whether thiazolidinedione or Vitamin D helps or harms.
- The fact that the previous data suggest opposing results is not made clear.
- There is no mention that GlaxoSmithKline was ordered by FDA to do the study.

continued

BOX 4-2 continued

- Some of the language is confusing. For example, in the following sentence on page 1 of the form, what the agents are being added to is not clear: "This study will compare adding a [thiazolidinedione] (either rosiglitazone or pioglitazone) to adding a placebo (a pill with no active ingredients)".
- The outcomes being studied are combined together in a run-on sentence, and will likely make little sense to someone reading it. A clear statement, perhaps in bullet form, of what the outcomes are would be preferable.
- The paragraph about ethics review is misplaced. It should be in a separate place, such as on Page 4 in the section titled "Monitoring".

3. Discussion of the Study Procedures

- Eligibility criteria should be clearly stated in a distinct section of the informed consent form to avoid patients automatically think that they will be enrolled in the study if they sign the consent form. Eligibility in the TIDE study is not clear. For example, the first sentence in the study procedures section mentions that "if you agree to be considered", whereas the first two sentences of the "Introduction" assert that, "You are invited to take part in a research project, You have been considered because [explain reason]".
- The second page of the "Procedures, Visits, Randomization Strategy" section contains lengthy paragraphs that are very difficult to understand. It would help to have better formatting or organization (for example, providing a timetable of visits and describing what would happen at each visit), and to include introductory sentences (such as "This study is scheduled to last 2 years, with a longer-term follow-up study planned as well. If you agree to participate you will be expected to participate for at least 2 years, with XX visits over that time").

4. Discussion of Long-Term Follow-Up

- The duration of follow-up is not clear. This section states that long-term follow-up is a maximum of 5 years, whereas elsewhere in the document it states that it is up to 10 years.
- This section contains the description of long-term follow-up, reminders that patients can withdraw from the study, and encouragements

to participate in the study. Those multiple messages dilute the key, simple message that this section is supposed to convey.

5. **Discussion of Possible Side Effects, Risks, Discomforts**
   - No explanation of the likelihood of the risks manifesting as harms is included in this section.
   - The lengths of some of the descriptions of risks are not commensurate with the severity of the adverse events. For example, there is a paragraph about low-risk blood draws and electrocardiograms, but only a brief description of other risks.
   - The organization of the discussion of risks is confusing. For example, discussing the risks from all thiazolidinedione first, and then discussing the risks specific to rosiglitazone and pioglitazone is confusing.
   - Although there is a paragraph devoted to the company's prior safety data about rosiglitazone, the importance of that information is not clear because of its wording and location. The paragraph reads more as a type of liability statement rather than a statement about risk of heart attack to those participating. Its location after the discussion of additional risks from rosiglitazone make it less likely that potential research participants will take not of it.
   - The consent form's disclosure about "important new information" is worded such that it is not clear if this information is about adverse events.

6. **Other Issues**
   - There is no mention of the 2007 FDA advisory committee vote, labeling differences between rosiglitazone and pioglitazone, or the American Diabetes Association recommendation against using rosiglitazone.
   - The trade names for Avandia and Actos should be mentioned by name earlier in the document.

---

[a] A number of these concerns were previously outlined by Graham and Gleperin (2010).
[b] The Thiazolidinedione Intervention with Vitamin D Evaluation (TIDE) study informed consent form is available at http://www.circare.org/consents/Avandia-TIDE-trial_consentform.pdf (accessed March 3, 2012).

cal justification for conducting a postmarketing trial. The other justifications for initiating a trial should be independently satisfied. People should not be asked to assume risks that are not justified in light of the benefits of the trial to participants or society. Particularly in research settings in which participants have low literacy, low income, and poor access to modern health care and medicines, even a robust consent process may do little to countervail the pressures that lead people to participate in research. Regulators, IRBs, and data-monitoring committees (DMCs) should serve as particularly strong bulwarks against unethical research in such settings.

Safety Monitoring in the Postmarketing Research

Among the ethical requirements for conducting postmarketing clinical trials (or other studies that alter the experience of participants in ways that pose risks of harm)—whether they are required by FDA or not—is a comprehensive and robust risk-monitoring plan. This is necessary to address a key criterion for continuing approval of the study by IRBs, that there is "adequate provision for monitoring the data collected to ensure the safety of subjects".[13] In the case of studies that FDA has required, it is also necessary to fulfill FDA's ethical responsibility to the research participants whose clinical experience its decision has affected. For example, despite significant concerns about risk, there was no DMC for the Vioxx trials of older adults, which was a surprise to FDA when it inquired about the trials' mortality findings (Psaty and Kronmal, 2008).

For all FDA-required postmarketing clinical trials, a properly qualified DMC should be appointed and given a written charter and pre-specified data-monitoring plan. The data-monitoring plan should include statistical guidelines for stopping the trial early (Ellenberg et al., 2003; Grant et al., 2005). The DMC should meet before trial initiation to review and approve the charter, protocol, and monitoring procedures and then at regular intervals to review not just outcomes and adverse events, but also indicators of whether the research team is adhering strictly to the protocol and of the quality of data being collected. The frequency and intensity of ongoing DMC review should be determined on the basis of the seriousness, incidence, and timing of known or possible harms of the study drug to research participants.

As discussed in the letter report (IOM, 2010), a critical issue for risk monitoring is the standard of evidence required to halt a study on the basis of harm. Typically, differences that cross pre-specified boundaries of statistical significance are required to halt trials for efficacy. However, depending on the type and degree of benefit, boundaries for harm may vary. The criteria for stopping a trial if the efficacy endpoint veers in the direction of harm are typically less stringent than the criteria for stopping for efficacy differences in the direction of benefit.

---

[13] 21 CRF 56.111(a)(6).

Modest evidence of an adverse effect on an efficacy endpoint may be sufficient to rule out a clinically meaningful benefit even if the point estimate does not exclude a null effect. On the other hand, if benefit on one endpoint is established (for example, cardiovascular health), but the trial is being done to assess a suspected harm on a different endpoint (for example, gastrointestinal bleeding), a higher standard of proof of the harm signal might be required. The Women's Health Initiative trial, for example, stopped its estrogen–progestin arm because the breast-cancer outcome crossed the pre-specified safety boundary and because the global index outcome just trended in the direction of harm, effectively ruling out a substantive net benefit (Rossouw et al., 2002; Wittes et al., 2007).

Other issues that affect the evidence threshold for stopping for harm are whether and how external information is used. If an emerging signal of harm is similar to that seen in external studies, it is ethically justified and may be ethically required to halt a study earlier than if such evidence did not exist (Pocock, 1996).

International Challenges

The ability of FDA to discharge its ethical obligations to ensure adequate oversight of the postmarketing studies it requires is complicated when studies are conducted outside of the United States (Office of Inspector General, 2010). During the past two decades, the volume of premarketing clinical trials conducted outside the United States has increased dramatically, with many of these studies occurring in economically developing countries (Thiers et al., 2008; Wadman, 2007). Particularly when studies are conducted in resource poor countries, concerns have been raised about the quality, reliability and transportability of research results, and about the adequacy of research participant protections (HHS, 2001; Kimmelman et al., 2009; Lavery, 2004; NBAC, 2001). The committee recognizes that these concerns may apply as well to FDA required postmarketing research.

As the TIDE experience suggests, FDA required postmarketing trials are also being conducted at sites outside the United States. For example, the TIDE trial was conducted at 190 sites in more than 20 countries. Some of the countries in which the TIDE trial was conducted had research and oversight infrastructures equivalent or superior to those in the United States, but others did not have equivalent systems. Concerns about research quality and participant protections in some non-US sites pose challenges for FDA's obligations to ensure adequate protection of the rights and interests of research participants in premarketing and postmarketing research that it requires and to ensure that such research can provide the evidence needed to identify the appropriate regulatory response to a public health question. The International Research Panel of the Presidential Commission for the Study of Bioethical Issues found that "ongoing international dialogue between U.S. and international bodies is critical to protecting human subjects in research" (PCSBI, 2011). FDA's Office of International Programs, through its Harmonization and Multilateral Relations Office, is tasked with the responsibility of coordinating and collaborating with other agencies and countries on international standards and harmonization issues (FDA, 2011c). It is critical that this office work to resolve the challenges with other federal offices and international counterparts and that it have sufficient resources and authority to do so.

Meeting Ethical Obligations: The Architecture of Ethical Review

To discharge its ethical obligations to ensure adequate oversight of the post-marketing studies that it requires, FDA can draw on both its internal resources for ethical review and relationships with external IRBs and DMCs. Potential roles for each type of organization are described below.

FDA has substantial statutory authority to regulate in the arena of human-subjects protection for studies that are related to its drug-approval process.[14] Parts 50 and 56 of Title 21 of the *Code of Federal Regulations* extend the authority to "all clinical investigations regulated by the Food and Drug Administration under sections 505(i) and 520(g) of the Federal Food, Drug, and Cosmetic Act, as well as clinical investigations that support applications for research or marketing permits for products regulated by the Food and Drug Administration".[15] The regulations include requirements for informed consent[16] and standards for the "composition, operation, and responsibility of an Institutional Review Board (IRB)".[17]

FDA has created several structures to support its ethics-oversight function. The Office of Good Clinical Practice, in the Office of Special Medical Programs of the Office of the Commissioner, addresses issues related to human research trials regulated by FDA. Its activities include drawing up policies and long-range goals, leading FDA's Human Subject Protection (HSP)/Bioresearch Monitoring (BIMO) council, acting as a liaison with other federal agencies, and contributing to international Good Clinical Practice harmonization activities.

The HSP/BIMO initiative was launched in 2006 as part of FDA's Critical Path Initiative. The initiative (FDA, 2010a)

> is aimed at modernizing and strengthening the agency's oversight and protection of subjects in clinical trials and the integrity of resulting data. . . . [The] overarching goals of the agency's BIMO program are to protect the rights, safety, and welfare of subjects involved in FDA-regulated clinical trials; to determine the accuracy and reliability of clinical trial data submitted to FDA in support of research or marketing applications; and to assess compliance with FDA's

---

[14] Pursuant to Sections 403, 406, 409, 412, 413, 502, 503, 505, 510, 513–516, 518–520, 721, and 801 of the Federal Food, Drug, and Cosmetic Act (PL 75-717, 52 Stat 1040 [1938]).

[15] 21 CFR 50.1(a).

[16] 21 CFR Part 50.

[17] 21 CFR 56.107(a).

regulations governing the conduct of clinical trials, including those for informed consent and ethical review.

A September 2010 report on the HSP/BIMO initiative (FDA, 2010a) highlights as progress the publication of a number of rules and guidance documents related to IRBs, safety reporting, and protection of study participants (FDA, 2009, 2010b) and work on the joint European Medicines Agency–FDA Good Clinical Practice (GCP) Initiative (EMA and FDA, 2011).

Finally, all "human subject research conducted, supported, or funded in whole or in part by FDA except for those categories of research specifically exempted or waived under HHS regulations and not otherwise included by FDA policy" must be reviewed and approved by an internal FDA IRB, the Research Involving Human Subjects Committee (RIHSC) (Human Subjects Research [45 CFR 46]). As previously noted, although Sentinel is funded by FDA, its activities have been determined to be public health activities and not research and thus do not require review by the RIHSC, because the federal Office for Human Research Protections "determined that the regulations that [the Office for Human Research Protections] administers (45 CFR 46) do not apply to the activities that are included in the Food and Drug Administration's Sentinel Initiative" (Rosati et al., 2010) (see Exhibit 1, letter from Dr. Jerry Menikoff); they are public health activities, not human research (McGraw et al., 2012; Rosati et al., 2010). In the future, FDA may choose to conduct or support more complex surveillance systems that include, for example, the capacity to contact patients, draw blood samples, and conduct genome-wide association analyses to identify generic variants associated with a serious adverse event. An independent review body to advise FDA on the ethics of postmarketing activities involving large datasets could play an important role in helping to ensure that more complex surveillance systems are designed appropriately. Some of these activities may well be determined to constitute research that requires oversight by the RIHSC or other IRBs.

Although the BIMO program and other internal resources provide FDA with considerable capacity in the ethical oversight of postmarketing studies, the agency must partner with external IRBs and DMCs to carry out oversight activities on studies it requires others to conduct. FDA should, however, retain several specific roles rather than delegating the entire oversight process to IRBs. Those roles are outlined below.

Some commentators challenge the capacity of IRBs to provide the independent peer-review function for which they are intended (Emanuel et al., 2004; IOM, 2002; Schluger, 2008), but IRBs, bolstered by DMCs as appropriate, remain the bulwark of our current system for the protection of research participants. The committee believes, however, that FDA cannot responsibly delegate the entire process of research ethics oversight to IRBs but retains some specific moral duties itself in that regard. The remit of IRBs is to protect research participants. Ensuring that the design of a proposed research study is scientifically acceptable is a component of IRB determination, but in practice IRBs' review of scientific aspects of study design is limited. Although federal regulations task IRBs with ensuring that "risks to subjects . . . are minimized by using study procedures that are consistent with sound research design",[18] IRBs tend to defer on scientific matters to investigators, study sponsors, and other reviewing bodies (such as study sections convened by the National Institutes of Health and foundations).

That deferral is generally appropriate, inasmuch as IRBs are not constituted with the aim of ensuring that their members have the full array of scientific expertise relevant to all the studies that they review. The perspective, responsibilities, and capabilities of FDA are quite different. Ensuring that studies are designed to return answers to scientific questions of regulatory and public health importance is central to the agency's mission and concordant with the expertise of its staff.

IRBs do, however, have expertise and capability at least equal to those of FDA to review the research-participant protection issues that FDA-required studies may raise. FDA should not attempt to displace IRBs' role in this realm, but it could do more to support IRB decision-making. Specifically, one role for FDA in the oversight process is to give each IRB (including any centralized IRBs and multiple IRBs) sufficient information to provide appropriate oversight. That should include information about the public health question at issue; the specifics of the study design intended to address that question, including any design features that it views as necessary to the ethical justification of the study; and any changes in clinical practice or professional standards that arise over the course of the study that might affect the benefit–risk profile of a drug and influence a person's decision to join or remain in the study, which the IRB should consider for dissemination to potential and current study participants. FDA should also communicate to IRBs what it is (and is not) requiring the investigators to do with respect to study design. Such information should minimize IRBs' attempts to alter study designs in ways that FDA would not approve and should ensure that investigators and pharmaceutical sponsors are not tempted to misrepresent FDA's requirements.

One potential mechanism for that kind of communication between FDA and IRBs would be for FDA to send a letter to the pharmaceutical manufacturer (and the study's principal investigator, if one has been identified) that sets forth the information that IRBs need to know about the study before initial IRB approval, as well as later letters as the study progresses if relevant information emerges and to require the manufacturer to submit such letters to each IRB involved with the study. FDA should also ensure that the relevant IRBs are provided with up-to-date Benefit and Risk Assessment Management Plans (BRAMPs) for the drugs under study.

With respect to clinical trials and other studies that alter the clinical experi-

---

[18] 21 CRF 56.111(a)(1).

ence of research participants in ways that pose a risk of harm, another role for FDA is to support the work of DMCs and data-monitoring committees. The latter can play a critical role in monitoring the safety of clinical-trial participants in both the postmarketing setting and the premarketing setting by providing DMCs with the same information that FDA provides to IRBs.

Thus, there is already an architecture in place for the ethical oversight of postmarketing studies required by FDA, but stronger relationships between the parts of the system are needed, including specific duties for FDA, to enhance its capacity to attend properly to the particular features of postmarketing research.

SUMMARY

Requiring drug manufacturers to conduct research is at the core of FDA's regulatory responsibilities before drug approval. After a drug has entered the marketplace, it is only one of a variety of actions open to FDA in monitoring the drug's benefit–risk profile. When FDA elects to pursue that action, the postmarketing setting poses a number of distinct challenges in considering which types of studies to require. One major challenge is created by the opportunity to require observational studies, an option that is generally not available in the premarketing setting. The statutory hierarchy in FDAAA that prioritizes observational designs is a starting point for the committee in providing guidance as to which kinds of study designs FDA should require. The committee finds that the presumption requiring that observational studies be ruled out before FDA can order an RCT is supported by ethical, practical, and scientific considerations. The committee concludes that there can be many circumstances when an observational design can provide evidence adequate to help to resolve the public health question at issue, but that there are also circumstances when only an RCT is able to provide the needed evidence. In theory RCTs provide the highest-quality evidence with respect to any outcome, but in practice observational studies may provide high quality evidence regarding a drug's risks sufficient for policy decisions. In many cases, practical, scientific, and ethical considerations make it difficult or impossible to conduct an RCT that contains all the elements that give the ideal RCT its evidential superiority. To be consistent with ethical, legal, and practical considerations, the required study should be designed to provide evidence that is as close as possible to the evidence that would be obtained if the ideal trial specific to the public health question at issue could have been implemented.

Much of the information about a drug's benefits and risks in the postmarketing context do not come from studies mandated by FDA. Therefore, FDA should endeavor to make the studies that it does require as informative as possible about both benefits and risks. FDA can do that by prospectively defining key endpoints, design aspects (such as details of drug administration), and covariates that postmarketing studies should use. FDA could develop such information internally or convene researchers for this purpose; the latter would maximize adherence to the recommendations and constitute a forum where logistics of data-sharing could be explored. That information should be included in the drug's BRAMP.

FDA has an obligation to ensure that the postmarketing studies that it requires are conducted ethically. The main mechanisms through which FDA can honor that obligation are requiring studies whose designs can provide the evidence needed to help to resolve a public health question, assessing the ethics of candidate designs as it makes its determination about what kinds of studies to require, and accepting specific responsibilities to work closely with IRBs and, when it is appropriate, DMCs to protect the rights and interests of research participants. It is the committee's view that FDA has expertise and information that are critical for research participants protection and that these must be routinely shared with IRBs and DMCs. Finally, in required postmarketing research, people are being asked to participate in research or to have information about them used to advance the public's health. An FDA decision to require postmarketing research is ethical only if the findings of the research are put to that common goal. FDA must take steps to ensure that postmarketing research that it requires is completed in a timely fashion and should use the findings of the research in making its regulatory response to the public health question.

FINDINGS AND RECOMMENDATIONS

Finding 4.1

A decision by FDA to require postmarketing research can put research participants at risk. It can also put patients and the public at risk by delaying a regulatory decision that might be protective of public health. Some conditions are necessary but not sufficient for an FDA decision to require postmarketing research to be ethical.

> **Recommendation 4.1.1**
> FDA should require postmarketing research only when (1) uncertainty about the benefit–risk balance is such that a responsible decision about the future regulatory status of the drug cannot be made on the basis of existing evidence; (2) it is expected that the research can be properly designed and implemented to reduce uncertainty about the benefit–risk profile to allow a responsible regulatory decision; (3) FDA has a plan for using the results of the research to make a regulatory decision in a timely fashion; and (4) the research can be conducted in a manner that provides sufficient protection of and respect for research participants.

Finding 4.2

For postmarketing investigations authorized under Section 901 of FDAAA,[19] FDA can require an RCT only if it is unable to obtain the data that it needs from an observational study or surveillance. Determining what kind of study will provide the information needed to answer FDA's public health question, however, is complex. In the postmarketing setting, both observational studies and RCTs have advantages and disadvantages. In some circumstances, the evidence provided by an observational study may be as good as or better for informing a public health question than the evidence provided by a feasible clinical trial; that is more likely to occur when the magnitude of the relative risk is large in contrast with the potential for confounding, which occurs with many drug harms. Observational studies also have a number of ethical and practical advantages over RCTs. In other circumstances, however, the evidence available from an observational study would not be able to provide the necessary additional information to help answer the public health question. Those instances are more likely to occur when the public health questions are related primarily to a drug's benefits.

> **Recommendation 4.2**
> When deciding which type of research to require in the postmarketing setting, FDA should carefully weigh the strengths of potential observational studies for evaluating risks and their ethical and practical advantages, including the timeframe within which the data are needed, against the limitations of potential observational studies for generating the data needed to answer the public health question. An RCT should be required only if FDA has concluded that an observational study could not provide the necessary information, that an RCT is likely to generate the information within the necessary timeframe, and that the necessary RCT is ethically acceptable.

Finding 4.3

When FDA requires a postmarketing RCT, the public health question is most likely to be properly addressed by a comparison of the target drug with the standard therapy for the condition involved—if there is a standard therapy. Such a trial would involve a "head-to-head" design, defined as a comparison of two active treatments that are indicated for the same patients who have the same condition. However, it is also important both scientifically and ethically for at least one clinically acceptable comparator in the required trial to have a well-defined benefit–risk profile.

---

[19] 21 USC § 355(o) (2010).

Recommendation 4.3
If FDA requires a postmarketing RCT for an indication for which there is an accepted active treatment that would probably be used if access to the drug under study were restricted, the alternative treatment should be used as at least one comparator in the trial.

Finding 4.4

When deciding whether to require a postmarketing study, FDA must balance its ethical obligation to protect the public's health with its ethical obligation to protect research participants. In some instances, FDA may be faced with a decision to require an RCT that might expose participants to more net risk than they would probably face if decisions about their drug treatment were being made in the context of clinical practice or that offers no reasonable expectation of clinical benefit to participants although its results may benefit society. Requiring such a study may be ethically justifiable but only under special circumstances.

Recommendation 4.4
FDA should require a postmarketing RCT that might expose research participants to more risk or less net clinical benefit than they would probably face if decisions about their drug treatment were being made in the context of clinical practice only if a question of pressing public health significance is at stake, if no other design with a better benefit–risk balance for participants could supply the evidence needed for a responsible regulatory response to the question, and if special safeguards are in place to protect the rights and interests of the research participants. Those safeguards should include the determination by an appropriately constituted review committee that the additional risk is small enough for it to be ethical to ask people whether they are willing to accept it *solely* to contribute to the public good; the minimization of additional risk by careful study design and implementation of a robust monitoring plan throughout the study; the inclusion of special measures in the process of soliciting informed consent to confirm that patients understand and willingly accept that they are assuming an additional risk, beyond what they are likely to face in clinical practice, solely in the interest of the public good; and the implementation of processes to ensure that over the course of the trial participants are regularly informed of any changes in clinical practice or the medical literature relevant to assessments of the comparative benefits and risks associated with trial participation and (nonresearch) clinical management.

Finding 4.5

Although regulations governing human subjects research do not apply if an activity is considered public health practice, as is the case with the Sentinel system, it is often not possible to draw a clear or ethically relevant distinction between some kinds of FDA-required observational research and public health practice. It is important that FDA, in conjunction with the Office for Human Research Protections (OHRP), clarify whether its human subjects regulations (21 CFR 50) govern required postmarketing observational studies and, if so, how FDA will address and will expect IRBs to address any differences between 21 CFR 50 and other potentially applicable human subject regulations (45 CFR 46 Subpart A) in oversight and research-participant protection, including consent requirements, in different observational designs so that its regulations are not a barrier to what would otherwise be ethically acceptable observational designs. FDA also needs to determine how best to ensure that it is feasible for drug companies and their contractors to conduct the postmarketing observational studies that it requires, in view of the Health Insurance Portability and Accountability Act of 1996 and other potential constraints, while protecting the privacy of the people whose data are used. It is also likely that the desirability of linking datasets and of obtaining additional information from patients or otherwise needing access to some identifying information about patients will increase, whether studies are conducted under the auspices of FDA-supported surveillance systems, such as Sentinel and deemed public health practice, or conducted by manufacturers as required by FDA and interpreted at least by some to be research, raising additional ethical questions about the adequacy of data security, authorization of access to different datasets, and different research and public health purposes.

Recommendation 4.5.1

FDA, in conjunction with the Office for Human Research Protections (OHRP), should clarify whether its human subjects regulations (21 CFR 50) govern required postmarketing observational studies and, if so, how FDA will address and will expect IRBs to address any differences between 21 CFR 50 and other potentially applicable human subject regulations (45 CFR 46 Subpart A) in oversight and research-participant protection, including consent requirements.

Recommendation 4.5.2

To assure the public that surveillance and required observational studies can proceed with appropriate controls and protections, and to facilitate the conduct of ethically acceptable surveillance and required observational studies that are important to the public's health, FDA should form an independent body to advise FDA, on an as needed basis, on the ethics of postmarketing research and surveillance activities that it conducts or requires. This advisory body should be positioned to provide guidance on emerging ethical challenges, with particular focus on activities that are determined not to require IRB oversight.

Finding 4.6

FDA has an ethical obligation to ensure that the rights and interests of participants in the postmarketing research that it requires are properly protected. IRBs and data-monitoring committees (DMCs) can play a critical role in assisting FDA with this obligation, but these bodies require information and guidance from FDA to be effective in their research-participant protection responsibilities.

Recommendation 4.6
For all postmarketing research that it requires and that is subject to IRB or DMC oversight, FDA should provide each IRB (including centralized IRBs and multiple IRBs) and each DMC with the up-to-date BRAMP document for the study drug and sufficient information in writing for the IRB or DMC to provide appropriate oversight, including information about the public health question at issue, the specifics of the study design intended to address the question, design features that FDA views as necessary for the ethical justification of the study, and any changes in clinical practice or professional standards that arise over the course of the study that might affect the risk–benefit profile of a drug and influence a person's decision to participate or remain a participant in the study.

Finding 4.7

There are heightened informed consent concerns in the conduct of FDA-required RCTs in the postmarketing setting. FDA has an ethical responsibility to ensure that postmarketing clinical trials include appropriate informed consent processes and oversight.

Recommendation 4.7
FDA should issue guidance for interpreting disclosure and informed consent requirements in applicable federal regulations in the context of postmarketing RCTs that it requires, using the authorities granted to it in Section 901 of FDAAA[20] to help oversight bodies (such as IRBs) to ensure that such trials include a comprehensive informed consent process. The guidance should emphasize that, in addition to standard disclosure requirements, the following information of particular importance in the postmarketing setting should be communicated to research participants: why a new study of an approved drug is being required; salient risks posed by participation in required postmarketing research, including whether new information suggests that the drug under study may pose serious risks; and whether medical practice has shifted or is shifting away from prescribing the study drug. The guidance should

[20] 21 USC § 355(o) (2010).

make clear that participants must be informed of any substantial changes in clinical practice and professional standards over the course of the trial and informed of any new research findings relevant to their willingness to accept or to continue to accept the risks associated with the trial. And the guidance should identify the conditions under which consent processes should include measures to validate the adequacy of participants' understanding, not only the adequacy of the disclosures made to participants.

Finding 4.8

During the last two decades, the volume of clinical trials conducted outside the United States has increased dramatically, and this has led to concerns about the quality, reliability, and transportability of research results and about the adequacy of protections for research participants. Those concerns apply as well to FDA-required postmarketing research that uses research sites outside the United States. FDA's Office of International Programs, through its Harmonization and Multilateral Relations Office, is tasked with the responsibility of coordinating and collaborating with other agencies and countries on international standards and harmonization issues and is therefore well positioned to address these concerns.

Recommendation 4.8
FDA should direct its Office of International Programs to include explicitly among its responsibilities working with counterpart agencies of other governments and with industry to resolve concerns about the ethics and quality of evidence in the conduct of FDA-required postmarketing research outside the United States.

REFERENCES

Appelbaum, P. S., L. H. Roth, C. W. Lidz, P. Benson, and W. Winslade. 1987. False hopes and best data: Consent to research and the therapeutic misconception. *Hastings Center Report* 17(2):20-24.

Campbell, M. K., C. Snowdon, D. Francis, D. Elbourne, A. M. McDonald, R. Knight, V. Entwistle, J. Gracia, I. Roberts, and A. Grant. 2004. *Recruitment to randomised trials: Strategies for trial enrollment and participation study. The STEPS study*. Vol. 11. London, England: Health Technology Assessments.

Castro, W. M. 2007. Selenium in critically ill patients with systemic inflammatory response. *Nutricion Hospitalaria* 22(3):295-306.

CHMP (Committee for Medicinal Products for Human Use). 2011. *Reflection paper on the need for active control in therapeutic areas where use of placebo is deemed ethical and one or more established medicines are available*. London, UK: European Medicines Agency.

Concato, J., N. Shah, and R. I. Horwitz. 2000. Randomized, controlled trials, observational studies, and the hierarchy of research designs. *New England Journal of Medicine* 342(25):1887-1892.

Danaei, G., M. Tavakkoli, and M. A. Hernán. 2012. Bias in observational studies of prevalent users: Lessons for comparative effectiveness research from a meta-analysis of statins. *American Journal of Epidemiology* 175(4):250-262.

DHEW (Department of Health Education and Welfare). 1979. *The Belmont Report: Ethical principles and guidelines for the protection of human subjects of research*. Washington, DC: Department of Health and Human Services.

Drazen, J. M. 2005. Patients at risk. *New England Journal of Medicine* 353(4):417-417.

Ellenberg, S. S., and R. Temple. 2000. Placebo-controlled trials and active-control trials in the evaluation of new treatments. Part 2: Practical issues and specific cases. *Annals of Internal Medicine* 133(6):464-470.

Ellenberg, S. S., T. R. Fleming, and D. L. DeMets. 2003. *Data monitoring committees in clinical trials: A practical perspective*. Chichester, UK: Wiley.

EMA (European Medicines Agency) and FDA (US Food and Drug Administration). 2011. *Report on the pilot EMA-FDA GCP Initiative*. European Medicines Agency and US Food and Drug Administration.

Emanuel, E. J., and F. G. Miller. 2001. The ethics of placebo-controlled trials—a middle ground. *New England Journal of Medicine* 345(12):915-919.

Emanuel, E. J., A. Wood, A. Fleischman, A. Bowen, K. A. Getz, C. Grady, C. Levine, D. E. Hammerschmidt, R. Faden, L. Eckenwiler, C. T. Muse, and J. Sugarman. 2004. Oversight of human participants research: Identifying problems to evaluate reform proposals. *Annals of Internal Medicine* 141(4):282-291.

Evans, B. 2012. The ethics of postmarketing observational studies of drug safety under Section 505(o)(3) of the Food, Drug, and Cosmetic Act. *American Journal of Law & Medicine* 38 (in press).

Faden, R. R., and T. L. Beauchamp. 1986. *A history and theory of informed consent*. New York: Oxford University Press.

Faden, R. R., T. L. Beauchamp, and N. E. Kass. 2011. Learning health care systems and justice. *Hastings Center Report* 41(4):3.

FDA (US Food and Drug Administration). 2001. *Guidance for industry: E 10 choice of control group and related issues in clinical trials*. Washington, DC: Department of Health and Human Services.

FDA. 2007. *Transcript: Sentinel network public meeting*. Rockville, MD: Department of Health and Human Services.

FDA. 2009. *Guidance for industry: Investigator responsibilities—protecting the rights, safety, and welfare of study subjects*. Washington, DC: Department of Health and Human Services.

FDA. 2010a. *Guidance for industry: Non-inferiority clinical trials, draft guidance*. Washington, DC: Department of Health and Human Services.

FDA. 2010b. *FDA's HSP/BIMO initiative accomplishments—update, September 2010*. Washington, DC: Department of Health and Human Services.

FDA. 2010c. *FDA issues final rule on safety information during clinical trials*. http://www.fda.gov/NewsEvents/Newsroom/PressAnnouncements/ucm227386.htm (accessed October 26, 2010).

FDA. 2011a. *Clinical trials guidance documents*. http://www.fda.gov/RegulatoryInformation/Guidances/ucm122046.htm (accessed November 13, 2011).

FDA. 2011b. *Access to investigational drugs outside of a clinical trial (expanded access)*. http://www.fda.gov/ForConsumers/ByAudience/ForPatientAdvocates/AccesstoInvestigationalDrugs/ucm176098.htm (accessed September 13, 2011).

FDA. 2011c. *Harmonization and multilateral relations office*. http://www.fda.gov/AboutFDA/CentersOffices/OC/OfficeofGlobalRegulatoryOperationsandPolicy/OfficeofInternationalPrograms/ucm243679.htm (accessed November 13, 2011).

Fisher, L. D. 1996. Comments on Bayesian and Frequentist analysis and interpretation of clinical trials. *Control Clinical Trials* 17(5):423-434.

Flory, J., and E. Emanuel. 2004. Interventions to improve research participants' understanding in informed consent for research. *JAMA* 292(13):1593-1601.

Golder, S., Y. K. Loke, and M. Bland. 2011. Meta-analyses of adverse effects data derived from randomised controlled trials as compared to observational studies: Methodological overview. *PLoS Med* 8(5):e1001026.

Graham, D. J., and K. Gelperin. 2010. *TIDE and benefit-risk considerations*. http://www.fda.gov/downloads/AdvisoryCommittees/CommitteesMeetingMaterials/Drugs/EndocrinologicandMetabolicDrugsAdvisoryCommittee/UCM224732.pdf (accessed October 11, 2011).

Graham, D. J., D. Campen, R. Hui, M. Spence, C. Cheetham, G. Levy, S. Shoor, and W. A. Ray. 2005. Risk of acute myocardial infarction and sudden cardiac death in patients treated with cyclo-oxygenase 2 selective and non-selective non-steroidal anti-inflammatory drugs: Nested case-control study. *Lancet* 365(9458):475-481.

Grant, A. M., D. G. Altman, A. B. Babiker, M. K. Campbell, F. J. Clemens, J. H. Darbyshire, D. R. Elbourne, S. K. McLeer, M. K. B. Parmar, S. J. Pocock, D. J. Spiegelhalter, M. R. Sydes, A. E. Walker, and S. A. Wallace. 2005. Issues in data monitoring and interim analysis of trials. *Health Technology Assessment* 9(7):1-238.

Greenland, S. 2005. Multiple-bias modelling for analysis of observational data. *Journal of the Royal Statistical Society: Series A.* 168(Part 2):267-306.

Halpern, S. D., P. A. Ubel, J. A. Berlin, R. R. Townsend, and D. A. Asch. 2002. Physicians' preferences for active-controlled versus placebo-controlled trials of new antihypertensive drugs. *Journal of General Internal Medicine* 17(9):689-695.

Hennessy, S., C. E. Leonard, and R. Platt. 2010. Assessing the safety and comparative effectiveness of follow-on biologics (biosimilars) in the United States. *Clinical Pharmacology and Therapeutics* 87(2):157-159.

Hernán, M. A., and J. M. Robins. 2006. Instruments for causal inference: An epidemiologist's dream? *Epidemiology* 17(4):360-372.

Hernán, M. A., A. Alonso, R. Logan, F. Grodstein, K. B. Michels, W. C. Willett, J. E. Manson, and J. M. Robins. 2008. Observational studies analyzed like randomized experiments: An application to postmenopausal hormone therapy and coronary heart disease. *Epidemiology* 19(6):766-779.

HHS (US Department of Health and Human Services). 2001. *The globalization of clinical trials: A growing challenge in protecting human subjects.* Washington, DC: Department of Health and Human Services.

ICH (International Conference on Harmonisation of Technical Requirements for Registration of Pharmaceuticals for Human Use). 1996. *ICH harmonized tripartite guideline: Guideline for good clinical practice.* Geneva, Switzerland: ICH Secretariat, International Federation for Pharmaceutical Manufacturers Association.

IOM (Institute of Medicine). 2002. *Responsible research: A systems approach to protecting research participants.* Washington, DC: The National Academies Press.

IOM. 2010. *Ethical issues in studying the safety of approved drugs: A letter report.* Washington, DC: The National Academies Press.

Joffe, S., E. F. Cook, P. D. Cleary, J. W. Clark, and J. C. Weeks. 2001. Quality of informed consent in cancer clinical trials: A cross-sectional survey. *Lancet* 358(9295):1772-1777.

Kass, N. E., and H. A. Taylor. 2008. *Empirical research on informed consent: A review of the literature prepared for the National Academies Workshop on Collecting, Storing, Accessing, and Protecting Data Containing Biological Measures* (unpublished).

Kimmelman, J., C. Weijer, and E. M. Meslin. 2009. Helsinki discords: FDA, ethics, and international drug trials. *Lancet* 373(9657):13-14.

King, N. M. 2000. Defining and describing benefit appropriately in clinical trials. *Journal of Law, Medicine & Ethics* 28(4):332-343.

Kleinschmidt-DeMasters, B. K., and K. L. Tyler. 2005. Progressive multifocal leukoencephalopathy complicating treatment with natalizumab and interferon beta-1a for multiple sclerosis. *New England Journal of Medicine* 353(4):369-374.

Kodish, E., M. Eder, R. B. Noll, K. Ruccione, B. Lange, A. Angiolillo, R. Pentz, S. Zyzanski, L. A. Siminoff, and D. Drotar. 2004. Communication of randomization in childhood leukemia trials. *JAMA* 291(4):470-475.

Langer-Gould, A., S. W. Atlas, A. J. Green, A. W. Bollen, and D. Pelletier. 2005. Progressive multifocal leukoencephalopathy in a patient treated with natalizumab. *New England Journal of Medicine* 353(4):375-381.

Largent, E., S. Joffe, and F. G. Miller. 2011. Can research and care be ethically integrated? *Hastings Center Report* 41(4):37-46.

Lavery, J. 2004. *Policy briefs: The challenge of regulating international research with human subjects.* http://www.scidev.net/en/policy-briefs/the-challenge-of-regulating-international-research.html (accessed November 13, 2011).

Lindegger, G., C. Milford, C. Slack, M. Quayle, X. Xaba, and E. Vardas. 2006. Beyond the checklist: Assessing understanding for HIV vaccine trial participation in South Africa. *Journal of Acquired Immune Deficiency Syndromes* 43(5):560-566

Lurie, P., and S. M. Wolfe. 1998. Ethics of HIV trials. *Lancet* 351(9097):220.

Mazor, K. M., J. E. Sabin, D. Boudreau, M. J. Goodman, J. H. Gurwitz, L. J. Herrinton, M. A. Raebel, D. Roblin, D. H. Smith, V. Meterko, and R. Platt. 2007. Cluster randomized trials: Opportunities and barriers identified by leaders of eight health plans. *Medical Care* 45(10 Suppl 2):S29-S37.

McClellan, M., B. J. McNeil, and J. P. Newhouse. 1994. Does more intensive treatment of acute myocardial infarction in the elderly reduce mortality? Analysis using instrumental variables. *JAMA* 272(11):859-866.

McGraw, D., K. Rosati, and B. Evans. 2012. A policy framework for public health uses of electronic health data. *Pharmacoepidemiology and Drug Safety* 21(Suppl 1):18-22.

Miller, F. G., and D. L. Rosenstein. 2002. Reporting of ethical issues in publications of medical research. *Lancet* 360(9342):1326-1328.

NBAC (National Bioethics Advisory Commission). 2001. *Ethical and policy issues in international research. Clinical trials in developing countries. Vol 1: Report and recommendations of the National Bioethics Advisory Commission.* Bethesda, MD: National Bioethics Advisory Commission.

Office of Inspector General. 2010. *Challenges to FDA's ability to monitor and inspect foreign clinical trials.* Washington, DC: Department of Health and Human Services.

PCSBI (Presidential Commission for the Study of Bioethical Issues). 2011. *Research across borders. Proceedings of the International Research Panel of the Presidential Commission for the Study of Bioethical Issues.* Washington, DC: Presidential Commission for the Study of Bioethical Issues.

Platt, R., S. U. Takvorian, E. Septimus, J. Hickok, J. Moody, J. Perlin, J. A. Jernigan, K. Kleinman, and S. S. Huang. 2010. Cluster randomized trials in comparative effectiveness research: Randomizing hospitals to test methods for prevention of healthcare-associated infections. *Medical Care* 48(6 Suppl):S52-S57.

Pocock, S. J. 1996. When to stop a clinical trial. *British Medical Journal* 305:235-240.

Psaty, B. M., and R. A. Kronmal. 2008. Reporting mortality findings in trials of rofecoxib for Alzheimer disease or cognitive impairment. *JAMA* 299(15):1813-1817.

Reskin, D. B. 2007. Beyond post-marketing research and MedWatch: Long-term studies of drug risks. *Drug Design, Development and Therapy* 1:1-5.

Robins, J. M., M. A. Hernán, and A. Rotnitzky. 2007. Effect modification by time-varying covariates. *American Journal of Epidemiology* 166(9):994-1002.

Rosati, K., B. Evans, and D. McGraw. 2010. *White paper: HIPAA and common rule compliance in the mini-sentinel pilot.* Mini-Sentinel Coordinating Center.

Rossouw, J. E., G. L. Anderson, R. L. Prentice, A. Z. LaCroix, C. Kooperberg, M. L. Stefanick, R. D. Jackson, S. A. Beresford, B. V. Howard, K. C. Johnson, J. M. Kotchen, and J. Ockene. 2002. Risks and benefits of estrogen plus progestin in healthy postmenopausal women. *JAMA* 288(3):321-333.

Schluger, N. W. 2008. Improving protection for human research subjects: Better oversight, not just more oversight. *American Journal of Bioethics* 8(11):13-15.

Stang, P. E., P. B. Ryan, J. A. Racoosin, J. M. Overhage, A. G. Hartzema, C. Reich, E. Welebob, T. Scarnecchia, and J. Woodcock. 2010. Advancing the science for active surveillance: Rationale and design for the observational medical outcomes partnership. *Annals of Internal Medicine* 153(9):600-606.

Stolberg, H. O., G. Norman, and I. Trop. 2004. Randomized controlled trials. *American Journal of Roentgenology* 183(6):1539-1544.

Strom, B.L. 2005. *Pharmacoepidemiology*, Fourth Edition. John Wiley and Sons: Hoboken, NJ.

Temple, R., and S. S. Ellenberg. 2000. Placebo-controlled trials and active-control trials in the evaluation of new treatments. Part 1: Ethical and scientific issues. *Annals of Internal Medicine* 133(6):455-463.

Thiers, F. A., A. J. Sinskey, and E. R. Berndt. 2008. Trends in the globalization of clinical trials. *Nature Reviews Drug Discovery* 7:13-14.

Truog, R. D., W. Robinson, A. Randolph, and A. Morris. 1999. Is informed consent always necessary for randomized, controlled trials? *New England Journal of Medicine* 340(10):804-807.

Van Assche, G., M. Van Ranst, R. Sciot, B. Dubois, S. Vermeire, M. Noman, J. Verbeeck, K. Geboes, W. Robberecht, and P. Rutgeerts. 2005. Progressive multifocal leukoencephalopathy after natalizumab therapy for Crohn's disease. *New England Journal of Medicine* 353(4):362-368.

Vandenbroucke, J. P., and B. M. Psaty. 2008. Benefits and risks of drug treatments: How to combine the best evidence on benefits with the best data about adverse effects. *JAMA* 300(20):2417-2419.

Wadman, M. 2007. Biomedical philanthropy: State of the donation. *Nature* 447(7142):248-250.

Wendler, D. 2009. Must research participants understand randomization? *American Journal of Bioethics* 9(2):3-8.

Wittes, J., E. Barrett-Connor, E. Braunwald, M. Chesney, H. J. Cohen, D. DeMets, L. Dunn, J. Dwyer, R. P. Heaney, V. Vogel, L. Walters, and S. Yusuf. 2007. Monitoring the randomized trials of the Women's Health Initiative: The experience of the Data and Safety Monitoring Board. *Clinical Trials* 4(3):218-234.

5

Synthesis

At the time that a drug is approved by the US Food and Drug Administration (FDA) for sale in the marketplace, uncertainties necessarily remain about the drug's benefits and risks. The research that is conducted before a drug's approval is limited in the numbers and types of patients who are involved and in the length of time that patients' experiences with the drug can be monitored (Borer et al., 2007; Hiatt, 2006; IOM, 2007; Ray and Stein, 2006). Ensuring that drugs continue to have an acceptable benefit–risk profile after they are approved for sale on the US market is as important to FDA's public health mission as ensuring the acceptability of the benefit–risk profile before it is permitted to enter the market. In support of the equal public health importance of regulatory oversight of drugs before and after approval, the authorities granted to FDA by the Food and Drug Administration Amendments Act (FDAAA) of 2007[1] provide FDA with the tools it needs to adopt a comprehensive lifecycle approach to the assessment of the benefits and risks associated with marketed drugs.

In the lifecycle approach, responding in a timely and responsible way to safety signals that emerge after a drug is on the market is among the most important and challenging public health responsibilities of FDA. Permitting a drug that is on balance harmful to stay on the market threatens public well-being, but so does limiting access to a drug whose benefits outweigh its harms. FDAAA provides FDA with greater statutory authority in the postmarketing setting than it had before, including the authority to require manufacturers to conduct studies of drugs in the postmarketing setting. That authority, however, presents a number of new challenges to the agency, including determining when it is appropriate for

[1]Food and Drug Administration Amendments Act of 2007, PL 110-85, 121 Stat. 823 (2007).

FDA to require a postmarketing study and what types of studies to require when that is the case, how best to protect the rights and interests of patients who serve as participants in the research that it requires, and how it should use the information from the required postmarketing studies and from other available research (for example, studies initiated by academic researchers) in making regulatory decisions. The present committee's charge to evaluate the scientific and ethical issues involved in conducting studies of the safety of approved drugs reflects those challenges.

In this chapter, the committee summarizes its responses to the specific questions in its charge (see Box 1-1) and gathers its broad findings and recommendations.[2]

RESPONSES TO THE CHARGE QUESTIONS

How should FDA factor in different kinds of safety evidence in considering different kinds of regulatory actions?

In response to this question, the committee notes that no single algorithm can determine how to factor different kinds of safety evidence into regulatory decision-making, but does specify processes and principles to guide how this should occur. The committee identifies five actions, discussed below, that FDA can take to improve its decision-making processes in response to different kinds of safety evidence: (1) adopt a specified decision-making framework; (2) create a Benefit and Risk Assessment and Management Plan (BRAMP) document for each drug that is maintained across the drug's lifecycle; (3) characterize the nature of any disagreements about the evidence of benefits or risks; (4) create effective multidisciplinary teams with wide-ranging expertise, including in observational study design and interpretation, outcomes research and pharmacoepidemiology, Bayesian methods and modern causal inference approaches, and (5) adhere to the principles of reproducible research.

The committee proposes that FDA use a three-stage framework—adapted from 2009 *Science and Decisions: Advancing Risk Assessment* (NRC, 2009) and consistent with a framework recommended by *A Risk-Characterization Framework for Decision-Making at the Food and Drug Administration* (NRC, 2011)—any time in the lifecycle of a drug that FDA needs to make a regulatory decision, and for planned reviews of regulatory decisions. Given its charge, the committee focuses on the use of the framework in the postmarketing setting where it could be employed, for example, when the emergence of a serious safety signal may

[2]The committee presents the questions in the order they are discussed in the previous chapters, not the order they are presented in the charge.

precipitate or require a regulatory decision, including the reaffirming of the drug's current regulatory status. The three stages of the adapted framework include (1) define the public health questions of importance, (2) assess the drug's benefits and risks, and (3) make, communicate, and implement the regulatory decision. The three-stage framework is designed to be broadly applicable to regulatory decisions, to support decision-makers' judgment, and to facilitate the resolution of disagreements about the scientific evidence and the best regulatory actions to protect public health. For FDA's regulatory decisions about approved drugs to be ethical and appropriate, FDA needs to consider the perspectives of patients; and the concerns of consumers, health care providers, and industry; securing this input is an important element of the proposed framework.

Establishing and maintaining a BRAMP document for each drug throughout its lifecycle would also enhance FDA's ability to respond appropriately to safety evidence. The document would summarize the benefits and risks of the drug, the rationale for FDA's decisions in light of those benefits and risks, and how any risks will be managed throughout the drug's lifecycle. The BRAMP document, as proposed by the committee, is designed to support the systematic implementation of the lifecycle approach to regulatory oversight of drugs, to foster collaboration between FDA and drug sponsors in that oversight, and to increase the transparency of FDA's decisions. Because the benefit–risk profile of a drug can change over time, the BRAMP document would become a living document that is updated when there is new information that warrants re-evaluation of the drug's benefit–risk profile. Each update would include summaries of the three stages of the decision-making framework discussed above and any plans for identifying or managing risks (such as a risk evaluation and mitigation strategy). In the *premarketing* setting, the drug sponsor would provide initial information about the benefits and risks of a given drug, uncertainties in the information relevant to the public's health, and detailed plans to decrease those uncertainties if they exist. FDA should review and finalize the BRAMP document. In the *postmarketing* setting, FDA staff who did not play a primary role in the drug's approval process and who have expertise in surveillance, epidemiology, and the evaluation of safety data collected from different observational and clinical trial designs, would review and modify the BRAMP document at pre-specified intervals throughout the lifecycle of the drug and when new information warrants re-evaluation of the drug's benefit–risk profile.

Disagreements among experts about scientific evidence lead to some of the more challenging regulatory decisions. When such disagreements occur, it is important for FDA to characterize the nature of the disagreements. These can occur because experts have different prior beliefs about the plausibility of a given benefit or risk in light of prior evidence, different views about the quality of the studies supplying the evidence or about the relevance of the new evidence to the public health question that calls for a regulatory decision, or different ideas about how to synthesize all the available evidence relevant to the public health question or about the threshold of certainty needed to justify concern or regulatory action.

Bayesian approaches to measuring the strength of evidence and to characterizing the uncertainty of scientific conclusions about the presence or absence of a drug benefit or risk can be enormously useful in decision-making, which should incorporate the chances of being wrong and the attendant consequences in the choice of regulatory option. Standard approaches to statistical analysis cannot provide those inputs.

Outside researchers can be key partners with FDA in identifying safety concerns, and FDA can greatly augment its own efforts in the safety arena by allowing the research community to be more fully engaged. FDA should explore, seek support for and implement practices that enhance the ability of the external community of scientists to both identify drug-safety issues and to assess the validity of FDA's attempts to do the same. These include policies and practices that contribute to transparency, reproducible research, and sharing of data from both the premarketing and postmarketing contexts. Few studies currently follow FDAAA requirements to publish even summary results in ClinicalTrials.gov within a year of drug approval; enhanced compliance with these requirements can facilitate that engagement.

What are the strengths and weaknesses of various approaches, including observational studies, including patient registries, meta-analyses, including patient-level data meta-analyses, and randomized controlled trials, to generate evidence about safety questions?

The strengths and weaknesses of the many ways to explore drug-safety questions depend critically on context-specific facts, priorities, data sources and the nature of the benefits and risks being considered. Whether an adverse event is rare or common, mild or serious, and known or unknown, and whether an anticipated drug effect is small or large could dramatically change the relative advantages of various designs. For example, the value of an observational study of a harm based on existing data depends on whether the harm was reliably recorded in the dataset being used. A clinical trial too short to find a delayed effect is going to provide less relevant safety evidence than a design based on patient registry data with long follow-up. The invocation of broad principles that are inapplicable to a specific case (for example, that randomized controlled trials [RCTs] always provide the best evidence) can sometimes impair the investigation of drug harms. In any specific case, regulators need to have the input of a wide variety of experts who can help to make context-specific judgments.

The committee does, however, outline some general considerations that are important for evaluating the value of various designs for decision-making purposes. The initial set of considerations is how strong the safety signal is that motivates the design, and whether it primarily involves an elevation in risk, a decrease in benefit, or both, for either the general population or a definable subgroup. Second is how time-urgent is the need for a regulatory response, based on the nature of the safety signal. The third involves how large the change in risks or benefits must be, on both relative and absolute scales, to justify a regulatory response. Fourth is what the other causes of a given adverse event (or failure of benefit) might be, and how strongly they are predictive. Fifth is the quality of data likely to be gathered as part of any given design on drug exposure, outcomes, confounders and other relevant patient, disease or contextual characteristics. Sixth is a judgment of how study design, conduct or context is likely to affect the transportability of the study results. Seventh is what the logistical requirements of a design will be, including data access, cost and feasibility. Finally, there are considerations of ethical burden, consent, confidentiality, and study oversight. These factors can lead to the choice of either a single design type or a combination of studies with counterbalancing strengths and weaknesses.

With the above considerations in mind, the committee made some general observations about the strengths and weaknesses of specific designs. The RCT is considered the gold standard for studies of a drug's benefits because of the ability of randomization to control for potential biases and confounders, both known and unknown. Although the committee agrees that a well-conducted, high-quality RCT has many theoretical advantages over other study designs, it also recognizes that what can be achieved in practice in assessing safety endpoints can fall short of the ideal. Noncompliance, cross-over and dropout, limitations in study size or duration, failure of the study population or procedures to adequately represent circumstances in the general population of users, and the realization that safety endpoints are sometimes unforeseeable and cannot always be specified in advance can decrease the advantages of RCTs over observational studies for evaluating the risks posed by approved drugs. In many cases, the latter may provide estimates closer to the actual risks in the target population if one considers the combination of bias, precision, and transportability of results.

In addition, because RCTs alter a patient's clinical experience, they may entail more ethical complications than observational studies. (That said, as part of the consent process, the information patients receive about benefits and risks of study treatment options, as well as alternative treatments, may be more complete than a typical health provider supplies.) Other disadvantages of RCTs are the cost and time required to conduct such studies; the duration of studies is particularly problematic when an urgent public health question needs to be answered. An advantage of an RCT, however, is the ability to ascertain moderate relative risk elevations of common outcomes with confidence. A small relative risk (for example, RR <1.5) increase in a common outcome (for example, MI) may represent a very large absolute increase in risk with great public health importance. The adequacy of confounding control in many observational designs may not be sufficient to estimate such risk elevations with high confidence. Additionally, RCTs have the potential ability to assess both benefit and risk in the same group of patients at the same time. While this is not frequently done, it sometimes can be necessary to find subgroups in which the benefit–risk balance may be unacceptable, to make finely-grained assessments of the benefit–risk balances when new risks arise, or to make fair benefit–risk comparisons with active comparators.

Observational studies can provide data on a large number of people under real-world conditions. They also typically have greater heterogeneity of participants and may be more likely to detect drug–drug interactions and adverse effects in populations that might not have been included, or specifically excluded from premarketing RCTs. Observational studies are more prone to confounding than RCTs but often have better transportability of results (that is, external validity or generalizability) to those populations that might not be included in RCTs. They are generally less prone to confounding for safety endpoints than they are for effectiveness endpoints, particularly when the harms were unintended or unsuspected at the time the drug was prescribed and don't share a common mechanism with benefit (Psaty and Vandenbroucke, 2008). Most important is the magnitude of the relative elevation in risk in relation to the potential for confounding; if the anticipated relative elevation in risk is quite large, beyond plausible degrees of confounding, observational designs with weak confounding control can be sufficient. As previously noted, modest relative risks, particularly those less than 1.5, can require substantial control of confounding that might only be achievable in a clinical trial. One way to ameliorate this problem is to conduct multiple observational studies with a variety of designs and data sources unlikely to share similar biases.

If observational studies can be based on existing data or can use data systems that are already in place, they typically are less expensive and, unless a drug is new to the market and is not in widespread use, can be conducted more quickly than RCTs. If the availability and quality of electronic medical records and other electronic data sources increase, the quality of information and the ability to identify and control for potential confounders will improve, and the cost and time needed to complete a study might decrease. In addition, observational studies, which by their nature do not interfere with the treatments that people would receive in the course of regular care, generally have fewer ethical complications than RCTs.

In meta-analysis, data from a number of studies—either RCTs or observational studies—are combined, in aggregate or at the individual patient level. Meta-analyses are observational studies that use other studies as the unit of analysis. Their advantages include the speed with which they can be conducted, the use of existing data with few ethical issues, increased statistical power, and the ability, because a large number of participants can be included from the pooling of data, to detect adverse events or groups at risk. Other than the larger sample size, however, the same limitations and biases of the underlying observational and randomized trials persist in meta-analyses, and publication and reporting bias may jeopardize the validity of meta-analyses that use only published studies. Finally, biases are potentially incurred by the criteria for study selection. FDA can improve the validity of later meta-analyses by providing, early in the post-marketing phase, guidance on common data definitions and other design features that will make subsequent safety research conducted by others more likely to be mutually informative and combinable.

The committee looked specifically at noninferiority and superiority studies; the former are increasingly used in analyses of safety. Noninferiority studies evaluate whether a new treatment is "no worse" than a previous, accepted treatment by a specified margin or, in the case of safety studies, poses no more than an "acceptable" excess risk of adverse effects compared with the accepted treatment. The definition of *acceptable* often implies a tradeoff against a known benefit, but the comparison must be made explicit in interpreting such studies. Superiority studies evaluate whether a new treatment performs better than a previous, accepted treatment or, in the case of safety studies, poses less risk of adverse effects than the accepted treatment. One concern with noninferiority studies is the consequence of poor study conduct. Poor study conduct that leads to data of poor quality may introduce bias toward no effect, that is, lead to an erroneous conclusion that there is no difference between the two treatments. In a noninferiority study, that erroneous conclusion may be incorrectly interpreted as supporting the claim that the risk of adverse effects is the same for both treatments. When interpreting noninferiority and superiority studies, it is important that FDA evaluate the magnitude of the differences between the drugs and not rely on the study's preset designation of what constitutes acceptable inferiority or sufficient evidence of superiority. Perhaps more important is for FDA to develop and implement performance standards for the conduct, analysis and interpretation of noninferiority studies for safety.

Finally, the committee found that it is critical to recognize that the analytic approach, not just design, is an important contributor to the strength of evidence provided by any study. For example, the use of causal inference and Bayesian methods—with sensitivity analyses and proper treatment of missing data—can produce estimates of benefit, risk, and the uncertainty associated with those estimates, that differ from estimates derived with standard frequentist approaches. Intention-to-treat approaches that are appropriate for the assessment of relative efficacy, may not be appropriate for the assessment of risk. Given the importance of using the optimal analytical technique to reap the advantages of various designs, bringing together teams that have broad and deep technical expertise in both the design and analysis of drug-safety studies is integral to having the best evidence to help answer the public health question.

Considering the speed, cost, and value of studies, what types of follow-up studies are appropriate to investigate different kinds of signals (detected pre-approval or post-marketing) and in what temporal order?

The optimal follow-up studies to investigate different safety signals, and the order of those studies, will depend on the specific circumstances of the safety signal. The committee does provide general guidance to FDA in making these determinations, beyond the statutory provision in FDAAA,[3] that permits FDA to require a clinical trial only if sufficient information cannot be obtained with an observational study, a presumption that the committee finds consistent with FDA's ethical obligations to research participants in the postmarketing context and to the public's health.

First, all research strategies will work best if anticipated and planned for early. As outlined elsewhere in this report, there are a number of characteristics that should signal heightened concern about the possibility that harm will outweigh benefit in the postmarketing context. Those characteristics might appear in the case of drugs that were approved on the basis of surrogate endpoints when different surrogate endpoints yield conflicting evidence about clinical effect or safety; drugs that are first-in-class and were validated on the basis of surrogate endpoints with drugs in a different class; drugs about which safety signals appear in premarketing data or postmarketing surveillance when there is a substantial public health concern, drugs where a severe adverse event is seen, or there is a strong biologic rationale for a particular adverse effect; drugs that are expected to have a different benefit–risk profile in a particular group or under real-world conditions; drugs in a class about which a substantial safety signal has previously been identified; and drugs of which evidence of a lack of benefit emerges in the postmarketing setting.

The earliest and easiest step that FDA can take is to ensure that it is making maximum use, perhaps through meta-analysis, of the data already in its possession, which often would have been submitted as part of a New Drug Application, or may pre-exist because of studies performed for a different indication. Recognizing that much postmarketing safety information will come from studies not specifically commissioned by the agency, through the BRAMP FDA can define how exposures, covariates, and outcomes are to be assessed in future safety studies conducted by industry or by independent researchers. That information is also available to other investigators. The agency can be yet more effective by bringing together researchers at the time of or shortly after approval to standardize various design dimensions to make studies appropriate for future data pooling, a process known as prospective or collaborative meta-analysis.

If at the time of approval it is judged that FDA must require new studies, the postmarketing study strategy should be incorporated into the BRAMP. A variety of study designs can be used early in the introduction of a drug that are much more difficult or impossible to implement once it is in wide use, and this underscores the need to plan and start such studies as early as possible. Early initiation of such studies can also allow longer followup, so both prospective observational studies and RCTs are more likely to provide necessary evidence close to the time

[3] 21 USC § 355(o)(3)(B) (2010).

when public health decisions have to be made, if postmarketing safety signals are indeed found.

This last point is critical for RCTs in that one of their main disadvantages cited is that they take too long. An alternative perspective is that they are started too late. If an RCT is considered only when very strong suspicion of a safety signal arises, it may be too late to initiate one, particularly if the adverse events occur long after exposure. In addition, some of the ethical difficulties that arise in trying to conduct an RCT of a widely used drug are minimized if the RCT is initiated soon after market introduction. In 1999, when rosiglitazone and pioglitazone had just been approved, the TIDE trial would have been an important, timely, and well-designed study. Because at that time there would have been populations of patients who were not on the drug, individual or cluster randomization poses fewer logistical and ethical difficulties than would exist later. However, because of FDAAA restrictions, a study could only be required when there were premarketing signals of a potential for serious risk (for example, adverse lipid alterations, or low frequency serious adverse events) and observational studies were deemed inadequate. Early initiation of postmarketing investigations can dramatically change both the scientific value and the ethical calculus of such studies, making the optimal sequence dependent on when in the lifecycle of a drug the studies are being contemplated.

One key determinant of the kinds of designs that might be considered is whether the safety signal is a harm to be offset by a known benefit or the harm is a failure to provide expected benefit, either overall or in specific populations. FDAAA defines the latter as a safety concern, or more specifically "any failure of expected pharmacological action of the drug".[4] A failure to provide expected clinical benefit is most likely to be observed if that benefit was not directly tested in the approval process, for example, if surrogate endpoints were used, or if non-responsive subpopulations were not well represented in premarketing trials. If the safety concern focuses on the issue of no or reduced benefit, an RCT is more likely needed because confounding by indication in observational studies of drug benefit can be difficult to overcome. Conversely, if the harm is distinct from the mechanism of benefit, is unforeseen and not strongly linked to patient or disease characteristics, or is strongly linked to conditions of general practice (such as cotreatments or inconsistent monitoring), observational studies can often provide sufficiently reliable evidence related to risk. As previously noted, that degree of sufficiency also depends on the relative degree of increase in the risk that is deemed important to detect, weighed against the likely magnitude of confounding.

The dimensions of quality that must be judged for each combination of study design, data source, and analytic approach are the precision, bias, and transportability of the result. Each of those contributes to the observed effect's potentially

[4]21 USC § 355-1(b) (2010).

differing from the true effect in the general population of patients taking the drug. The intrinsic design qualities must be weighed with extrinsic issues, such as the time that it will take for a given design to deliver a result, the cost and complexity of various designs, and the ethical dimensions of the study. Some of the ethical dimensions depend on how uncertain the benefit–risk profile of the drug in question is, so properly assessing the uncertainty before the studies begin is quite important.

At every step in the process, FDA is faced with the choice between making a decision on the basis of evidence already gathered, and waiting for more or higher-quality evidence. If there is strong evidence of a safety problem, or new evidence about the benefit–risk balance for the population or a definable subset of it, FDA's decision can be extraordinarily difficult. Methodologies such as Bayesian analyses or other approaches to incorporate prior relevant information with newly emerging information could provide decision-makers with better quantitative assessments of evidence. An example would be through sensitivity analyses of clinical trials data that illustrate the influence of prior probabilities on estimates of probabilities that the intervention induces unacceptable safety risks. These insights can help enlighten judgments, allowing for more rational decision-making, and permitting input from multiple stakeholders and experts.

What are the ethical and informed consent issues that must be considered when designing randomized clinical trials to evaluate potential safety risks?

An assessment of the ethics of FDA's requiring a postmarketing RCT is inextricably intertwined with an assessment of the science related to the underlying public health question and regulatory decision. There are circumstances in which FDA is ethically justified in requiring a postmarketing clinical trial, and there are circumstances in which a clinical trial is required by statute.

When a trial is not required by statute, a decision to require a trial to resolve a postmarketing benefit–risk profile question should be based on the determination that (1) uncertainty about the benefit–risk balance is such that a responsible decision about the future regulatory status of the drug cannot be made on the basis of existing evidence, or evidence that could be obtained from new observational studies; (2) an RCT can be properly designed and implemented to reduce uncertainty about the benefit–risk balance sufficiently to inform a responsible regulatory decision; (3) FDA will use trial results in making a regulatory decision in a timely fashion; and (4) the RCT can be carried out in a manner that provides sufficient protection of and respect for research participants.

In making the fourth determination—that the RCT can be carried out in a manner that provides sufficient protection of and respect for research participants—FDA must attend to multiple considerations, including whether the trial should be designed to include an active medical intervention as the comparator (in contrast, for example, with a placebo) and issues of consent. The ethics of selecting an appropriate comparator for an FDA-required RCT are discussed under Question 4, below.

Informed consent obligations may be especially salient in the context of required postmarketing trials because patients may be asked to submit to a drug regimen about which a safety signal has prompted concerns about risk, and potentially about the acceptability of the drug's benefit–risk profile. FDA should work with manufacturers, investigators, and institutional review boards (IRBs) to ensure that the following occur as parts of the informed consent process:

- Information is provided about why a new study is required, particularly to persons already taking the drug who might have to undergo a change in regimen as a result of study participation. Prospective research participants need to understand why additional research is important even though the drug they are currently taking was found by FDA to have a favorable benefit–risk profile on the basis of existing evidence and why it is reasonable to ask them to consider participating in the study.
- Special care is taken to ensure that prospective participants understand the potential risks of study participation in the postmarketing context. When a substantial amount of information indicating that a drug to be studied may involve serious risks has already accumulated, there is a heightened obligation to ensure that potential participants understand the risks posed by study enrollment. At a minimum, the disclosure of risks should include any boxed warnings, the "major statement" currently listed in direct-to-consumer advertisements, any formal conclusions about adverse effects made by FDA staff or an FDA advisory committee, and a summary of evidence from published peer-reviewed studies or relevant, quality studies submitted to FDA. Special efforts should be made to ensure that people who have low health literacy or educational attainment, who have shown poorer understanding of disclosed information on consent forms (Flory and Emanuel, 2004; Kass and Taylor, 2008; Lindegger et al., 2006), understand this and other study information.
- In addition to considerations of benefits and risks, people who are considering participation in research need to know how the care that they will receive in a protocol may differ from the care that they would ordinarily receive. Thus, information about "alternatives to participation" should convey the current standard of care for the health condition that the study drug targets. That is particularly crucial in cases in which medical practice has shifted away from prescribing the study drug because accumulating evidence from passive surveillance, observational studies, and small trials or meta-analyses suggests that another therapy is as effective and has a more favorable benefit–risk profile. It should be communicated in this situation that a potential participant who does not enroll in the trial

is more likely to have a different drug prescribed. If clinical practice continues to shift during the trial period, the latter statement should be strengthened; researchers have an ethical obligation to disclose all new developments that may affect a person's willingness to continue to participate in a research study.

Comprehensive informed consent processes can help to ensure that trial participants understand the potential consequences for them of study participation, in addition to what they are contributing to the advancement of public health in the regulatory arena. These processes cannot, however, serve as exclusive or sufficient ethical justification for conducting a postmarketing trial. The other conditions for initiating a trial should be independently satisfied. People should not be asked to assume risks that are not justified by the potential benefits of the trial to participants or society. Particularly in research settings in which participants have low literacy, low income, and poor access to modern health care and medicines, even a robust consent process may do little to countervail the pressures that lead people to participate in research.

Informed consent and other ethical considerations become more complex as the clinical risks to participants increase and the clinical benefits decrease. In making the determination that an RCT that FDA is considering requiring can be carried out in a manner that provides sufficient protection of and respect for research participants, FDA must always balance its ethical obligations to protect the public from unsafe drugs with its ethical obligations to safeguard the rights and interests of people who participate in research supporting the agency's decisions about drug benefits and risks. Difficult choices must be confronted when the study design that seems to offer the greatest potential for obtaining knowledge relevant to the public health question also involves the greatest burden on and risks to research participants.

If uncertainty about the benefit–risk profile of a marketed drug exists, there may be circumstances in which it is ethically acceptable to ask patients to participate in an RCT that exposes them to risks that are not likely to be outweighed by any prospect of clinical benefit to them and that are readily avoidable with treatment options available to patients outside research participation. These circumstances may be a satisfied when a question of pressing public health importance cannot be properly answered without the conduct of the study, the study may be appropriately designed to provide high-quality evidence that is needed to answer the question, and other conditions that are intended to safeguard the rights and interests of participants can be satisfied. Those safeguards should include but are not limited to:

- Determination by an appropriately constituted review committee that the additional net risk is small enough for it to be ethical to ask people whether they are willing to accept the risk *solely* to contribute to the public good.

- Minimization of additional net risk by careful study design and implementation of a robust monitoring plan throughout the study.
- Inclusion of special measures in the process of soliciting informed consent to confirm that patients understand and willingly accept that they are assuming an additional net risk—beyond what they are likely to face in clinical practice—solely in the interest of the public good.
- Implementation of processes to ensure that over the course of the trial participants are regularly informed of any changes in clinical practice or the medical literature that are relevant to assessments of the comparative benefits and risks of trial participation and (non-research) clinical management.

External IRBs and data monitoring committees (DMCs) overseeing FDA-required postmarketing RCTs should have all the information necessary to ensure that the trials they oversee are ethically acceptable and adequately monitored. To that end, FDA should provide all relevant IRBs (centralized and multiple IRBs) and DMCs with sufficient information to permit appropriate continuing oversight of the RCT in accordance with their roles. That should include information about the public health question at issue, the specifics of the study design that it has deemed suitable to address the question—including any design features that it views as necessary for the ethical justification of the study, and any changes in clinical practice or professional standards that arise over the course of the RCT that might affect the benefit–risk profile of the drug and influence a person's decision about whether to continue to participate.

Under what circumstances should head-to-head randomized clinical trials for safety be required?

The committee's answer to this question assumes that it has already been determined, according to the criteria and processes outlined elsewhere in this report, that it is appropriate for FDA to require a postmarketing study and that this study should be an RCT.

A head-to-head trial involves a comparison of two active treatments that are both indicated for the same patients who have the same condition. The committee considered study designs in the context of a public health question about the benefits or risks associated with a drug. The public health question is most likely to be addressed by comparing the drug at issue with the therapies likely to be used if the drug were removed from the market or its use were restricted; that is the decision-relevant public health question. However, for such a study to be scientifically valid and ethical, the active comparator must have a well-defined benefit–risk profile and be a clinically acceptable alternative. The dose of the comparator needs to be carefully defined so neither the benefits nor risks differ appreciably from what would be expected in common use. Unless precluded by toxicity or tolerability, it would be expected that the dose of the comparator should be at least equal in effectiveness to the target agent. If no comparator treatment exists or no comparator has a well-defined benefit–risk profile, then typically at least one arm of the study should be some form of "usual care" or a placebo if usual care is not a proven or active treatment. If there are ethical reasons for not having a usual-care or placebo arm in the study—for example, if the treatment in question is for an irreversible and fatal disease—a treatment that does not have a well-defined benefit–risk profile might be the only ethically acceptable comparator. In such cases, FDA should take the questionable benefit–risk profiles of the drug and its comparator into account when interpreting the results of the study.

REFERENCES

Borer, J. S., H. Pouleur, E. Abadie, F. Follath, J. Wittes, M. A. Pfeffer, B. Pitt, and F. Zannad. 2007. Cardiovascular safety of drugs not intended for cardiovascular use: Need for a new conceptual basis for assessment and approval. *European Heart Journal* 28(15):1904-1909.

Flory, J., and E. Emanuel. 2004. Interventions to improve research participants' understanding in informed consent for research. *JAMA* 292(13):1593-1601.

Hiatt, W. R. 2006. Observational studies of drug safety—aprotinin and the absence of transparency. *New England Journal of Medicine* 355(21):2171-2173.

IOM (Institute of Medicine). 2007. *The future of drug safety: Promoting and protecting the health of the public.* Washington, DC: The National Academies Press.

Kass, N. E., and H. A. Taylor. 2008. *Empirical research on informed consent: A review of the literature prepared for the National Academies Workshop on Collecting, Storing, Accessing, and Protecting Data Containing Biological Measures* (unpublished).

Lindegger, G., C. Milford, C. Slack, M. Quayle, X. Xaba, and E. Vardas. 2006. Beyond the checklist: Assessing understanding for HIV vaccine trial participation in South Africa. *Journal of Acquired Immune Deficiency Syndromes* 43(5):560-566.

NRC (National Research Council). 2009. *Science and decisions: Advancing risk assessment.* Washington, DC: The National Academies Press.

NRC. 2011. *A risk-characterization framework for decision-making at the Food and Drug Administration.* Washington, DC: The National Academies Press.

Psaty, B. M., and J. P. Vandenbroucke. 2008. Opportunities for enhancing the FDA guidance on pharmacovigilance. *JAMA* 300(8):952-954.

Ray, W. A., and C. M. Stein. 2006. Reform of drug regulation—beyond an independent drug-safety board. *New England Journal of Medicine* 354(2):194-201.

A

Other Elements of the Food and Drug Administration Amendments Act

Chapter 1 discusses three sections of the Food and Drug Administration Amendments Act (FDAAA) of 2007[1] that are integral to the US Food and Drug Administration's (FDA's) ability to take a lifecycle approach to drug oversight: the authority to require postmarketing studies; the authority to require risk evaluation and mitigation strategies; and the requirement to develop a large-scale active surveillance system. This appendix discusses additional sections of FDAAA that improve FDA's ability to oversee drugs in the postmarketing setting: increased authority to enforce submission of clinical-trial registry and database information; increased authority over the contents of direct-to-consumer advertising; increased authority to order labeling and warning changes in a timely manner; increased resources directed toward identifying and mitigating drug risks both premarketing and postmarketing; and increased requirements for agency transparency and risk communication. Those five elements are described briefly below.

CONTENTS OF CLINICALTRIALS.GOV

ClinicalTrials.gov is a clinical-trial registry and database website that is supported and housed by the National Institutes of Health (NIH) and provides public access to information regarding clinical trials. ClinicalTrials.gov was initially mandated by the FDA Modernization Act of 1997,[2] and required that clinical trials for effectiveness conducted under an investigational new drug application (IND) for "serious or life threatening diseases" must be registered in

[1]Food and Drug Administration Amendments Act of 2007, PL 110-85, 121 Stat. 823 (2007).

[2]Food and Drug Administration Modernization Act of 1997, PL 105-115, 111 Stat. 2296 (1997).

ClinicalTrials.gov; there was no enforcement capability to ensure that privately funded trials were included, and study results were not included in the database.[3] FDAAA expanded the requirements for registration of clinical trials to include all trials beyond Phase 1 that are parts of new drug applications,[4] required the reporting of results of those trials,[5] and gave FDA the ability to enforce registration by allowing penalties if drug sponsors failed to comply with submission of information to ClinicalTrials.gov.[6] The statute directs NIH to ensure that the information submitted is truthful and not misleading.[7] Sponsors must submit any changes in the information to NIH. FDAAA also increased FDA's regulatory responsibility for the form of and methods for reporting serious adverse events in ClinicalTrials.gov.[8]

CONTENTS OF DIRECT-TO-CONSUMER ADVERTISING

FDAAA provides FDA with the authority to require that direct-to-consumer radio and television advertisements include a "major statement relating to side effects and contraindications" of the drug and that the "major statement" be "presented in a clear, conspicuous, and neutral manner".[9] FDAAA stipulates that in the absence of such a statement, FDA can determine that the advertisement is "false or misleading",[10] and establishes civil penalties for dissemination of such advertisements.[11]

On March 29, 2010, FDA published in the *Federal Register* the following proposed standards for evaluating a "major statement":

- Information is presented in language that is readily understandable by consumers.
- Audio information is understandable in terms of the volume, articulation, and pacing used.
- Textual information is placed appropriately and is presented against a contrasting background for sufficient duration and in a size and font style that can be read easily; and there are no distractions—such as statements, text, images or sounds—that detract from the communication of the major statement.[12]

---

[3]42 USC § 282(i) (2010).
[4]42 USC § 282(j)(1)(A) (2010).
[5]42 USC § 282(j)(3) (2010).
[6]42 USC § 282(j)(5)(E) (2010).
[7]42 USC § 282(j)(5)(D) (2010).
[8]42 USC § 282(j)(3)(I) (2010).
[9]21 USC § 352(n) (2010).
[10]21 USC § 352(q) (2010).
[11]21 USC § 352(r) (2010).
[12]Direct-to-Consumer Prescription Drug Advertisements; Presentation of the Major Statement in Television and Radio Advertisements in a Clear, Conspicuous, and Neutral Manner, 75 *Fed. Reg.* 15376-15387 (March 29, 2010) (amending 20 CFR § 202.1).

Final standards for evaluating a major statement are not yet published.

Under FDAAA, FDA also has the authority to require a company to disclose a drug's approval date for up to 2 years after a drug is approved if it "determines that [an] advertisement would otherwise be false or misleading".[13] FDA has declined to require an indication that a drug is new out of concern that "new" will be wrongly interpreted by consumers to imply "new and improved" (FDA, 2009a).

LABEL AND WARNING CHANGES

Before the passage of FDAAA, FDA could not require a drug manufacturer to change a label even if FDA became aware of new safety information about a marketed drug. FDA negotiated with the manufacturer about the language of the label, and its recourse was to use a claim of "misbranding" to revoke, or threaten to revoke, approval if a company was not willing to change a drug's label (Carpenter, 2010). Under FDAAA, FDA can require changes in the label of a drug to reflect new information about its benefit–risk profile. Those changes can include "boxed warnings, contraindications, warnings, precautions, or adverse reactions".[14]

INCREASED RESOURCES FOR DRUG SAFETY

In addition to increasing FDA's postmarketing responsibility and authority, FDAAA specifies that user fees will be "dedicated toward expediting the drug development process and the process for the review of human drug applications, including postmarketing drug safety activities".[15] Much of the funding comes from a specific authorization of $225 million over 5 years for "drug safety".[16] The funds are being used by the Center for Drug Evaluation and Review (CDER) and others in FDA to increase the number of staff dedicated to the safety evaluation of marketed medications and to administer CDER's new safety-related authority under FDAAA, including the implementation of REMSs, postmarketing requirements (PMRs), safety-related labeling changes, and active postmarketing risk identification (such as Sentinel) (FDA, 2009b).

TRANSPARENCY AND COMMUNICATION

FDAAA requires FDA to improve the availability and transparency of information about the drug-approval process, approved drugs, and, in particular, drug

[13] 21 USC § 353b(e) (2010).
[14] 21 USC § 355(o)(4)(B) (2010).
[15] 21 USC § 379g note (2010).
[16] 21 USC § 379h(b)(4)(B) (2010).

safety. To that end, the website *MedWatch: The FDA Safety Information and Adverse Event Reporting Program* (http://www.fda.gov/Safety/MedWatch) now includes information on new package inserts and labels, recent safety information and alerts, quarterly reports on potential safety issues identified by using the Adverse Event Reporting System database, and links to other FDA-approved safety information. FDA has recently taken advantage of new technology by making electronic subscriptions available to MedWatch via e-newsletters, safety alerts, and Twitter (FDA, 2012).

Under FDAAA, FDA is also required to include on its website the approval package, which contains FDA staff reviews of a drug with proprietary information redacted, for any new molecular entity. For drugs that are not new molecular entities, it is required to provide the same material upon request. That approval information is now posted for each drug on FDA's website at Drugs@FDA.[17]

As suggested in the 2007 Institute of Medicine report, FDAAA called for FDA to form an Advisory Committee on Risk Communication,[18] which was established in 2008. The role of the advisory committee is to improve how information on drugs and drug safety is communicated to health care professionals and the public.[19]

REFERENCES

Carpenter, D. 2010. The other side of the gate: Reputation, power, and post-market regulation. In *Reputation and power. Organizational image and pharmaceutical regulation at the FDA*. Cambridge, NY: Princeton University Press.

FDA (US Food and Drug Administration). 2009a. *IOM recommendations: FDA actions update*. http://www.fda.gov/Safety/SafetyofSpecificProducts/ucm184598.htm (accessed March 20, 2012).

FDA. 2009b. *FDAAA implementation—highlights two years after enactment.* http://www.fda.gov/RegulatoryInformation/Legislation/FederalFoodDrugandCosmeticActFDCAct/SignificantAmendmentstotheFDCAct/FoodandDrugAdministrationAmendmentsActof2007/ucm184271.htm (accessed March 20, 2012).

FDA. 2012. *MedWatch: The FDA safety information and adverse event reporting program*. http://www.fda.gov/Safety/MedWatch (accessed August 17, 2011).

[17]Drugs@FDA is located at http://www.accessdata.fda.gov/scripts/cder/drugsatfda (accessed on February 13, 2012).

[18]21 USC § 360bbb–6 (2010).

[19]21 USC § 355(r)(6) (2010).

B

Committee's Letter Report

ETHICAL ISSUES IN STUDYING THE SAFETY OF APPROVED DRUGS: A LETTER REPORT

Margaret Hamburg, MD
Commissioner
US Food and Drug Administration
10903 New Hampshire Avenue
Silver Spring, MD 20993-0002

Dear Dr. Hamburg,

In April 2010, the US Food and Drug Administration (FDA) asked the Institute of Medicine (IOM) to respond to five questions about ethical and scientific issues in studying the safety of approved drugs. FDA requested a final report on the five questions in 2011. In light of the scheduling of a joint meeting of FDA's Endocrinologic and Metabolic Drugs Advisory Committee and Drug Safety and Risk Management Advisory Committee on July 13–14, 2010, FDA further requested a letter report addressing question 1 of the charge—"What are the ethical and informed consent issues that must be considered when designing randomized clinical trials to evaluate potential safety risks?"—by July 2010. The attached letter report, which has been reviewed in accordance with IOM review procedures, addresses that question.

Sincerely,
Ruth R. Faden
Steven N. Goodman
Cochairs, Committee on Ethical and Scientific Issues in Studying the Safety of Approved Drugs

CONTEXT OF THE INSTITUTE OF MEDICINE STUDY AND CHARGE TO THE COMMITTEE

Public Law 110-85, the Food and Drug Administration Amendments Act of 2007 (FDAAA 2007; PL 110-85) expanded the US Food and Drug Administration (FDA) authorities and responsibilities over drugs[1] during the postmarketing period (that is, after a drug is approved to enter the US market). The expanded authorities, many of which were recommended in *The Future of Drug Safety: Promoting and Protecting the Health of the Public* (IOM, 2007), provide FDA with additional regulatory tools, such as requiring clinical trials or other studies after a drug has been approved, to protect the health of the public. With the expanded postmarketing authorities comes the recognition that critical decisions regarding the study of drugs after approval raise new challenges and questions, both ethical and scientific, for the agency to consider. FDA therefore asked the Institute of Medicine (IOM) to "convene a committee to evaluate the scientific and ethical issues involved in conducting studies of the safety of approved drugs." The specific questions that the committee was asked to evaluate are presented in Box 1. In light of the scheduling of a joint meeting of FDA's Endocrinologic and Metabolic Drugs Advisory Committee and Drug Safety and Risk Management Advisory Committee on July 13–14, 2010, FDA requested a letter report addressing question 1 of the charge—"What are the ethical and informed consent issues that must be considered when designing randomized clinical trials to evaluate potential safety risks?"—by July 2010.

COMMITTEE'S APPROACH TO ITS CHARGE

In response to FDA's request, IOM convened a committee of persons who had expertise in clinical trials, epidemiology, pharmacoepidemiology, bioethics, law, patient safety, biostatistics, public health, and health policy. Those experts agreed to prepare both this letter report, which focuses on question 1 of the charge, by July 2010 and a final report that addresses all the questions in the charge by 2011.

For the present letter report, the committee held one meeting, which included an open session in which it heard from representatives of FDA and representatives of the Agency for Healthcare Research and Quality (AHRQ) and the National Institutes of Health (NIH), which funded this report with FDA. The committee provided an opportunity for other stakeholders to present their perspectives and concerns at the meeting. The committee conducted searches of the literature on the ethics of clinical trials and informed consent relevant to postmarketing clini-

[1] For simplicity, the committee uses the term *drugs* throughout this report, but similar considerations would apply to biologics.

BOX 1
Charge to the Committee

The Food and Drug Administration (FDA) has requested that the Institute of Medicine convene a committee to evaluate the scientific and ethical issues involved in conducting studies of the safety of approved drugs. Questions to be explored by a committee include:

1. What are the ethical and informed consent issues that must be considered when designing randomized clinical trials to evaluate potential safety risks?
2. What are the strengths and weaknesses of various approaches, including observational studies, including patient registries, meta-analyses, including patient-level data meta-analyses, and randomized controlled trials, to generate evidence about safety questions?
3. Considering the speed, cost, and value of studies, what types of follow-up studies are appropriate to investigate different kinds of signals (detected pre-approval or post-marketing) and in what temporal order?
4. Under what circumstances should head-to-head randomized clinical trials for safety be required?
5. How should FDA factor in different kinds of safety evidence in considering different kinds of regulatory actions?

cal trials. This letter report does not, however, present a comprehensive literature review of the subject.

Given the short period available for preparing this letter report, the committee focused on identifying a conceptual framework to guide its analysis of the ethics of the design and conduct of postmarketing safety research required by FDA, including key issues that need to be taken into account in assessing ethics and informed consent in randomized controlled trials. In developing this framework, and in its explication in this letter report, the committee relied on the extensive body of codes, regulations and guidance on the ethics of research involving human participants, much of which is built around a commitment to several basic moral principles, including beneficence, respect for persons and their autonomy, and justice. The committee did not enumerate all the ways in which the issues raised in this letter report can affect the ethics of a study, did not detail how the various issues should be weighed against one another, and did not explore in depth issues related to the ethical and scientific justifications of randomized controlled trials. A more detailed analysis of those issues and their implications and effects will be included in the committee's final report.

BOX 2
Conceptual Framework for Analyzing the Ethics of Postmarketing Randomized Clinical Trials Required by the Food and Drug Administration: Four Central Classes of Considerations and Recommendations

I. **The Public Health Context.** The Food and Drug Administration (FDA) should determine that there is a substantial public health question about the nature or acceptability of the risks, or the risk–benefit profile, of a marketed drug—a question that requires a policy decision from FDA.

II. **Regulatory Science and Public Accountability**. FDA should use regulatory-science principles and practices that include processes of public accountability and transparency to determine the need for a policy decision, the need for new knowledge to support a policy decision, and the policy decision based on the new knowledge.

III. **Design Considerations.** It is appropriate for FDA to require that a randomized controlled trial be conducted to provide additional evidence about an approved drug's efficacy and safety only when (i) uncertainty about the risk-benefit balance is such that a responsible policy decision cannot be made based either on the existing evidence or on evidence from new observational studies, and (ii) the trial is properly designed and implemented to reduce uncertainty about the risk-benefit balance sufficiently for a responsible policy decision to be made.

IV. **Additional Ethical Obligations to Trial Participants.** FDA should ensure that the trial will answer the public health question with a design that minimizes risks to trial participants and involves ongoing monitoring of risks. The risks should be judged to be acceptable by appropriate oversight bodies before and during the trial and by trial participants at enrollment and as appropriate during the trial. Specifically, FDA and appropriate oversight bodies should ensure that the trial includes a comprehensive and meaningful informed consent process that continues during the trial and that takes into account any substantial changes in clinical practice and professional standards and any new research findings relevant to a participant's willingness to accept the risks associated with the trial. The FDA and appropriate oversight bodies should ensure that those conducting the trial convey such changes to participants in a timely and understandable fashion.

The committee's conceptual framework consists of four classes of considerations, as shown in Box 2. In accordance with the framework, the remainder of this letter report is organized in four major sections: the public health context of drug safety, regulatory science and public accountability, design considerations, and additional ethical obligations to research participants.

THE PUBLIC HEALTH CONTEXT OF DRUG SAFETY

The ethics of any postmarketing study required by FDA, including randomized controlled trials, should be assessed in the context of FDA's mission to promote and protect public health. The safety of the US drug supply contributes to the nation's health, and FDA is the agency responsible for ensuring this safety. As stated by the FDA commissioner and deputy commissioner, "to be healthy, people need access to . . . innovative, safe, and effective medical products" and "FDA's job is to support this access and, in doing so, to promote health, prevent illness, and prolong life" (Hamburg and Sharfstein, 2009). With specific reference to drugs, FDA's job includes (FDA, 2010a)

- "Protecting the public health by assuring the safety, effectiveness, and security of human and veterinary drugs, vaccines and other biological products"
- "Advancing the public health by helping to speed product innovations"
- "Helping the public get the accurate, science-based information they need to use medicines and foods to improve their health"

The committee believes that FDA, to fulfill its public health mission, should allow a drug to enter and remain on the market only if the balance of the risk to the benefit is appropriate for its intended use. The committee also believes that it is critical to FDA's public health mission that the agency: provide information needed by clinicians to prescribe a drug responsibly and needed by patients to take it appropriately; foster innovation and drug development by using decision-making processes that are predictable, clear, and timely; and conduct its responsibilities in a way that fosters public trust in the drug oversight system.

Ensuring the acceptability of the risk–benefit profile of a drug after it is approved for the US market is no less central to FDA's public health mission than ensuring the acceptability of the profile before it is permitted to enter the market. As discussed later in this letter report, because of the infrequency and delayed occurrence of some adverse events, there is often more uncertainty about the risks posed by a new drug at the time of approval than there is about its efficacy. In addition, when an agent is approved on the basis of surrogate end points, the estimated degree of benefit may change when the effect on clinical end points is studied. Postmarketing research may be important for examining such clinical end points. Therefore, the committee agrees with a previous IOM committee that a drug-safety system "has at its core a lifecycle approach to drug risk and benefit" and that such a system "would require continuous availability of new data and ongoing, active reassessment of risk and benefit to drive regulatory action (responsive to the accumulating information about a given drug), and regulatory authority that is strong both before and after approval" (IOM, 2007).

The new authorities and regulatory tools provided in FDAAA 2007 (PL 110-85) expanded the possibilities for FDA to adopt a comprehensive life-cycle approach to the assessment of the risks and benefits associated with marketed drugs. FDAAA 2007 mandated that FDA establish an active surveillance system for monitoring drugs by using electronic data from health-care information holders and gave FDA new authorities that include the ability to require revisions to a product label, to require further study of a drug, to restrict the use of a treatment to specified populations, and to require a formal Risk Evaluation and Mitigation Strategy (REMS). Those authorities provide new regulatory opportunities that are short of the pre-existing option of drug withdrawal. Under FDAAA 2007, FDA can require postmarketing studies and clinical trials under the following circumstances (PL 110-85):

> "To assess a known serious risk related to the use of the drug involved."
> "To assess signals of serious risk related to the use of the drug."
> "To identify an unexpected serious risk when available data indicates the potential for a serious risk."

The ability to require further study of a drug is a powerful tool for FDA to use in acquiring additional information to make informed, science-based decisions as part of its public health mission. In making a decision whether to require a postmarketing study, however, FDA not only should consider the ethical issues that arise in obtaining information to clarify a policy decision[2] but should bear in mind that such issues vary among types of studies.

The committee concludes that for FDA-required postmarketing research to be ethical, a critical first step is the determination by FDA that it is facing a policy decision of importance to public health that cannot satisfactorily be resolved with existing evidence.[3,4]

---

[2]When referring to a policy decision the committee means choosing among the range of responses available to the FDA when safety signals emerge—including the decision to continue a drug's monitoring plan without modification, the decision to add a warning to a drug's label, the decision to require a postmarketing trial, and the decision to remove a drug from the market—some of which are not mutually exclusive.

[3]The committee's conclusion is consistent with that of a previous committee of the National Research Council that was related to Environmental Protection Agency consideration of research involving human subjects (NRC, 2004).

[4]This conclusion, and this entire letter report, is specific to research on postmarketed products required by FDA. In this regulatory and public health context, it is critical from an ethics standpoint that existing evidence be insufficient to make an appropriate policy determination. Scientific studies

REGULATORY SCIENCE AND PUBLIC ACCOUNTABILITY

As noted above, FDA can require a postmarketing trial "to assess signals of serious risk" (PL 110-85). The key to the ethics of a postmarketing safety trial is a determination that a safety signal, if it represents a true risk, would warrant a policy decision and that new knowledge is needed to determine the existence and magnitude of the risk and thereby inform the nature of the decision. If, for example, the existing information about a safety risk is sufficient to warrant the removal of a drug from the market, then it would be unethical to conduct a trial. On the other hand, existing evidence about a new safety signal may be sufficient to warrant a change in labeling but not sufficient to warrant removal from the market, a policy decision that may be appropriate once the risks, or risks in relation to potential benefits, are better characterized. In such a context, it may be possible to design and implement an ethically acceptable trial. The same reasoning applies to judgments about whether a current trial should be stopped. If new evidence from any source, including the trial itself, is determined to be sufficiently compelling to ground a policy decision without waiting for additional new information, allowing the trial to continue would be unethical.

The ethics of postmarketing studies requires that the kinds of determinations outlined above be based on the best principles and practices for making policy decisions under conditions of uncertainty, including appropriate processes for transparency in decision making and public accountability. Those principles and practices, sometimes referred to as the emerging field of regulatory science,[5] require that policy decisions reflect the best available scientific evidence and analytic techniques drawn from a wide array of disciplines and technical expertise, including decision sciences, behavioral economics, and cognitive psychology. Public accountability and transparency increase the likelihood that the perspectives of stakeholders,[6] who have kinds of knowledge different from those of technical experts, are included in the making of policy decisions. Transparency and other public accountability processes also may increase the likelihood that the public will view regulatory and policy decisions, including the conduct of a trial and a decision to continue or discontinue a clinical trial, as fair and acceptable.[7]

---

of approved and marketed medical products outside this FDA context are an increasing component of biomedical and health services research and also can contribute significantly to population health.

[5]FDA defines regulatory science as "the development and use of new tools, standards and approaches to more efficiently develop products and to more effectively evaluate product safety, efficacy and quality" (FDA, 2010b).

[6]Relevant government stakeholders include FDA, NIH, AHRQ, and the Centers for Disease Control and Prevention. Relevant nongovernment stakeholders include industry, academe, health-care providers, payers, patients, and other members of the public.

[7]As the committee has already noted, FDA and those advising FDA therefore should have access to all information relevant to a given public health question, whether or not the information is deemed proprietary information or trade secrets. One tension in meeting acceptable standards of transparency with stakeholders is managing public access to such information.

Accurately assessing the risks posed by and the potential benefits of a drug requires the use of a wide variety of scientific data, including findings from animal studies of toxicology, basic research (for example, mechanistic studies and structure–activity relationships), clinical trials, high-quality epidemiologic and health-services research (such as observational studies and meta-analyses), and postmarketing surveillance systems that detect and analyze adverse events. FDA and those advising FDA therefore should be able to consider all data, and the design and analyses that led to those data, that are relevant to a given public health question, whether or not they are deemed proprietary information or trade secrets.

Judgments about the adequacy of available evidence for FDA decisions require input from a multidisciplinary team acting through a process that can integrate and take advantage of the different kinds of knowledge and perspectives that reside in clinical practice, biologic science, ethics, biostatistics, epidemiology, and research design. The decision-making process should also minimize and correct for potential cognitive and intellectual biases that arise from previous policy decisions or strongly held opinions—for example, the human tendency to focus on evidence that confirms a pre-existing belief or decision and to discount evidence that contradicts it.

Modern tools for risk communication and public engagement should be used to ensure that all stakeholders—including physicians, other health professionals, interested patients and their families, and members of the public—understand the decision problem facing the agency, including what is known about the benefits and risks associated with the therapy in question and the pertinent uncertainties. Uncertainties could pertain to the quantity and quality of evidence, the risk–benefit profile, or the effect of policy decisions on future risks. Engagement with stakeholders is required to explain the types of uncertainties at issue and how the agency is dealing with the uncertainties in making its policy decision and to permit the agency to understand how those affected by its actions weigh risks and benefits.[8]

In using best practices to determine whether additional research is required, the agency should also keep in mind that one aspect of its mission to advance public health involves accelerating the evolution of effective new therapies from bench to bedside by encouraging product innovation (FDA, 2010a). That is most likely to occur when FDA's regulatory regime facilitates industry's ability to make informed research-and-development decisions—for example, by applying consistent requirements and criteria for assessing risks and possible benefits, by making decisions in accord with a clear and understandable framework, and by

[8]The committee acknowledges that there are significant challenges to implementing policy making and regulatory processes that appropriately balance scientific evidence and stakeholder input (Lomas et al., 2005).

responding in predictable ways to different kinds of information, including new information about risk.

DESIGN CONSIDERATIONS

It is never ethical to involve research participants in an inappropriately designed or inappropriately conducted study or any study that does not have a reasonable prospect of answering the research question under study. Without a reasonable prospect of contributing to scientific knowledge, the exposure of research participants to even minimal risk or inconvenience can never be justified. In the case of postmarketing clinical trials required by FDA, that ethical precept requires further specification and strengthening. In particular, before a clinical trial is selected as the design of choice, it should be determined that no other research or information gathering effort—including a new observational study—can reduce the uncertainty about a drug's risk–benefit profile sufficiently to support a responsible policy decision.[9] It is also critical that the clinical trial be designed to provide precisely the data needed to facilitate the policy decision that needs to be made. Finally, there should be sufficient continuing monitoring of the trial to ensure that the associated risks (if any) continue to be acceptable.[10]

A comprehensive assessment of risks associated with a drug is often impossible in the premarketing-study phases because of small samples, short followup, and the selected nature of the populations included in preapproval trials. In addition, across the lifespan of a drug, the benefit profile and consequently the acceptability of risks in relation to benefits can change with the development of alternative treatment or prevention methods or even with the evolution of the disease or causative agent, such as the development of resistance to a given antibiotic. The assessment of benefits and risks is a dynamic process that requires continual revisiting and monitoring, and changes in evidence about risks should be considered against evidence about benefits at the time of the reassessment. Postmarketing safety studies constitute an important part of understanding the dynamics of the risk–benefit balance.

The most important features of any research are that the research question is properly conceived and that the proposed study is designed appropriately to address the question that has been specified. In the postmarketing context all such questions pertain to the risk–benefit profile of an approved treatment. However, not all changes in the risk–benefit balance are policy concerns, although they might merit alterations in medical practice. For example, the introduction

[9]This observation is again specific to the FDA context under consideration in this letter report.

[10]Continuing monitoring of a trial is essential to ensure that risks (if any) to participants continue to be acceptable. How monitoring should be conducted is also an essential feature of a properly designed trial. In this letter report, we have elected to discuss monitoring in the section on design considerations. It would fit equally well in the section on other obligations to trial participants.

of lower-risk therapies of similar or greater efficacy would justify changes in medical practice; without a new safety concern about the old agent, however, this situation might not require action by FDA.

A number of questions of policy relevance can remain or arise after approval. They include:

- Whether treatments approved on the basis of surrogate end points or biomarkers—such as lipid concentrations, blood pressure, or glycated hemoglobin—show improvement in clinical end points.
- Whether benefits seen in preapproval studies are not experienced by identifiable patient groups, in which case the acceptability of risks in these groups might be altered.
- Whether additional safety concerns that affect the risk–benefit profile arise from
  - Newly identified serious adverse events.
  - More serious or more frequent harms than expected in the intended population or in identifiable patient groups that may be defined by co-treatments, patient characteristics or co-morbidities, or disease or treatment-delivery characteristics.

New safety signals may arise from various sources: spontaneous reports of adverse events, safety-surveillance systems, observational studies, meta-analyses, and randomized trials. FDA can require new research to address key safety questions if the existing evidence is insufficient to infer causality or to characterize the frequency and severity of observed harms with adequate confidence or if such evidence is not complete enough to judge the acceptability of the risk–benefit profile for a drug's intended use.

The first step in deciding whether new research is needed is to assess the strength of the existing evidence related to new safety or risk–benefit concerns. The traditional hierarchies of evidence based on study design, which are regularly used in determinations of efficacy (Barton et al., 2007; Owens et al., 2010), might not apply in a straightforward manner to safety evidence. Randomized controlled trials are optimal for efficacy determinations because the randomization of large numbers of patients creates groups that have similar average risks of the outcome of interest. Observational studies designed to evaluate the efficacy or anticipated effects of treatment, either intended benefits or expected harms, are often liable to confounding by indication (Vandenbroucke and Psaty, 2008). That is, the reasons that physicians treat patients differently or that patients prefer particular treatment options are often related to factors that themselves affect outcomes. For example, if sicker patients choose medical care more often and avoid surgery, observational studies of surgical vs medical care could provide false evidence that surgery has more favorable results than medical care. Similarly, if an adverse effect of a drug is known, physicians may avoid prescribing it for patients who are at higher risk for the effect. Thus, in observational studies of the anticipated effects of treatment, it may be difficult to determine whether differences in outcomes are due to the treatments themselves or to the other factors that led to the treatment choices. Although such differences due to other factors can often be minimized through design and analysis, they cannot be eliminated with the same confidence as one would attach to a high-quality randomized trial.

In the evaluation of unintended or previously unsuspected effects of drugs, however, observational safety studies are less likely than studies of known effects to be influenced by confounding by indication. Under specific circumstances, observational studies may be adequate not only to identify the presence of an important safety issue but, if the findings are replicated, to provide convincing evidence that an association is causal. For instance, a well-designed and well-conducted observational comparison of two similar drugs that came onto the market at the same time, that are used for the same condition at the same stage, and that have similar side-effect profiles could provide useful and valid estimates of the risk associated with a safety signal (Vandenbroucke and Psaty, 2008). In addition, some observational studies of safety may have distinct advantages over trials. They can often be much larger than randomized controlled trials, involve longer patient followup, include a broader diversity of patients and care settings, and be completed more quickly. Because of those features, observational studies evaluating infrequent outcomes that occur long after exposure and in which confounding by indication is unlikely can sometimes provide higher-quality safety evidence than randomized controlled trials, if the trials were not optimally designed to capture such safety outcomes.

The relative strength of other research designs may be different between safety and efficacy determinations. Meta-analysis of randomized controlled trials can increase the ability to detect rare events, but if the trials encompassed by the meta-analysis were not well designed or well conducted to capture safety outcomes or reported them inconsistently (Ioannidis and Lau, 2001), the meta-analysis may produce misleading results. An unexpectedly low incidence in the control group of a randomized trial may signal a problem with the conduct of the study.

All observational studies and meta-analyses of randomized trials may be affected by confounding or bias. If the estimated relative risks are small, selection bias, confounding, and measurement error may be alternative explanations for associations found in an observational study. But small relative risks of serious outcomes associated with widely used agents can have substantial public health consequences. Under such circumstances, if there is substantial uncertainty about a safety signal, a well-designed and well-conducted postmarketing randomized clinical trial is the best approach for characterizing the risk–benefit profile. The opportunity to evaluate both risks and benefits in the same study is an important advantage of randomized trials.

In evaluating or proposing a postmarketing randomized trial, the design and conduct should be closely scrutinized for quality and relevance to the US context. Findings from trials conducted in countries where medical care differs substantially from that in the United States may be less relevant to US populations (HHS, 2010).

Non-inferiority studies—designed with the one-sided intent to show that a therapy is not worse than another by some predetermined margin—pose some special challenges compared with the superiority trials traditionally used to evaluate efficacy (Fleming, 2008; Kaul and Diamond, 2006, 2007). The implications of poor quality in the design or conduct of a non-inferiority study are often the opposite of those in a superiority trial (Temple and Ellenberg, 2000). Low-quality study conduct, such as poor compliance with treatment regimens, usually biases a superiority trial toward a finding of no difference between treatments but often biases a non-inferiority trial toward a finding of "equivalence" or "non-inferiority" between treatments. Thus, the findings of a poorly conducted non-inferiority trial may inappropriately support a conclusion that the treatments under study are "equally" efficacious or "equally" safe. Non-inferiority trials may therefore require special oversight and scrutiny by FDA, as well as appropriate adjustment for poor compliance, to ensure valid inferences.

Another critical, and perhaps underappreciated, aspect of non-inferiority designs that makes them problematic for safety assessments is the rationale for the choice of the non-inferiority margin. The selection of a margin that is too large can result in a finding that the two treatments are "equally safe" even if their risks are substantially different. Regardless of the hypothesis-test verdict in such a trial, FDA should look carefully at the estimated difference and its confidence interval in deciding whether meaningful differences in safety have truly been ruled out (Kaul and Diamond, 2006).

All those considerations also apply to the assessment of existing evidence and to a determination of what kind of research design is needed to generate new evidence. Because observational designs usually generate fewer ethical concerns than randomized controlled trials, a decision to require a randomized controlled trial to resolve safety questions should be based on the determination that neither the existing evidence nor new, prospectively conducted observational studies can provide safety evidence sufficiently reliable for FDA to make a sound policy decision.

If a randomized controlled trial is deemed necessary for an FDA-policy decision, its characteristics should include the following:

1. **The evidence gap should be clearly present and specifically identified, and the research question and study design should be precisely crafted to address the gap.**

This effort involves not only the review of the quantity, quality, and consistency of the existing evidence but careful selection of a study population, end points, treatments, comparators, and setting.

2. The trial should be adequately powered, and the trial procedures and the pre-specified analytic plans should be appropriate to provide answers to the study questions.

If a study addresses more than one question or end point, it should be powered so that all major outcomes of interest can be adequately studied. If the proposed trial uses a non-inferiority design, the non-inferiority margin should confidently exclude small risks of serious events, especially for widely used drugs. The analytic plan should be laid out in detail at the time the study protocol is approved by the sponsor and institutional review boards (IRBs). The data-management and quality-assurance plans should be fully described and adequate both for the protection of research participants and for the trial to achieve its aims.

3. The inclusion and exclusion criteria should reflect the best available knowledge about risks and potential benefits in the population.

From a public health perspective, it is desirable to test the effectiveness and safety of a drug for its intended use in a sample that is representative of the population receiving the drug. However, the ethical obligation to minimize risks to research participants may require excluding some who are at a high risk of adverse events. It is never ethically justified to include in a postmarketing trial participants for whom the drug is contraindicated by the currently approved product label unless their involvement is necessary to answer a specific question and the risks to them posed by participation are acceptable.[11] The exclusion of participants for whom more moderate safety warnings or precautions have been issued presents a more difficult case and involves a tradeoff among several considerations: the prevention of possible harm to participants, the generalizability of the trial's findings to patient populations in which the drug is being used, and the ability to reach an answer to the study's safety questions more quickly (if the participants are likely to experience the outcome of interest at a higher rate).[12]

4. A comprehensive and robust safety-monitoring plan should be in place.

Every postmarketing clinical trial should have a properly qualified data-safety monitoring board (DSMB) in place with a written charter and a pre-specified data-monitoring plan, which includes statistical guidelines for stopping the trial

[11] If new information raises substantial uncertainty about the appropriateness of the current product warning, suggesting that it may be in the interest of patients to have the warning removed, it may be ethically acceptable to mount a trial that involves patients who are the subject of the warning to resolve this question.

[12] If such a trial is otherwise determined to be ethically justifiable, the consent process should emphasize to potential participants the existence of safety warnings or precautions.

early (Ellenberg et al., 2003; Grant et al., 2005). The frequency and intensity of DSMB review should be determined on the basis of the seriousness, incidence, and timing of known or possible harms. The DSMB should meet before trial onset to review and approve the charter, protocol, and monitoring procedures and then at regular intervals to review not just outcomes and adverse events but the various aspects of trial conduct and data quality.

A critical issue for trial monitoring is the standard of evidence required to halt a trial on the basis of harm. Typically, differences that cross pre-specified boundaries of statistical significance are required to halt trials for efficacy. However, depending on the type and degree of benefit, boundaries for harm may vary. The criteria for stopping a trial if the efficacy end point veers in the direction of harm are typically less stringent than the criteria for stopping for efficacy differences in the direction of benefit. Modest evidence of an adverse effect on an efficacy end point may be sufficient to rule out a clinically meaningful benefit even if the point estimate does not exclude a null effect. On the other hand, if benefit on one end point is established (for example, cardiovascular health), but the trial is being done to assess a suspected harm on a different end point (for example, hepatic failure), a higher standard of proof of the harm signal might be required. The Women's Health Initiative trial, for example, stopped its estrogen–progestin arm because the breast-cancer outcome crossed the pre-specified safety boundary and because the global index outcome just trended in the direction of harm, effectively ruling out a substantive net benefit (Wittes et al., 2007).

Other issues that affect the evidence threshold for stopping for harm are whether and how external information is used. This matter is not a settled methodologic issue, but if an emerging signal of harm is similar to that seen in external studies, it is ethically justified and may be ethically required to halt a trial earlier than if such evidence did not exist (Pocock, 1996).

Although vigorous safety monitoring is crucial for minimizing risks to participants in postmarketing trials, it is but one of multiple ethical considerations that must be addressed and satisfied if ethical obligations to research participants are to be fully honored.

ADDITIONAL ETHICAL OBLIGATIONS TO RESEARCH PARTICIPANTS

In the context of FDA-required randomized controlled trials, the need for a well-designed randomized controlled trial to determine the proper policy decision in response to a new drug-safety concern is a necessary but not sufficient condition for a trial to be ethically acceptable. Obligations to protect the rights and welfare of participants in a trial—to whom special duties of care and compassion may be owed because of illness, disability, or threat of illness—should be respected.

The general ethical principles governing research that involves human participants are well established and apply to the postmarketing context as they do to all human research (Council for International Organizations of Medical Sciences, 2002; DHEW, 1979). In the present letter report, the committee specifies aspects of those principles that have particular relevance to postmarketing research. In a postmarketing study, the risks to participants should be kept to the minimum that can be achieved while the trial is still able to answer the motivating policy question. The risk–benefit balance should be judged to be acceptable by FDA, participating IRBs, and the DSMB before initiation and throughout the course of the trial. That balance should also be acceptable to trial participants. To ensure that patients view the risks as acceptable in relation to any potential benefits, the trial should include a meaningful informed consent process that continues over the course of the trial and that includes prompt communication to participants of relevant new evidence or developments in clinical practice or professional standards that might affect their evaluation of the risks and benefits associated with continued participation.

Although the risks to research participants in randomized controlled trials are expected to be reasonable in relation to anticipated benefits, there is substantial consensus in both domestic regulatory and other guidance documents that different ways of balancing risk and benefit can be ethically justified. For example, both FDA regulations (21 CFR 50/56) and the Common Rule (45 CFR 46 Subpart A) distinguish among research that does not present greater than minimal risk, research that involves greater than minimal risk but offers the prospect of direct benefit to individual subjects, and research that involves greater than minimal risk and no prospect of direct benefit to individual subjects but is likely to yield scientific knowledge about the subjects' disorder or condition. A trial in which the risks to participants are not outweighed by the prospect of direct medical benefits to participants may be justifiable if a question of pressing public health importance cannot be properly answered without the conduct of the trial and if other conditions intended to safeguard the rights and interests of participants are satisfied. Those conditions include but are not limited to determination by appropriately constituted review committees that the risks are small enough to make it ethically acceptable to ask people whether they are willing to be exposed to the risks in the service of contributing to the public good, minimization of the risks through careful study design and a robust monitoring plan that is in place throughout the course of the trial, and implementation of a thorough informed consent process that adheres to the highest standards of respect for participants.

The informed consent process should provide an accurate, comprehensible explanation of the available knowledge about the risks and benefits associated with being assigned to the treatment and control groups. It is a bedrock principle of research ethics that participants who put themselves at risk in human research should receive an understandable, unbiased, accurate, and comprehensive disclosure of the potential benefits and risks attached to study participation (DHEW, 1979; ICH, 1996). A comprehensive disclosure is important to fulfill the substantive moral requirement of informed consent that participants have a meaningful *understanding* of what is being asked of them, including the risks and benefits (if any), not merely that information is provided to them (Faden and Beauchamp, 1986).

When a substantial amount of information indicating that a drug to be studied may involve serious safety risks has already accumulated, there are heightened obligations to ensure that potential participants understand the risks posed by study enrollment. Those obligations may include special efforts to communicate complex risk information clearly and to establish that participants have sufficient understanding of what the risks mean to them.

The emphasis given to risk information in the consent process should increase with the severity of risk and the level of certainty about the causal association between the drug and the adverse outcome. At a minimum, risks that should be disclosed should include any black-box warnings, the "major statement" currently listed in television advertisements, any adverse-event findings of an FDA advisory committee, and a summary of evidence from published peer-reviewed studies.

Communicating complicated risk information and research findings to participants poses challenges. It is critical that the information be conveyed in a manner that can be understood and weighed by participants. A "kitchen sink" approach to consent-form drafting, in which voluminous information is included with little attempt to distill it into a short format that is useful to participants, is unfortunately increasingly common in clinical trials and should be avoided. Participants are likely to be overwhelmed by a long and complex form and unable to weigh conflicting study findings or findings about different types of risk.

Verbal disclosures and written consent documents (both consent forms and information sheets) should help potential participants to understand how experts weigh the available evidence about the safety profile of the drug being studied. Moreover, there is a growing set of additional resources (for example, decision aids, videos, and interactive electronic presentations) to supplement written materials that may enhance participants' understanding of complex clinical information. Although evidence about the effectiveness of techniques designed to improve and document understanding among potential research participants is mixed (Kass and Taylor, 2008), such interventions as engaging in additional interpersonal conversations with potential participants and asking them to explain the study to a friend have been shown to be helpful (Flory and Emanuel, 2004; Kass and Taylor, 2008; Lindegger et al., 2006). Whatever efforts are employed to communicate with potential participants, it is key that they include information that is useful to participants about where the weight of the evidence falls with regard to serious risks and the level of confidence that experts have in drawing conclusions about the risks. A statement that "Some studies have found that the drug causes X, whereas others have not" may be true but misleading if nearly all well-designed studies have reached the same conclusion and there is little or no reliable evidence on the other side.

In addition to safety risks, people who are considering participation in research need to know how the care that they will receive in a protocol may differ from the care that they would ordinarily receive. Thus, information about "Alternatives to Participation" should convey the current standard of care for the health condition that the study drug targets. That is particularly crucial in cases in which medical practice has shifted away from prescribing the study drug because accumulating evidence from passive surveillance, observational studies, and small trials or meta-analyses suggests that another therapy is as effective and has a more favorable safety profile. A statement that if a potential participant does not enroll in the trial, he or she is more likely to have a different drug prescribed should be communicated in this situation. If clinical practice continues to shift during the trial period, the statement should be strengthened; researchers have an ethical obligation to disclose all new developments that may affect a person's willingness to continue to participate in a research study.

Comprehensive informed consent processes can help ensure that trial participants understand the potential consequences of study participation in addition to what they are contributing to the advancement of public health in the regulatory arena. They cannot, however, serve as an exclusive or sufficient ethical justification for conducting a postmarketing trial. The other ethical bases for initiating a trial should be independently satisfied. People should not be asked to assume risks that are not justified in light of the benefits of the trial to participants or society. Particularly in research settings in which participants have low literacy, low income, and poor access to modern health care and medicines, even a robust consent process may do little to countervail the pressures that lead people to participate in research. Regulators, IRBs, and DSMBs should serve as particularly strong bulwarks against unethical experimentation in such settings.

RECOMMENDATIONS

The committee recommends that the ethical and informed consent issues related to FDA-required postmarketing clinical trials should be evaluated according to the considerations identified in the conceptual framework summarized in Box 2 as explicated in this letter report.

Given the timeframe of this letter report, the committee does not detail all the issues within the framework or discuss how various considerations should be weighed. The committee plans to provide further details in its full report in 2011.

REFERENCES

Barton, M. B., T. Miller, T. Wolff, D. Petitti, M. LeFevre, G. Sawaya, B. Yawn, J. Guirguis-Blake, N. Calonge, R. Harris, and U.S. Preventive Services Task Force. 2007. How to read the new recommendation statement: Methods update from the U.S. Preventive Services Task Force. *Annals of Internal Medicine* 147(2):123-127.

Council for International Organizations of Medical Sciences. 2002. *International ethical guidelines for biomedical research involving human subjects*. Geneva, Switzerland: World Health Organization.

DHEW (Department of Health Education and Welfare). 1979. *The Belmont Report: Ethical principles and guidelines for the protection of human subjects of research*. Washington, DC: U.S. Department of Health and Human Services.

Ellenberg, S. S., T. R. Fleming, and D. L. DeMets. 2003. *Data monitoring committees in clinical trials: A practical perspective*. Chichester, UK: Wiley.

Faden, R. R., and T. L. Beauchamp. 1986. *A history and theory of informed consent*. New York City: Oxford University Press.

FDA (Food and Drug Administration). 2010a. *What does FDA do?* http://www.fda.gov/AboutFDA/Basics/ucm194877.htm (accessed June 15, 2010).

———. 2010b. *NIH and FDA announce collaborative initiative to fast-track innovations to the public*. http://www.fda.gov/NewsEvents/Newsroom/PressAnnouncements/ucm201706.htm (accessed June 21, 2010).

Fleming, T. R. 2008. Current issues in non-inferiority trials. *Statistics in Medicine* 27(3):317-332.

Flory, J., and E. Emanuel. 2004. Interventions to improve research participants' understanding in informed consent for research: A systematic review. *JAMA* 292(13):1593-1601.

Grant, A. M., D. G. Altman, A. B. Babiker, M. K. Campbell, F. J. Clemens, J. H. Darbyshire, D. R. Elbourne, S. K. McLeer, M. K. B. Parmar, S. J. Pocock, D. J. Spiegelhalter, M. R. Sydes, A. E. Walker, and S. A. Wallace. 2005. Issues in data monitoring and interim analysis of trials. Health Technology Assessment 9(7):1-238.

Hamburg, M. A., and J. M. Sharfstein. 2009. The FDA as a public health agency. *New England Journal of Medicine* 360(24):2493-2495.

HHS (Department of Health and Human Services). 2010. *Challenges to FDA's ability to monitor and inspect foreign clinical trials*. Washington, DC: Department of Health and Human Services, Office of the Inspector General.

ICH (International Conference on Harmonisation of Technical Requirements for Registration of Pharmaceuticals for Human Use). 1996. *ICH harmonized tripartite guideline: Guideline for good clinical practice*. Geneva, Switzerland: ICH Secretariat, International Federation for Pharmaceutical Manufacturers Association.

Ioannidis, J. P. A., and J. Lau. 2001. Completeness of safety reporting in randomized trials: An evaluation of 7 medical areas. *JAMA* 285(4):437-443.

IOM (Institute of Medicine). 2007. *The future of drug safety: Promoting and protecting the health of the public* Washington, DC: The National Academies Press.

Kass, N. E., and H. A. Taylor. 2008. *Empirical research on informed consent: A review of the literature prepared for The National Academies' Workshop on Collecting, Storing, Accessing, and Protecting Data Containing Biological Measures*.

Kaul, S., and G. A. Diamond. 2006. Good enough: A primer on the analysis and interpretation of noninferiority trials. *Annals of Internal Medicine* 145(1):62-69.

———. 2007. Making sense of noninferiority: A clinical and statistical perspective on its application to cardiovascular clinical trials. *Progress in Cardiovascular Diseases* 49(4):284-299.

Lindegger, G., C. Milford, C. Slack, M. Quayle, X. Xaba, and E. Vardas. 2006. Beyond the checklist: Assessing understanding for HIV vaccine trial participation in South Africa. *Journal of Acquired Immune Deficiency Syndromes* 43(5):560-566.

Lomas, J., T. Culyer, C. McCutcheon, L. McAuley, and S. Law. 2005. *Conceptualizing and combining evidence for health system guidance: Final report for the Canadian Health Services Research Foundation*. Ottawa, Canada.

NRC (National Research Council). 2004. *Intentional human dosing studies for EPA regulatory purposes: Scientific and ethical issues*. Washington, DC: The National Academies Press.

Owens, D. K., K. N. Lohr, D. Atkins, J. R. Treadwell, J. T. Reston, E. B. Bass, S. Chang, and M. Helfand. 2010. AHRQ series paper 5: Grading the strength of a body of evidence when comparing medical interventions-agency for healthcare research and quality and the effective health-care program. *Journal of Clinical Epidemiology* 63(5):513-523.

Pocock, S. J. 1996. The role of external evidence in data monitoring of a clinical trial. *Statistics in Medicine* 15(12):1285-1293.

Temple, R., and S. S. Ellenberg. 2000. Placebo-controlled trials and active-control trials in the evaluation of new treatments. Part 1: Ethical and scientific issues. *Annals of Internal Medicine* 133(6):455-463.

Vandenbroucke, J. P., and B. M. Psaty. 2008. Benefits and risks of drug treatments: How to combine the best evidence on benefits with the best data about adverse effects. *JAMA* 300(20):2417-2419.

Wittes, J., E. Barrett-Connor, E. Braunwald, M. Chesney, H. J. Cohen, D. Demets, L. Dunn, J. Dwyer, R. P. Heaney, V. Vogel, L. Walters, and S. Yusuf. 2007. Monitoring the randomized trials of the Women's Health Initiative: The experience of the Data and Safety Monitoring Board. *Clinical Trials* 4(3):218-234.

C

Open Session Agendas

First Meeting of the Committee on
Ethical and Scientific Issues in Studying the Safety of Approved Drugs
Keck Center, 500 Fifth Street NW, Room 100
Washington, DC

Monday, June 7, 2010

OPEN SESSION

11:00 AM	**Welcome and Introductions** Ruth R. Faden, Ph.D., M.P.H., Co-Chair Steven N. Goodman, M.D., Ph.D., Co-Chair
11:10 AM	**Presentation of Charge, Food and Drug Administration (FDA)** Dr. Margaret A. Hamburg, M.D., Commissioner, FDA Dr. Janet Woodcock, M.D., Director, Center for Drug Evaluation and Research, FDA
12:00 PM	**Committee Charge—Perspective of the Agency for Health-care Research and Quality (AHRQ)** Dr. Carolyn M. Clancy, M.D., Director, AHRQ
12:15 PM	**Committee Charge—Perspective of the National Institutes of Health (NIH)** Francis S. Collins, M.D., Ph.D., Director, NIH

12:30 PM **Open Microphone**

1:25 PM **Closing Remarks**
Ruth R. Faden, Ph.D., M.P.H., Co-Chair
Steven N. Goodman, M.D., Ph.D., Co-Chair

1:30 PM **Adjourn Open Session**

Third Meeting of the Committee on
Ethical and Scientific Issues in Studying the Safety of Approved Drugs
Keck Center, 500 Fifth Street NW, Room 110
Washington, DC

Tuesday, November 9, 2010

OPEN SESSION

8:50 AM **Welcome and Committee Introductions**
Ruth R. Faden and Steven N. Goodman, Co-Chairs

9:00 AM ***Panel A—Interpreting Safety Signals in the Context of Regulatory Science***

9:00 AM Freda Lewis-Hall, M.D., FAPA, Senior Vice President and Chief Medical Officer, Pfizer Inc.

9:20 AM Susan Ellenberg, Ph.D., Professor of Biostatistics and Associate Dean for Clinical Research, University of Pennsylvania School of Medicine

9:40 AM **Panel Questions**

10:00 AM Break

10:10 AM ***Panel B—Emerging Data Sources and Methods for Pharmacovigilence***

10:10 AM Jesse Berlin, Ph.D., Vice President, Pharmacoepidemiology, Johnson & Johnson Pharmaceutical Research and Development

10:30 AM Richard Platt, M.D., M.Sc., Professor and Chair, Department of Population Medicine, Harvard Pilgrim Health

Care Institute and Harvard Medical School. Principal Investigator of the FDA Mini-Sentinel Project and a member of OMOP Executive Board

10:50 AM Andrew Bate, Ph.D., Senior Director, Analytics Team Lead, Epidemiology, Worldwide Safety Strategy (formerly with the WHO Collaborating Centre for International Drug Monitoring, Uppsala Monitoring Centre)

11:10 AM Dan O'Connor, Ph.D., Greenwall Foundation Postdoctoral Fellow in Bioethics and the History of Medicine, Berman Institute of Bioethics and the Institute for the History of Medicine, Johns Hopkins University, Baltimore, MD

11:20 AM **Panel Questions**

11:45 AM Break

12:00 PM ***Panel C—Patient and Public Interest Group Perspective***
Sydney Wolfe, M.D., Director of the Health Research Group, Public Citizen's Health
Marc Boutin, J.D., Executive Vice President and Chief Operating Officer, The National Health Council.

12:30 PM Lunch

1:15 PM **FDA Representatives**
Joshua Sharfstein, M.D., Principal Deputy Commissioner, FDA
Dr. Janet Woodcock, M.D., Director, Center for Drug Evaluation and Research, FDA

2:30 PM **Adjourn Open Session**

D

Decision Conferencing and Multicriteria Decision Analysis

Benefit–risk assessment characterizes information regarding estimates of benefits, estimates of risks, and the severity and comparability among health endpoints associated with benefits and risks. Much has been published about methods for quantitative benefit–risk assessment (Coplan et al., 2011; Guo et al., 2010). Such assessments are widely used in decision-making contexts, particularly with regard to environmental regulation, and the mode of their particular application varies (NRC, 1994, 2009). The committee does not wish to prescribe a particular method for conducting benefit–risk assessment, particularly inasmuch as formal quantitative approaches are likely to be used only in select circumstances when disagreements about potential regulatory actions arise. Instead, the committee highlights in this appendix two decision tools that incorporate key considerations of benefit–risk assessment relevant to regulatory decision-making: *decision conferencing*, which is a social process intended to engage all the relevant stakeholders to provide scientific judgments at key points in the decision-making process, and *multicriteria decision analysis* (MCDA), which is a technical model for making decisions that have multiple objectives (Walker et al., 2005). Decision conferencing and MCDA have been used in other contexts and are offered here as examples of potentially useful approaches that integrate analytic and deliberative processes for in-depth evaluation and informed assessments of the benefit–risk balance of approved drugs (Phillips, 2006; Walker et al., 2005). Both processes, when used in a transparent way that documents the inputs into the process, can help to identify the underlying sources of scientific disagreements that are discussed in Chapter 3.

DECISION CONFERENCING

Decision conferencing is a tool that brings key experts and stakeholders together to generate a shared understanding of a challenge, create a sense of common purpose, and gain commitment to a way forward (Phillips, 2006) to aid evaluation and assessment of the benefits and risks associated with a drug (Walker et al., 2005). Decision conferencing has four basic elements: attendance by key stakeholders (for example, regulators; methodologists who have expertise in design, conduct, and analysis of observational studies and clinical trials; decision scientists; physicians who have relevant clinical expertise; patients; and the public); impartial facilitation to guide discussions of estimates of benefit and risk, degree of uncertainty, and values and preferences for health endpoints; on-the-spot modeling with continuous display of the developing model; and an interactive and iterative group process (Phillips, 2006). When quantitative benefit–risk assessments are needed in situations in which disagreements about appropriate regulatory action arise, a neutral facilitator can guide the group through the stages of discussing the issues, developing models for evaluating the issues, and eliciting assumptions about the quality of evidence regarding benefits and risks and about underlying ethical values and preferences for health endpoints without contributing to the content of discussions. Although quantitative estimates resulting from benefit–risk assessment may appear to provide objective information about optimal regulatory decisions, assumptions used in the model are often based on individual judgments about the quality of evidence related to benefits and risks, as discussed in Chapter 3, or based on individual values or preferences for different health endpoints. Using a process like decision conferencing helps to frame the issues and identify the relevant data and evidentiary gaps to guide later data-gathering and thereby improves the efficiency and transparency of the benefit–risk assessment process (Phillips, 2006).

The decision-conferencing process could be integrated into FDA's current processes and requirements under the Federal Advisory Committee Act,[1] and it is similar to initiatives that FDA currently has planned. For example, FDA is working with stakeholders, using faculty of the George Washington University as facilitators, to develop guidance material for approving obesity drugs (McCaughan, 2011). Decision conferencing in benefit–risk assessment has four advantages:

- It facilitates and focuses thinking about a complex challenge.
- It helps to establish common purpose among participants and commitment to move forward.
- It promotes transparency and a shared understanding of how stakeholders define benefits, risks, degree of uncertainty, ethical values regarding outcomes, and potential regulatory actions for managing risk.

[1]Federal Advisory Committee Act, PL 920-463, 86 Stat. 770 (1972).

- Because decision conferencing can generate both the outcome and a description of the process that leads to the outcome, it can improve stakeholders' and the public's understanding of a regulatory decision.

MULTICRITERIA DECISION ANALYSIS

MCDA is a set of methods designed to bring together evaluations of options on different criteria into one overall decision (CHMP, 2008). There are many variants of MCDA, some of which may be adapted to consider the uncertainty of the decision-maker (Linkov and Seager, 2011), and MCDA can be used to provide either a qualitative or a quantitative assessment. The basic methods of MCDA are scoring and weighting (CHMP, 2008). Scoring involves the process of assigning numerical values to options according to particular criteria. Weighting ensures the comparability of the numerical values assigned to all criteria, which allows comparison of different health states with a single metric (Linkov and Seager, 2011). The weights assigned to scores reflect the relative importance of the underlying criteria for the benefit–risk assessment outcome (Walker et al., 2005).

MCDA uses four steps (Linkov and Seager, 2011):

1. Defining the problem and the decision context.
2. Identifying stakeholders, decision-makers, assessment criteria (for example, health outcomes of interest), and the relative importance of different health outcomes.
3. Defining and assessing management alternatives whereby the effects of different regulatory decisions on each criterion, or health outcome, are assessed.
4. Allowing for variability in weighting of different criteria and accounting for the stochastic nature of data through the use of probabilistic sensitivity analysis to provide a rank order of different alternatives for distinct stakeholder groups.

Those four steps help to ensure that all participants understand and are in agreement about the need for a regulatory decision, the criteria by which benefit–risk balance is judged, the evidence and its uncertainties, the values and preferences of different stakeholders, and the consequences of different regulatory decisions. The outputs or information synthesis of the benefit–risk assessment stage of the framework should include model inputs and model outputs (Linkov and Seager, 2011). The model inputs would include estimates of benefits, estimates of risks, the degree of uncertainty, and preferences for health outcomes based on ethical values. The model outputs may be characterized quantitatively, for example, the benefits of a drug outweigh the risks 85 percent of the time; or qualitatively, for example, there is clear and convincing evidence that the benefits of a drug outweigh its risks. The synthesis should also discuss any uncertainty analyses that were conducted and the process by which the benefit–risk assessment was performed—that is, a description of the "decision conferencing" or other process that FDA used to seek and include stakeholder input as necessary. Useful information includes statements of who provided the inputs and who moderated the process. Both the process and the outcome should be documented as a way to set the stage for understanding the regulatory decision. The outcome of the assessment process, whether quantitative or qualitative, becomes the evidentiary basis of the regulatory decision-making that is at the heart of the next stage—benefit–risk management.

LIMITATIONS OF USING MODELING APPROACHES FOR BENEFIT AND RISK ASSESSMENTS

MCDA is a useful tool for benefit–risk assessment, but it has its limitations, both in its own right and as an aid to regulatory decision-making. Using a quantitative MCDA approach to benefit–risk assessment forces participants to be explicit about how they evaluate existing evidence regarding the effectiveness of a drug and its associated harms and about the degree of uncertainty regarding benefits and risks. Such a quantitative assessment, however, can obscure underlying interpretations of scientific findings. The interpretations should be explicitly described, and decision conferencing can mitigate some concerns by describing differences in underlying assumptions. In addition, quantification of intangible factors, such as a patient's preferences that might be based on various degrees of dread for different diseases, may be difficult in MCDA models although relevant for the decision-making process.

Preferences regarding the relative importance and severity of health states associated with the disease or the treatment may also vary widely among stakeholders and could potentially be obscured by using modeling approaches. However, decision conferencing can serve as a useful tool for conducting MCDA by explicitly describing stakeholders' values and preferences and how they may affect regulatory decisions.

Even with the aid of social and technical decision tools, benefit–risk assessment is unavoidably limited by the quality and quantity of available evidence. Uncertainty analysis may identify the key information needed to support a particular regulatory action, but such data may not be available in the time needed to address the public health issue at hand. The available data may lead to multiple interpretations and contribute to decision-making gridlock. That delay could compound limitations of the resources and expertise available in FDA to conduct benefit–risk assessments and result in a backlog. Such risk-assessment backlogs have occurred in the Environmental Protection Agency (NRC, 2009). If tools like decision conferencing and MCDA are used to enhance transparency, the rationale for regulatory decisions can at least be understood by stakeholders even if disagreements about optimal regulatory action remain. The transparency allows stakeholders to have a shared understanding of differences in scientific assessment of preferences regarding health outcomes, which can help to determine whether additional data are needed and whether those data will meet thresholds for influencing future regulatory action. Decision conferencing and MCDA, however, may not be appropriate for every situation, and benefit–risk assessments should be scalable to the severity and scope of the particular public health concern at issue, the level of controversy surrounding it, and FDA resource constraints.

REFERENCES

CHMP (Committee for Medical Products for Human Use). 2008. *Reflection paper on benefit-risk assessment methods in the context of the evaluation of marketing authorisation applications of medicinal products for human use.* London, UK: European Medicines Agency.

Coplan, P. M., R. A. Noel, B. S. Levitan, J. Ferguson, and F. Mussen. 2011. Development of a framework for enhancing the transparency, reproducibility and communication of the benefit-risk balance of medicines. *Clinical Pharmacology & Therapeutics* 89(2):312-315.

Guo, J. J., S. Pandey, J. Doyle, B. Bian, Y. Lis, and D. W. Raisch. 2010. A review of quantitative risk-benefit methodologies for assessing drug safety and efficacy-report of the ISPOR risk-benefit management working group. *Value Health* 13(5):657-666.

Linkov, I., and T. P. Seager. 2011. Coupling multi-criteria decision analysis, life-cycle assessment, and risk assessment for emerging threats. *Environmental Science and Technology* 45(12):5068-5074.

McCaughan, M. 2011. FDA rethinking weight loss standards: A test case for patient-focused drug development. *"The Pink Sheet" Daily*, June 6, 2011.

NRC (National Research Council). 1994. *Science and judgment in risk assessment.* Washington, DC: National Academy Press.

NRC. 2009. *Science and decisions: Advancing risk assessment.* Washington, DC: The National Academies Press.

Phillips, L. D. 2006. *Decision conferencing. Operational research working papers, LSEOR 06.85.* London, UK: Operational Research Group, Department of Management, London School of Economics and Political Science.

Walker, S., L. Phillips, and M. Cone. 2005 (unpublished). *Benefit-risk assessment model for medicines: Developing a structured approach to decision making.*

E

Benefit and Risk Assessment and Management Plan Document Template

This appendix serves as a template for the committee's proposed Benefit and Risk Assessment and Management Plan (BRAMP) document. For some drugs, much of the information that the committee recommends be recorded in a BRAMP is available in various summary reviews and other documents. However, these documents can be difficult to locate, are often highly technical in language and level of detail, and are not necessarily easily linked or connected. By contrast, a key aspect of the recommendation for a BRAMP document is that it will be a single, easy to read, living document that is updated at periodic intervals, including whenever the benefit–risk profile of a drug is questioned or evaluated in the postmarketing setting, and therefore that will serve as a comprehensive source of information about a drug.

This BRAMP template is for a fictitious Drug X, approved by Food and Drug Administration (FDA) in 2005. Later regulatory decisions, documented in the BRAMP for this drug, are: a labeling change in 2006, the addition of a risk evaluation and mitigation strategy (REMS) requirement in 2009, and removal of the REMS requirement in 2011.

BRAMP DOCUMENT TEMPLATE

Contents Page

SECTION 1
DRUG X—APPROVAL
11/10/2005

1. Public Health Question

This section of the BRAMP document specifies the public health problem or question that prompted a review of the benefits and risks associated with a drug. At the time of approval for marketing, the public health question is whether the benefits of Drug X outweigh its risks and, therefore, whether the drug should be approved for marketing.

This section also should include a discussion of the context in which the public health question is asked. That is, it includes characteristics of the condition that the drug is approved to treat for, patients' perceptions and concerns, practical considerations, availability of other treatments, and any other issues that should be considered in addressing the public health question.

2. Summary of the Benefit and Risk Assessment

This section should include a description of the process used to assess the benefits and risks, including how stakeholder input was sought and incorporated. It should also include, in the sections below for benefit and for risk assessments, a summary of the available evidence used, the quality and uncertainty of the different studies, and the judgments made about the different studies, including how the studies were factored into decisions. The description of the evidence should include a characterization of the overall consistency and uncertainty of that evidence. All assumptions used in estimating benefits and risks should also be described.

a. Benefit Assessment

This section should include a description of the evidence used in the assessment of the benefits of the drug, including the quality, consistency, and relevance of the data.

b. Risk Assessment

This section should include a description of the evidence used in the assessment of the risks posed by the drug, including the quality, consistency, and relevance of the data.

c. Overall Benefit–Risk Profile

This section should include a description of the evidence used in the assessment of the benefit–risk profile of the drug, including the quality, consistency, and relevance of the data. It should also include a characterization of the uncertainty around the estimates of the benefits and risks.

3. Regulatory Actions and Rationale

This section should have a clear statement of the regulatory decision, and the rationale for that decision, including not only the final output of the benefit–risk assessment process but a description of any other factors that affected the decision, such as ethical issues, timeframe issues, the lack of an available treatment for a disease, or the risk posed by a drug in a specific population. It should also include a description of any VOI analysis, decision conferencing, or multiple-criteria decision analysis that was conducted

If there are any regulatory requirements that are meant to highlight or mitigate a drug's risks, such as labeling changes, boxed warnings, or a REMS, those requirements should be described in this section. This section should also include a description of any postmarketing surveillance, studies, or trial requirements or commitments.

a. Regulatory Decision

This section should include a statement of the regulatory decision, such as approval of the drug or the requirement for a postmarketing requirement.

b. Rationale

This section should discuss the rationale for the regulatory decision, including a description of any factors other than the benefit and risk assessment that might have affected the decision, such as ethical issues, patient perspectives, timeframe issues, the lack of an available treatment for a disease, and the risk posed by the drug in a specific population.

c. Concomitant Actions

This section should discuss any actions needed to highlight or mitigate a drug's risks, including labeling, boxed warning, REMS, and postmarketing study requirements. It includes a discussion of the rationale for requiring these changes, and any remaining public health questions that need to be answered by postmarketing requirements.

4. Schedule of Future Reviews

This section should include a schedule of future evaluations of the benefit–risk profile, taking into account when additional information on the benefits or risks associated with the drug might be expected. This section should also outline any plans to review the decision, and the decision-making process used for the drug. For example, if the approval of Drug X was controversial or difficult, this section should include a schedule for reviewing the affect of the decision on the public's health, and reviewing the process used for the decision to identify ways to improve the decision-making process in the future.

SECTION 2
DRUG X—LABELING CHANGE
11/29/2006

This section of the BRAMP document should contain a discussion of the labeling change that was made for Drug X on 11/29/2006. It should outline the public health question that prompted the label change, summarize the benefit and risk assessment that supported the change, and outline the regulatory change.

1. Public Health Question

This section should detail the problem, or public health question, that led FDA and the sponsor of Drug X to consider changing the drug's label. For example, if problems with administration of Drug X were reported, FDA should include a discussion of the problems in this section.

2. Summary of the Benefit and Risk Assessment

This section of the document should include a description of the evidence used in the assessment of the risks posed by the drug and the benefits of the drug, including the increased risks or decreased benefits associated with improper use.

3. Regulatory Actions and Rationale

a. Regulatory Decision

This section should include a statement of the regulatory decisions considered to respond to the public health question.

b. Rationale

This section should discuss the rationale for the regulatory decision, including a description of any factors other than the benefit and risk assessment that might have affected the decision, such as ethical issues, patient perspectives, timeframe issues, the lack of an available treatment for a disease, and the risk posed by the drug in a specific population. It should include a discussion of how the label changes are expected to increase the drug's benefits, decrease the drug's risks, or both.

c. Concomitant Actions

If the label change is the only regulatory action considered and taken at this time, this section should indicate that no other regulatory actions were considered and taken at this time.

4. Schedule of Future Reviews

This section should include a schedule of future evaluations of the benefit–risk profile, taking into account when additional information on the benefits or risks associated with the drug is expected. This section should also outline any plans to review the decision, and the decision-making process used for the drug. For example, if the approval of Drug X was controversial or difficult, this section should include a schedule for reviewing the affect of the decision on the public's health, and reviewing the process used for the decision to identify ways to improve the decision-making process in the future.

SECTION 3
REQUIREMENT OF A REMS
05/21/2009

This section of the document should contain a discussion of the decision to require a REMS for Drug X. It should outline the public health question that prompted consideration of the REMS requirement, summarize the benefit and risk assessment that supported the requirement, and outline the regulatory requirement.

1. Public Health Question

This section should detail the problem, or public health question, that led FDA to consider requiring a REMS for Drug X. For example, if there is new evidence from postmarketing surveillance that the risks posed by Drug X outweigh its benefits, the evidence should be briefly introduced in this section.

2. Summary of the Benefit and Risk Assessment

This section should include a description of the evidence used in the assessment of risks and benefits associated with Drug X, and an assessment of the effects of a REMS on the benefits and risks.

3. Regulatory Actions and Rationale

a. Regulatory Decision

This section should include a statement of the regulatory decisions considered to respond to the public health question.

b. Rationale

This section should discuss the rationale for the decision to require a REMS, including a description of any factors other than the benefit and risk assessment that might have affected the decision, such as ethical issues, patient perspectives, timeframe issues, the lack of an available treatment for a disease, and the risk posed by a drug in a specific population.

c. Concomitant Actions

If the REMS requirement is the only regulatory action considered and taken at this time, this section should indicate that no other regulatory actions were considered and taken at this time.

4. Schedule of Future Reviews

This section should include a schedule of future evaluations of the benefit–risk profile, taking into account when additional information on the benefits or risks associated with the drug is expected. It should include a discussion of FDA's plans to assess the effectiveness of the REMS. This section should also outline any plans to review the decision, and the decision-making process used for the drug. For example, if the approval of Drug X was controversial or difficult, this section should include a schedule for reviewing the affect of the decision on the public's health, and reviewing the process used for the decision to identify ways to improve the decision-making process in the future.

SECTION 4
REMOVAL OF REMS REQUIREMENT
09/05/2011

This section of the BRAMP document should contain a discussion of the decision to remove a REMS requirement for Drug X. It should outline the public health question that prompted consideration of removal of the REMS requirement, summarize the benefit and risk assessment that supported the change, and outline the regulatory change.

1. Public Health Question

This section should detail the problem, or public health question, that led FDA to consider removing the REMS requirement for Drug X, for example, if there is evidence that the potential risks that prompted the previous requirement for a REMS were not as high as estimated or there is evidence that the REMS is not effective in mitigating those risks.

2. Summary of the Benefit and Risk Assessment

This section of the document should include a description of the evidence used in the assessment of the effects of the REMS on the risks and benefits associated with the drug.

3. Regulatory Actions and Rationale

a. Regulatory Decision

This section should include a statement of the regulatory decisions considered to respond to the public health question.

b. Rationale

This section should discuss the rationale for the regulatory decision, including a description of any factors other than the benefit and risk assessment that might have affected the decision, such as ethical issues, patient perspectives, timeframe issues, the lack of an available treatment for a disease, and the risk posed by the drug in a specific population.

c. Concomitant Actions

If the removal of a REMS requirement is the only regulatory action considered and taken at this time, this section should indicate that no other regulatory actions were considered and taken at this time.

4. Schedule of Future Reviews

This section should include a schedule of future evaluations of the benefit–risk profile, taking into account when additional information on the benefits or risks associated with the drug is expected. This section should also outline any plans to review the decision, and the decision-making process used for the drug. For example, if the approval of Drug X was controversial or difficult, this section should include a schedule for reviewing the affect of the decision on the public's health, and reviewing the process used for the decision to identify ways to improve the decision-making process in the future.

F

Committee Biosketches

Ruth R. Faden, Ph.D., M.P.H. (*Co-Chair*), is the Philip Franklin Wagley Professor of Biomedical Ethics and executive director of the Johns Hopkins Berman Institute of Bioethics. She is also a senior research scholar at the Kennedy Institute of Ethics of Georgetown University. Dr. Faden is the author and editor of numerous books and articles on biomedical ethics and health policy, including *A History and Theory of Informed Consent* (with Tom L. Beauchamp), *AIDS, Women, and the Next Generation* (Ruth R. Faden, Gail Geller, and Madison Powers, editors), *HIV, AIDS and Childbearing: Public Policy, Private Lives* (Ruth R. Faden and Nancy E. Kass, editors). Dr. Faden is a member of the Institute of Medicine and a Fellow of the Hastings Center and the American Psychological Association. She has served on several national advisory committees and commissions, including the President's Advisory Committee on Human Radiation Experiments, which she chaired. Current research interests include bioethics and public policy; ethics and cellular engineering; ethics and neuroscience; ethics and bioterrorism; ethics, genetics, and public policy; research ethics; and justice.

Steven N. Goodman, M.D., M.H.S., Ph.D. (*Co-Chair*), is associate dean for clinical and translational research and professor of medicine and health policy and research at Stanford University School of Medicine. Before joining Stanford in 2011, Dr. Goodman was professor of oncology in the division of biostatistics of the Johns Hopkins Kimmel Cancer Center, with appointments in the departments of pediatrics, biostatistics, and epidemiology in the Johns Hopkins Schools of Medicine and Public Health. He was also on the core faculties of the Johns Hopkins Center for Clinical Trials, Berman Bioethics Institute, Graduate Training Program in Clinical Investigation, and co-directed the epidemiology doctoral program. He is the editor of *Clinical Trials: Journal of the Society for Clinical Trials* and is statistical and associate editor of the *Annals of Internal Medicine*, since 1987. He served on the Institute of Medicine's the Committee to Review the Health Effects in Vietnam Veterans of Exposure to Herbicides: Second Biennial Update, Committee to Review the Evidence Regarding the Link between Exposure to Agent Orange and Diabetes, Immunization Safety Review Committee, the Committee on Alternatives to the Daubert Standards ,and the Committee on Treatment of Post-traumatic Stress Disorder in Veterans. Dr. Goodman also served on the Surgeon General's committee to write the 2004 report on the Health Consequences of Smoking. He is a scientific advisor to the Medical Advisory Panel of the National Blue Cross/Blue Shield Technology Evaluation Center, and was appointed to the Methodology Committee of the Patient Centered Outcomes Research Institute. Dr. Goodman received a B.A. from Harvard, an M.D. from New York University, trained in Pediatrics at Washington University in St. Louis, and received an M.H.S. in biostatistics, and Ph.D. in epidemiology from Johns Hopkins University. He writes and teaches on evidence evaluation and inferential, methodologic, and ethical issues in epidemiology and clinical research.

Alasdair Breckenridge, M.D., FRCP, is chairman of the United Kingdom Medicines and Healthcare products Regulatory Agency (MHRA). The MHRA is the executive agency of the UK Department of Health, which is responsible for protecting and promoting public health and patient safety by ensuring that medicines, health care products, and medical equipment meet appropriate standards of safety, quality, performance, and effectiveness and are used safely. In 2004, he was awarded a knighthood for his services to medicine in recognition of his role in ensuring that British patients receive safe medical treatment. Dr. Breckenridge has played a leading role in monitoring the safety of medicines for many years. He previously was chairman of the UK Committee on the Safety of Medicines (CSM) and was a member of the CSM Adverse Reactions Group and Subcommittee on Adverse Reactions to Vaccines and Immunization. He is a former professor of clinical pharmacology at the University of Liverpool and headed its Department of Pharmacology and Therapeutics for 26 years. Dr. Breckenridge has also been both a member and chairman of a regional health authority and a member of a local health authority. His research interests include the pharmacology of HIV drugs.

Lisa Egbuonu-Davis, M.D., M.P.H., M.B.A., is an executive adviser in Booz Allen Hamilton's health care practice. Her focus includes business implications of health care reform, strategies to support the product-value proposition from development through commercialization, and practices to ensure compliance and transparency while delivering business impact. Dr. Egbuonu-Davis joined Booz Allen after 18 years in the pharmaceutical industry, including 13 years at Pfizer Pharmaceuticals, where she served as vice president for global outcomes research and vice president of US Medical. She built and led a multinational health economic and outcomes research function, developing and implementing processes to provide clinical and comparative-effectiveness research and generate data needed to support pricing, reimbursement, formulary coverage, and acceptance. She has been involved in comparative-effectiveness research policy, previously serving as a member of the National Advisory Council for the Agency for Healthcare Research and Quality and the Steering Committee for the Centers for Research and Education on Therapeutics. She played a leadership role in the integration of medical–regulatory and clinical research functions during several mergers. She created a US field-based medical team that supported clinical research and communication with medical opinion leaders. As vice present of US Medical, she had responsibility for marketed-product clinical and outcomes research, medical information, public-health and academic partnerships, and regulatory promotional review. Dr. Egbuonu-Davis earned a B.S. in biology from the Massachusetts Institute of Technology, an M.B.A. in health care management from Wharton, and an M.D. and M.P.H. from Johns Hopkins and is a fellow of the American Academy of Pediatrics.

Miguel A. Hernán, M.D., Sc.M., Dr.P.H., is professor of epidemiology at Harvard School of Public Health and an affiliated faculty member of the Harvard–Massachusetts Institute of Technology Division of Health Sciences and Technology. He is an editor of *Epidemiology* and a Fellow of the American Association for the Advancement of Science. He writes and teaches on methods of causal inference, including comparative effectiveness of policy and clinical interventions. His current research interests include the optimal use of antiretroviral therapy for HIV disease, clinical strategies for the reduction of mortality in people who have kidney failure, and the effects of lifestyle and pharmacologic interventions in reducing the incidence of cardiovascular disease.

Grace M. Lee, M.D., M.P.H., is an associate professor of population medicine and pediatrics at the Harvard Pilgrim Health Care Institute, Harvard Medical School, and Children's Hospital Boston. She is also an assistant professor of pediatrics in the Division of Infectious Diseases at Children's Hospital Boston. Dr. Lee's research focuses on vaccine economics, vaccine safety, and infectious-diseases epidemiology. She recently completed a study funded by the Centers for Disease Control and Prevention (CDC) on emerging gaps in vaccine financing for underinsured children in the United States. She is working on a study funded by the Agency for Healthcare Research and Quality (AHRQ) to determine the potential effects and cost-effectiveness of using a group A streptococcal vaccine and a CDC-funded study of influenza-vaccine safety. Dr. Lee joined the faculty of Harvard Medical School, Harvard Pilgrim Health Care, and Children's Hospital Boston in 2003 after completing an AHRQ postdoctoral fellowship. She received her M.D. from the University of Pennsylvania School of Medicine and her M.P.H.

from the Harvard School of Public Health. She completed her pediatric residency and subspecialty training in pediatric infectious diseases and pediatric health services research at Children's Hospital Boston. Dr. Lee is currently serving on the Institute of Medicine Committee on Review of Priorities in the National Vaccine Plan.

Michelle Mello, Ph.D., J.D., M.Phil., is a professor of law and public health in the Department of Health Policy and Management of the Harvard School of Public Health. She holds a J.D. from the Yale Law School; a Ph.D. in health policy and administration from the University of North Carolina at Chapel Hill; an M.Phil. from Oxford University, where she was a Marshall Scholar; and a B.A. from Stanford University. Dr. Mello conducts empirical research on issues at the intersection of law, ethic, and health policy. She is the author of more than 100 articles and book chapters on the medical-malpractice system, medical errors and patient safety, research ethics, the obesity epidemic, pharmaceuticals, clinical ethics, and other topics. Among other current projects, Dr. Mello is studying disclosure of and compensation for medical injuries as the recipient of a Robert Wood Johnson Foundation (RWJF) Investigator Award in Health Policy Research, and she is also the recipient of the Alice S. Hersh New Investigator Award from AcademyHealth for contributions to the field of health-services research. Dr. Mello is director of the Program in Law and Public Health of the Harvard School of Public Health and chair of the school's institutional review board. She teaches courses in public-health law and public-health ethics. Dr. Mello serves as a key consultant to RWJF's Public Health Law Research Program.

Eric M. Meslin, Ph.D., is director of the Indiana University (IU) Center for Bioethics, associate dean for bioethics in the Indiana University School of Medicine, and professor of medicine, medical and molecular genetics, public health, and philosophy. He also codirects the IU Center for Law, Ethics and Applied Research in Health Information (CLEAR) and the IU-Moi Academic Research Ethics Partnership, an innovative bioethics-research training program in Eldoret, Kenya. He came to Indiana in 2001 from Washington, DC, where he directed bioethics research for the Ethical, Legal and Social Implications program of the Human Genome Project and then served as executive director of the US National Bioethics Advisory Commission established by President Clinton. Born in Canada, Dr. Meslin received his B.A. in philosophy from York University in Toronto and his M.A. and Ph.D. from the Bioethics Program in Philosophy of the Kennedy Institute of Ethics at Georgetown University. He has held academic positions at the University of Toronto (1988–1996), as a visiting fellow at Green College, Oxford University (1994–1995), and as professor-at-large at the University of Western Australia (2008–2010). He has more than 150 published articles and book chapters on topics from international health research to science policy. His most recent book is *The Sage Handbook of Health Care Ethics* (coedited with

Ruth Chadwick and Henk Ten Have, published in 2011). Dr. Meslin sits on several boards and committees, including the Institute of Medicine's Committee on Ethical and Scientific Issues in Studying the Safety of Approved Drugs, the Board of Directors of the Indiana Public Umbilical Cord Blood Bank, and the Board of Directors of Genome Canada. On May 9, 2007, he was appointed a Chevalier de L'Order Nationale du Mérite (Knight of the National Order of Merit) by the French ambassador to the United States for his contributions to French bioethics policy.

Larry I. Palmer, L.L.B., (retired June 2011), is professor of law emeritus at Cornell University. He previously served as a professor of law at Virginia Commonwealth University and professor of law at the William & Mary Law School. He also has appointments at the College of William & Mary in the Marshall-Wythe School of Law as a law professor and in the Thomas Jefferson Program in Public Policy's Schroder Center for Healthcare Policy as a research professor. He served 4 years as the Endowed Chair in Urban Health Policy at the University of Louisville and 27 years at Cornell University as law professor, vice president, and vice provost. He has been a visiting professor at Georgetown University and the University of Virginia. He is the author of *Endings and Beginnings: Law, Medicine, and Society in Assisted Life and Death, Law, Medicine and Social Justice*, and numerous articles dealing with law, medicine, and health policy. He is also the executive producer and author of the study guide of the prizewinning educational video *Susceptible to Kindness: Miss Evers' Boys and the Tuskegee Syphilis Study*. He was a director of the Hastings Center in Garrison, New York, and a member of the National Institute on Alcohol Abuse and Alcoholism Advisory Council. Previously, Mr. Palmer served as a director of the National Patient Safety Foundation, a trustee of the Phillips Exeter Academy, and a member of the American Bar Association's Special Committee on Bioethics and Law. He has been a member of the Institute of Medicine Committee on Ethical Considerations for Revisions to DHHS Regulations for Protection of Prisoners Involved in Research and Committee on Establishing a National Cord Blood Stem Cell Bank Program.

Bruce M. Psaty, M.D., Ph.D., M.P.H., is a professor of medicine, epidemiology, and health services; co-director of the Cardiovascular Health Research Unit of the University of Washington; an investigator at Group Health Research Institute, Group Health Cooperative; and a practicing general internist at Harborview Medical Center, Seattle, WA. He received his M.D. and a Ph.D. in English language and literature from Indiana University and his M.P.H. in epidemiology from the University of Washington. His research interests include cardiovascular epidemiology, hypertension, diabetes, epidemiological methods, drug safety, pharmacoepidemiology, genetics, genomics, and pharmacogenetics. Dr. Psaty is the principal investigator on several large epidemiologic studies and has had major roles as a cardiovascular disease epidemiologist at the coordinating centers of National Institutes of Health (NIH)–funded multi-center studies, including the Cardiovascular Health Study, the Multi-Ethnic Study of Atherosclerosis, and the Women's Health Initiative. In these settings and others, he has used case-control, cohort, clinical-trial and meta-analytic methods to evaluate the risks and benefits of a variety of medications, including hormone therapy, non-steroidal anti-inflammatory agents, and drugs used to treat hypertension, diabetes, dyslipidemia, asthma, heart failure, atrial fibrillation, osteoporosis, chronic pain, and other conditions as well as drug-gene interactions that may influence the occurrence of the risks or benefits of selected medications. Recently, Dr. Psaty collaborated with investigators from other national and international cohort studies to establish the CHARGE (Cohorts for Heart and Aging Research in Genomic Epidemiology) consortium, which has published more than 70 meta-analyses of genome-wide association studies of a variety of phenotypes. Dr. Psaty has served on various NIH working groups, data-safety monitoring committees, review groups and study sections, including as chair of the NIH Cardiovascular Disease and Sleep Epidemiology Study Section (2004–2006), Institute of Medicine's Committee on the Assessment of the US Drug Safety System (2005–2006), the Executive Committee of the National Heart, Lung, and Blood Institute's Strategic Planning Effort (2006–2007), and the Scientific Advisory Board of the Netherlands Biobank Infrastructure (2010–present). In 2005, he received the University of Washington Outstanding Public Service Award for his work on drug safety. The American Heart Association's Epidemiology and Prevention Council selected Dr Psaty as the Remington Methodology Lecturer (2004) and as the Ancel Keys Memorial Lecturer (2009). Elected memberships include American Epidemiological Society, Association of American Physicians, and fellow of the American Heart Association. Currently, Dr. Psaty is a member of the FDA Science Board and the Safety Science Committee of the Mini-Sentinel Initiative. He also teaches and mentors students, fellows and junior faculty in medicine and epidemiology. With more than 500 articles, editorials and commentaries in the medical literature, Dr. Psaty publishes regularly, serves on the editorial board of several journals, and is a contributing writer at *JAMA*.

Thomas R. Ten Have, Ph.D., M.P.H.,[*] was a professor of biostatistics, Perelman School of Medicine, University of Pennsylvania, director of the Biostatistics-Data Core, and coinvestigator of the National Institute of Mental Health–sponsored Advanced Center for Interventions and Services Research for Depression in the Aged. In the latter capacity, Dr. Ten Have was collaborating on trials involving the prevention of suicide in elderly primary-care patients; the treatment of postmenopausal women with estrogen for depression; the treatment of substance abuse, anxiety, and depression in elderly veterans; and disparities of screening

[*]Deceased May 1, 2011.

and treatment for mental-health disorders in participants of color. In addition to investigating methods for accommodating dropout in longitudinal studies, Dr. Ten Have focused on other methodologic issues, including accounting for different sources of nonadherence in randomized trials, such as patient and physician nonadherence to randomized treatment regimens; analyses of data from practice-randomized studies; and designs and analyses of clinical trials of complex multicomponent, adaptive treatment regimens. His previous Institute of Medicine service included membership on the Committee on NASA's Bioastronautics Critical Path Roadmap. Dr. Ten Have was a member of the American Statistical Association, the Institute of Mathematical Statistics, the International Biometrics Society, the Society for Epidemiological Research, and the American Public Health Association. He was associate editor of *Biometrics* and of the *Journal of the Royal Statistical Society, Series C*, statistical consulting editor of *Bipolar Disorders*, and guest editor for *Statistics in the Biosciences*.

William K. Vaughan, B.A., has recently retired as a senior policy analyst in the health sector for Consumers Union, the nonprofit, independent publisher of *Consumer Reports*. Starting in 1965, he worked for various members of the House of Representatives Committee on Ways and Means; he retired in 2001 as Subcommittee on Health staff director for the minority. From 2003 to May 2005, he was director of government relations for Families USA, a national health-advocacy organization.